FLANNELS ON THE SWARD

HISTORY OF CRICKET IN AMERICAS

JAYESH PATEL

Cover: Untitled Lithograph which is most likely of the 1872 Robert Fitzerald's amateur English cricket team showing W.G. Grace at bat.

All images that are not credited to their respective owners are part of the author's collection.

In memory of my father – R. A. Patel.

CONTENTS

ACKNOWLEDGMENTS

Research, is by no means an easy task, it requires the expertise of librarians and historians who have compiled information before me and collating it all together, takes time, effort and tons of patience. No book is complete without the help of these unsung individuals and institutions and regrettably, cannot acknowledge them individually.

However, mention must be made for the Bristol Historical Society in Connecticut, and its former President Bob Montgomery, who led me to the few surviving 'Wicket Bats' in existence at the Manross Library in Forestville and also to the Windsor Historical Society, who also have a Wicket bat & ball in their museum. Another local source was the New Britain Public Library. It all began with the collection at Ridley College in Canada and others in the region. Thanks to St Pauls' School in New Hampshire for providing great pictures and information on their cricketing days, the Baseball Hall of Fame Library in Cooperstown, New York for their pictures and insights. Various libraries/historical societies/museums across the United States who willingly provided digital images and reference material such as the Library of Virginia, Allen County Public Library Foundation in Fort Wayne, Indiana, Brown University in Rhode Island, the Harry T. Peters 'America on Stone' Collection from the National Museum of American History, Smithsonian Institution. Mention must be made of the Hargrett Rare Book and Manuscript Library at the University of Georgia Libraries for the copy of the rare handwritten note by Levi Sheftall and to Lilly Library at Indiana University in Bloomington for an image copy from the 'Pretty Little Pocket Book.'

Special thanks to the National Museum of Australia for providing the images at no cost, the National Library of Ireland for a copy of the extremely rare book of the first tour by the Irish to America, and other Australian Libraries for their prompt attention. A special thanks to Judy and Victoria at Choate Rosemary Hall in Connecticut, for digitizing the wonderful pictures of the girls playing cricket (and letting me in on more than one occasion) and also to Smith College and Mount Holyoke. Last, but not the least, thanks to Ann Upton at Haverford College, for going the extra mile (next door) to get some great pictures from CC Morris Cricket Library. Finally, there is John Thorn, the 'Official Baseball Historian' who provided the earliest 'Wicket' sketch and other helpful information related to baseball, and to the wonderful digital online world, which has made it easier for me to become a (armchair) historian...I hope!

INTRODUCTION

The seeds for this book were sown, when I acquired part of the 'KA Auty Library of Cricket' collection. Thus, began my pursuit into the wonderful history of cricket in the United States, Canada, and Latin America. My research would not have been possible without the internet, with its vast resources of information available at my fingertips, and the gratitude goes to Google's vast compilation of digitized books and reference material.

This book is dedicated to every kid - old or young - on every street corner, alleyway, terrace, fields, hallways and driveways, any open space was our field of dreams, where victories were conjured up under fertile imaginations! If I was tired or knocked down, forget the smelling salts, just hold a used smelly cricket gear to my nose and I would be wide awake, ready to be battered and bruised again on the 22 yards of paradise – the cricket pitch! The smell of used sweaty glove, the dirty pads and the 'aroma' of a used leather ball, would conjure up imaginary victories achieved singlehandedly on the hallowed grounds of Eden Gardens in Calcutta, the Lord's (MCC) in London or the Melbourne Cricket Ground (MCG) in Australia. When we played on the terrace of our five storied building, the tennis or rubber ball would invariably fall down to the streets below and the batter who hit the ball, would have to run down the flight of stairs, mind you – there were no elevators, and the rule was to throw the ball up to the terrace from the street, so as not to hold up the game for the others. One required a good arm to throw that high and when you are 10 years old, the building does look taller than it actually is. Also, while running down the stairs one would pray and hope that some kid on the street did not run away with the ball as that would create a bigger headache - who was going to pay for the new ball?

In my hometown we would play on the street with an empty barrel/drum, a poor substitute for stumps and when the tractor or a car would pass by, we would have to move our stumps out of the way. I remember how difficult it was to play without proper gear, the gloves would not fit, or they would be old and smelly (it still triggers the olfactory sensory cell and I can recall *the* 'smell') or they would have holes in them and the pads would not fit properly. Many a times we played without pads and when the ball hit the shin bone - ouch! Right now I am sure those who have played without pads can 'feel' the pain, just thinking about it. In the villages, kids would make bats from a piece of wood to resemble the general shape and the handle would be a rectangle or a square with plenty of splinters to spare - try holding that without gloves! Growing up in Calcutta, India, every year I looked forward to a test match at Eden Gardens, the Mecca of cricket. (Lord's may have started the game, but Eden Gardens was *the* place!)There is no stadium quite like it, in terms of the appreciative crowd that would fill up the 80,000 capacity stadium even on the last days play. I remember during a match against England in the late 70's, where they required only a few hours play on the final day. The match was over before lunch with India losing the test match, still, not an empty seat was to be found in the stadium! Sadly, it does not hold true today.

I would get up early on match days in the crisp winter morning, and as we made our way towards the stadium, a light fog would be wafting low across the 'maidan' which is an open ground or park in the city. Preparations for attending the game would start days in advance and the agonizing wait and anticipation, holding the tickets in my hands, and looking at it over and over again, telling myself – yes, tomorrow, I will be sitting in the stadium watching the match! The city itself would come to a standstill, the attendance at the companies would be sparse, everyone would be glued to the radios – yes radios, and this was in the nascent years of television so a privileged few had televisions. In those days, the antennas would sprout up sporadically on the rooftops, like metallic foliage on a concrete jungle and we would know who had a brand new, two color TV as I would say, or generally referred to as black and white televisions which bordered towards grey and white. The lucky kid with a brand new TV in his home would wear a huge toothy grin for days and it would be difficult to wipe that skewed silliness of a grin, off his face!

After my college days, the best cricketing experience I ever had was during the final of a local tournament in my hometown and to make matters worse, we were having the 25th anniversary dinner celebrations for the club, the same evening. I went in at number 6 and we still required about 125 runs to win, which the tail-enders were normally not expected to make. It was a monumental task; even getting 50 runs would have been respectable! That day was turning out to be good for me as earlier I had taken about 3 wickets and when I came in to bat, I somehow had supreme confidence and told the other batsman, just don't lose your wicket and we will make it through! Wonder where that came from, well it turns out we chipped away at the improbable score and we were lucky as my team mate was dropped twice by the fielder and I happened to play a perfect game without any mishaps and the two of us remained not out. I must have scored about 65-70 and my team mate made up the rest, what a victory that was. The big dinner of course was the high light of the day, for before the match one of the team mates had said to me, *"If we lose, I won't be able to eat tonight!"* I think that summed it all up – what was important, the game or the gastronomical delights that awaited us in the evening.

After the match, as I was making my way home to change for the evening celebrations, the bus with the visiting cricketers sped by and as I inhaled the tobacco laced village dust (tobacco is the winter crop there) kicked up by the tires, one of the players leaned out and yelled, *"Don't come back next time*!" I think that was the best compliment I ever received *and* his wishes were fulfilled too, as the following year I immigrated to America. Little did I realize, that twenty five years later, I would be travelling back into the labyrinths of history to dig up and discover that Golden age of American Cricket.

One of the fond recollections of playing during childhood is the fact that whoever brought the bat would get to bat first! If there was any opposition, then all he had to do was threaten to walk away and then the kid with the bat would ask again, "who bats first?" unified voices would say – you! Thus the batting order was decided upon by a popular *free* and *unimpeded* vote or as I liked to call it, "a Singularly Democratic Vote."

Another noteworthy match that I recall took place in high school against St. Paul's in Darjeeling. I was on the school team during my senior year and we travelled up to Darjeeling, which is situated at an elevation of 6700 feet. Coming up from sea level, we struggled with our breathing especially when it came to running on the field, the enviable part was seeing our opponent absolutely relaxed and we were sure they were enjoying every bit of it. Even though we struggled with the thin air, we put up a fight, but I think what did us in ultimately was the excellent lunch in the Principal's garden. No one was going to pass up on such a gourmet meal and when the time came to put the spring back into those feet, one could see it in our lumbering run!

Our trip back would have been uneventful, had it not been for one of our team mate who had to answer natures call and needless to say, the pleasant trip across the rolling green hills came to a halt. He had managed to hold off long enough to burst through the doors of the bus even before it stopped and disappeared into the fields in a flash. This was not the end of it though, a grazing animal nearby did not like his company (I would say it was the smell) and as it took threatening steps towards our 'cricketer' who was neither standing nor crouched, and undecided as to complete his business or run when the animal inched towards him. The animal was not going to allow a two legged city dweller to encroach on his sanctuary. It was comical to see and quite a spectacle I must say, for us to watch his predicament from the comfort of our bus. He was holding his pants with one hand and with the other, blindly trying to find a stick or a branch (as though that would have solved his problem) to ward off the beast! After a few minutes of back and forth, I believe both the 'contestants' lost their patience with, 'let's see who makes the first move' and our friend ran back towards the bus and in the process rendering the pants un-wearable as they were covered with the "processed food" that he had so thoroughly enjoyed only a day earlier!

We almost creamed him, when he threw the very same pair on the roof of the bus, where all out luggage was stored. Buses in those days had a 'carrier' on top to hold the luggage. Needless to say, some un-fortunate few were not happy when they found out their bags had come in contact with his, "boy, do I have a story to tell" trousers!

St. Paul's Darjeeling school grounds where the match was played – notice the absence of any grass and the Himalayan mountain range in the background.

One fine sunny afternoon out of boredom, I was doing a search for cricket books on a sports bookseller's website and I came across a listing for, "A 'Bawl' for American Cricket" by Jones. A. Wister, right away I perked up as if a shot of caffeine had been injected thru my sleepy veins. "American Cricket" I said to myself! All kinds of question and exclamation marks were randomly swirling in the cramped cranium, trying to organize in a fashion my grey cells could decipher!

'America' and 'Cricket' were poles apart (or so I thought) and the notion of them being used in the same breath, was as alien as having a coffee break during a cricket match instead of a tea break with cucumber sandwiches– an absolute sacrilege!

I bought the hardcover book and awaited its arrival with bated breath! It had a signature, "G.S. Patterson 29th May 1893", and the book was stamped, "K. A. Auty Library of Cricket, Ridley College, Ontario." G. S. Patterson was part of the Philadelphia's English tour of 1889 and later captained the team in 1897 on another English tour. Another jumble of question marks arose, who, or what was KA Auty and a cricket library in Ontario! First America, now Canada? I was being bowled too many googlies. The more I dug in for a long inning, the deeper I got, or rather; it took me further south – to South America that is! Cricket, and in Latin America too! What a silly point, or was it? As it turns out, Argentina, Brazil, Chile, Costa Rica, Mexico, Peru and Uruguay have cricketing history going back to the 1800's! The islands of Hawaii also did not escape its' clutches!

Here began my most gratifying journey into the game's history in Americas, of this, time tested gentlemen's sport which is played in countless climes by wide eyed boys with a gleam in their eyes, of making it big one day and the great future that lay before them. As soon as a bat or ball was held by their grubby little hand's, the impressionable minds would instantly wander into the magical world of their cricket heroes in the hopes of one day, emulating them! All the troubles were forgotten as soon as they reached an open patch of land, planted the stumps and the game had begun.

I started looking for this 'Auty Library' and an internet search yielded a valid name and location for Ridley College which came up as, St. Catherine's in Ontario, Canada, close to Niagara Falls. It had been a while since I had last visited the falls, and was thinking of using this as an excuse for a trip. Little did I know one would be coming up soon! I decided to get in touch with them, by reviving the old art of letter writing! So began the laborious process, with a touch of angst I might add, penned my thoughts in the slimmest of hopes, that they still had some books left! Maybe the curator had misplaced some, maybe some were in storage, maybe, just maybe, and everything had not been sold off! A thin sheet of processed wood on which my thoughts were penned, were left in the capable hands of the men in blue, the US Postal Service! A few weeks later, a big white envelope arrived in the mailbox.

"Securing the future for Ridley" was printed on the top left in large blue letters.

Everything stood still; I don't think I was breathing for a few seconds. I opened the door to the complex and hurried towards the elevator, that day, for some strange reason, it took longer than usual to traverse the short distance, or so it seemed. Hurriedly I read that, the majority of collection was sold off as the game was no longer played at the college and… *and*…whatever remaining books they had, I was welcome to acquire. Was this happening to me, did I read it correctly, they still had some books left and *I* could buy them! Hope had given way to reality! A few books were listed, but none that stood out as the ones I was looking for. Still, here was an opportunity to own the books that once belonged to Karl Auty himself, a true cricketer who tirelessly promoted the game in the Chicago area and beyond.

Karl Andre Auty was born at Dewsbury, Yorkshire, England in 1878. In 1909 he emigrated to Vancouver, Canada. In 1915 Karl moved to Chicago, Illinois, where he was employed by the Commonwealth Edison Company as Sales Manager until his retirement in 1946. He was an active cricketer well into his sixties, and was reputed to be an excellent fielder. He was President of the Chicago Cricket Club and the Illinois Cricket Association for 25 years and did a great deal to promote cricket in the area. He was also the publisher of a newspaper *The British American* and *The Illinois Cricket Annual.* Karl Auty passed away from a heart attack in Chicago in 1959 at the age of 81. (Source: Canada Cricket Association)

AUTY, MR. KARL ANDRE, who died in Chicago on November 30, aged 81, was the owner of an outstanding cricket book collection. Educated at Wheelwright Grammar School, Dewsbury, and on H.M.S. Conway Training Ship, he accomplished a Military and General course at the Sorbonne, Paris, and obtained a B.Sc. at Nottingham. He was an active participant in cricket until his late sixties in New England, B.C., and in North America. In the thirties he published a weekly newspaper, The British American, and for some years issued a cricket annual containing full details of Chicago cricket. He was celebrated for his Christmas cards, one of which included the following information: "It is interesting to note that a Surrey (England) team on its way to play exhibition games in Paris in 1789 was at Dover ready for the crossing, but turned back when met there by their host, the Duke of Dorset, H. B. M. Ambassador, who had fled from Paris before the coming outbreak of the French Revolution. Otherwise this would have been the first team ever to leave Britain's shores to play cricket abroad, thus depriving the 1859 team of that distinction." From the Wisden Obituaries 1959.

I did not waste any time in getting in touch with Ridley College and after exchanging a few emails (yes, I moved up the communication chain), I met the curator and collected the material from him. Now I had a unique cricket memorabilia collection and my friend also suggested casually, *write a book*. Now, after three years, I fully understand the true meaning of the expression, 'talk is cheap!'

FOREWORD

Sir Robert Menzies once said, *"The world would have been a much happier abode had America and Russia played cricket!"* I reckon the political restlessness of our world might have prompted the popular Australian Premier to make the statement when he did. Also, the emphasis was deliberately on 'playing cricket' implying the fairness of it all in just about every possible manner.

Be that as it may, I'm aghast that only in the American continent the impact of early 'cricketing pioneers' does not quite show up in the social milieu as it does in two other continents - Asia and Australia. Again, be that as it may, if the Yankees didn't find a game of cricket socially viable, it is a Yankee loss! For all my reverence for the willow game, I'm reasonably sure I may be barking up the wrong tree! But my humble attempt to write a 'foreword' for Jayesh Patel's well researched analogy of "History of Cricket in Americas" is mainly to extol the virtues of a man I've never met, and yet it seems I've known Jayesh for as long as I can remember! Thanks to 'Twitter' we got to know each other and then one tweet led to another, until I became very absorbed with Jayesh's obsession, which was getting to the bottom of cricket played by Americans - North and South!

And then one day I receive the manuscript from Jayesh. It was both heavy in weight and words and demanded a sincere scanning. I tried to catch up with Jayesh's flight of fancy and to some extent taxed my own patience. It was all worth the effort I thought, considering he had put in so many hours of relentless digging of cricket's archives in a non-cricketing nation. Of late, we've been awfully pre-occupied with Sachin Ramesh Tendulkar's farewell series, an event which gripped the entire cricketing globe, but it would be well-nigh impossible to convince an American what a great void will be felt by the sport. Even so, an attempt is being made, in all sincerity, to bring about some cricketing awareness in the land of basketball and baseball by a cricketer.

It is a tough task for Jayesh Patel, for my personal experience tells me that Americans do not possess the patience for a game of cricket! Having played club cricket in the Valley in Los Angeles and also in San Diego, I'd noticed only Asian and West Indian expats were willing to have fun via cricket, but not the locals! Way back in the 70's, the cream of cricketers formed the 'Rest of the World' team, indulged in a game of cricket at the Shea Stadium in New York, whence yours truly, nailed the matting surface! Barely a couple of hundred turned up to witness this strange spectacle. We've also played fun games in

Toronto and Vancouver without really getting down to spreading the virtues of the game of cricket.

Now, this is not an attempt to discourage my twitter-mate, Jayesh Patel! If anything, my aim is to highlight Jay's love and passion for cricket. History of any sort cannot be passed on without enduring ties binding not many, but a Commonwealth of countries. If I'm able to convince Jayesh that cricket, indeed has a strange power of uniting men and women (yes, Lasses too have taken up cricket in a big way!) of all castes and creeds and degrees, skilled and unskilled, binding them together in a common devotion to the game, then I will have done my job of writing this humble foreword. I write therefore, as one of those who only stand and wait! As the title of the book indicates, it is a story of digging of historical archives with sustained values of patience and passion. I wish Jayesh reaps a good harvest in terms of spreading the gospel of cricket in both the Americas and if in the process Jayesh can improve upon the awareness, then he would have earned his cap.

Bishan Singh Bedi

November, 2013

Delhi, India.

COLONIAL COUSINS, THE YANKEE GAME OF WICKET

ajority of the modern bat and ball games arrived with the settlers, and the game of Wicket which was predominant in the New England states, was no exception, though its' a mystery why it did not find a home elsewhere. Was this the precursor to modern cricket, going solely by the evolution of the stump design – it looks probable. Wicket stumps were 5 to 6 feet wide and 3 to 4 inches high and defended by a tubular bat, whereas the stumps used in cricket as per the diagram below, were 2 feet wide and 1 foot high, and the bat was curved and almost came up to the chest, give or take a foot based on the rendering by the artist. Gradual changes were introduced and the stumps became narrower and taller and the bat became shorter and straight. There is no evidence of wicket being played in England, nor is it a Native American game, so where did it originate?

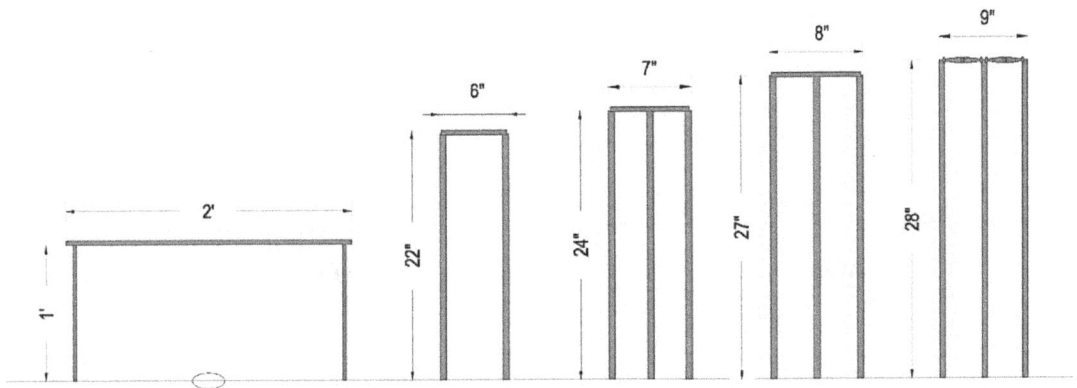

The Evolution of Stumps.

This diagram is based on the book, *'The English Game of Cricket'* by Charles Box 1877, *(p. 382 shown below)* which depicts the evolution of the stumps. *"The stumps must be three in number, twenty-seven inches out of the ground, the bails eight inches in length, the stumps of equal and sufficient thickness to prevent the ball from passing through."* So, the stumps were 27" x 8" before the present dimensions (Fig 6) were settled upon. Describing the origins, the book sates that #1 appeared about 1700, and *'about 1775 a third stump was introduced, making the breadth of the wicket six inches and its height twenty-two inches.'* There is conflicting description of the stump dimension as given in the text on page 383 of the book and the description as given in the diagram below. The text is referring to #2 which has only 2 stumps. The 27" x 8" came about in 1818 which now had two bails, while the current standard is 28" x 9".

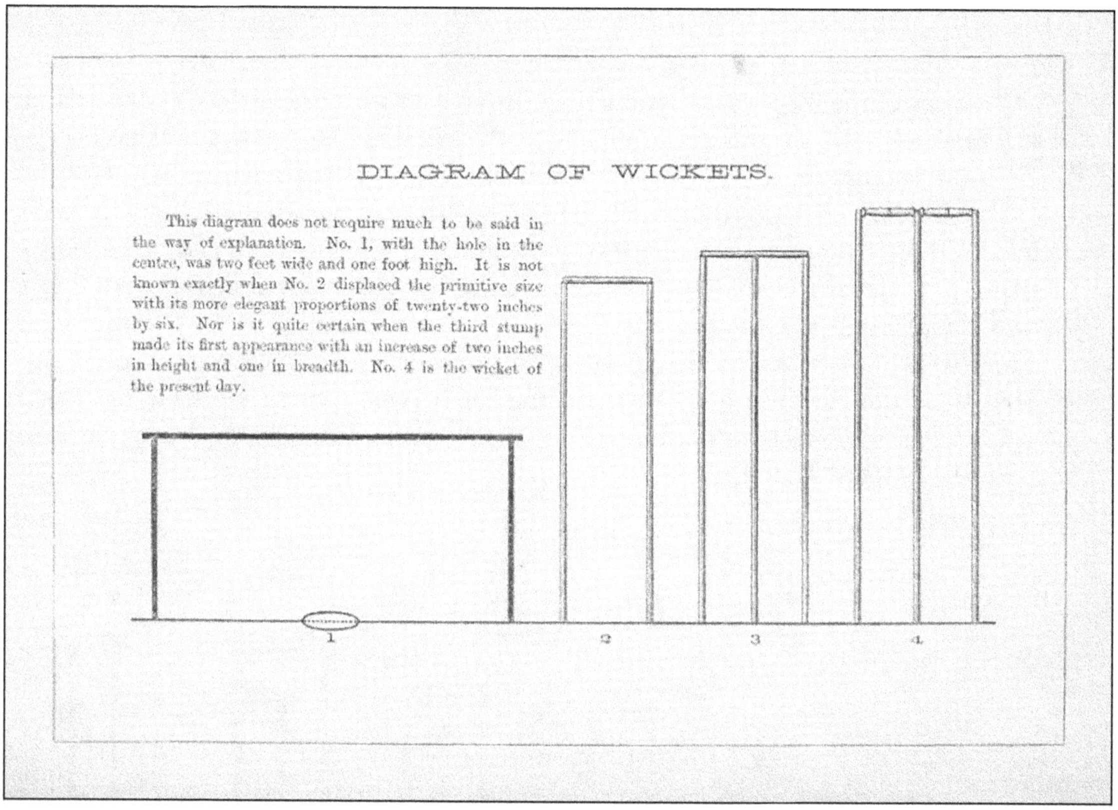

DIAGRAM OF WICKETS.

This diagram does not require much to be said in the way of explanation. No. 1, with the hole in the centre, was two feet wide and one foot high. It is not known exactly when No. 2 displaced the primitive size with its more elegant proportions of twenty-two inches by six. Nor is it quite certain when the third stump made its first appearance with an increase of two inches in height and one in breadth. No. 4 is the wicket of the present day.

Wicket diagram from, 'The English Game of Cricket.'

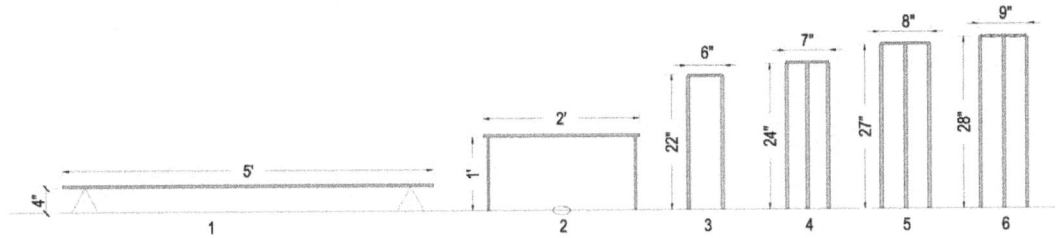

© *Wicket/Stumps comparison.*

Now thrown in the New England wicket 'stump' to the evolution mix and the progression looks logical.

"The field is laid out with what is known as an alley, a smooth space of ground, at each end of which is the wicket. This consists of two wooden pyramid on top of which is a slender stick about five feet in length. The other end of the alley is the bowler who stands outside of the wicket. The bat resembles a tennis racquet without the net and the wood replacing the netting area. There was another batsman of the same team at the opposite end of the alley which was 75 feet long and also a bowler. The bowler can throw the ball from either end as many times as he wishes, and at times a good bowler will completely mix up a batsman." [1]

Could this have been the original form of cricket (I know traditionalist will be up in arms over this), or, evolved entirely on its own as a similar game is shown to have existed in Hamburg, Germany in the 1790s.[2] Wicket may have its origins in Europe and arrived with the settlers who brought their customs and way of life. In America, the origins are found in Bristol, Connecticut, the nutmeg state in the early 1700s and continued to be played till about the 1910s. (An exhibition match was played in Newington, Connecticut as late as 1940s) The game was however confined to Connecticut and Massachusetts but occasional mention is found in, New York, New Orleans, Hawaii and Ohio. The boys from Bristol were the undisputed champions, and no organized team in the state has beaten the men and boys from the Clock Town. When Connecticut emigrants settled in the Western Reserves of Ohio and Michigan, or with the Congregational missionaries to Hawaii, the game of Wicket followed [3] and in Hawaii it was known as 'Aipuni.' [4] The country's first President – George Washington is documented playing wicket with the troops at Valley Forge, Pennsylvania, on May 4, 1778. A letter written by a soldier, George Ewing states, *"this day His Excellency (Washington) dined with General Knox and after dinner did us the honor to play at Wicket with us."*

In this Yankee version of cricket, a batsman defends a wicket which is about five feet wide and is placed on two wooden pyramids or blocks just 3 to 4 inches off the ground, and the object of the bowler is to knock down the wicket. Someone watching the game for the first time is struck by the number of people on the field as there are 30 players to a side and it seems impossible to score or play a game with so many crowding the field all

3

at once. The bowler takes a running start and when he reaches the wicket he *jumps over it* and *throws the ball along the ground* towards the other end of the alley (pitch) in an effort to prevent the other batsman from hitting and getting a run and to displace the wicket.

If the wicket is knocked off, by the ball or some mistake on the part of the batsman, he is out and the next one in the batting order takes his place. When the ball is hit and it's not caught on the fly, the batsman runs to the opposite end of the alley, and a run is counted. The bowler can change ends any time and various tricks are resorted to put the batsman off his guard. The ball can be delivered by any bowler from any end! The field placing was similar to cricket, except, more hands were around to catch a flying ball or prevent runs. The ball when bowled along the ground must touch the ground before it passes the central line of the alley – or halfway mark to avoid being a no ball. When the ball hops a little before reaching the batsman, only then is the batsman able to hit it over the fielders and the batsman can run and meet the ball also to make a hit. A run can only be made after a hit and not on a bye or a wide as in cricket. There are three umpires, one for each side and the third one act's as a judge to oversee the other two in case of a dispute.

One of the memorable games played in Bristol was on Federal Hill Green against Waterbury on September 9th, 1858. The Waterbury players hired a special train to bring them to Bristol and the press at the time, the *Waterbury Journal* carried the news in detail. A band from Forestville provided the music and the game ended in Bristol's favor where the visitors were defeated by 110 runs. The band lead a procession down Main Street following the game where the visiting team was loudly cheered as they marched to the center of town and this was followed by a banquet. The game generated a lot of attention and it was carried extensively in New York *Sunday Mercury* and again 22 years later when Bristol went to Brooklyn and defeated a local club there.

The most important game ever played in Bristol was against New Britain on a warm Monday on July 18th 1859, for the championship of the State. Prior to this, Bristol had advertised that they were willing to meet, "a team from any town or city in the State or any combination" to determine who was the better team. (Was this a championship of a league or a game that was challenged? The theme is familiar here as teams were often challenged to games thru advertisement in the newspaper which was *the* medium for communication). The challenge was accepted by New Britain and on the day of the event, a holiday was practically declared. The whole town was afoot and the plot on Federal Hill Green presented a scene that was never forgotten by those who were present.

So much interest had been generated that a special train had to be arranged in Hartford and when it reached New Britain, the four cars were quickly filled with eager people – all this for a game of wicket! The cars were trimmed with flags and buntings and the visitors brought a band with them and were greeted by a large crowd at the station. About 4000 people were estimated to be at the grounds (present day Federal Hill Green would never be able to hold that many people as its smaller now than what it might have been in those days). All available windows in the surrounding homes were occupied by people watching the game all day long, including the Congregational Church. Thousands stood all day long in the hot July sun to watch a contest that was to decide the supremacy in Connecticut!

The ground was, 'clear, hard and fine' according to the local newspaper of the day. The *Hartford Press* reported, *"the most remarkable order prevailed during the game and the contestants treated each other with faultless courtesy, the good natured cheers at each other's mishaps being given and received in the best of spirits. The judges required the umpire but a few times during the game and the decisions were yielded to promptly. Toward the close of the day a number of outsiders were unnecessarily vociferous towards the New Britain players but they were an exception. The sole drink was cold water for the New Britain Club and mixed water and milk for the Bristol's, rum was at a discount."*

The following were the scores from the game in which Bristol won by a score of 190 to New Britain's 152.

Bristol	1st Innings	2nd Innings	3rd Innings
George Hendrick	0b	0b	0b
Elijah Manross	2b	0c	7b
Franklin Wordworth	0c	4b	6b
Charles Alpress	0b	1b	12c
Russell Fellows	1b	0b	0c
Lucius Osborne	1b	0b	0b
George H Mitchell	0b	0b	0b
J. Fayette Douglass	0b	0b	5b
Eli Manross	8c	0c	0
Harry S Bartholomew	11c	2b	1c
Franklin Steele	4t	2t	0b
William Jerome	5b	7c	0c
Hiram Wilcox	1c	0t	0b
Henry I Muzzy	1c	0c	4c
John Williams	3c	4c	6c
T. B. Robinson	4b	0b	1c
Henry. A. Peck	5b	5c	0c
Volney Bradley	0b	0c	1
Josiah Tracy Peck	1c	4c	2c
Rufus Sherman	1b	0b	3b
Hobart A. Warner	7b	0b	0b
Orrin Tuttle	2t	1b	0b
Warren McIntire	2c	12c	0b
Albert Woodruff	0b	0b	0b
William Carpenter	0b	0b	1c
Horace Grey	0b	0b	4c
Charles Smith. Jr.	0b	6c	3
John Manross	5	0b	0b
John C. Mack	5b	1	2c
Total	75	55	60

New Britain	1st Innings	2nd Innings	3rd Innings
William Maitland	4c	0b	5b
William H. Hart	2c	0c	0b
Charles W. Andrews	2b	4b	1t
Samuel Moore	3b	0b	2c
Henry Mather	7c	9c	5b
William Burritt	4t	0c	0c
Andrew E. Hart	11b	1c	0t
Monroe Stannard	0b	0b	0b
W. H. Riley	2b	1b	1c
William Hotchkiss	0b	0b	2b
John Stannard	1t	1c	1c
Charles Gilbert	1c	0b	5c
Daniel Gilbert	0b	1b	7c
John Burritt	2b	0b	0b
Walter Parsons	2b	0b	0b
Philip Corbin	0c	0b	0b
C. Myron Talcott	0c	0	2b
Andrew Corbin	0c	2b	0b
Thomas Brigham	0b	1b	0b
George Gilbert	1t	3b	0b
Frank W. Beckley	0b	5b	0b
Robert Kenyon	0b	15	1c
Walter Stanley	4b	2	2c
F.W. Stanley	0b	0c	0c
Valentine B. Chamberlain	0b	0b	5b
Edward Stanley	0c	3c	1c
Thedeus Butler	4b	5t	3
I.S. Lee	0b	0b	0b
Walter Judd	0b	0c	0b
Thomas Hart	1	0b	5c
Total	51	53	48

'b' bowled out – 't' ticked out – 'c' caught out

The New Britain crowd left for the train station after the loss of the game to return home and the festive decorations from the morning gave way to black bunting on the cars as if a famous personality was being sent on his final journey. The player's remained behind for the customary banquet at the Kilbourn House.

An interesting fact of many a game for thirty years was 'Gus' Smith, without whom Bristol could not think of playing. Gus always had a tricky way of bowling and the batsman had a hard time reading him and on majority of occasions they could not score. It wasn't the bowling that stood him apart – it was the fact that he was always sent for before a game, from the Connecticut Hospital for the Insane at Middletown! He had become 'imbalanced' and remained at the asylum for a long time and Gus would be sent for whenever Bristol played and he would be sent back after the game! Even when he was moved to the Soldier's Home in Togus, Maine, he would be called for an important match to bowl his opponents out.

On August 27, 1880, the boys and men of Bristol Wicket Club defeated the Ansonia Wicket Club of Brooklyn (employees of Ansonia Company of South Brooklyn) on the lacrosse field of the Brooklyn Athletic Grounds on Ninth Avenue and Ninth Street. A great deal of curiosity was created around the game amongst the New York reporters and the *Brooklyn Eagle* reported,

"There were many greybeards on both sides, but what was most striking in the contest to the spectators present, accustomed to witnessing games and matches of all kinds in the metropolis, was the entire absence of that spirit of partisan malice of continuous disputing and quarreling, which is so frequent at the local contest on the local ball fields. There was plenty of good natured chaffing, but the behavior of the contestants throughout the game was that of educated, intelligent, American workmen. It is rather rough re-creative exercise, well calculated to give a man a healthy old appetite after a match, besides making him sleep well that night."

There was also a 'Brooklyn Wicket Club' that was formed on 24th July as reported by the *Brooklyn Eagle* of August 12th 1858 and their grounds were at Bedford opposite Halder's Hotel. About 25 years before the 1880 match, the boys from Windsor had first played a match there. In describing the wicket gear, the paper notes that the 'stumps' were two pieces of white wood which were six foot long and an inch square, which was placed on two blocks three inches off the ground. The ball was almost double the size of a cricket or baseball but weighed only 9 ounces.

The Brighton Beach Hotel was the venue for supper that evening and the day ended joyfully as it had begun. A book with the record for all the matches played over 30 years was maintained by Henry B. Cook, beginning with the October 3rd, 1874 game between Bristol and Forestville. Bristol won by a score of 122 to 111. A game from the previous year is also mentioned between Wolcottville (now Torrington) scoring 109 to Bristol's 312. A September 24, 1873 game between Bristol and Ansonia resulted in Ansonia scoring only 45 runs to Bristol's 282, which must have been a boring game! July 1876 saw Bristol taking on the old friends from the Brass City – Waterbury, on their grounds. At the end of two innings the score was ties at 147 and the Bristol team pulled forward in the last innings to win with a score of 230 to 193.

Other matches played by Bristol were:

- July 29th, 1876 – Burlington lost 135 to 305
- August 5th, 1876 – Burlington lost 109 to 409 a one sided loss for the farmers from the hill town.
- September 9th, 1876 – Forestville lost 130 to 153
- September return match against Waterbury, Bristol winning 318 to 230
- August 15th, 1887 – Winsted lost 100 to 184
- September 1887 – Winsted lost again to Bristol.
- October 6th, 1892 – Newington lost 164 to 280
- October 27th, 1892 – Newington lost 111 to 191
- August 18th, 1893 – Newington lost 125 to 164
- September 8th, 1893 – Newington lost again 80 to 84, a near win.
- October 13th, 1893 – Torrington lost 107 to 168
- September 7th, 1894 – Newington lost 122 to 215
- September 20th, 1895 – Newington lost 76 to 79 another close one as the 1893 game.

On September 4th, 1903, Bristol took on an old rival - New Britain, on the Center street baseball grounds. Governor Chamberlain consented to do the judging and William H. Hart and Captain Henry A. Peck, both veterans of the 1859 game were appointed as umpires. The first inning went in Bristol's favor – 57 to 4, the second half resulted in New Britain losing 81 to 109. (There is no mention of a 3rd inning!) The evening banquet was presided by the Governor at Gridley House, while Miles Lewis Peck was the toast-master and speeches were given by the Governor, William H. Hart, New Britain Mayor, Samuel Basset and John H. Kirkham.

REWARD OF MERIT.

The earliest depiction for the game of Wicket. This 'Reward of Merit' was intended as a prize for school achievement, engraved by John Cheney 1821. Courtesy: John Thorn

This vignette also appears in, 'A Century of Philadelphia Cricket' which was provided by Newton. C. Brainard, who was the Mayor of Hartford, (Connecticut) in the 1920's. Lester acknowledges the contribution by the Mayor in his introduction. (p. XIV)

A one page note provided by the "Connecticut Historical Society" from the *"Manuscript Collection of Newton C. Brainard Papers, 1941-1964"* talks of the origins of the wicket game and the above print came from an exhibit of prints by early Hartford engravers and artists. The book image is reportedly a 'second plate' though the above image was acquired by John at an auction. The note dated April 14th 1949 mentions of an exhibition game played in Newington with old equipment that may have been in existence at the time. It further goes on to say that it was played for the first time in more than half a century and probably the last time also. Notice the striker or batsmen crossing to get back to tick his bat down on or over the tick mark to have the cross count. The 'wicket' can be seen on both ends, inches off the ground resting on blocks. The ball is up in the air and the striker's fate rests in the capable hand of one of the catchers!

Fourth of July Picnic of the Poquonock Drum Corp 1889-90. Picture taken at a clambake and Wicket game played in J.M. Brown's pasture at Poquonock.

Windsor Historical Society, Windsor, Connecticut

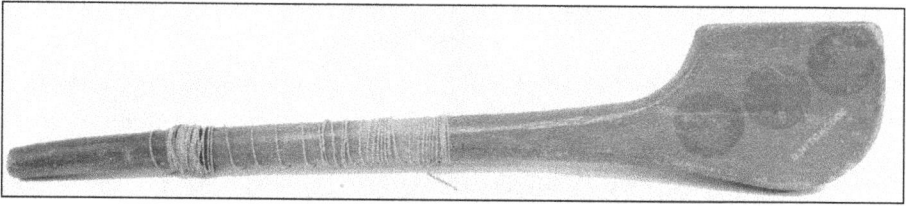

Bat and Ball from the same game.
Windsor Historical Society, Windsor, Connecticut

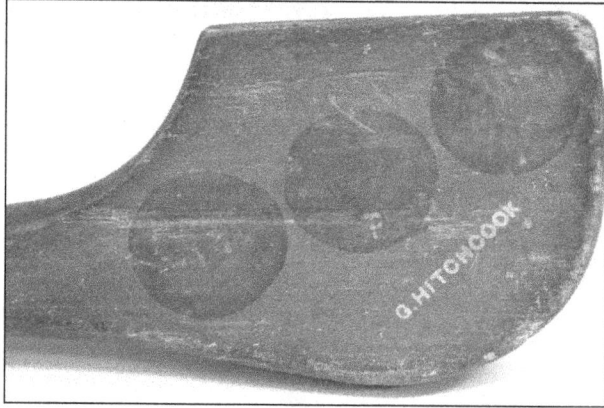

Close-up of the bat with the owners' name?
Windsor Historical Society, Windsor, Connecticut

A close up of the same Wicket Ball from the game.
Windsor Historical Society, Windsor, Connecticut

The bats from Bristol were heavier than the Windsor bats, and the wicket balls were also different in size and weight, as the ones from Windsor were smaller (3.25") and lighter.

Rules of the game of Wicket, when Bristol played New Britain in 1865.

1. The ball shall be from 3 ¾ to 4 inches in diameter and weigh from 9 to 10 ounces.
2. The wicket (pitch) shall be 75 feet apart. (10 feet wide)
3. The wicket shall be six feet long. (6 feet wide & 3 inches high)
4. The tick marks shall be six feet from the wickets.
5. The ball shall strike the ground on or before it reaches the center, to be a bowl.
6. The bowler must start from behind the wicket and pass over it in bowling.
7. The bowler shall be within ten feet of the wicket, when the ball leaves his hand.
8. A throw or jerk, is in no case a bowl, but the arm in bowling must be kept perfectly straight.
9. In ticking, the bowler must stand astride or back of the wicket striking it off from the inside, retaining the ball in his hand.
10. When the bowler has received the ball, it shall be bowled by him before it is passed to the other bowler.
11. The striker shall in no case molest the ball when it is being thrown in, so as to hinder the bowler from ticking him out.
12. There shall be no crossing the alley when the ball is being bowled.
13. There shall be no unnecessary shinning. (See the paragraph below)
14. In catching, flying balls only are out. A ball caught before striking any other object but the catcher is out.
15. In crossing, the striker shall tick his bat down on or over the tick mark to have a cross count except when caught or ticked out.
16. No striker shall strike a ball more than once except in defense of his wicket, neither shall he stop the ball with his bat and then kick it.
17. No one shall get in the way of a striker to prevent his crossing freely.
18. Lost ball may have four crosses run on it.
19. No one but the judge may cry "no bowl."

Another rule that came about early on was *'shinning,'* it meant stopping the ball with your shins without having made any effort to hit it with the bat. Sometimes players who had very tough shins would try to tire out a bowler of the opposite team by shinning ball after ball and a rule was made to prevent this. When, however, the batter struck at and tried to hit the ball, but failed, and the ball hit the shins, it was not called shinning. (An early instance to Leg Before Wicket?) Adrian James Muzzy was 29 years old in 1880 when he participated in the wicket game against Brooklyn in New York. Later on, Muzzy became a successful dry goods businessman. His Riverside Avenue store was an institution and the most popular destination in town for shoppers for nearly anything from women's hat to carpets and other house furnishings. When Fenway Park opened in 1912 in Boston, the same year Bristol Public Welfare Association received its first land donation when Muzzy offered five acres within Hickory Park, north of Park Street in memory of his two sons, who had died in early childhood.[5]

The same Muzzy field was the scene of a baseball game which saw the legendary 'Babe' Ruth hit home runs in October of 1920 (*New Departure News*, Bristol). It was also here where Vince Lombardi participated in a fundraiser in 1936 while playing for Fordham University. He went on to become the head coach for the Green Bay Packers and the coveted National Football League Trophy would be renamed after him in 1970 - The Vince Lombardi Trophy, which is now given to the winning team in the Super Bowl.

This old Connecticut method of playing cricket – very similar to what cricket was when the New England colonies were first established, was exhibited in Brooklyn on August 27th, and it was like old times again to see the veterans of the Bristol Wicket Club in the field again, on the occasion of their visit to play a friendly match with the Yankee clockmakers of the Ansonia Clock Company of South Brooklyn. The scene of the contest was the lacrosse field of the Brooklyn Athletic Club.

The weather was all that could have been desired, and a capital 'alley' was laid out on the field, the fences at each end being an effective backstop, which necessarily decreased the chances for scoring on the ends. That veteran bowler of the Bristol team of twenty odd years ago, Mr. Cornelius Day, acted as an umpire, and did his duty with thorough impartiality. Among the Bristol thirty were Messer's Eli Mauross, H. Bartholomew, Henry Peck and Tim Robinson, who took part in the celebrated three inning match at Bristol in September 1858, when the

14

Bristol team defeated the Waterbury's by 340 runs to 230. Bartholomew scoring 29 runs in the match, Mauross 15, and Cornelius Day 8, WM Jerome topping the score with 31. That was a great day for Bristol, and an era in the history of the old Bristol Wicket Club, which was then in its palmy days. The twenty odd years which have passed since then have made veterans of youthful players, but still the old Yankee spirit prevails. The old "boys" in this match showed the youngsters how they used to handle their bats and win fields in the merry olden time. The Ansonia's included several novices, who though well up in baseball fielding, were necessarily green in handling the willow. Nevertheless, they gave the old Bristol players a very good fight, especially in the first inning.

From the word, "play the ball" by the umpire all was life and activity on the field, and the sport was fully enjoyed throughout. With the doings of sixty players to record in bowling, batting and fielding in a match of two innings on each side we should require columns to describe the match, therefore we must be brief, leaving the score to give the somewhat meager details it affords, in as much as the score-sheet used by the tally-keepers contained no records of how and by whom each batsman was put out, such as who bowled him, who caught him, who threw him out. Play was called shortly after 10 a.m. at which time the Ansonia went to the bat, and before they were all put out, 71 runs had been tallied. H. Rossiter having the most 'crossings', viz — runs, his score being 11. In the first inning of the Bristol thirty they scored 78, thereby leading the younger club by but 7 runs, Hart's 10 being the best score of the inning. In the second inning both sides woke up to their work, the Bristol fielders disposing off their opponents for 56, of which P. Gillersen's 16 was the top score. This left the Bristol batsmen but 50 runs to win, and this number they obtained with the loss of ten men, Cook topping the score with 20 runs. Before the inning was over they ran the total up to 84, which left them victorious in the match by 162 to 127. Fine fielding was done by Green and Stocking on the part of Ansonia, and by Newell on the other side. The match lasted for 5 hours and 25 minutes.[6]

A Queer Game called Wicket: An Invention of the Nutmeg State Brought to New York, is how the New York Times article of August 28, 1880, refers to a Wicket match played at the Brooklyn Athletic Club, while the April to September issue of Brentano's for the same year describe the game in detail as shown above, a difference in sporting perspective? Wicket was also played in the hill towns of Western Massachusetts including Westfield, Granville, Tolland and Sandisfield in the 1850's. Wicket was a favorite pastime long before the revolution.

OUT-DOOR SPORTS.

In the absence of any reports or incidents of this kind, during such a sloppy, slushy, foggy weather—or term—as we have had lately, we give place to the following communications in relation to the game of " WICKET," of which we have ourselves no personal knowledge or experience :

TROY, *Feb. 5th*, 1857.

EDITORS OF PORTER'S SPIRIT : — *Gentlemen*,—On the 25th of January, I wrote you a letter requesting you to answer the following questions in your valuable paper :—1. If there is any work published on the game of " *Wicket*," and if so, where it can be procured ?   2. If there are any Wicket Clubs formed east of the Hudson, or in the city of New York, and if so, what are their addresses ?   3. If there are any published rules in the game of Wicket, and if so, where they can be procured ?   As I can find no mention of the subject in your two issues since that date (25th), I infer that you either did not receive the letter, or you thought that the "Troy Wicket Club" was a "myth."   To show you such is not the case, I attach a list of the officers. The Club has been playing under a set of rules during the last fall, which were compiled from different sources.   By answering this, you will confer a great favor on the

Officers and Members of the TROY WICKET CLUB.

President, J. F. CALDER ; Vice President, ——; Treasurer, P. A. CARTER ; Secretary, G. P. GRIFFITH ; Assistant Secretary and Treasurer, F. COIT ; Referee, A. D. McCONCHIE.   Tellers (2), J. L. LANE ; 2d, ——.

NEW YORK, *February* 5, 1857.

To THE EDITOR OF PORTER'S SPIRIT OF THE TIMES :—I would like to see the old game of WICKET (not Cricket), played.   It is a *manly* game, and requires the bowler to be equal to playing a good game of ten pins.   The ground is made smooth and level, say six feet wide by sixty to ninety in length.   The ball from five to five and a-half inches in diameter, hand wound and well covered.   The *bat* of light wood, say bass.   The ground plan as follows :

A. A. The bowlers.
O. O. The batmen.

B. B. The wicket.
* * * * Fielders.

The wicket is placed at each end, and on the top of a peg drove in the ground, just high enough to let the ball pass under the wicket, which is a very light piece of wood lying on the top of the pegs.   The rules are ver similar to those of cricket.   Can a club be started ?

Yours,   WICKET.

Porter's Spirit of the Times, New York, Saturday, February 14th 1857.

Even during the height of the games popularity in the mid nineteenth century, newspapers tended to ignore the game while cricket was covered extensively in newspapers, journals etc. In 1857, unhappy proponents of the game voiced their anger in a letter to the editor of *Porter's Spirit of Times,* and a wicket player from Troy, New York, complained on the lack of response to his earlier query on wicket in his letter, *"I infer that you either did not receive the letter, or you thought that the 'Troy Wicket Club' was a myth."* Another wrote, *"I would like to see the old game of WICKET (not cricket) played. It is a manly game, and requires the bowler to be equal to playing a good game of ten pins."*

The first definite reference to ball playing in America shows up in 1622 from the Journal kept by William Bradford the Governor of Plymouth, of the new colony in America. Governor Bradford had an amusing encounter with some of his new recruits, who had arrived on the ship 'Fortune' a month earlier. It was on a Christmas day that the Governor had asked them to work, but most of them excused themselves saying that it went against their conscience to work that day. The Governor in his own words, *"One ye day called Christmas-day, ye Govr caled them out to worke, (as was used), but ye most of this new-company excused them selves and said it wente against their consciences to work on yt day. So ye Govr tould them that if they made it mater of conscience, he would spare them till they were better informed. So he led-away ye rest and left them; but when they came home at noone from their worke, he found them in ye streete at play, openly; some pitching ye barr, & some at stooleball, and shuch like sports. So he went to them, and took away their implements, and tould them that was against his conscience, that they should play & others worke. If they made ye keeping of it mater of devotion, let them kepe their houses, but ther should be no gameing or revelling in ye streets. Since which time nothing hath been atempted that way, at least openly."*[7]

I wonder what the 'implements' looked like, and what were the 'such like sports,' was it wicket or cricket and did they bring over the early curved bats or did the wicket bats exists from the very beginning for as we see from the 'new' recruits, ball playing was definitely on top of their list, even though they were in a new and unchartered territory.

The next reference to a ball game shows up in 1704 from the journal of Madam Knight in her journey from Boston to New York wherein she witnesses ball playing in Connecticut – again, what kind of ball game? Another reference comes in Judge Sewall's dairies dated March 15th, 1725-26 where he writes, *"Sam Hirst got up betimes in the morning and took Ben Swett with him and went into Boston Common to play at Wicket. Went before anybody was up, left the door open, Sam came not to prayer, at which I was much displeased."* Two days later the offence was repeated and he was asked to lodge elsewhere! Sam Hirst was the grandson of Judge Sewall, was born in 1705 and graduated from Harvard in 1723. Besides using the Boston Common for settling disputes by dueling in the early period, it was also a playground where the favorite games played were *'wicket and flinging the bullet.'*[8]

Was Cricket ever known as Wicket in early England? The bats were similar and early cricket pictures show a curved bat, though not as big of a bulge as the wicket bats and the bowling was underhand. The 'stumps' also had two vertical sticks with a third stick placed horizontally on top, wicket also had two blocks (Waterbury and Meriden used 3 blocks and 2 sticks) for support and a 5 or 6 foot long stick was placed horizontally only 3 or 4 inches off the ground. The origin itself suggests that at one point the game was played defending the wicket – which was a small gate that swung in or out, besides or inside a larger one. The gate was replaced with two vertical sticks and the play moved to open fields and a third (middle) stick was introduced around 1775. The word as defined is, "a small gate, and etymologically it denotes something that turns – presumably on a hinge in opening and closing." It was borrowed from the Old Northern French *wiket*, which in turn came from Germanic root of Old Norse – *víkja* - to turn, move (Swedish - *vika*, to fold or turn). The date of origin is around 13th century.

Cricket, comes from the old French *criquet*, 'goal post, stick' or its possible Flemish source, *krick*. Though it's not clear whether the original reference may have been to the stick at which the ball was aimed or to the stick/bat used to hit the ball. Another possible candidate is also Flemish - *krickstoel*, a long low stool with a shape reminiscent of the early types of wicket. Another explanation to the origin theory I have come across is that, maids, while waiting for the men to deliver milk would turn the stool upside down and use it as a wicket, but that was called stool ball.

The first certain reference to the word and possibly the early form of cricket anywhere originates in north eastern France, in Flanders, near St. Omer, from a document found in the *Archives de France*, dated at Thouars in December 1478. "*On the 11th day of last October, a servant was requesting leave in the Castle of Leat, which was near to the town of Theroune. He wanted to go and spend time in the town of Liettes and arrived at place where people were playing a ball game.*"[9]

Wicket was so widely played that it did not even escape the clutches of the law. In Richard Vosburgh vs. John W. Moak & others, the defendants were engaged in a game of wicket on 8th of April 1846, on a public highway and the plaintiff, while travelling in a one horse wagon with his wife in the village of Great Barrington, was struck in the pit of his stomach thereby causing injury. Apparently, the ball was wet and it slipped from the thrower's hand and did not go in the intended direction and struck the plaintiff.[10]

Coming back to some of the recorded instances of wicket in New England, an American traveler to England in 1810, "*drew a sharp distinction between cricket as played in England and 'our cricket', and referred to the old long low wicket still used in America.*"[11] Interesting to note that even in 1810 wicket was considered an 'old' game that had been played for years! A great reference to Wicket chronology can be found at 'Retrosheet' website, which mostly deals with the baseball, but I was surprised by the amount of wicket related information that has been contributed, some of which is given below.[12]

1757 September 9th – Diary of Jabez Fitch Jr. (This is not on their website)

"In the afternoon I see a number of the Royal American Officers playing at Wicket."

-The Mayflower Descendant: A quarterly magazine of Pilgrim – By Massachusetts Society of Mayflower Descendants.

In July 1779, an American soldier in Pennsylvania reported playing bandy wicket. Bandy wicket was "old-fashioned" cricket played with a "bandy" (a thick, curved club) rather than with the flat cricket bat introduced into English cricket during the 1760s. In America, the term bandy wicket was seen in the Mid-Atlantic region until the mid–19th century

1781 March – Journal of Enos Stevens mentions playing Wicket in the afternoon.

1790 – A description of a game from Hamburg, Germany was similar to American 'Wicket' based on the observation of the author. The ball was bowled alternatively from each end and that it had to be rolled and a striker is out if he tries to stop the ball with his foot or body.[13] So, did Wicket have European roots?

1791 – Pittsfield, Massachusetts.

A by-law is enacted to bar "any game of wicket, cricket, baseball, bat ball, football, cats, fives, or any other game played with ball" within eighty yards of the windows of the newly built meeting house. However, the law does not exclude the playing of the game in the lawn of "Meeting-House Common."

At a legal Meeting of the Inhabitants of the Town of Pittsfield qualified to vote in Town Meetings, ~~on the~~ holden on Monday the fifth day of Sep.r 1791 ~~Voted,~~ The following Bye-Laws, for the Preservation of the Windows in the New Meeting House in said Town — viz.

Be it ordained by the said Inhabitants, that no Person an Inhabitant of said Town, shall be permitted to play at any Game called Wicket, Cricket, Base ball, Bat ball, Foot ball, Cat, Fives or any other Game or Games with Balls within the Distance of Eighty Yards from said Meeting House — And every such Person who shall play at any of the said Games or other Games with Balls within the Distance aforesaid, shall for every Instance thereof, forfeit the sum of five shillings to be recovered by Action of Debt brought before any Justice of the Peace to the Use of the Person who shall sue and prosecute therefor —

And be it further ordained That in every Instance where any Minor shall be guilty of a breach of this Law, his Parent, Master, Mistress, or Guardian shall forfeit the like sum to be recovered in Manner and to the Use aforesaid —

The 'Broken Window' by-law, Courtesy: Berkshire Athenaeum & City of Pittsfield, Massachusetts.

1830 – When the Western Reserve of Ohio was settled from Connecticut, Wicket also followed. Professor Thomas Day Seymour of Yale mentions that it was the favorite game of the students at the Western Regional College in Hudson, Ohio. The students were of the same stock and were already familiar with the game. Till 1861 the standard games were Wicket and Baseball with Wicket being in the forefront.[14]

1830 – Wicket ball in Buffalo NY.

The Indians would lounge on the steps of the 'Old First Church', where they could look at young men playing wicket ball in front of the church.

1840 – Hartford Daily Courant June 27, 1840.

Ball players from the city met 25 players from Granville, MA for a nine game challenge, but as they were beaten five games in a row, the rest of the games were not played.

1841 – Bloomfield, Connecticut, Wicket challenge. *Hartford Daily Courant* June 23.

"The ball players of Bloomfield and vicinity respectfully invite the Ball Players of the city of Hartford to play at Wicket Ball, the best in nine games for dinner and trimmings. Rules to be as follows: (1) The ball to be rolled and to strike once or more before it reaches the wicket. (2) The ball to be fairly caught flying or at the first bound. (In the Bristol, New Britain game in 1865, a catch was not allowed on the first bounce.) (3) The striker may defend his wicket with his bat as he may chooses (4) One shamble shall be out (5) Each party may choose one judge or talisman."

1844 – Wicket in New Orleans, Louisiana! *Times Picayune*, November 7.

"The members of the New Orleans Wicket Club are requested to meet at the field, this day, Thursday at 5 o'clock PM, precisely."

1846 – An Amherst Alumni recalls how Wicket was played.

Dr. Edward Hitchcock describes the wicket as being 8 to 10 feet long (wide). We have seen lengths of 5 to 6 feet, which are more in line with other descriptions and besides, a 10 feet wide wicket would be impossible to defend. A picture taken at a Wicket game played in J.M. Brown's pasture at Poquonock , Connecticut shows a player holding the wicket stick which looks to be about 5 to 6 feet long. The width of the 'alley' or the 'pitch' was 10 feet wide and 75 feet long.

1854 – Samuel Robert Calthrop who taught at Mr. Such's school in Bridgeport.

It was in the spring of 1854, carrying a letter of introduction from my friend Dr. Osgood to President Walker that I stepped into the Harvard College yard close to the park. There I saw several stalwart looking fellows playing with a ball about the size of a small bowling ball, which they aimed at a couple of low sticks surmounted by a long stick. They called it a wicket. It was the ancient game of cricket and they were playing it as it was played in the reign of Charles the First (1600s). The bat was a heavy oak thing and they trundled the ball along the ground, the ball being so large it could not get under the sticks.

They politely invited me to take the bat. Any cricketer could have stayed there all day and not been bowled out. After I had played awhile I said, "You must play the modern game cricket." I had a ball and they made six stumps. Then we went to Delta, the field where the Harvard Memorial Hall now stands. We played and they took to cricket like a duck to water. I think that was the first game of cricket at Harvard.[15] (The first 'image' of cricket being played at Harvard dates to 1795 and *the 'customs' at Harvard College in 1735 declared that "Freshmen are to find the rest of the scholars with bats, balls, and foot-balls."*)[16]

Here, Cambridge educated clergyman, Samuel Calthrop, provides a direct link for wicket, calling it the forerunner of modern cricket which puts the origins of wicket in England! So when I theorized in the beginning of the chapter that the wicket/stump evolution looks not only logical, but probable, the idea was not too farfetched. (Has Calthrop's suggestion been debated upon or refuted, I do not know). Brentano's article earlier also alludes to the origin of Wicket as, *'this old Connecticut method of playing cricket – very similar to what cricket was when the New England colonies were first established.'* Now, 'Club-Ball' is believed to be the earliest name for cricket in thirteenth century England, (The Cricket-Field, James Pycroft 1922 p.1) and the 'bat' used in Wicket does look like a 'club,' albeit, a flat one, so the name at least gives a tantalizing possibility that Club-Ball may be Wicket's sibling who changed names in the new colony! As Pycroft puts it, *"games commonly change their names…and bear different appellations in different places!"* He also mentions that Club-Ball may be identical to *'Hondyn* and *Hondoute'* (Hand-in & Hand-Out) played during the same time frame. David Block links it to 'cat and dog' (based on another author's observation) which was similar and that in turn was the likely precursor to 'two-old-cat.' *Porter's Spirit of the Times* (November 15, 1856 p.176) editorial in venturing into the origins of cricket writes that the game may have been, *"termed 'Wicket' as per the old chroniclers, to have been invented by the Druids, and was first played at Stonehenge!"* Druids or not, wicket does have a place in the early history and there is no denying that it has been around a lot longer than any other bat and ball innovation.

However, David has debunked Joseph Strutt's (who chronicled sports in 1801 in *Sports and Pastimes of the People of England*) description of 'club-ball' which identified it as an ancestor to cricket. Strutt's Latin translation of *pilam bacculoreum* as 'club-ball' is simply not accurate according to Block, it means, *'ball playing with a stick or staff.'* Robert W. Henderson in *Ball, Bat, and Bishop* takes similar liberties in describing a game as 'stool-ball' and *'la soule.'* The unsuspecting culprit in both Strutt's and Henderson's ball game origins theory is a Flemish parchment of 1344 from Tournai titled, *'Romance of Alexander,'* housed with the Bodleian Library at University of Oxford and easily accessible on their website. Block has correctly surmised that they may not have seen the actual manuscript and Henderson in turn would have interpreted Strutt's writing as fact, just as I have relied on others before me. On checking with the library, Dr. Martin Kauffman from the Department of Special Collections and Western Manuscripts clearly states that, *"what I can say is that, as far as we can see, the text on this page – part of the medieval French Romance of Alexander the Great – is entirely unrelated to the scene or scenes depicted in the lower margin. This is a common feature of marginal imagery in medieval manuscripts of this period. So, there is no authoritative textual key to what is depicted, and the identification of the picture as depicting a game of cricket, or any kind of game involving a bat and ball, should be treated with the greatest caution!"*

When comparing the overall illustration, the image on the left is described by the library on their website as *a group of nuns being taken in a wheelbarrow by a naked man to a brothel* (given into temptation?). I can interpret 'the ball playing image' on the right (in comparison to the image on the left) of the folio as one nun coming back having resisted the temptation and returned to the 'fold' by giving up that proverbial apple that seduced Adam. The head monk is about to punish her as she hands the 'apple' and the other monks and nuns have raised their hands as if to say, 'no, don't punish her, or pleading with folded hands!' Just because it shows a stick and a round object, it cannot be construed as a bat and ball game. There is no dearth in speculating the origins of the bat and ball games and they will forever be mired in history, as no conclusive evidence can be presented.

Another intriguing imagery can be seen in the Flemish calendar from the Book of Hours of John III, Lord of Ghistelles and Ingelmunster 1299 (Walters Art Museum, Baltimore). It depicts two boys playing with a club and a ball 'supervised' by an adult, whereas the text is totally unrelated (similar to *Romance of Alexander*) and the calendar is for the month of September wherein the names of saints are listed for the 'liturgy of the hours,' often referred to as the Breviary, which sets forth an official set of daily prayers. Majority of the imagery in the different months depicts a peasant going about his daily routine or a butcher slitting the throat of a pig or a nobleman riding his horse and only the month of September depicts any kind of leisure activity which begs a question – why September?

Wicket was a popular ball game during the Civil War as seen here (along with Base Ball) and in a journal kept by James B. Lockney dated 30th September, 1863 in a camp near Little Rock, Arkansas, he writes about watching a Wicket game for the first time.

A lithograph clearly depicting a game of Wicket in progress on the left. A scene from the Camp of the 37th Massachusetts Infantry Regiment near Brandy Station, Virginia in 1864. The voluntary infantry regiment, primarily of men from the far western counties of Massachusetts and was organized at Camp Briggs. (M. Sutherland)

Courtesy: Harry T. Peters 'America on Stone' Collection, National Museum of American History, Smithsonian Institution.

The games had gained such popularity that it even reached the 'eyes' of a fair damsel with the initials E.B.P. residing in the town of Modbury, in Devonshire, England. She wrote a poem, for this was the age of Emily Dickinson, Alfred Tennyson, George Eliot, and one would be expressive through poetry, so it was sent in honor of the 'Boys' who came out victorious against the 'Men' in one of the matches. A weekly called The North and South, (August 7th, 1858) was avidly followed by her and she writes, "*The North and South interest us so much, not only for its political aims, but also for it making us so familiar with your native town.*" She further goes on to say, '*I have been much interested in the cricket news, as it is a game I am very fond of watching, and waited quite anxiously to see the great result of the proposed match, when I found that the 'boys' had won, my thoughts slipped into a few lines of rhyme, which I send for your own amusement.*' Elihu Burritt, one of the prominent citizens of New Britain at the time issued a regular newspaper called, "North and the South" and as you would have guessed from the title, the news talked and discussed about the '*subject of compensated emancipation, and other matters relating to the freedom of the blacks in the South.*"[17] From November 6th 1858 onwards, the weekly was called, "The North and South and New Britain Journal."[18]

TO THE CRICKETERS OF NEW BRITAIN

Up, up! ye stalwart cricketers!
    Ye men of married fame!
Nor let the youthful bachelors
    Be victorious in the game!

Enter once more with the lists,
    And throw the gauntlet down,
Nor rest until your manly arms
    Have won yourselves renown!

Think ye not shame that 'boys' should be
    Victorious over 'men'?
Sons of New Britain! Seize your bats,
    And try the fight again!

Nerve your strong arms with manly skill,
    Ye men of married joys,
And in the conflict may ye be
    Triumphant o'er the 'boys'!

What is interesting to note is that she is referring to cricket and not wicket, I guess 'wicketers' would not sound right! Was she aware of the difference between the two, or just took it as an error on part of the paper in typing wicket and not cricket. The 'Weekly' also on its part did not make any correction when printing her poem. (As this was the peak period for wicket, I would tend to lean towards a wicket match, rather than cricket.) The match was played between the 'Married Men' and 'Bachelors' and the club in New Britain was called 'Phoenix Club'. The staying power of wicket lasted well into the very early 1900s, a game that arrived with the settlers was concentrated mostly in New England and survived the onslaught of cricket and baseball, is a feat in itself.

The *Hartford Daily Courant* of June 21, 1858 carried a detailed write-up on the same 'Wicket Ball' match played between the 25 married and un-married men of New Britain. The grounds where the match was played belonged to David C. Osborn Esq. which was about a mile and a half from the village and the losing team would pay for the supper for both teams (listed under rule 13 of the match) including the umpires/tallymen at Humphrey House. The unmarried were victorious by 20 runs and the honors for high scores went to Albert Corbin for the married with 26 tallies and John Burrit scoring 24 tallies for the bachelors.

"New Britain athletes have always excelled in their favorite sport, else the town will not support the particular pastime and it speedily goes out of favor. Thus it was with baseball." (Wonder what the current minor league baseball team, 'New Britain Rock Cats' would say to that) In reminiscing about a wicket game played on August 12th 1858, the *North & South* paper recalls how the home team, Phoenix Club beat the Winstead Club at Waterbury by a score of 310 to 141. After the winners were dined at the Scoville House by the vanquished, the victors reached home by midnight by a special train and were received by the citizens with a band, torch lights and a bonfire burning on the green! There were pockets of resistance to baseball in the country depending on which game was popular to the people at the time, Wicket, no doubt was the ruling game in Connecticut. Hon. Orville H. Platt of Meriden, judged/umpired the match, he went on to become the Connecticut Senator for 26 years, beginning in 1879. Some names that are still seen around town may have originated from these players: William H Hart, John and William Burritt, Walter Stanley, Andrew Hart, C.M. Talcott, Andrew and Phillip Corbin, Robert Kenyon, etc.

Another interesting tidbit comes from John Thorn who writes in his blog about a colored man's recollection of playing Wicket which was in an August 19, 1881 interview in the *Daily Freeman*, of Kingston, New York.

A Colored Resident. Henry Rosecranse Columbus, Jr. Some Incidents in the Life of an Old Resident of Kingston, NY. Born in 1801 per federal census or 1804 per Daily Freeman.

Mr. Rosecranse evidently believes in the good times of a half a century ago. He said, "We used to have a great deal better time than that you do now. We didn't have a big city with lamps and curb stones and paved walks, and had to go round through the mud, but we had more holidays. There was the Pinkster holiday, the Great Holiday for the colored men. They used to meet at Black Horse Tavern (the building still stands on the lower end of Wall street) and shoot for turkeys. Then the colored men raced horses on Peter Sharpe's lane. They used to come a great many of them with horses of their bosses, and run them. (This lane was where Albany avenue now runs, and the race ground was from Kiefer's to the lane that runs in to the house of William M. Hayes). The bosses used to come and bet on the horses, and they had a great deal of fun. After the races they used to play ball for eggnog." Reporter—"Was it base ball as now played?"

Mr. Rosecranse—"Something like it, only the ball wasn't near so hard, and we used to have much more fun playing." He further said a great game of those days was wicket.

The bats used in the game of 'Wicket' had a rounded bottom akin to a tennis racket, did they get the idea from the Hurling stick, the Irish game which is older than the recorded history of Ireland itself.[19] Madam Knight's journal on her travels from Boston to New York provides an early eyewitness account of ball playing in Connecticut in 1704. What was the ball game that she witnessed, was it wicket or cricket and what was the equipment like? All ball games originated outside the American continent and were brought over by the settlers, so then why is there so little mention of wicket anywhere else but New England? Wicket is a microcosm of cricket, just as cricket did not find favor in America; similarly, wicket did not find favor outside of New England.

The Wicket 'bats' at the Manross Memorial Library in Forestville, Connecticut.
Courtesy: Bristol Historical Society, and Manross Memorial Library, Bristol, Connecticut.

CRICKET IN CANADA

By the time Canada became a nation in 1867, cricket had become so popular that it was declared a national sport by the first Prime Minister, Sir. John A. Macdonald. There were cricket clubs in almost every city, town and village.[1] Canadian cricket has its roots in the Upper Canada region from the town of York (Toronto) in Ontario province. A young English schoolmaster and a publisher at the Toronto Herald, George A. Barber, encouraged the game in the early nineteenth century and who is today considered the father of Canadian cricket. In 1827 he helped in formation of the Toronto Cricket Club and was instrumental in starting the historic series between the Club and Upper Canada College in 1836.

The earliest reference to Canadian cricket is of a match played at Île Ste-Hélène in the Province of Quebec in 1785 on the site where the Montreal Exposition buildings now stand. It is generally believed that the game was introduced into the country by British soldiers following the historic battle at the Plains of Abraham near Quebec City, between the armies of General Wolfe and General Montcalm in 1759.[2] However, Donald King, ex-executive Secretary of 'Canada Cricket Association' provides a more conservative timeline as to the beginnings of the game, placing it around 1795.[3]

"After tea we took a walk with Mr. Lilly to a place they call Vauxhall. They have a very good assembly room and a pretty good garden. The Canadians were playing at bowls and cricket."

Another early reference comes from an entry in the diary of Robert Hunter, Jr. a twenty-year-old, son of a Scottish merchant from London who had come in 1785-1786 to collect overdue debts of his father's mercantile firm. He kept a diary of his travels and of business and adventure that took him to Canada, New York, Pennsylvania, Maryland, Virginia, North Carolina, and South Carolina.

References on Canadian cricket History were gleaned from the following books and without further acknowledgement in detail, they are:

1. Sixty Years of Canadian Cricket by John E. Hall and R. O. McCulloch 1895.
2. The Canadian Cricketers Guide 1858, by Member of the St. Catharines Cricket Club.
3. The Canadian Cricketer's Guide, Compiled and Edited by Rev. T.D. Phillipps and H.J. Campbell. 1876 & 1877.
4. Cricket across the Sea, or the Wanderings and Matches of the Gentlemen of Canada, by Two of the Vagrants 1887. GGS Lindsey & Dyce Saunders.
5. The Pleasures of the Game, The Story of the Toronto Cricket, Skating and Curling Club, by Stanley Fillmore 1977.
6. Seventy One Not Out, The Reminiscences of William Caffyn 1899.
7. Wickets in the West or The Twelve in America by R. A. Fitzgerald. 1873.
8. The English Cricketers Trip to Canada and United States by Fred Lillywhite, 1860.
9. History of Upper Canada College 1829-1892, George Dickson, Graeme Mercer Adam.

By 1825 a cricket field had been built in York and it was on the grounds of the Home District Grammar School. A book published in 1893 by George Dickson and Adam Mercer wrote:

"The ground surrounding the school which, in primitive times, was slightly undulating, had been cleared of the stumps, and a space for a few hundred square feet, was selected for the good old English sport of cricket, which was cultivated from 1825, under the enthusiastic direction of Mr. George Anthony Barber, who accompanied Dr. Thomas Phillipps to York as his principal assistant in the school, and who was well known as the father of cricket in old Upper Canada."

Prior to 1840 the game was played in Toronto, Guelph, Kingston, Woodstock, Montréal and Hamilton. The Duke of Richmond is reported to have played cricket at Kingston in Upper Canada in 1819.[4] The first recorded match took place at Hamilton, Ontario in 1834 between teams from Guelph and Toronto and the next recorded match was also between the same teams on August 15th, 1835. The scores for Toronto in the two innings were 74 and 37, while Guelph scored 108 and 7. In 1822-1823, during his second expedition in search for the north-west passage, from the Atlantic to the Pacific, explorer Captain William Edward Parry and his crew on board the HMS Fury and HMS Hecla were stuck on ice in winter near the island of Igloolik, close to the Arctic Circle. When the weather had improved in spring the captain set up various games for his crew, like cricket, foot-ball and quoits which was enjoyed for a number of hours.[5]

The engraving depicts the two ships, HMS Fury and HMS Hecla anchored in icy seas while some sailors are standing around and others playing cricket while an Esquimaux/Eskimaux (Eskimo or Inuit) is shown in the background with a small child and dogs.

wn by Captn Lyon R.N. — Engraved by Edwd Finde

SITUATION OF H.M. SHIPS FURY & HECLA AT IGLOOLIK.

1822 23.

15th July, 1836 saw cricket being played for the first time at Upper Canada College which started the historic series against Toronto Cricket Club. Toronto was able to score only 44 in two innings while Upper Canada College scored 60, winning by an innings and sixteen runs. The team scores are worth mentioning here since this is the first encounter and it gives an idea into the difficulty of getting big scores in the early development of the players and the game itself.

TORONTO

First Innings	Runs	Second Innings	Runs
Draper b White	0	caught White	8
Murray not out	9	bowled Barron	0
Lane b Barron	0	b White	0
Nash stumped Phillpotts	0	run out	2
Loring c Barber	0	c Kent	2
Boulton b White	7	b Barron	4
Head b White	0	c Barron	3
Roswell b Barron	0	b White	1
Maddock b Barron	1	b Barron	0
Humphreys b White	0	b Barron	0
Wakefield run out	0	not out	1
Total	19	Total	25

UPPER CANADA COLLEGE

First Innings	Runs
White c Head	6
L Robinson b Lane	7
Phillpotts b Lane	0
Kent b Draper	7
A Keefer b Lane	0
Barber struck out	0
J Robinson b Draper	7
Barron b Draper	18
Dyett c Boulton	0
Hale not out	2
T Keefer b Draper	3
Extras	10
Total	60

These two public schools, Upper Canada College and Trinity College School at Port Hope, fostered the climate and influence of cricket in its early years. Upper Canada College took the lead and consistently nurtured the spirit of cricket since it opened its doors in January 1830. Though George Anthony Barber has been called *the* father of Canadian cricket, F.W. Barron and John Kent together formed the *triumvirate* or the fathers of Canadian cricket.

More teams were being formed in different parts of the province and as a result, added to the list of items of import were Clapshaw Cricket bats and Duke's Cricket Balls! In an April 8th 1844 issue of the Toronto Herald, an advertisement for an upcoming cricketer's Handbook by a member of the Toronto Club was to be released but no such book has been found. The first published Cricket book in North America appears to be the Canadian Cricketer's Guide of 1857 edited by T.D. Phillips of St. Catherine's Cricket Club. The other recorded matches found, were between, Toronto and Guelph, 11th and 12th August 1837, Brantford and Hamilton, 14th August 1837, Eleven Officers of the 85th and 43rd Regiments played against Toronto, who came out victorious on August 8th, 1838. Cricket was beginning to take hold in the region with the influx of more English settlers.

By 1847 cricket at Upper Canada College had vastly improved and they were able to defeat the eleven of The Province of Upper Canada, which led the *Herald* to comment, *"We think it may justly be asserted that such another two-and-twenty could scarcely be brought together in Canada."* Some of the players who excelled were, Heward and Helliwell, they were good with the bat, while Barron and Parsons or "Little Ben" were excellent bowlers. Phillpots was one of the best wicket keepers in Canada and one whose name was forever linked to the International series between the Canadians and the Americans that came about as a hoax, though he had no hand in it! He was also a successful bowler. 1854 saw the emergence of T.D. Phillipps, who was later on known as Rev. T.D. Phillipps, the highest run getter at the Halifax Tournament in 1874. He made 197 runs, though his average was second best at 39.4. The Canadian Cricket Guides were compiled and edited by him and later in life he retired to Chicago. In the 1860s the officers of the garrison would coach the boys at the college and Captain Wallace, a former captain at Harrow and Captain Northey, an old captain at Eaton were amongst those who trained the boys. It's interesting to note that there were two Americans, Ellard and Kemper who were trained by Wright, were also part of the coaching roster for the eleven at the college. Looking at the scores from the period shows that college cricket was much stronger than before. In 1867 the college won all its matches as they defeated Toronto twice, then Hamilton, the Royal Artillery, Hussars, the Trinity College and Trinity School who were all beaten. The Intercollegiate matches between Trinity College School and Upper Canada College as recorded in Sixty Years of Canadian Cricket went on from 1867 to 1894.

The distinction of having scored the first recorded century goes to Hon. M.B. Daly who scored 106 at Halifax, Nova Scotia during the 1858 season and who went on to become the Lt. Governor of Nova Scotia. R.K. Leisk of Hamilton is the first to score 202 against Hamilton in the July 23rd, 24th match in 1877.

Canadian and American Matches

The match of 1844 between eleven representing Canada and United States has the distinction as being the first ever international match between two countries, in reality it was their *fourth* engagement! However, the first encounter took place in 1840 in Toronto due to a prank or a hoax perpetrated by a certain 'Mr. Phillpotts' who claimed to be a representative of The Toronto Cricket Club. There was a G. A. Phillpotts, a wicketkeeper on the club roster at the time and he had no involvement in the matter. Here you have a team that has travelled 500 miles and keeping in mind that in those days they had to traverse the distanced by carriage, railway, stage coach, river boat before they could reach their destination and then to be told that they had not been invited – I am sure they were annoyed, to say the least!

Here are the details of the fiasco as narrated by the *Cobourg Star* taken from the *British Colonist* of September 10th.

In the *Spirit of the Times* of the 22nd, it was mentioned that a match at cricket was made with the Toronto club for $500 dollars, and that the New York players would arrive around the 1st. Since there was no official communication it was considered as one of the unauthorized articles that found their way in newspapers, and the news was soon forgotten. When eighteen gentlemen players from the St. George's Cricket Club arrived, all were astonished and a committee of three, Colonel McKenzie Fraser, W.H. Boulton and John Barwick were appointed to meet the Americans and offer a profound apology and make offer to repair the damage and were instructed on behalf of the club to:

a)   To express their ignorance of the whole affair.
b)   The regret of the Toronto Club that the New York gentlemen had received such a disappointment.
c)   That in order the visit should be made agreeable the Toronto club would be happy to play the St. George's Club of New York at a friendly game, say for 50 pound sterling, and to request the pleasure of entertaining the Club at dinner after the game is finished.

This was accepted and on the appointed day Friday (September 4th), the match commenced at 10 a.m., a large and respectable crowd had gathered to watch the noble and manly game of cricket that went off with the greatest éclat! The day ended with a loss for the host but it was soon forgotten on a sumptuous banquet in honor of the guest with delicacy of the season and fine wine. Here are the scores of the <u>first ever cricket engagement, between teams of two nations.</u>

TORONTO

First Innings	Runs	Second Innings	Runs
Goring c Wilde	3	caught Groom	3
Barber b Gill	1	run out	10
Warren b Gill	2	bowled Groom	0
Bliss run out	7	bowled Groom	9
Birch run out	10	bowled Groom	6
Maddock run out	9	bowled Russell	2
Winckworth run out	1	caught Stead	0
Harrington c Gill	0	caught Green	1
Girdlestone run out	4	not out	7
J G Spragge c Wright	0	bowled Groom	1
Marryatt not out	6	bowled Groom	7
Extras	9	Extras	8
Total	52	Total	54

ST. GEORGE'S CLUB NEW YORK

First Innings	Runs	Second Innings	Runs
Gill c Maddock	1		
W Russell c barber	6		
Wright b Winckworth	2	not out	3
H Russell b Winckworth	17		
Tinson b Winckworth	0		
Wilde c Harrington	22	not out	5
Wheatman b Winckworth	17		
Stead b Winckworth	2		
Groom b Maddock	1		
Wyville b Winckworth	0		
Green not out	4		
Extras	26	Extras	1
Total	98	Total	9

After their first meeting of 1840, there were no matches between the two nations till 1843 when the St. George's team was again in Toronto – this time, they were actually invited! Before the game could begin, the guests learnt that the visitors had included three players from Philadelphia in their team, and after discussions and agreement from New York, Guelph added six players from Upper Canada College. The only score mentioned is that Guelph scored 71 while the American's scored 33. Toronto returned the hospitality the same year on September 13th and 14th and beat St. George's on their home turf by four wickets.

Meanwhile there were other clubs being formed, like the Woodstock Cricket Club who played against Guelph in 1840. In the same year, Carelton Cricket Club was formed in Ottawa, but no records have been found. The first reference to a Toronto University and Upper Canada College Cricket match is given as being played on July 8th 1843. Other matches were played between the UC College and Royals, the Garrison versus the Kingston on July 29th 1843, the 43rd Light Infantry versus Montreal Garrison on the same day played on St. Helen Island, Montreal. Single wicket format was also popular at the time and for a $100 wager, D. Winckworth of Toronto Club beat H. Groom of St. George's by an innings and 22 runs. Yes, even though it was one on one, it was an innings defeat and the score – Groom scored 5 and 0, while Winckworth scored 21 and had the benefit of 6 wide balls added to the score!

The dawn of September 24th and 25th 1844, saw the staging of the first International match between eleven of American and Canada on the grounds of St. George's Club, at the Red House that stood near the corner of Third Avenue and 105th street, Harlem near Bloomingdale Rd, and the grounds extended to the Harlem River. (Another reference puts the location at the current New York University Medical Center at East 31st street and 1st Avenue and another, at the corner of 2nd Avenue and 106th Street in Harlem, today this corner is marked with a Cold Cut House Caterers NYC, a Chase bank and a Triangle Pizzeria). *The Red House was one of the famous resorts for New Yorkers of sporting proclivities, NY Times April 11, 1909.*

"We wish the Torontowegians every success," read the *Toronto Patriot*, which was very economical in its expression in contrast to the *New York Herald* which carried a lengthy article befitting the occasion.

"Grand Cricket match for one thousand dollars between the players of Canada and the St. George's Club, of this city."

Excitement had been building up for some time and a large crowd of about 5000 had gathered and the visitors were sent in to bat as the toss was won by St. George. In the team was George Barber, the only international appearance by the school master who had worked tirelessly to promote cricket in Canada. The wicket keeper was none other than G.A. Phillpotts, the unfortunate player whose name was linked to the embarrassing 'fake' invitation episode, four years earlier.

Canada was dismissed for 82 runs on the first day and America replied with a score of 64 for the first innings. Betting, which was common during those days, was rumored to be about $100,000 – a huge amount for that era! The odds were 5 to 4 on Canada and as they scored only 63 in the second innings, the betting changed in favor of St. George! The target was set at 82 but America managed to get 58 and Canada was victorious in its first International match by 23 runs. James Turner who opened the bat for America has the distinction of being the first in North America to score a recorded century – 120 for Union Club of Camden, New Jersey against St. George earlier in the year.[6] The second International match was played at Montreal on July 30th, 1845, and Canada was again victorious by 61 runs. The third match was arranged at New York, August 28th and 29th, 1845 and again Canada defeated the United States by two wickets.

Following are the scores from the very *first International Cricket Match.*

CANADA v. UNITED STATES

New York, September 24th and 25th, 1844

CANADA

First Innings	Runs	Second Innings	Runs
Winckworth run out	12	b Wright	14
Wilson b Wright	0	b Groom	0
Birch c Page	5	c Turner	0
Barber b Wright	1	b Groom	3
Sharpe b Wright	12	b Groom	5
Phillpotts lbw b Groom	1	b Wright	13
Robinson J Beverly lbw	1	b Wright	4
Maddock not out	7	b Groom	7
Freeling c Dudson	12	not out	7
French b Groom	9	b Wright	0
Thompson b Wright	5	lbw	3
Byes 11, wides 6	17	wides	7
Total	82	Total	63

UNITED STATES

First Innings	Runs	Second Innings	Runs
Turner, b Winckworth	7	c Barber, b Sharpe	14
Wheatcroft, b Winckworth	9	absent	0
Ticknor, J., lbw	0	b Sharpe	0
Symes, c Thompson	1	b Sharpe	11
Groom, c Thompson	0	b Winckworth	0
Bage, not out	1	not out	5
Ticknor, R., c Thompson	5	b Sharpe	8
Wright, S., c Barber	4	b French	3
Tinson, st. Phillpotts	14	lbw, b Sharpe	0
Dudson, c Freeling	4	c Winckworth, b Sharpe	0
Wild, b Winckworth	10	c Maddock	8
Byes 7, wides 2	9	Byes 3, wides 6	9
Total	64	Total	58

CANADA wins by 23 runs.

The match played at New York on August 27th and 28th, 1846, resulted in bad blood, which prevented any more engagements till it was revived in 1853! For the first time, the United States eleven on this occasion included players from Philadelphia and the Canadian team included players from Montreal and Toronto. The incident was reported in *Bell's Life*, London, England, of October 14th, 1846, which in turn relied on the *New York Mercury*. Samuel Dudson of Philadelphia was bowling to Helliwell who hit the ball high in the air towards the bowler. The batsman ran towards the bowler on purpose, a good two feet away with the bat handle pointing towards him in fervent hope of preventing a catch, which he failed. Helliwell admitted he ran towards him on purpose thinking that the laws of the game allowed it! Dudson had fallen down with pain but got up and ran towards Helliwell who was returning to the tent and threw the ball at Helliwell which hit him on the thigh after one bounce, but did not cause any harm. Rest of the players intervened but the Canadians ultimately did not return to play and the match was forfeited. The Canadians also had to pay the bets, as the laws regarding betting at the time stated, *"the bets are not payable unless the match be played out or given up."*

The matches were resumed in 1853 and the match ended up in America's favor at St. George's ground. The umpire was none other than Mr. Barber of the Toronto Herald. The following year, Canada won at home in Toronto, though no match was played in 1855 (Canada could not field eleven players due to the Crimean War). United States won the next year at Hoboken but lost to Canada in 1857 but won again in 1858. It's as if they had decided that they would win on alternate years.

An article in the 1856 *New York Clipper* summed it up best.

"Whatever may be the cricketing scores of these noble games their general results are eminently social and manly, exhilarating and elevating. As a charmingly elegant lady writer has eloquently observed: "What a glorious sensation it is to be for five hours together winning-winning-winning! Always feeling as a whist player feels when he takes up four honors or seven tricks! Who would think that a little bit of leather and two pieces of wood had such a delightful and delighting power?"

If only there were more like minded individuals during the antebellum era, cricket then surely would have been the National Game of America! In 1859 and 1860 United States won both matches, till it resumed again in 1865 where they played with 10 players and still won. After a long gap, the matches were again restarted in 1879 where United States won by five wickets, and from 1879 to 1894, regular matches were held except on a couple of occasions. A series of matches were started in 1847 when the Province was challenged by the ex-pupils of Upper Canada College, this lasted till 1892 (up till the publication of Sixty Years of Canadian Cricket). Out of the 20 games played, UCC won 12 and Province took home 5 victories and 2 ended in a draw. No scores were recorded or found for the match played in 1870.

The First English team in Canada and America

The *first ever* overseas tour began when the English team boarded the ship, Nova Scotia on 7th September 1859 at Liverpool, and headed for Quebec. The twelve consisted of H.H. Stephenson, Julius Caesar, Tom Lockyer and William Caffyn from Surrey, George Parr, Grundy and Jackson from Notts (Nottingham), T. Hayward, Carpenter and Diver from Cambridge, while Wisden and John Lillywhite were from Sussex. Fred Lillywhite accompanied them as a reporter with his trademark scoring tent and printing press! The team comprised of six All England players and six players of United England[7] and they were to receive 50 pounds each and have all their to and fro expenses paid for.

Since none of them were sailors, it took then a few days to get their sea legs and would pass the time playing 'shuffle-board' during the day and some 'vocal' entertainment in the night with the help of Captain Borland (of the ship), Diver and Grundy were the other vocalist. The crew in the galley seemed to be the busiest as breakfast was served at half past eight, lunch at noon, dinner at four, tea at seven and supper from nine to eleven. I suppose that did not leave time for much else! As the horizon disappeared in the distance and the waves got bigger, John Lillywhite, Caffyn, Stephenson and Jackson were not in their elements and during one fierce gale, Caffyn and Stephenson lost balance and fell to the bottom of the stairs and were not seen again for two and a half days! As the days progressed and the seas got rougher, the players wished they had not made the journey. The fast bowler wished for a back door to Ollerton his home in Notts and Caffyn vowed never to leave England under any circumstances and if he did, he would forfeit 100 pounds. John Lillywhite was ill, Grundy, Lockyer and Diver were seldom seen and Julius Caesar did not fancy himself as a sailor. Parr, Wisden, Hayward, Carpenter and Fred Lillywhite were equally at home on the sea. Wisden, a thorough sailor enjoyed both his tobacco pipe and meals.

After being on sea for sixteen days, they finally reached Quebec on 22nd September, and proceeded to Montreal by a special train and were put up at the St. Lawrence Hotel. Friday the 23rd September was to have been the first day of play, but it was postponed for a day due to rain. A large and anxious crowd had gathered for days and finally the wait was over, reporters were also present from all parts of the States, who were very 'pressing' in their demand for information. The weather cleared up by noon and on losing the toss, George Parr's English Eleven took to the field against the twenty two of Lower Canada. A stand on the right was filled with ladies and on the left there were many carriages and by the time play commenced, there were about 3000 spectators or 'natives' as they were referred to by Lillywhite in his book. One side of the ground had a tent set up to provide refreshments' and a smaller one for the 'English' only.

The first ball of the first All England, Canada match was bowled by Caffyn and it was promptly dispatched to the ropes for a boundary by G. Swain and the very next delivery he was walking back to the pavilion! Canada did not get off to a good start and lost 6 wickets for only 12 runs and cries of *"Bravo England!"* rang out from the crowd. After four and a half hours, Canada was all out for 84 runs. When the English went in to bat, the light conditions were bad and they lost an early wicket of Grundy and Hayward and Wisden played on till the play was called off. That evening a big dinner was held in their honor at the St. Lawrence Hotel. The Chairman gave a toast to the guest and he could not refrain from giving a speech on this momentous occasion of having the "Elevens" of Old England in their midst. Mr. Pickering was given due credit for having arranged this tour successfully. The next day being a Sunday, they were taken around for sightseeing to the nearby mountain by members of the Montreal Club and they were treated to the spectacular fall foliage.

On Monday there was a great crowd and the English eleven scored 117 runs in their first innings. Georg Parr was the top scorer with 24 and was bowled by Fisher. The Twenty Two of Lower Canada scored only 63 runs in their second innings and the visitors were left with 30 to win which was achieved with the loss of two wickets. Since the game was over early, they decided to play another match but this time it was eleven-a-side. Six All-England players with five of the Gentlemen of Lower Canada against six of the United with five of Canada made up the team. The All England team combination, lost by an innings and 54 runs.

The scores for the ***first ever overseas tour by an English Team***.

ALL ENGLAND vs. TWENTY TWO OF LOWER CANADA

Played at Montreal on September 24th, 26th, and 27th, 1859.

THE TWENTY TWO OF LOWER CANADA

First Innings	Runs	Second Innings	Runs
G Swain b Caffy	4	c Jackson, b Caffyn	1
Lt. Surman c Caffyn b Jackson	4	lbw, b Caffyn	7
Lt. Symons c Jackson b Caffyn	2	run out	1
Lt. Bonner b Jackson	0	st. Lockyer b Jackson	6
F Fisher lbw b Jackson	0	run out	3
F Foudrinier c Grundy b Jackson	6	b Jackson	5
S Hardinge b Caffyn	0	c Lillywhite b Parr	0
Ravenhill c Jackson b Caffyn	2	b Jackson	0
Capt. Earle run out	4	c Lillywhite b Jackson	6
WP Pickering b Caffyn	8	c Lockyer b Jackson	0
Capt. King b Jackson	3	c Stephenson b Jackson	3
JG Daly b Parr	19	run out	0
W Smith b Jackson	8	hit wicket b Parr	2
G Bacon run out	4	b Parr	2
S Morgan c Wisden, b Stephenson	0	hit wicket, b Parr	0
WS Swettenham b Parr	3	c Lockyer b Parr	1
JW Smith c Stephenson b Parr	6	b Parr	17
W Napier St. Lockyer b Parr	0	c Grundy b Parr	0
W Ellis c and b Parr	2	b Parr	0
BS Prior b Jackson	3	c Caffyn b Parr	1
CHE Tilston c Lockyer b Parr	0	not out	0
JM Kerr not out	1	c Caesar b Parr	2
Extras, byes 4, leg byes	6	Extras, leg byes 4, wides 2	6
Total	85	Total	63

ALL ENGLAND

First Innings	Runs	Second Innings	Runs
J Grundy b Hardinge	2		
Wisden, J. c Hardinge, b Fisher	7		
T Hayward run out	17	c Bonner b Smith	10
W Caffyn b Fisher	18	not out	4
G Parr b Fisher	24		
J Caesar b Fisher	0		
A Diver c Pickering b Napier	3	not out	1
J Lillywhite b Napier	4		
T Lockyer not out	19	b JU Smith	10
HH Stephenson b Fisher	2		
J Jackson c Smith	10		
Extras, byes 5, wides 6	11	Extras, byes 2, wides 5	7
Total	117	Total	32

The players from left to right are:

Carpenter, Caffyn, Lockyer, Wisden, Stephenson, G. Parr, Grundy, Caesar, Hayward and Jackson.
The two sitting on the matt are Diver and John Lillywhite.

This was photographed aboard the "Nova Scotia" at Liverpool on September 7th 1859.

Photographed by T.H. Henna and W.H. Mason.

On 17th October, the English team returned to Hamilton to play 22 of Upper Canada after playing in New York and Philadelphia and by this time the weather was cold. Two innings were played with the visitors being victorious and they left for Rochester on the 20th. The Hamilton match would have been the last one on this maiden tour, but at New York it had been agreed to play one last match with the 22 of the American and Canadian players combined.

They arrived at Rochester amid really cold weather conditions, the combined team was bowled out for 39 on the first day, and the 2nd days play had to be called off due to snow. This would be the first and last time play was stopped due to snow! During the break the visitors tried their hand at base ball, this would be the first instance of cricketer's playing base ball. (Later on in 1874, during a World Tour organized by Albert Spalding, a baseball game was organized at the 'Oval' in Kensington, London, for the very first time). At this time in baseball history, the rule of catching the ball on the first bounce was permitted, which the English thought was childish. Henry Chadwick was instrumental in changing that rule in 1864.

On Sunday they were taken to Niagara Falls which they were finally able to view from the Canadian side, and according to them, *it was worth the trouble of getting there.* When the match resumed on Monday the 24th, the Englishmen scored 171, and concluded the next day in their favor with a win by innings and 68 runs. When they took to the field for the last time, most of them had their gloves and coats on, not the ideal condition for cricket or baseball for that matter! Some of the batsmen aptly commented when they lost their wicket, *'Shiver me timbers, I'm out!'* The victorious visitors returned to England on November 11th after the successful tour and each player was 90 pounds richer! One of the players, Grundy, was delayed at the customs; apparently he had some 'weed' in his possession!

Harper's Weekly engraving dated October 15th, after an ambrotype by Brady portraying the "Eleven of All England". John Lillywhite and John Jackson are not pictured.

Meanwhile, 'Canadians and other Players' as it was called out, played against the St. George's Club of New York in Hoboken on August 9th, 1860. St. George won the match by 4 wickets. One exciting match of the time took place in Toronto in 1861which elicited much excitement and interest due to the presence of H.R.H. Prince Alfred, Duke of Edinburgh and one of the player who later went on to become Sir S.W. Des Voeux, Governor of Hong Kong.

Various matches were played, not only between clubs, but between military officers of Canada and United States, Eleven of the Military versus 'All Comers', military against civilians etc. Detroit played Toronto on their home grounds on July 19th and 20th 1865, where Toronto won by 110 runs. A return match was played at Detroit on August 18th and 19th where Toronto won again, but by a smaller margin of 35 runs. The other teams during the period that played were, United Eleven (consisting of players from Port Hope and Cobourg), 16th Regiment, Hamilton Clubs, Upper Canada College, 13th Hussars, Garrison and Trinity College.

A Canadian Eleven made a trip to New York to play St. George on July 13th 1868, the visitors were called 'The Knickerbockers' of Montreal who won by four wickets. The

Philadelphian's played an interesting game at Montreal against the Montreal Garrison Knickerbockers on July 28th, 1868. The knickerbockers scored an impressive 326 out of which 101 was scored by a player named Pepys. In reply, Philadelphia scored 59 and the match was abandoned as there was not enough time to complete the match.

The All England Eleven returned to Canada in 1868 for their second tour after a nine year gap. The team comprised of Edgar Willsher (Capt.), John Smith, G. Tarrant, James Lillywhite Jr., H. Charlwood, E. Pooley, G. Griffith, T. Humphrey, H. Jupp, J. Rowbotham, G. Freeman and A. Shaw. This again was a late season tour and only ONE match[8] was played in Canada at Montreal on September 22nd, 23rd, and 24th against the twenty two. Fortunately for the Canadian's, they had to face them only once as they were all out for 28 under the bowling pressure of Willsher and Freeman. In reply, the English eleven scored 310 runs for the loss of nine wickets. As this was late September, the match was declared a draw (of all things) due to the cold wet weather.

WG Grace in America

The year 1872 saw the return of the English back on the Canadian shores under the captaincy of Fitzgerald and in the ranks was the young and soon to be legendary W.G. Grace, the catalyst for drawing large number of spectators. During the 1870's, two of the most popular figures in cricket were, Capt. N. Willoughby Wallace of Halifax with the 60th Rifles, and T.C. Patteson of Toronto who was instrumental in bringing the English on their third tour across the pond, or as the 1877 Canadian Guide put it, *by the indefatigable labors of Mr. Patteson.* To commemorate the 1872 English visit, a lithographic view of the match was made by Rolph, Smith & Co, for Mr. R.B. Blake, Lessee of the Toronto Cricket Ground. The match was played on the Taddle grounds against the backdrop of the new University of Toronto buildings. The University College and Croft Chapter House are shown on the right. A few of the professors are noticeable with their academic caps mingling with the players. Grace is shown on the left ready to face R. B. Blake and Ottaway is on the non-strikers' end.

The Cricket Match at Toronto, Canada, 2nd & 3rd September, 1872, played between twelve of the Gentlemen of England and twenty two of the Toronto Club.

R.A. Fitzgerald was the Captain and manager of the amateur 12 to Canada and America who sailed on August 8th 1872, aboard the S.S. Sarmatian and they reached Quebec on August 17th after a nine day trip, the fastest at the time.[9] The team comprised of :

R.A. Fitzgerald then secretary of the M.C.C.
WG Grace aka *Leviathan*
VE Walker replaced by Edgar Lubbock
RD Walker replaced by F Pickering
CI Thornton replaced by WH Hadow aka *Saint*
A Lubbock
AN Hornby aka *Monkey*
A Appleby aka *Unassuming* – left hand bowler from Lancashire
Hon. G Harris (later Lord Harris)
RA Mitchell
JW Dale replaced by WM Rose
RD Balfour replaced by CJ Ottaway aka *Ojibway*
CK Francis

Five matches were played in Canada and three in America and the English won all, save for the last one in Boston which was played on a swampy land and it ended in a draw. Arthur Appleby, the left arm pacer from Lancashire was the only first class bowler in the side. WG was about 24 years old on this tour and Grace developed a different sort of talent during this tour with his anticipated speeches wherever they went and he did so by substituting certain phrases and the team mates would look forward to the next word or phrase that would be inserted into the standard speech. Towards the end of the tour, phrases were getting harder to come by and he would use, "such beautiful grounds" or "such splendid companions" or even "such pretty ladies." By the time they reached Philadelphia and New York it was down to the food group, "such good oysters!"

On August 17th they met with Mr. J.C. Patteson and members of the Toronto Club at Quebec and after some fishing and hunting they reached Montreal on the morning of 21st. The grounds were on Catherine St, and after the rains had stopped around 1 pm, the much awaited 3 day match began on the 22nd against the twenty-two of Montreal. With the toss being won by England, the opening pair of WG and Ottaway put up 100 runs without loss of a wicket at stumps and compiled a 1st innings total of 255 runs. The twenty two replied with a score of 48 and 67, thus the visitors won by an innings and 140 runs. Grace observed that, *"neither the reporters nor the spectators seemed to understand the game very thoroughly, and we were often amused at the excitement when a catch was made off a bump ball,"* someone should have informed the guest about the base ball rule of catching a ball on the first bounce, that would have elicited an 'ah-ha' from the visitors.[10]

Source: Spalding baseball collection, 1845-1913, bulk (1860-1900). Henry Chadwick papers / B. Chadwick Scorebooks, 1856-1907. New York Public Library. Handwritten score from the 1872 Montreal match.

49

The second match took place on August 27th/28th at Ottawa, and it was played under clear skies with a great crowd in attendance. The visitors scored 201 at stumps on the first day. Matches in those days began very late in the morning and the 2nd day's game started at 11.20 am! "It was a slaughter of the innocents," describes the captain in his book, *Wickets in the West*. The butcher's bill or bowling analysis read – Rose, 8 wickets for 35 runs and Appleby, 12 wickets for 3 runs! The host team managed to score 43 and 49, and the game was summed up thus by a local paper, *"The wickets of the Canadians are going down rather more like shelling peas even than at Montreal."* (Shelling peas was a community effort where peas were brushed out of the pods, in other words, they were losing players at a rapid pace, though I did not find an explanation/meaning for 'even than at Montreal.')

On September 2nd 3rd and 4th the third match of the tour was played at Toronto, and the toss was won again by Fitzgerald following which, the innings was opened by WG and Ottaway. Grace scored his first century on Canadian soil, but broke his bat in the process and was finally out at 142. The roar of the crowd was enough to let the neighborhood know that WG was finally out. At 319 the English were all out and the twenty two of 'Torontoes' went into bat around noon, and by lunch they had lost 8 wickets for only 27 runs! The first innings total amounted to 97 and when stumps were drawn at 6.30 p.m. for the day, the 2nd innings total stood at 12 for 83 and the next day, they went on to score 118, thus ensuring a victory for the visitors by an innings and 104 runs.

The last fixture in Toronto was on September 6th and 7th, a regular even sided match with combined payers was held between Grace's twelve and Fitzgerald's twelve, where Grace's team came out victorious. A week of stay had come to an end and after the customary speeches and acknowledgements, the English team left for London, (Ontario) minus three of the players as they were allowed to stay behind in the company of their lady friends, provided they showed up before the next match. Needless to say, the trio failed to show up on the appointed hour, but did manage to trudge in later in the day to bat as rain had delayed the start of the match. As expected, the cockneys of London were defeated by the English and later the members of the London Cricket Club organized a ball in their honor at city hall after which they departed for Hamilton.

On September 12th, England played against Hamilton which went in England's favor as expected and the match was finished in the 'dark' and as Grace admitted to, he got the last man out with an 'underhand sneak!' [11] Once during a break in the game, a tall figure strode up to them and introduced himself as "Last of the Mohicans" and he was chief of the Iroquois Nation and also an attorney in Hamilton. He extended an invitation to the visiting twelve but it had to be declined due to the current engagements and I am sure this would have been one of the highlights of their visit. As in London, a ball was organized in their honor at the Royal Hotel and the ball and supper were, as Fitzgerald put it, *'on the most handsome scale.'* A most heartwarming letter was written to Mr. T.C. Patteson by Mr. Fitzgerald at the conclusion of the tour, thanking the hosts for the generous reception and hospitality bestowed on them during their stay. *"We came to your shores as strangers, we have been welcome as friends, we leave your Dominion as if we were leaving a second home."*

Cricket continued on the home front and due to the tireless efforts of Capt. Nesbit Willoughby Wallace of the 60th Royal Rifles, who was stationed at the Citadel in Halifax, he proposed a tournament which resulted in the Silver Halifax Cup that was started in 1874 where Philadelphia were the winners in this inaugural tournament. Captain Wallace played against the Philadelphians a number of times and also when the Gentlemen of Philadelphia toured England for the first time in 1884. Now a Major, he played for the Gentlemen of Hampshire on 27th June where they defeated Philadelphia by 5 wickets.[12] The following year in September, the Cup was retained by Philadelphia and in 1880 the cup was turned over to a committee to be awarded yearly to the winning team. The Young America Cricket Club were the winners in the first two years - 1880 and 1881, while the Belmont Cricket Club won it in 1882 and the Halifax Cup tournament continued till 1926.

CANADIAN ELEVEN, HALIFAX TOURNAMENT, 1874

The All Canada Cricket team: Halifax tournament in 1874.
M.C. Hebert, Ed. Kearney, M.B. Daly, G. Brunel, J. Gorham
Hon. W.P.R. Street, John Brunel,
Reverend T.D. Phillipps is seated extreme left. W. Snider, C.B. Brodie
W.H. Powell, J.H. Park

In the 1870's regular matches were played not only in the country, but across the border against leading clubs to test their mettle. Cricket was played in almost every town and city in Ontario, Nova Scotia and New Brunswick were prominent at the time, the Northwest Territories and Quebec contributed to the games development. The game had spread to the west and in 1864 the North West Cricket Club was formed in Winnipeg and in 1876, the famous United Victoria Cricket Club was established. Following the formation of the two historical clubs, others appeared in the Prairie Provinces and in Alberta and British Columbia. The game was now beginning to take a strong hold west of

Ontario and cricket was being played nationwide. *Victoria Daily Colonist*, a paper that was established during the Fraser river gold rush of 1858, carried the results of the matches played between the navy and the local Victoria Cricket Club. The modern printing press arrived on this tiny community from San Francisco during the gold rush and it brought along with them, prospectors, storekeepers and of course the opportunistic anti-social elements and land sharks and those who could not make it in San Francisco.

Colonel Wallace of Bishopstoke, England, who was stationed at Montreal and Halifax with the 66th Rifles from 1868 to 1878, was asked to contribute to "Sixty Years of Canadian Cricket" from memory, contradicts the fact that Cricket Clubs in Nova Scotia were few and far between, and that most of the cricket was held between the garrison, navy and the civilian clubs in Halifax, maybe the colonel did not consider the teams outside the garrisons to be worthy of competition. After the English visit of 1872, there was talk that the Philadelphians and St. George's Club of New York may visit and it was hoped that it would materialize soon. It hoped to re-establish the "United States vs. Canada" as an annual event. The Peninsular's of Detroit had been making yearly visits to Toronto and Toledo also had made an appearance in 1876. A common malady that infested cricket matches whether it was in America or Canada, was that a large portion of the matches were left unfinished, which point to a greater need for punctuality and discipline. This was one of the leading factors in the demise of the game on the American continent. There was fervent hope that this practice would stop.

Upper Canada College (U.C.C.) was one of the colleges to have produced a great number of cricketers, as did Hellmuth College, London. The other schools/colleges during the period were Bishop's College School, Lennoxville, Berlin High School, Galt Collegiate Institute, Ottawa Collegiate Institute (Rev. T.D. Phillipps, was the Mathematical Master and President of the club), Wentworth School, Hamilton and Trinity College School. Since 1858 U.C.C. has been the nursery of cricketers, no other institution has produced so many players and the annual fixture against Ontario has resulted in U.C.C's favor. From 1846 to 1876 only four matches have gone against them and 1875 saw the passing away of G.A. Barber a former master at U.C.C. and "the father of Canadian Cricket."

The same year they received an invitation to send a dozen representatives to Philadelphia, and the Rev. Phillipps informed the Canadian Cricket Clubs of organizing a conference to select a team representing players from all provinces. After a match on 2nd July in Ottawa, over 50 cricketers representing Quebec, Eastern and Western Canada met on the grounds and it was decided that the Reverend would select the Canadian XII. On 26th August a circular was issued to the clubs informing them of the selection based on the following principles.

   a.) Each province was to be represented.
   b.) Have plenty of change bowling without sacrificing the batting.
   c.) Select players who were steady in their fielding and *other habits*. (???)
   d.) Avoid *cause of jealousy* by taking more than 2 players from one place!

As mentioned later, we see here the underlying issues with Canadian cricket – namely 'jealousy amongst teams and individuals' and 'other habits' to put it mildly. The team selected was:

F.W. Armstrong	Orillia, Captain.
W.B. Wells	Chatham.
J. Whelan	London.
R.K. Hope	Hamilton.
A.J. Greenfield	Toronto.
E.W. Spragge	Toronto.
G.F. Hall	Port Hope.
C.B. Brodie	Ottawa.
C. McLean	Montreal.
L.V. Bristow	Montreal.
E. Kearney	Halifax, N.S.
Colonel Morris	Fredericton, N.B.

The team arrived in Philadelphia around noon on 13th Monday (day of their match) as they were delayed at a way station for 18 hours! Captain Wallace of the British Officers offered to play the England vs. America match, thus providing an opportunity for rest to the Canadian side, but the Philadelphians insisted on the order of the program. The first match was played on September 13th, 14th and 15th, the score being 117 and 114 for Philadelphia and Canada scoring 68 and 76, thus losing the match by 87 runs.

The second match commenced the same afternoon (15th to 18th) against the British Officers who were no match for the Canadians, though credit must be given to the Canadians as they trained with little instruction and support from clubs as compared to their opponent who are trained at the great public schools of England under the professionals. Also, putting together players from such towns as Chatham, Ontario and Halifax who are separated by a distance of about 1500 miles with little practice together and to travel so far to play for the country is noteworthy, and the Canadian fielding turned out to be the best in the tournament. Two bats were given out as prizes for scores over 50, and one went to Whelan, one of the strongest all round players in Canada. The scores were 162 and 191 for the British Officers and 123 and 167 for the Canadian side, thus losing by 63 runs, an impressive display against a strong team. The third match was won by Philadelphia by 8 wickets, which was played from 18th to the 22nd against the British Officers.

The detailed scores can be found from pages 105 to 115 of the 1876 Canadian Cricket Guide, The International Matches by Rev T.D. Phillipps.

On May 10th 1876, the Centennial Exhibition opened at Philadelphia where 37 nations displayed their industrial exhibits in over 250 pavilions for six months. It was the first major international exhibition to be held in the United States and a significant event in the history of the young republic, and an opportunity to display to the world, the technological and industrial progress it had made in its first hundred years.

Against this backdrop, 'International Series of Cricket Matches' were held in June and September. On the invitation of the Merion Cricket Club of Philadelphia, Rev. Phillipps arranged for sixteen players from different clubs in Canada to join him in New York, but unforeseen circumstances forced most of them to cancel at the last minute. Only four from Toronto were able to make it, they were A.M. Baines, E.H. Baines, H.J. Campbell and C.H. Sproule. The 'Canadian' team was augmented by local talent who were available at the time and they played their first match against St. George's Club of New York. The next two matches were against Merion with the first ending in a tie and the second game was left unfinished! New arrivals in the form of A.H. Hope of Hamilton and C.B. Calvert and F.C. Irvine of Detroit strengthened the visiting team. The last outing was against the Germantown Club of Philadelphia, where the Reverend had to return home with an injury. A wicket that favored batting, enabled Germantown to amass an amazing score of 356 runs with 163 (highest at the time) coming from Joseph Hargreaves and 108 by J.B. Large.

A team of eleven cricketers from Virginia, played several matches but unfortunately no records were kept. A team from St. Louis was to have taken part in the tournament and they were encouraged by none other than S.M. Graffen, the Manager of Brown Stockings, first professional baseball club of St. Louis. Graffen also held the presidency of the Union Cricket Club.[13] The exhibition was a great attraction as well as the hospitality shown by the host, but all good things must come to an end.

In 1878 for the first time, a team of Australian cricketers arrived in North America after playing a series of matches in England. They easily out played the 22 of Toronto and the 22 of Montreal as the Canadians were no match for a team that had just beaten the English (MCC) by 9 wickets just a few months earlier. The team comprised of: J. Conway (manager), W.C.V. Gibbes (assistant-manager), D.W. Gregory (captain), F.E. Allan, G.H. Bailey, Alec Bannerman, Charles Bannerman, John McCarthy Blackham, (wicket-keeper), H.F. Boyle, T.W. Garrett, T.P. Horan, W.E. Midwinter, W.L. Murdoch, (along with Charles Bannerman, the side's best batsman) and, F.R. Spofforth, the original 'Demon Bowler.'

The tourists played the following games: Against Ontario, at Toronto, on 8-9 October, where Australia won by 10 wickets and against Montreal and District on 10-11 October, this match was drawn.

T. Horan, F.R. Spofforth, J. Conway (Secretary) F.E. Allan.
G.H. Bailey, T.W. Garrett, D.W. Gregory (Captain), A. Bannerman, H.F. Boyle.
C. Bannerman, W.L. Murdoch, J. M. Blackham.
The 1878 Australian team.

An Introspection of the Canadian Performance after the Australian visit

An article by 'T.C.' in Rose-Belford's *Canadian Monthly and National Review* of 1878, goes into an in depth analysis on the debacle of Canadian Cricket and how it could be saved if it were to prosper as a national game. This came about after they had lost badly to the Australians.

The game against the Australian Eleven was *unjustifiably dignified with the title of an International contest*! The Toronto twenty two put up a respectable score of 100 and the Australian's were ahead by 23 only, which led the Aussies to compliment on their excellent bowling, and hinted that it was the best on the continent (this was after the American matches). As 'TC' put it, the second day proved, the *Waterloo of Canadian Cricket*! The visitors were left with a target of 32 only which was met in no time. The wickets went down like chaff before the demon bowler, 'Fred the Demon' Spofforth. The defeat was called disgraceful and humiliating, and *The Globe* which covered cricket extensively, went on to say that, either cricket is given up in Canada or to avoid such exhibition in the future. The recent match showed the weakness of cricket as a national sport in Canada.

How is it that, one colony sends out an eleven and the other has to field two and twenty and still get a sound thrashing. On comparing the two in regards to cricket, Australia has an eight month cricket season while Canada gets four months, or five at the most. Similar to the English, Australian wealth was found to be more concentrated so as to afford more leisure time to the sport. Whereas even the best Canadian players neither have the time nor the money to indulge in it full time, most of them are engaged in business which is their livelihood. This leads the clubs to arrange and play matches on the availability of the players and not have a fixed yearly schedule or league matches at different venues. Another stumbling block in the development of the game was that unlike in Australia where cricket is a national institution and receives help from the shopkeepers to the Government, such similar endorsement is not given to the Canadian cricket. The grounds were provided by the Government to be held forever and free of taxes and Melbourne at the time had a dozen clubs, each with their own enclosed grounds, with a pavilion and grand stand! At the beginning of each season the matches would be arranged amongst the clubs and also with outside teams, which led to thorough knowledge of the main players at various clubs. Spectators were also aplenty numbering 12,000 during a regular Sunday match and Toronto in contrast had nearly empty seats, which speaks volumes of the cricket culture between the two countries.

Help of the general public was required in marshaling the troops and the prosperous and leading citizens of the dominion should lend support in organizing clubs and supporting them with donations and time. Just as in other strong cricketing nations, the club is supported by non-playing members who make up the bulk of the membership and are happy to take the cause forward for the next generation.

To surmise, a strong club comprising of the best players of the district along with non-playing members should be organized along with an independent ground of its own where the players could practice at all times and arrange matches. Without an exclusive ground to play on, a club can be no more than a scattered entity trying fervently to organize matches based on available playing grounds and players. 'TC' puts forth an important point – '*where the American game of Baseball has been allowed, solely through want of organization on the part of cricketers, to usurp the place held of hereditary right by cricket as the national game of Canada!*"

T.C. Patteson in *Sixty Years of Canadian Cricket* also opined that the lack of funds and talent was a handicap in drawing large crowds. The imported talent was mediocre save a few exceptions. The other games that are played in Canada are better understood than cricket, the finer points are lost on the majority and this could change if an English professional is brought in who can be useful and instructive.

A trait that did not go unnoticed was the absolute unanimity amongst the Australian players. They performed as a single entity and were led by an able Captain whose instructions were followed to the letter. In comparison, the Canadian performance was the total opposite and the true state of affairs of cricket in Canada in general, is laid bare for the first time. 'TC' uses the word 'jealousy' to enumerate the differences that existed between the clubs in the same town or between different towns. The players in the club themselves would not get along with his fellow player and does not take lightly at not being asked to play in every match. Quarrels between players, clubs and towns abound which harms the overall ethos of the game.

"In the present condition of affairs it is hardly too much to say, that if eleven Canadian cricketers, chosen from various Provinces and strangers to one another, started on a twelve month's tour, such as that which the Australian's are now bringing to a close, before the end of three months every man would be at daggers drawn with every other man, and by the end of six months, like the Kilkenny cats, nothing would be left of them but their tails." I hope this was an exaggeration on the part of TC.

Though cricket was popular and numerous clubs abound all over Canada, this kind of portrayal by 'TC' puts the early Canadian cricket in a different light and the public was also losing interest in the game. Credit was given to the current twenty two as the discipline on the whole was admirable which shows that the Canadian cricketers can rise to the occasion. The Australians set a noteworthy example which was sorely lacking in the Canadian as well as in the Americans - punctuality. This has been observed time and again by Henry Chadwick and Newhall as one of the many reason for the game losing interest with the masses. The Australian's were on the ground and ready to play at the given time, whereas not a single match that has been played on the Toronto Cricket Ground has begun on the appointed hour as players on either team have failed to assemble on time.

"Without some support from without and some reform from within, the game can never really flourish here. But of these two the first is the most important, because if it be granted, the second would inevitably follow."

The same sentiments were echoed by the *1877 Canadian Cricket Guide* which lamented about the unfinished matches. Playing for a trophy or prizes *"led to absurd display of jealousy, and had the most demoralizing effect on the game."* Paucity of punctuality resulted in a large number of unfinished matches.

The year that Edison invented the light bulb, saw the English back on Canadian shores for the fifth time under the captaincy of Richard Daft. Earlier during the year in May 1879, Lord Harris's amateur eleven played against an eleven chosen from the clubs of New York and Philadelphia at Hoboken, on their way back home from Australia. They were defeated in one innings with 113 runs to spare. In Brentano's *Aquatic Monthly and Sporting Gazetteer* of May 1879 (pg.107), it mentions of a planned July visit to New York, by an eleven from Lascelles Hall Cricket Club of (Huddersfield in West Yorkshire) England. In going thru their website it does not reveal that any such tour took place. A town of handloom weavers would not have had the means to send a team to America. This club was founded in 1825 and is the oldest club still in existence in Kirklees, and the most famous player of the time was George H. Hirst, a Kirkheaton who went on to become an Yorkshire legend.

The team included:

W. Oscroft
John Selby
Arthur Shrewsbury
W. Barnes
Alfred Shaw and
Fred Morley of Nottinghamshire.

Ephraim. Lockwood
T. Emmett
George Ulyett
George Pinder and
W. Bates of Yorkshire.

On August 28th they set sail on the *Sardinian* at the end of the English season, and played twelve matches in Canada and America, winning nine with the rest being drawn. The captain stayed in his berth most of the time as he was seasick and stuck to 'gruel' and since the rest of them were so concerned about his health, they would come down and tell him what a great meal they had! Another instance shows their mischievous side was when they were under the Niagara Falls and as the day was hot, Tom Emmett had taken off his boots and socks to dip his toe in the water. Ulyett filled Tom's socks with snails and worms and put it back without Tom noticing. Earlier on they had noticed a snake which they had talked about it, so as soon as Tom put his socks on and felt the squirmy creatures, he let out a scream thinking it was a snake! It's always fun to have pranksters' around to lighten up the things a bit, especially when you are not on the receiving end!

Hardly anything has been described of the actual matches by Daft in his book, '*Kings of Cricket*' but Mr. E. Browne, Assistant Secretary of Notts County who accompanied the team has provided a brief account of the tour in '*Sixty Years of Canadian Cricket.*'

Three matches were played at Toronto, the first was against the native Canadian twenty two, and the next was against the twenty two English residents and the third against the twenty two of Ontario. The performance of the home teams was more like a 'procession' as one player after another would depart without putting up a fight and one member of the Provincial Parliament was so upset that he knocked down the stumps with his bat and ran off the field as fast as he could. He must have been the talk of the evening and an amusing sight to behold! The match at Hamilton boasted of a telegraph station on the premise to send out the latest scores and the last match in Canada was held in London where the visitors notched another easy victory.

Here are the scores in brief from the *New York Clipper Annual* of 1879.

September 10th & 11th - Defeated the twenty-two of Canada at Toronto, with 10 wickets to spare.
September 12th & 13th - Drew against the English twenty-two at Toronto.
September 15th & 16th - Defeated the Anglo-Canadian's twenty-two in one innings with 3 runs to spare.
September 18th, 19th & 20th - Defeated the Hamilton's seventeen at Hamilton in one innings with 103 runs to spare.
September 22nd & 23rd - Defeated London's twenty-two by 133 runs.
September 25th & 26th - Drew against the Peninsular Club's eighteen at Detroit, Michigan.
September 30th & October 1st - Defeated Central New York's twenty-two at Syracuse, N.Y. in one innings, with 70 runs to spare.
October 3rd, 4th & 6th - Defeated New York City's twenty-two at Staten Island, N.Y. in one innings with 27 runs to spare.
October 10th, 11th & 13th - Defeated Philadelphia's fifteen at Philadelphia, by 145 runs.
October 14th - defeated eighteen *baseball* players by 43 runs at Brooklyn, N.Y.
October 17th, 18th & 20th - Defeated the Young America Club's eleven at Philadelphia in one innings with 60 runs to spare.
October 21st & 22nd - Drew against the Merion Clubs twenty-two at Ardmore, P.A.
October 23rd & 24th - Played a farewell game Yorkshire vs. Nottinghamshire at Philadelphia, Notts winning with 10 wickets to spare. The next day they set sail for England after a financially successful tour.

I have come across a few instances where the dates of the matches played don't match up from two different sources. As an example, the dates as given in the NY Clipper above mention the first game being played on 10th & 11th, whereas in the recollections of the game by E. Browne, he puts the date for the 1st match as 11th & 12th September. Similarly, the match with the Anglo-Canadians in the NY Clipper is given as 15th & 16th whereas, Browne says it was on the 14th & 15th. Judging by the location & duration, the 'NY Clipper' dates looks to be the actual dates.

Before the Irish visited North America for the first time, they had their first international exposure against the Gentlemen of England at home in Dublin in 1855 and against the M.C.C in 1858. George Colhurst's Irishmen visited the Dominion (Canada) in 1879 and they played four games, all against local teams from Ontario. Of these only Hamilton were accorded the honor of playing the tourists on level terms, though losing the match by 60 runs in a two innings contest. The scores in brief:

October 10th & 11th - Defeated the Toronto fifteen at Toronto in one innings with 85 runs to spare.
October 13th & 14th - Defeated the Hamilton, Ontario eleven by 60 runs.
October 16th & 17th - Drew against the Whitby sixteen at Whitby, Ontario.
October 18th resulted in a draw against the Cobourg eighteen at Cobourg.

The Irish were to visit Canada and USA again in 1888 winning 11 out of the 13 fixtures, the two loses were against a strong Philadelphia side. In September and October of 1892, Ireland visited Canada and USA for the third time, playing seven keenly contested matches in Boston, Lowell, New York, Baltimore and, three against the Gentlemen of Philadelphia. Only one match was played at Toronto on September 12th and 13th which was stopped by rain. Besides the foreign teams, American clubs paid regular visit to their northern neighbor as seen from some of the matches played in 1880.

Young America v. Port Hope July 5th & 6th - won by an innings & 5 runs.
Young America v. Toronto, July 7th & 8th - won by an innings & 142 runs.
Young America v. Hamilton CC, July 9th & 10th - won by 157 runs.
Staten Island v. Toronto, July 21st, Toronto won by an innings and 63 runs.
Staten Island v. Hamilton, July 23rd & 24th, Hamilton won by 10 wickets.
Longwood (Boston) v. Hamilton, August 9th & 10th, Boston wins by 9 runs.
Longwood v. Toronto August 11th & 12th, Toronto wins by 44 runs.
Longwood v. Cobourg, August 14th, Longwood wins by 59 runs.
Longwood v. Montreal, August 16th, Longwood wins by an innings and 87 runs.
Chicago v. London, August 15th 1881, London wins by 6 wickets.
Chicago v. Hamilton, August 16th 1881.
Chicago v. Guelph, August 18th 1881, Guelph wins by seven wickets.
Chicago v. Toronto, August 19th 1881, Chicago wins by an innings and 38 runs.
Chicago v. Windsor, played at Detroit, July 6th 1882, rain stopped further play.
Pittsburgh v. Canadian Zingari, August 9th 1885, Zingari wins by 8 wickets.
Pittsburgh v. Toronto, August 10th 1885, Pittsburgh wins by 82 runs.
Pittsburgh v. Hamilton, August 12th & 13th 1885.

An English team under the captaincy of Rev. RT Thornton played in September of 1885 with another visit the following year by Mr. EJ Sander's English Eleven in 1886. Rev. Thornton's team played against Toronto on September 11th as the previous day was washed out due to heavy rain. The Ontarians were no match against the formidable bowling of Bruen, Roller and Whitby and lost to them by an innings and twenty runs and during the next match at Montreal, even the Stock Exchange was adjourned for the day. For the English the outing was a success as they defeated the team from Toronto and the fifteen of Montreal twice each. EJ Sanders eleven played against Ontario on

September 8th and 9th winning by eight wickets and against Montreal on the 11th and 13th where the sixteen of Montreal managed to score 85 and 55 against a score of 257 put up by the English.

1887 Canadian Tour to Ireland and England

An unofficial and first tour by a Canadian side to England in 1880, ended in the arrest of their Captain, Trooper Dale, a deserter from the Royal Horse Guard who was arrested on the field. He was sentenced to one month's imprisonment, but tried to escape by jumping into the street, only to be caught by a passerby! Rotten luck I guess, and this time the sentence was 300 days! Even the arrival of Rev. T.D. Phillipps, could not help save the tour.[14] It was abandoned midway and a dejected group of cricketers returned home. Despite that, they had managed to play seventeen matches, out of which they won 5, lost 5 and 7 ended in a draw.[15]

The matches were played against:

Edinburgh High School at Edinburgh in May - Lost
Hunslet Cricket Club at Leeds on May 31st and June 1 - Drawn
Leicestershire on June 1st and 2nd – Drawn (2 matches on June 1 at two different places?)
MCC and Ground (?) at Lord's in June - Lost
West of Scotland at Partick in June - Won
Greenock Cricket Club at Greenock in June - Drawn
Crystal Palace at Sydenham in June - Drawn
Stockport Cricket Club at Stockport in June - Lost
Fifteen Wallsden Cricket Club at Wallsden in June - Won
Twelve of Cheltenham at Cheltenham on June 22, 23 - Drawn
Surrey C and Ground at Kensington Oval on June 25, 26 - Won
Halifax on June 28, 29 - Drawn
Orleans Club at Twickenham on June 28, 29 - Lost
Longsight Cricket Club at Manchester on July 2, 3 - Drawn
Gentlemen of Derbyshire at Derby on July 5, 6 - Lost
Wavertree Cricket Club at Liverpool on July 9, 10 - Won
Stourbridge Cricket Club at Stourbridge on July 12, 13 - Won

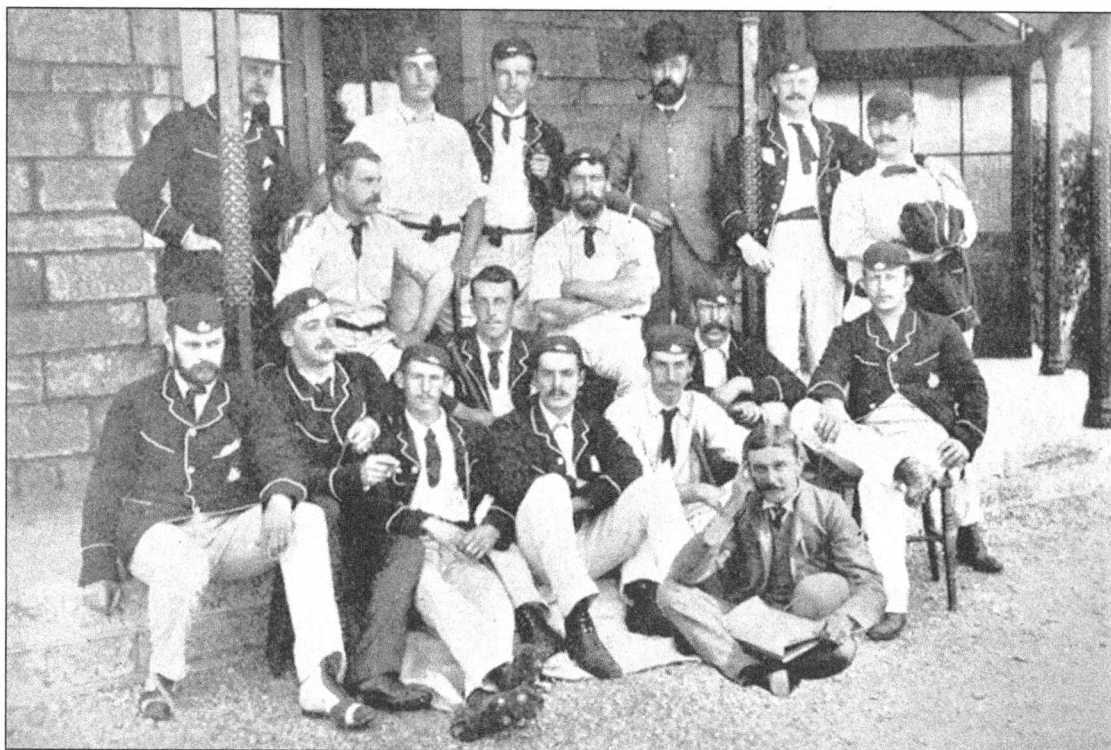

1887 Canadian Gentlemen in England.
C.N. Shanly (Umpire), W.W. Jones, W. J. Fleury, L. Ogden,
George Lindsey, Dyce. W. Saunders
C.J. Annand, George.W. Jones, W.A. Henry, W.W. Vickers (Reporter), R.B. Ferrie
A. Gillespie, R.C. Dickson (Scorer), Dr. E.R. Ogden (Captain), Arthur C. Allan,
W.C. Little, Lyon M. Lindsey (Correspondent), aka "Shrimps."

George Lindsey's eleven toured England in 1887, after convincing the Toronto Cricket Club committee that for the last three years they have been winning the International matches against the US, and that they had a strong roster comparable to the Philadelphia eleven that toured England in the summer of 1884. The tour memories were captured in *'Cricket across the Sea, or the Wanderings and Matches of the Gentlemen of Canada, 1887, by Two of the Vagrants.'*

The team comprised of:

Arthur C. Allan, Trinity College, Toronto.
W. C. Little, Ottawa.
W. A. Henry, Wanderer's Club, Halifax. (Canadian Bonner)
W. W. Vickers, Toronto Cricket Club.
W. W. Jones, Toronto Cricket Club. (Parsees)
G. W. Jones, St. John, N.B. (Bluenoses)
Dr. E. R. Ogden, Toronto Cricket Club - Captain

R. B. Ferrie, Hamilton.
A. Gillespie, Hamilton.
D. W. Saunders, Toronto.
C. J. Annand, Halifax. (Gunner)
W. J. Fleury, Toronto. (The Baby)
Lyon Lindsey, Correspondent (Shrimps)
R.C. Dickson
C.N. Shanly (Butcher Bob)
H.J. Bethune
George G. Lindsey, Toronto. (Manager)

C. J. Logan, B.T.A. Bell, F. Harley and M. Boyd could not commit to the tour. The team comprised of all native born Canadians and it represented an "All Canadian" team in the true sense. The average age of the players was under 23.

On July 2nd, they set sail on the S.S. Furnessia, from New York after having defeated the 'All New York' team and reached Derry, Glasgow after a ten day trip. The team arrived in Dublin on the evening of July 12th and was driven to Shelbourne Hotel in Stephen's Green. Here they were met by "Teddie" Ogden who was to be their captain, and also Mrs. Ogden, who faithfully kept scores throughout the trip. Next morning after a little rest, they set out for the Phoenix Club grounds for practice. The team color was maroon, for the coats, caps and sashes. The peak of the cap and the coat pocket depicted a maple leaf in white silk and a white silk cord binding the coat completed the ensemble. Besides the fancy uniform, they did not have much to show for in terms of the game as they were out of practice and not in good form after the trip.

Against Ireland at Dublin: July 14th & 15th, they lost by an innings and 102 runs.

The first day of the match commenced on July 14th with the visitors losing the toss to host Ireland, and took to the field at the Leinster Cricket Ground in Rathmines at the stroke of noon. Emerson and Trotter opened the innings for Ireland, with Ferrie bowling to Emerson. An unusual drought had been going on for six weeks which rendered the wicket hard and Ferrie strained himself after five overs and could not bowl for the rest of the match, in fact, he would not regain his form till the middle of the tour. He was replaced by Gillespie the famed medium pacer of his time and the following year in 1888 the Irish captain called Gillespie the, 'Canadian Bonner.' The host team put up a score of 319 runs and the visitors stepped onto the field to play their first innings at 5.40 pm! The Irish struck in the first over by removing Allan's stumps. Gillespie and Vickers played out the remainder of the time, and at stumps the score was 20 for the loss of one wicket.

One would think the young lads would turn in early for the night so as to face the next morning with vigor, but, Mr. Barrington and a group of ladies took the boys to Bray, a fashionable watering hole of the time, and returned to their hotel by midnight after much merriment. The next day's play saw the Canadians being bundled out for 88 and a follow-on ensued, and all the wonderful match news was relayed back to the newspaper offices by – carrier pigeons! Gillespie's score of 54 was the highlight of the second innings and they buckled under for 129, still 102 runs short of the target, thus ending the first engagement of the tour. In, 'Cricket across the Sea' the author points out that the poor showing was a result of, lack of practice, being out of shape due to the long voyage and the wicket which was unusually quick, a condition with which they were not accustomed to. After the very first day's play, they were out with their host till late at night, which is understandable as the host were eager to show their new friends around and the visitor too were also eager to experience the sights and sounds of a new country. Since a day and a half remained, it was decided to have another match which turned in the visitor's favor, the final score being 202 for the Canadians against the Irish score of 166. An observation which struck my mind was that after a banquet – a constant recurrence, the visitors were more successful the next day than the host, too much merriment and Guinness on the part of the Irish maybe? Earlier that morning, they had been taken on a tour to see how the green water of the Liffey, which runs through the center of Dublin, is *made into brown porter by the Guinness's*. They had hoped to return to Dublin by August end, but that was not in the cards.

Gentlemen of Ireland: July 16th, a return match won by Canada by 5 wickets based on 1st inning scores. At Edinburgh v. Gentlemen of Scotland: July 18th & 19th, they lost by 10 wickets.

A four hour sail across the Irish Sea took them to Holyhead and an all-night journey took then to Edinburgh along with their seventy eight pieces of luggage, that in itself must have required a full time player/baggage handler. Sunday was spent in sightseeing of, as the authors put it, "Athens of modern Europe."

The match was played during the Scottish week in Edinburgh and was held on the Grange ground at Raeburn Place. Dr. Ogden having lost the toss again took to the field and L.M. Balfour and R.J. Pope opened for the Gentlemen of Scotland. While Captain Balfour was from the Grange Club, Pope was a member of the last visiting Australian team to England, now attending Edinburgh University. The host scored a respectable 253 runs and since the Canadian captain had agreed to play till seven o'clock, they still had two hours of play and started on a disastrous note by losing 2 wickets for eight runs and ended up with 138 for seven at stumps, all this in just two hours! After the customary banquet which the team claimed was their most delightful, they could not muster enough runs the next day and ended the innings at 146, conceding a follow-on.

At one point in the second innings both the left hand batsmen, Ogden and Allan, were facing two left arm bowlers, Macnair and Thornton. When the last man went in to bat, two runs were still required to avert an innings defeat, which they managed by adding a dozen to the final tally which left the Scots six runs to win which they easily achieved and the Canadians had lost by 10 wickets.

The next few matches on the tour were against:

At Newcastle v. Gentlemen of Northumberland: July 22nd & 23rd.

Played on the South Northumberland Club Grounds at Gosforth Park, Newcastle, where they lost by 212 runs. (Ogden losing the toss for the third time).

At Sunderland v. County of Durham: July 25th & 26th, match drawn.

Played on the Ashbrooke Grounds where the match ended in a draw. (The toss - well, Ogden was on a roll with the losing streak!)

At Buxton v. Gentlemen of Derbyshire: July 27th & 28th.

The toss was finally won and the jinx broken and with that, they won the match by an innings and 40 runs!

At Brighton v. Gentlemen of Sussex: July 29th & 30th.

Match played on the county grounds at Hove where they lost by 9 wickets. The Canadians fielded first after losing the toss again and here the future Hollywood actor and knighthood recipient, Sir Charles Aubrey Smith, left an indelible mark on the young impressionable minds by taking 8 wickets for 19 runs!

Gentlemen of Marylebone Cricket Club, London: August 1st & 2nd, Lord's Cricket grounds, match drawn.

Except for one earlier anomaly at Derbyshire, Dr. Ogden loses the toss again! The tourists were suitably impressed by its appearance and excellent appointments. At the time, the covered area could seat sixteen thousand people. The main scoring apparatus impressed the visitors as it was able to provide the scores at a glance, it showed the total number of runs, wickets lost and also the individual scores of the two batsmen which increased run by run! The manicured ground resembled a billiard table and it was on this surface that the Canadians played their most important match of the tour.

Even though the match started just before noon, MCC finished their innings before four o'clock with a score of 306 and keeping in mind these were shorter overs - four balls per over. The London press described the fielding as brilliant, which helped keep the scoring in check as the bowling was poor. The Canadians went in to bat at four o'clock and had amassed 161 at close of play and required 69 to avoid follow-on the next day. The follow-on was easily avoided and they put up a score of 254 and the match ultimately ended up in a draw, a most satisfying performance, where the captain took 9 wickets in one innings.

Portsmouth, against the Gentlemen of United Services, played on August 5th and 6th.

This time the toss was won by Canada and they elected to bat on the United Service Recreation Grounds and scored only 159 in the first innings and 267 runs in the second innings. Major Bethune from the United Service had the distinction of scoring the first century against the Canadians, having scored 105, and the teams total stood at 351, which resulted in a draw.

Gentlemen of Surrey, August 8th and 9th at the Oval - match drawn.

The toss now being won twice in a row, the Canadians went into bat first, scoring 141 runs. The Gentlemen of Surrey put up a massive score of 432, which included 102 from L.A. Shuter, and the visitors replied with only 149 runs. The Oval at one time was a cabbage garden as remembered by a Mr. 'Billy' Burrup, who was instrumental in making the Oval from its' earlier days. He was a prominent member of the Surrey club and was a guide to the visitors during their stay in Surrey.

At Southampton v. Gentlemen of Hants, August 10th and 11th - match drawn.

A hat trick of sorts, as the toss is won for the third time by the Canadian captain, and they take to the bat scoring 219 and 211. The Gentlemen of Hants score 225 and 145 respectively.

At Yatton v. Mr. Tankerville Chamberlain's Eleven (Gentlemen of Gloucestershire), August 12th and 13th, match drawn.

While practicing at the nets, Dr. W.G. Grace shows up and as youngsters many of them had watched him play at the Toronto Cricket Ground back in 1872 and little did they dream that one day, they would be, *"bearding the lion in his den."* WG was suitably impressed with the immense strides taken by Canadian cricket and saw no reason why it should not be successful as the sister colony in far off Australia. Ogden was on a roll now winning the coin toss again and electing to bat and the team put up a score of 140 and 283, while the Gentlemen of Gloucestershire replied with 239 and 103.

At Stoke-on-Tent v. Gentlemen of Staffordshire, August 15th and 16th - match drawn.

The Gentlemen of Staffordshire won the toss and elected to bat, scoring 229 and 145 runs. The visitors replied with 313 and 37 for 8 wickets. Captain Ogden, the only one to score over a hundred (133) on the tour, was the best all-rounder in the team, and was most successful as a bowler too.

At Birmingham v. Gentlemen of Warwickshire, August 17th and 18th.

The toss being won by Bainbridge, he elected to bat first and they could only muster 106 and the second innings was even worse where they scored a measly 73 runs. Canada had scored 204 in their first innings thereby giving them an easy victory by an innings and 25 runs. Much of this could be attributed to the fact that the rain has slowed down the pace of the pitch, the likes of which the Canadians were accustomed to and this made it their fourth win of the tour.

At Leicestershire v. Gentlemen of Leicestshire, August 19th and 20th.

Arnall-Thompson, the Leicester Captain wins the toss and elects to field. The Canadians being put in to bat scored 228 and were replied with 209. The Canadian second innings brought up 141, leaving the opponents a target of 158 to win in an hour. They scored 40 for 3 wickets as time ran out, which resulted in another draw, the eighth draw of the tour.

At Liverpool v. Gentlemen of Liverpool and District, August 22nd and 23rd.

Liverpool, the future home of the Beatles, here the toss was lost and the visitors were sent in to field. Gentlemen of Liverpool and District scored 233 and 76 for the loss of 4 wickets, and the boys from Canada scored, 78 and 229, thus losing the game by 6 wickets. The tour was nearly coming to an end and this was to be the last night where all the team members would be together. The following morning after a night of dinner and speeches, Saunders left for home, Gillespie went to Scotland, Ferrie to Weston and the rest moved on to their next venue at Oxton Park, Cheshire.

At Oxton v. Gentlemen of Cheshire, August 24th and 25th match drawn.

This was a twelve-a-side match. Mr. C.I. Thornton's XI, August 27th at Norbury Park, match won by 13 runs. The last fixture on the tour was a one day match – toss and match won by the young lads from Canada!

Overall, the 1887 tour was a success in terms of their improvement over the previous engagements. They won 5, lost 5 and 9 ended in a draw. It took them a few games getting used to the fast wickets which they were not accustomed to, their batting which they regarded as their weak point, turned out to be better than expected, whereas the bowling left much to be desired. The fielding throughout the tour was appreciated by one and all. The best batting average on the tour went to W.A. Henry who scored 879 runs in 34 innings, with an average of 25.85 (88 being the highest in an inning). The best bowling average belonged to Captain Ogden, who bowled 817.3 overs, 311 maidens, gave away 1520 runs for 91 wickets - an average of 16.7.

(Match dates and scores were taken from Red Lillywhite of 1888)

Dyce Saunders was later on termed as the 'Grand Old Man' of Canadian cricket and he died in London, Ontario, on 12th June 1930. He is the only Canadian cricketer to grace the walls at Lord's. At 19 he took part in his first International match against America in 1881 and at the young age of 60 in 1922, he went on his last tour with Norman Seagram's team to England. During the 1887 tour he scored 613 runs with an average of 23.58 and was one of the greatest wicket-keepers for Canada.

Below is another picture of the 1887 team showing G.G.S. Lindsey, standing extreme left and Dyce Saunders who is seated second from right. They were co-authors of, *Cricket Across the Sea, or the Wanderings and Matches of the Gentlemen of Canada, 1887, by Two of the Vagrants.*' The young woman in the picture is Mrs. Ogden and her husband, the team captain E. R. Ogden, is to the right of her.

Courtesy: Upper Canada College Archives, Toronto, Canada.

Between the visits by International teams there were also regular exchange of matches between the American and Canadian teams, and also university matches between Trinity and Toronto University. Lord Hawke on his first visit to the American continent in 1891 played two matches in Canada. They easily beat the Western Ontario XI at Toronto on October 20th and 21st by an innings and 24 runs. Similarly, they beat Eastern Canada at Ottawa on the 23rd and 24th by an innings and 84 runs. The only high scorer of substance was MG Bristowe who single handedly scored almost half the teams' total. In the first innings he was run out at 35 (total 106) and remained not out in the second innings at 47 with the teams total at 90, and oh, he was the opening bat!

Tours and visitors at the turn of the Century

Three years later in 1894, Lord Hawke was back for another visit. After playing the Americans, the English arrived in Canada on 2nd October 1894, and played their first match the very next day making a low score of 147. When the Canadian's went in to bat, the field was set as they had never seen before — there was only one man on the off side! A. J. Hill, the slow underhand bowler enticed the opponent into hitting the ball and they were bundled out for 55. The follow on resulted in a respectable score of 125 for the loss of 5 wickets, though the two day match resulted in a draw.

It was on March 28, 1892 that the Canadian Cricket Association was setup, (since 2007 it is known as Cricket Canada, and headquartered in Toronto, Ontario). One of the earliest provincial associations was Ontario which was formed in 1880. Other provinces followed, Manitoba in 1895 followed by Quebec in 1902. Alberta and Saskatchewan joined in 1910 followed by British Columbia in 1922, Nova Scotia in 1967 and New Brunswick in 1980.

After touring England in 1893, the disappointed Australians led by Jack Blackham who had hoped to win the ashes, returned home via North America, hoping to steamroll the cricketers here on the continent though they were in for a rude awakening against the Philadelphians. The only match in Canada was played at Toronto on October 17th and 18th that afforded little resistance and the Canadians lost by an innings and 70 runs, but the match was contested evenly in terms of equal number of players and they reached triple digits in both innings. John M (Jack) Laing of Toronto and one of the greatest Canadian cricketers of his time, a counterpart to John B King of Philadelphia, scored 1 and an unbeaten 43 in the second innings, but failed to take a single wicket in his 31 overs. The Australian innings of 298 had a generous helping of 52 extras, the second highest 'score' of the innings, the top scorer being Coningham with 69, who was run out and batted at number 10!

In September of 1897, Pelham F Warner then just 23 years old, brought a team over to Canada and the United States. Little did he know back then that he would forever be linked to the infamous Bodyline Tour (1932-33 Ashes in Australia) as the manager of that English team. During the following year in 1898 the team included Bernard (Bosie) Bosanquet who is credited with creating the googly.

Bosanquet wrote, *"About the year 1897 I was playing a game with a tennis ball, known as 'Twisti-Twosti.' The object was to bounce the ball on a table so that your opponent sitting opposite could not catch it. After a little experimenting I managed to pitch the ball which broke in a certain direction; then with more or less the same delivery make the next ball go in the opposite direction! I practiced the same thing with a soft ball at 'Stump-cricket.' From this I progressed to the cricket ball. I devoted a great deal of time to practicing the googly at the nets, occasionally in unimportant matches."*[16]

The Canada-USA tour may have been the initial 'guinea pig' where he was able to experiment his new technique much to the discomfort of the recipients in those 'unimportant matches' as he called it.

Although WW1 was nearing, Australia toured the United States and Canada in 1913 for the last time under the captaincy of Austin Diamond, and played a staggering 53 matches, experiencing one lone defeat at the hands of the Germantown Cricket Club of Philadelphia. The side contained several famous names, including Charlie Macartney, Warren Bardsley, Arthur Mailey and Herbert Collins. During a match against Vancouver, the Australians put on a massive 633 runs for the loss of 8 wickets, to record the highest innings total ever achieved in Canadian cricket. At the other end of the spectrum, the Winnipeg Cricket Association was dismissed for a measly 6 runs against the visitors, the lowest score in Canadian cricket.

The turn of the century saw the game being elevated to a new level. Two players emerged and are considered to be the greatest all-rounder cricketers in North American Cricket history as Canada and United States matches reached new heights of popularity. John Barton (Bart) King of the United States and John M. (Jack) Laing of Canada, were two high class players that dominated the local scene for almost two decades. Kings performance with the bat and ball was legendary and ahead of his time as he was one of the best in the world. John M. Laing played for a total of 13 occasions for Canada against the United States, Ireland, Australia and England. During this short career he captured a total of 77 wickets.

In the match between the United States and Canada at Toronto in 1895, he devastated the American batting line-up to capture 7 for 21 in the first innings, to record the first hat-trick in the International Series when he clean bowled J. W. Sharp, S. Goodman and L. K. Mallinkrodt. The following year he did even better when he captured 6 for 17 and 8 for 37 against the United States at Manheim in Pennsylvania, to set a Canadian bowling record. Laing, also a capable batsman, scored 249 and with J. G. Davis's 103 not out, helped establish a 4th wicket partnership record of 313 runs for North American cricket. This was while playing for Wanderers Cricket Club against the Douglas Park Cricket Club in the Chicago competition of 1903.

With the advent of WWI of 1914-18, Canadian cricket further waned and the last International Series against America was played in 1912 and twenty years would elapse before another major cricket tour took place. Following the war, Norman Seagram who came from a prominent Waterloo, Ontario family of distillers and horse racers, also a stockbroker and basically a man of means, put up a strong national side which included A.E. Mix, C.R. Somerville, H.J. Lounsborough, H. Dean (Manager), G.E.D. Greene, A.M. Inglis, H.S. Reid, R.D. Hague, the grand old man of Canadian cricket Dyce Saunders who was sixty at the time, H.W. Wookey, and V.R. Mustard. Seven of the players were old boys of Trinity College School, they included:-

Norman Seagram went to TCS from 1890 to 1893
Dyce Saunders, captain of the school XI of 1878
Percy E Henderson, school XI of 1894 and 1895
Stuart R Saunders, school XI of 1897-1899
L. Marvin Rathbun, school XI of 1898-1900
Tom W Seagram, school XI of 1904-1905
Selwyn R Harper, school XI of 1916-1918

Besides the matches, plenty of social activities took up their free time. As soon as 'Melita' docked at Southampton, Major Wynyard and Dr. Bencraft received them on behalf of the President of M.C.C, Lord Chelmsford, who also happened to be the Viceroy of India at the time. The highlight of their tour was an evening spent at the House of Parliament where practically all the cabinet ministers were to be present for dinner. In all there were about hundred people and after dinner they listened to the debates, one of the debater was Winston Churchill.[17]

Out of the eleven matches played, seven were drawn and they lost four, but the dominant theme was that high praises were given for their play and sportsmanship, a far cry from the 1878 team that faced the first Australian team at home. Seagram was one of the principals in Cricket Development Limited who purchased about thirteen acres of property on which now stands the Toronto Cricket Club and one of the most dedicated cricketers of the time. In 1910 he was a member of the Canadian Zingari to tour England. On his return from the 1922 tour, Seagram devoted his time to the organization of Cricket Development Limited and in 1926 the club opened on Wilson Avenue. On more than one occasion he was the saviour of TCC as in the initial years the finances were strained. A fire in 1952 partially destroyed the building and along with it, priceless archives were lost! [18]

Norman Seagram's Canadian Cricket XI, 1922 tour of England.
Courtesy: J.D. Burns Archives, Trinity College School, Port Hope, Ontario, Canada.

Norman Seagram's Canadian Cricket XI vs. Royal Navy at Chatham, 1922 tour of England. Courtesy: J.D. Burns Archives, Trinity College School, Port Hope, Ontario, Canada.

The 'Don' in North America

On 6th July 1932, the Australian XI took on Ridley College where they piled up 309 runs for loss of 6 wickets in a short span which included 109 by the Don. In reply the school with 18 past and present players could only muster 112 runs. L.C. (Clarke) Bell, a left-hander who had scored 109 not out the previous day, (only one to score a century against the visiting Aussies) put up 39 the highest score for the college before being bowled by Fleetwood-Smith.[19] He went on to become one of the finest batsmen in Canadian cricket history. In his brief career, he scored 1401 runs during his 25 stays at the crease which included 16 centuries and with a personal best of 193 not out for the Toronto Cricket Club against the Bell Telegraph Cricket Club in 1930. He died during World War II just short of his 32nd birthday.[20]

The images of the depression era are indelibly ingrained in our subconscious, yet, against this backdrop, a team from Australia embarked on a tour of Canada and United States in 1932. *Fifty-one matches, more than 20 towns & cities, over 76 days, 12 players, a round trip of almost 10,000 kilometres and all this for a fee of 100 British Pounds per player!* [21]

Arthur Mailey and his friend in America, 'Foxy' Dean who acted as the go between the Canadian Pacific Railway, the tour's major financial backer, were the people behind this operation. There was one stipulation in the sponsorship which was non-negotiable – the team must include 'Don'. Arthur Mailey had a couple of issues to iron out before the tour could progress. Bradman had a three way post with Associated Newspapers, 2UE Radio Station and F.J. Palmer & Sons, outfitters for men's and boys'. There was also this matter of him promising to marry his, *'schoolboy sweetheart, Jessie Menzis'* as Sir Don puts it, on April 30th.

It was finally agreed upon that the new employers would allow Don leave of absence without pay and Mailey in return, offered to reimburse Don for the lost pay and also cover for his wife's travel and accommodation. This was to take place in June, July and August and Bradman was not too keen on going as England was slated to tour Australia in the winter of 1932-33, and as we all know now, it came to be known as the infamous 'Bodyline' Tour. Though Bradman did not play in the first test, he was bowled for a 'duck' in the first innings of the second test played at Melbourne Cricket Ground. He redeemed himself with an unbeaten century in the second innings, this being the only test win for Australia out of the 5 that were played. A noteworthy snippet was the maiden test century by the Nawab of Pataudi on his test debut and his *only* one. He was dropped after the second test for refusing to go along with the bodyline tactics. He did not take a fielding position on the leg side and Jardine is said to have commented, *"I see his highness is a conscientious objector."*[22] The bodyline bowling tactics did not sit well with the public and in 1934, Douglas Jardine stepped down as England's captain and never played another Test. Harold Larwood also gave up playing for England after returning home from the bodyline tour.

The pioneering credit of bowling straight to a batsman though goes to an Australian, Frederick Robert Spofforth, the 'Demon Bowler.' This was the first and only Test Match at the Oval between England and the visiting Australians to be played in 1882 and only the second ever to be played in England. In just under two and a quarter hours the Australians were bowled out for a mere 63 runs and England replied with just 101 ending day one with a slim first innings lead of 38 runs. This was a three day test where four balls per over were bowled. After a rain delay the play finally commenced at noon on the second day and by 3 o'clock the Australians were out for an improved second innings total of 122 leaving England with only 85 to win and they had an impressive batting line up, which included, W.G. Grace, Hornby, Barlow, George Ulyett, Maurice Read, Barnes, and C.T. Studd.

Spofforth began the innings with a singular aim of decimating the line-up, an uphill task. *He bowled deliberate and directly to Grace – the first recorded instance of bodyline bowling in Test Cricket.*[23] Bookmakers were offering 60-1 against an Australian win as Grace had provided a good start and a loss was unthinkable. Cricket can be so unpredictable, at one point they were 65 for 4, requiring only 20 to win in an hour plus they had the luxury of another whole day. Eight runs were required to win and they were down to the last two,

Arthur Mailey's Australian Cricket XI at Ridley College

July 1932

Courtesy, Ridley College Archives.

Studd and Peate who went for a hit and missed, thus being bowled by Boyle, and handing the Australians an improbable victory. Studd, who had scored two centuries against them earlier in the year, never faced a ball. The excitement of this close match was too much for one fan to bear and he passed away in the stands!

During this bodyline tour Victor Richardson suggested to his captain, Bill Woodfull: "Why don't we do it back to them?" Woodfull refused. He wasn't going to lower himself to Douglas Jardine's tactics. Cricket was bigger than a mere win-loss ratio. Victor Richardson was the grandfather of Ian Chappell, under whose captaincy sledging started. Greg Chappell was so panicked about losing a one-day match, he forced his younger brother, Trevor, to bowl underarm. It worked. We won. Over the past 30 years, countless former players, under the Chappell mantle, have produced modern cricketers, and the tide of childish antics has continued unabated. (S Baldwin, The Sydney Morning Herald, January 28th 2003.)

Before the tour could commence, there was also this issue of getting permission from the Australian Board of Control. A resolution passed earlier in 1927 stated that no team or first class cricketers were to tour overseas without prior approval. The tour was blessed provided few conditions were fulfilled. The board was to approve the players chosen by Mailey, a complete set of financial records were to be provided on completion of the tour and no player was to receive a fee of more than 100 pounds.

The team under the captaincy of Vic Richardson (grandfather to the Chappell brothers, Ian, Greg and Trevor) departed on Thursday the 26th May aboard the liner RMS Niagara, and three weeks later reached Victoria in British Columbia. On the way it had stopped at Auckland in New Zealand, Suva in Fiji and Honolulu, Hawaii. Besides Bradman, the team comprised of:

Vic Richardson, Captain, South Australia, Shield & Test Player.
Arthur Mailey, NSW, ex Shield & Test Player.
Alan Kippax, NSW, Shield & Test Player.
Stan McCabe, NSW, Shield & Test Player.
HS (Sammy Carter), ex Australian XI wicket-keeper.
Leslie Fleetwood-Smith, Victoria, Shield Player.
Dick Nutt, NSW, first grade player.
Phil Carney, Victoria, stockbroker.
Keith Tolhurst, Victoria, stockbroker.
Edgar Rofe, NSW, solicitor.
Dr. RJ Pope, Hon. Medical Officer.

The matches in Canada were played in British Columbia, Ontario, Quebec, Manitoba, Saskatchewan and Alberta. The American matches were held in New York, Detroit, Chicago and California, notice the absence of Philadelphia? The visitors won 4 matches outright, won a further 39 on first innings basis, drew 7 and lost just one. Bradman's average on the tour was 3777 runs, at an average of 102.01. The previous high by an Australian was Charlie G. Macartney's, 2390 runs at an average of 45.92 during his 1913 North American tour and also claimed 189 wickets for an average of 3.81. The bowling figures were another matter, Stan McCabe taking 189 at 6.0, Fleetwood-Smith took 238 wickets at 7.5 and Mailey, 203 wickets at 8.6.[24] Bradman's best was the six wicket haul in one 8-ball over (4 overs, 43 runs & 7 wickets) against Vancouver Island XV in the 2nd innings, this was their very first engagement of the tour on June 18th.

Six Wickets For Bradman In One Over

Vancouver Sun: Provincie June 19 1932

Famous Australian Batsman Has Remarkable Spell Without Hat Trick

---

ALSO SCORES 94

Tourists Easily Beat Vancouver Island Eleven in Second Game.

Ric Sissons in his book, 'Don meets the Babe', writes that Don got a hat-trick in the over, but the Vancouver Sun of June 18th, had a different headline of the match results as shown in the picture. The book does quote another reporter's description of the over as: *wicket-run-wicket-wicket-ball-wicket-wicket-wicket.* In the first innings, Vancouver Island had fifteen players whereas in the second innings there were only nine where they scored 7 for 99 at stumps, all 7 wickets going to Bradman!

The only defeat of the tour was handed to the Australians by the Mainland All Stars XV on 22nd June at Brockton Point Grounds in Vancouver, *"the prettiest ground in the world"*, as observed by Don. (The mainland side batted with 15 but fielded 11 players). The Australians were bundled out for 129 runs while chasing a target of 147. Besides the unending matches and travels, there were a couple of amusing incidents which stood out. Both the incidents happened at a place called Moose Jaw, close to the wheat growing region of Regina. Due to very windy conditions the bails were 'stuck' to the stumps with the help of chewing gum. This worked well till a batsman was stumped and the bail hung to the side by the gum thread and the umpire waited a very long time before giving the verdict. He explained that a verdict could not be given till the bail had reached the ground! In another match against the Moose Jaw XVII, the umpire seemed to be the biggest threat. The umpire in his 70's insisted on standing at mid-on. *"You can't give me out LBW from that position,"* Bradman informed him. *"Oh can't I, you just wait and see." The second ball from a spinner hit Bradman on the pads and up went the old boy's finger. "I told you I could",* he proudly commented to the departing batsman."[25] Don wished that he had kept his mouth shut!

Bradman against the West Indians in New York, July 14, 15 & 16, 1932.
Played at Innisfail Park, Bronx. (Literary Digest July 30, 1932)

July 20th saw two of the greatest hitters of the ball come together in New York, Babe Ruth, the Sultan of Swing and Don the 'Anzac Babe Ruth' as the American press called him, met at the private box of the Babe at Yankee Stadium. When Babe asked Don what he thought of Baseball, he famously commented, *"Cricket could learn a lot from baseball… there is more snap and dash to baseball."* According to newspaper accounts, the Babe told Don, *"Why don't you put on a Yankee Uniform and see what you can do against our kind of pitching?"* Apparently Don tried the uniform only, but surprised Ruth with his baseball knowledge as he had watched Baseball in Australia and was interested in it.[26] The visitors also toured the Empire State Building which had just opened a year earlier.

BRADMAN—in a "Babe" Ruth outfit.

SLSA:PRG 682 – Bradman in Baseball Outfit.

Don Bradman and Babe Ruth watching baseball in New York.

Courtesy of the SLSA & Bradman Digital Library
SLSA:PRG 682 – Bradman & Babe Ruth, New York 1932.

Another high light of their social calendar was the visit and cricket matches with the Hollywood stars, Clark Gable, Leslie Howard, Charles Aubrey Smith, Boris Karloff, Ronald Coleman, and the heart throb of millions, Jean Harlow, Myrna Loy, Joan Crawford, and Jeanette MacDonald.

Boris Karloff
A. Mailey, (actor), V. Richardson, (Director)
H. Carter
E. Rofe, R. Nutt, W. Ives, S. McCabe
P. Carney, L. Fleetwood-Smith, Myrna Loy, K. Tolhurst, A. Kippax, D. Bradman
Desmond Roberts, (actor), Aubrey Smith

Courtesy of the SLSA & Bradman Digital Library
SLSA:PRG 682 – Australian cricketers & cast of Fu Man Chu, Hollywood, 1932.

The still existing Hollywood Cricket Club was started by C.A. Smith in 1932, captain of the first English team to tour South Africa in 1888-89. Due to his strange run up while bowling, he was known as, 'round the corner' Smith, the moniker may have been given by WG Grace during their county match playing days. This idyllic tour was soon to be shattered into the realization of the bodyline tour and the harsh realities of competitive cricket. *Mailey's 1932 North American tour was the last gasp of crickets' old sporting order.*[27]

"The best Cricket in America is now Canadian. The most successful team from this continent that ever toured England was the Hon. R.C. Matthews' Canadian XI of 1936," wrote Lester.[28]

Canada toured England in 1936 under the patronage of the Hon. R. C. Matthews, the side was captained by W. E. N. Bell and they were the first Canadian team to defeat M.C.C. at Lord's by 76 runs. In 1954 H.B.O. (Basil) Robinson led Canada on a tour of England and they played 18 matches in all, including one against Pakistan, who were also touring England at the same time. Pakistan visited North America in 1958 led by Captain A. H. Kardar. The Canada U.S.A. series continued in the 1960s as the historic international series between the two nations was revived at Toronto in 1963 and an informative book on North American cricket, *'The International Series, the History of the United States and Canada at Cricket,'* was written by John I. Marder. In 1979 Canada took part in their first ICC Trophy reaching the finals which qualified them for their first ever World Cup in 1979 played in England.

A talented right-handed Canadian batsman, W. R. G. (Reg) Wenman of British Columbia, was probably the most prolific run-getter in Canadian cricket. During a career which spanned some 40 years, he scored a record of 37 centuries, including 3 centuries in 4 days at the Western Canada tournament held at Regina in 1929. The only cricketer in North America to record more centuries than Wenman was American, John Barton King who scored 38. The bowling record against Canada in international cricket is held by Bart King. On a rainy afternoon in Philadelphia in 1906, King bowled into a slight breeze to capture 8 for 17 against the Canadians. JB King has several spectacular bowling performances during his long and illustrious career. During the 1908 tour of England by Philadelphia, he took 87 wickets for 958 runs at an average of 11.01 to lead the English first-class averages for the season and become the only North American player to achieve such a feat!

The 1975 season produced an upset when Eastern Canada defeated the touring Australian World Cup side led by Ian Chappell by five wickets. Eastern Canada's Ontario batsman, Franklyn Dennis scored 57 not out against the attack of Dennis Lillee, Max Walker and Allan Hurst. The stage was set early in this historic event when Canadian bowlers, Jitu Patel, Rick Stevens (both from Ontario) and Roy Callender (Quebec) bowled out the powerful Australian side for a modest 159 runs to pave the way for victory. The Australian team comprised of the Chappell brothers, Ian and Greg, Ross Edwards, Gary Gilmour, Jim Higgs, Alan Hurst, Bruce Laird, Rick McCosker, Ashley Mallett, Rodney Marsh, Richie Robinson, Alan Turner, Doug Walters and the 'terrible trio' of bowling, Max Walker, Dennis Lillee and Jeff Thomson! John W. Cole, President of the Canadian Cricket Association reflecting on the previous years' win, reminiscences that, since defeating the Australians and they having defeated the English, and Canada maybe heading towards a tie in the current series with the West Indies, *"would it be impossibly frivolous for me to assume that Canada has some claim to be World Champions?"* A positive approach indeed.

SOUVENIR PROGRAMME OF THE
SECOND AUSTRALIAN CRICKET TOUR OF CANADA
MAY 19 - MAY 29th 1975

The 1989 United Way Cricket Match held at the Toronto Sky Dome between the West Indies and a Rest of the World X1 drew a crowd of 40,570 to set a new attendance record for North America. During the summer of 2001 another milestone occurred in the annals of Canadian cricket when Canada played host to the International Cricket council Trophy tournament in the Toronto area. Twenty two nations took part, making it the most important cricket event ever staged in the Americas. Canada finished 3rd behind Holland and Namibia to advance to the 2003 World Cup in South Africa, and also in 2007 and as recent as 2011.[29] Unlike United States which has sputtered along the way, Canada has continuously engaged other cricketing nations on International levels with a national team and has steadily improved and prospects are there of becoming a test playing nation.

A Prelude to Cricket
in the Colonies

Thirteen years before the Pilgrims landed in Plymouth Massachusetts, Jamestown in Virginia was the first permanent English settlement in North America in 1607 *(a fort was built at a place called Point Comfort),* though the 'Lost Colony of Roanoke' was an even earlier settlement of 1585. (A Spanish fort established at St. Augustine, Florida in 1565, claims the title as *the earliest* settlement in America!) It may have been here in Virginia that cricket was first played in the New World along with other ball games. A wonderful read in the form of Protoball Chronology[1] which delves into the origins of baseball and ultimately other games involving a bat and ball, provides the first reference to some form of recreation in the new colony. The year is 1609 and Polish craftsman (glass blowers) take time off from the daily routine to indulge in a little game of bat and ball which they called *'pilka palantowa'* or bat and ball. The memoir written by one of them reads, *"soon after the New Year we initiated a ball game played with a bat…we rolled rags to make balls…our game even attracted the savages who sat around the field, delighted with this Polish sport."*[2] Palant, as the folk game is more commonly known in Poland, may be linked to an ancient family of northern European bat and ball game that Danish historian, Per Maigaard broadly categorized as 'longball.' There were different variations throughout the Scandinavian countries, and also Germany and Poland. It was a game with two bases, *batting home* and *running home*, a batter was delivered or thrown a ball and if hit, he could run to the running home where he could stay or run back to the batting home (running between wickets). Outs were by a fielder catching the ball in the air, or 'soaking' the runner between the two homes. According to David Block, Long ball seems to have been played in America for more than two centuries and yet it has not been talked about or known by many.[3] Wicket is another game that lasted well over three hundred years, yet not much was written or known outside the immediate vicinity of Connecticut and Massachusetts, though we do find mention of it being played in other areas.

The first reference to ball playing in America shows up in *1622* from a journal kept by William Bradford the Governor of Plymouth, of the new colony in America. (Another reference puts the date as 1621 and is referred to as 'a primitive game of cricket' so, was it Cricket or Wicket?[4]

The next reference[5] comes from an ordinance that was passed in New Netherland dated 26th October 1656, where the Director-General Peter Stuyvesant and the council passed another ordinance for the better observance of the Sabbath Law in New Netherlands. It forbade, *"all persons from performing or doing on the Lord's day of rest, by us called Sunday, any ordinary labor, such as plowing, sowing…which may be lawful on other days, on pain of forfeiting one pound Flemish for each person; much less any lower or unlawful exercise and amusement… dancing, playing ball, cards, trick-track, tennis, cricket (balslaen) or ninepins etc., before, between or during divine service, on pain of a double fine."*

> 50   *THE REFORMED CHURCH, DUTCH.*   [CHAP. I.
>
> allowed, under a penalty of twenty-five florins. In 1656 these Sunday laws were still more fully elaborated, showing a growth of healthy sentiment for a stricter observance of the Sabbath. The director-general and council forbade "all persons from performing or doing on the Lord's day of rest, by us called Sunday, any ordinary labor, such as plowing, sowing, mowing, building, wood-sawing, smithing, bleaching, hunting, fishing, or any other work which may be lawful on other days, on pain of forfeiting one pound Flemish for each person; much less any lower or unlawful exercise and amusement, drunkenness, frequenting taverns or tippling-houses, dancing, playing ball, cards, trick-track, tennis, cricket, or ninepins, going on pleasure-parties in a boat, car, or wagon, before, between, or during divine service, on pain of a double fine; especially, all tavern-keepers or tapsters from entertaining any clubs, or tapping; bestowing, giving, or selling, directly or indirectly, any brandy, wine, beer, or strong liquor to any person before, between, or during the sermons, under a fine of six guilders, to be forfeited by the tavern-keeper or tapster for each person, and three guilders for every person found drinking at the time aforesaid.

This image from the *Manual of the Reformed Church in America* creates misrepresentation by using the word 'Cricket', whereas the actual document does not use the word cricket. According to historian Rowland Bowen, he comments in his book, 'Cricket, A History of its growth and Development throughout the World' that, *"he sees no reason why the Dutch of New Amsterdam or the English colonist moving in from New England should not have been playing cricket there eight years before the town became New York."* The original document pictured in his book, draws attention to the word *balslaen* (hitting a ball) which he says is, *"too general a word to be necessarily confined to cricket, but the possibility cannot be excluded."*

The original document resides at the New York State Library in Albany, New York. The Dutch had a few unsavory games in the form of 'clubbing the cat' and 'pulling the goose.' As one can imagine from the names, in the former game, a loosely tied barrel was suspended by a rope between two poles with a live cat in it. The object was to free the cat by throwing clubs from an agreed distance and thus winning the game, but the cats were not so lucky all the time. For the other game, the goose had its head greased and tied lightly to an object and the participants would ride towards it on a horse and lean over to grab the goose and thus winning it if it came loose, one can only imagine what happened if the neck did not come loose!

Madam Knight while travelling through Connecticut in 1704 writes of a ball game in her diaries but does not allude to the type of game she witnessed. It could have been any type of ball game, we can all but speculate. The first *written* account on cricket is provided by William Byrd on April 25th 1709, where he talks of an early morning game before breakfast.

"I rose at 6 o'clock and Colonel Ludwell, Nat Harrison, Mr. Edwards and myself played at cricket, and I won a bit. (A 'bit' is one-eighth of a Spanish dollar) Then we played at whist and I won. About 10 o'clock we went to breakfast and I ate some boiled rice. Then Colonel Ludwell went to Jamestown court and then we played at {l-n-s-n-t} (maybe Lansquenet, a card game of German origin) and I lost £4 (English pounds) most of which Nat Harrison won."[6]

This was the May 6th 1709 entry in William Byrd II diaries. He had studied at the Felsted School in England and returned to Virginia upon the death of his father in 1704.[7] He was the founder of Richmond and provided the land where the city was laid out in 1737. He lived in Virginia on his Westover Estate, a plantation on the banks of James River and in a secret diary written in short-hand penned between 1709 and 1712 (The Secret Diaries of William Byrd of Westover), he refers to playing cricket that day with family and friends for a friendly wager. The original diary, resides at the Huntington Library in Los Angeles, California.

Picture an early morning game on a clear spring day, on the banks of the James River which flowed barely a hundred yards away. Byrd with his wealthy neighbors on his front lawn engaged in an informal game of cricket for a bit or English pound, and since there would be few players based on availability, I am sure the slaves and indentured servants would have been in attendance to gather the equipment and retrieve the ball if it was hit too far and also to serve tea coffee or refreshments. Though the beverages may not have been served there, Byrd does mention a coffee house (1709- earliest reference to a coffee house in America), *which was located on the east end of Duke of Gloucester Street near the capital.*[8] The 'Penny Universities' as the London coffeehouses were know, (anyone with a penny could enter) were opened in the 1650s in London after new and exotic beverages appeared in Europe – coffee, tea and chocolate. As with everything English, it soon followed to Colonial Virginia, though it did not survive after 1767 when the last one owned by Richard Charlton was converted into a tavern.[9] Cricket in England during this timeframe was beginning to be played by Lord's and locals alike and shared the same space on the playing field as equals, if this had taken root early on in colonial America, the social structure may have undergone change at faster pace and cricket may have been *the* game of choice. Gambling was one impetus that made strange bed-fellows of the Master and the Servant in England and since a lot of money was at stake, even the head gardener could be the captain of the team.[10]

Another entry from March 28th 1710 reads, *"I rose at 6 o'clock and read a chapter in Hebrew and some Greek in Anacreon. I ate milk for breakfast and said my prayers. About 10 o'clock Major Harrison, Hal Harrison, James Burwell and Mr. Doyley came to play at cricket. Isham Randolph, Mr. Doyley, and I played with them three for a crown. We won one game, they won two. Then we played at billiards till dinner, before which Colonel Ludwell came on his way to Mr. Harrison's. They all dined with us and I ate boiled pork. Soon after dinner the company went away and I took a nap. Then we walked to Mr. Harrison's, whom we found better. We played a game at cricket again."*[11]

Cricket news began to appear on the American scene in bits and pieces in the form of advertisements in gazettes, newspapers and journals. There were diaries, kept by well to do people, who during their travel would capture their 'eyewitness' accounts, and the landowners who could afford to indulge in such leisurely activities. Cricket was played long before any other bat and ball game was established as a team sport in America.

Cricket is believed to have originated in the 16th century during Saxon or Norman times by children living in south east England. The first definite reference to cricket or creckett (name may have derived from the Middle Dutch krick(e), meaning a stick or Old English cricc or cryce meaning a crutch or staff),[12] was found in a court case in a dispute of a school's ownership of a plot of land. John Derrick, one of Queen Elizabeth's coroner for Surrey, testified that, *"When he was a schooller in the free school of Guldeford, he and severall of his fellowes did runne and play at crickett and other plaies,"* on that site fifty years earlier. Royal Grammar School in Guilford was the location in Surrey and the year was 1550.[13] *That was generally accepted on the authority of Russell, a local historian who had transcribed it from the borough of Guildford's old records. A more careful reading has shown that Russell must have, innocently or intentionally, substituted crickett for quitos.*[14] A, 1611 account mentions that two men in Sussex, England were prosecuted for playing cricket on Sunday instead of going to church[15] and around the same time, Jamestown in Virginia was coming to life in the new world.

If cricket started so early in England, is it not plausible that cricket was played by the settlers in Jamestown during their early years, (earlier than 1709) just because there is no 'written evidence' does not mean cricket may not have been played by them. As early as 1611, Captain John Smith on his return to Jamestown found the starving colonist engaged in 'lawn bowling' inside the fortress.[16] The same year Sir Thomas Dale the governor instituted, 'Laws Divine, Moral and Martial' as the survival of the colony was jeopardized by the settlers unwillingness to work and he forbade them from playing bowls.[17] If this started so early, could other ball games have been far behind?

The youthful games popular at the time in 1723 were quoits, football, stool ball, ball and bat, cricket, marbles, tag, penny pinching, 'Button Button', and 'Break the Pope's Neck'. Taverns which were a popular feature at the time provided facilities for the adults, including skittle alleys, shuffleboards, billiards and bowling. Card games were so popular that they were imported in large quantities and taverns provided the cards and the tables for the patrons.[18] In a statement made by William Stephens in 1737, who was educated at Winchester and King's College in Cambridge states that, *"Many of our Townsmen, Freeholders, Inmates and Servants were assembled in the principal square, at Cricket and diverse other athletick Sports."* (*A Journal of the proceedings in Georgia*, II, p. 217)[19]

As time went by and the print media became an acceptable and affordable medium of communication, cricket news began to appear sporadically. A 1739 New York newspaper carries an advertisement looking for players for a cricket match.[20] The *Chronological History of Savannah, Georgia,*[21] mentions a *"game of cricket played, and next day, rifle match, and raffle for horse at £12,"* the entry is dated March 30th 1741. Georgia had an on and off love affair with cricket for various reasons well into the late 1800s when the fairer sex also took up cricket in petticoats.

William Stephens was sent to Savannah in 1737 by the trustees of Georgia who resided in London to report back on the condition and situation there. A year earlier he had travelled to South Carolina from England for land survey, where he met James Edward Oglethorpe (in charge of the colony) whom he had known in the British Parliament.[22] Impressed with his report, he was sent as the secretary of the Province of Georgia from 1737 to 1750 and also became the President of the entire colony from 1741 to 1751.[23] Besides the regular letters, a journal appraising of the local situation both trivial and important pertaining to the province, were sent to London periodically. He was in his mid-sixties and cricket finds a lot of mention in his journals and would have loved to play, but, *"thinking myself not altogether so fit at seventy, as heretofore, for such sports."*[24] Most of the games were played on holidays such as Easter, St. Andrew's Day, New Year etc. One such entry reads:

Tuesday, November 30th 1742, *"This being the Titular Saints day of Scotland, I order'd the usual Compliment to be paid of hoisting the flag, when most of North Britons in town assembled in the (Johnson) square, diverting themselves at Cricket &c, with a barrel of New York Ale placed near, to regale them as they saw fit, which they purchased at their own expense and no disorder happen'd. Nothing offer'd that I thought worth noting this day more."*[25]

Was cricket played in South Carolina and Georgia before 1736 when William Stephens first came to America? Absolutely! *'Various athletick sports'* did not appear overnight, they would have been in existence for some time and were it not for the journals, the allusion to cricket would have appeared much later. (William Byrd was already playing in Virginia in 1709 and possibly earlier after he returned from his studies in England).

"We hear that this day a great Cricket match is to be play'd on our Commons, (today's Fulton Fish Market in Manhattan) *by a company of Londoners against a Company of New-Yorkers."* (N.Y. Gazette, Revived in the Weekly Post Boy, April 28, 1751).

"Last Monday afternoon, a match at Cricket was play'd on our commons for a considerable wager, by eleven Londoners, against eleven New Yorkers. The game was play'd according to the London method, (a likely reference to the 1744 Laws of Cricket) *and those who got most notches in two hands, to be the winners. The New Yorkers went in first and got 81, then the Londoners went in got but 43. Then the New Yorkers went in again and got 86, and the Londoners finished the game with getting only 37 more."* (N.Y. Gazette, Revived in Weekly Post Boy, May 6th 1751) *This so far, is the FIRST recorded public report of a Cricket match in America.*

We find a mention of a 'South River Club' that may have existed near Annapolis Maryland, as early as 1754, who played cricket against men from other counties.[26] This was the year when Benjamin Franklin brought back from England a copy of the 1744 Laws of Cricket. It was this very copy that was presented to 'Young America Club' by Miss Mary D. Fox on June 4, 1867.[27]

"We hear that there is to be a great cricket match for a good sum played on Saturday next, near Mr. Aaron Rawling's Spring, between eleven young men of this city (Annapolis) and the same number of Prince George's County."

A May 1st 1809 pamphlet containing the 'Bye Laws for the Government of the Boston Cricket Club', was thought to be the introduction point of cricket in America, till a reader of, 'The American Cricketer', a Mr. Bunford Samuel of Philadelphia drew the readers' attention to the above notice that appeared in *Bradford's Journal* of 1st August, 1754. This was eighty years before the first recorded match between Guelph and Toronto in Canada, played at Hamilton, Ontario in 1834.[28]

"Last week, a cricket match was play'd, in Mr. Murdock's old field, in Prince George's County, between eleven of that county, and eleven South River Gentlemen (Anne Arundel County) and that the Prince Georgians were beat." (Another advertisement from the *Maryland Gazette* – Annapolis, November 14, 1754).

With the passage of time, more references to the game begin to appear and not just in idyllic situations, like the game on a town green or an open field, but also in the theater of war. Major General Edward Braddock a Commander-in-chief of the British forces in North America, who was killed during the 1755 July 9th failed expedition against the French and Indian War to capture the French Fort Duquesne (modern day down-town Pittsburgh) as he had supposedly taken cricket equipment and heavy rollers with him to create a cricket pitch as he was confident of defeating them. A certain *George Washington* then just 23, was part of his command, who served as a volunteer officer, an aide-de-camp.[29]

"*. . . no person shall use the exercise of playing or kicking of foot-ball, or the Exercise of Bat-and-Ball, or Cricket, within the Body of the Town, under a penalty of One Shilling and Six Pence.*" A New England reference to cricket is revealed in the form of an ordinance that was passed by the town of Salem, Massachusetts on July 26, 1762.[30]

When London was the watering hole for the American wealthy in the eighteenth century, many rich families from New England, Virginia and Carolinas found themselves in that vibrant city. Their offspring's were placed in well to do schools and guided them to right careers and trade with the London elite. Benjamin West an Anglo American artist well-known for his large scale historical paintings captured a glimpse of this privileged life during the heyday of the Britain's American Empire, and also a time of growing political rift over Britain's right to tax the colonies.[31] His oil on canvas painting titled, 'The Cricketers' shows five youths resting after a game of cricket. It seems there is a disagreement over the identity of the youths but are generally identified from left to right as Ralph Wormeley V from Virginia, brothers James and Andrew Allen of Philadelphia, Ralph Izard and Arthur Middleton from S. Carolina.[32] The Smithsonian identifies the figure on the right as Peter Beckford or possibly Arthur Middleton, another reference identifies him as a member of the large Beckford clan of Jamaica. A local history of Wiltshire on BBC website talks about a young Peter Beckford from England making their fortune from the sugar plantations in Jamaica, hence Arthur Middleton an American may be the right person in the painting (along with his dog). In the background is the Kew Bridge over the river Thames.

'In Pursuit of Refinement: Charlestonians Abroad, 1740-1860 by Maurie D, McInnis, Gibbes Museum of Art (Charleston, S. C.), Historic Charleston Foundation (Charleston, S. C.) 1999.'

This book further delves into the origins of the painting and identifies the subject more accurately than what I had uncovered in the previous paragraph from various sources. Since this is from a museum and the Charleston foundation, the information here would be more trustworthy and is expanded upon (information from the previous paragraph is left as alternate information). There are reportedly two versions of the painting, the first was not signed nor dated and the second was painted the following year in 1764. The 'friends' are identified from left to right as, James Allen (1742-78), Ralph Wormeley (1745-1806), Andrew Allen (1740-1825), and Ralph Izard (1741/42-1804). The Allen brothers were from Pennsylvania while Wormeley was from Rosegill Plantation, Virginia and Izard was from 'The Elms' of the Goose Creek Plantation, South Carolina, the traditionally wealthy

THE CRICKETERS - a painting by Benjamin West (Ralph Izard and his friends) 1764.
Courtesy Smithsonian Institute Archives.

plantation families. The identity of the last 'friend' on the right is not confirmed – is it Arthur Middleton (1742-87) or Peter Beckford (1739-1811) from the wealthy Jamaican Plantation. As Middleton and Benjamin West were in London at the same time for a short duration of four months, the undated version may have been painted in that short period. The 1764 painting was done after Arthur's departure and there are minor differences between the two versions. The Beckford name was provided by the Izard and Middleton families as they may have studied together.[33]

The American Revolutionary War (1775-1783) changed their fortunes and showed where their loyalty lay, Andrew Allen fought in the British Army and had to flee to London after his property was confiscated in Philadelphia and younger brother retired to the country during the war opposing the independence. Ralph Izard had stayed behind in London after his schooling but left for Paris in protest in 1776 and returned to South Carolina and was elected to the Continental Congress. Arthur Middleton was one of the 56 signatories for the Declaration of Independence and also a member of the Continental Congress. He was a British prisoner of war during 1780-81.[34] Ralph Wormeley was staunchly loyal to England, he was arrested and confined to family property in Berkley County (now West Virginia) for several years.[35] A June 16th 1709 entry in William Byrds' diary talks about a visit by Ralph Wormeley III, of Rosegill, the sheriff of Middlesex in 1704, while he was at dinner. He would be the granduncle to Ralph shown in this painting.

"*A match is proposed to be played tomorrow. Those who chuse to be of the party must meet at the exchange precisely at eight o'clock in the morning,*" Georgia Gazette, January 7th 1767.

Advertisement from "The Connecticut Courant" June 1, 1767

"*Whereas a challenge was given by Fifteen Men South of the Great Bridge in Hartford, to an equal Number North of faid Bridge, to play a Game at Cricket the Day after the laft Election – the Public are hereby inform'd, that the Challenged beat the Challengers by a great Majority. And faid North do hereby acquaint the South Side, that they are not afraid to meet them with any Number they fhall chufe, and give them not only the Liberty of picking their Men among themfelves but alfo the beft Players both in the Weft-Divifion and Wethersfield. Witnefs out Hands (in the Name of the whole Company) William Pratt, Niell McLean, Jr.*" (Language not corrected)

The 'Great Bridge' (pictured below in 1870, on Main Street) as it was referred to after 1750 was over the Mill River (mills were built along the river) or Little River, the Rivulet or Riveret, as it was differently named, and Park River, (sometimes called the Hog River, as there were also pig farms along the river) as it is known today. It was diverted underground by the Army Corps of Engineers in 1940 and now flows under the city of Hartford. To stop the dumping of human, animal and industrial waste in the 1900s, a park was created by Hartford Minister Horace Bushnell, which led to the current name, Park River.

Main-Street Bridge, Hartford

The Great Bridge, then (1838) and now (2013).

From the *'Memorial History of Hartford County, Connecticut, the Social Life after the Revolution,'* a passage describes the holiday after the Election:

"The rest of the week was observed as a holiday season in the State, particularly among apprentices, who went zealously into turkey-shooting and athletic sports. In 1766 William Pratt, Daniel Olcott and eighteen other young men living north of the bridge challenged Ashbel Steel, John Barnard and eighteen others on the south side, "to play a game at Bowl for a Dinner & Trimmings" on Friday after Election. In 1767, and on the same day, a match game of cricket was played in Cooper Lane, now Lafayette Street. 'The Southside', which had given the challenge, were beaten."

When early reference to cricket is alluded to in Connecticut, a question will always arise – was it Wicket or Cricket? Here they talk of 20 players, 10 short of the customary 30 for a wicket game, (9 more if it were cricket, but, when the All England team visited American in 1859, 22 played against the English XI) are we to believe there was only wicket when the neighboring states played cricket? The *'game of bowl'* is certainly not cricket as an article relating to activity in England talks of gentlemen engaged in *'Cricket and Bowls'*.[36] It may or may not have been played early on for some inexplicable reason, even searching thru *'Connecticut Courant'* newspaper (started in 1764) for advertisements etc. have not yielded much in reference to early cricket. Even the Wickets matches in early 1850s were referred to as cricket. A case in point – A Collinsville player, who went by the initial 'C', writes a letter to the *'Hartford Daily Courant'* published on July 7th, 1855, after a match against the Phoenix Club of New Britain. (The name of Phoenix Club appears in a Wicket article also).

A match was played at Canton on July 3rd, where Collinsville lost to the Phoenix Club. Subsequently after another article had appeared in the New Haven Register a few days later which prompted this article from the Collinsville player and suggested that the Phoenix Club was not happy after defeating them but had a long standing grudge going back two years. It describes the possible causes to this animosity and maybe some faulty decision by the Judges (Wicket umpires were always referred to as Judges) resulting from some *'underhand tricks played on that day'*, by the New Britain team, but could not be attributed to them. He further goes on to make the public 'aware' that the Phoenix club, not only has 30 members but, *"they have some three times that number to select from, to make up the number which the rules of the game required"*. Having a 'Judge' and thirty players on a team is definitely Wicket and not Cricket as headlined in the article.

Though 'Cricket' played with XI players, *does appear* in a game between Bridgeport Cricket Club XI and St. George Cricket Club of New York played in Fairfield County, Connecticut, where one innings was played with Bridgeport emerging victorious by a score of 100 to St. George's 77.[37] Cricket continued to be played by the British troops at the Ferry House Tavern near Fulton and Elm Street in Brooklyn, their headquarters, till their departure from Manhattan in 1783. Regular practices were held on Mondays' near the Jewish Burial Grounds and the Bowling Green ground is where the Brooklyn and Greenwich Cricket Clubs played near Cannon's Tavern, overlooking the East River on Corlear's Hook.[38] *"The game of Cricket, to be played on Monday next, the 14th inst., at Cannon's Tavern, at Corlear's Hook. Those Gentlemen that choose to become Members of the Club are desired to attend. The wickets to be pitched at two o'clock."*[39]

"Match between Brooklyn and Greenwich Clubs. A Set of Gentlemen propose playing a cricket match this day, and every Monday during the summer season, on the Cricket Ground near Brooklyn Ferry. The company of any Gentlemen to join the set in the exercise is invited. A large booth is erected for the accommodation of spectators," New York Mercury, August 9th 1779.[40]

There is evidence that George Washington played wicket (maybe cricket too) with his troops at Valley Forge during the summer of 1778. According to an entry of May 4th in the diary of first lieutenant George Ewing, *"This day His Excellency dined with General Nox, and after dinner did us the honor to play at Wicket with us."* During the first Congress of the United States, on April 23rd 1789, John Adams obsessively argues against the ordinary title for the highest office in the country for a few days, they were simply referred to as President and Vice President.[41] He was in favor of a more opulent title.

Now that there is so much evidence that cricket and other ball games were part of the downtime of the war theater, that it should not come as a surprise to find that, *"this day I was very much fatigued playing cricket"* writes Lieutenant William Feltman in his 1782 diary after playing with his army friends in South Carolina.[42] Majority of the officers kept detailed diaries which now enables us to glimpse into their time and state of mind. An April 19, 1786 advertisement for, *'bats and balls to sell'* appear in the *New York Independent Journal*, addressed to the Cricket Clubs. By 1794 the Batten's Tavern was a regular meeting place for the New York Cricket Club.[43] Reports at the time frequently mention, 'young gentleman' and 'men of fashion' taking up the sport!

As games became more proliferated, laws had to be enacted and one such example took place in Pittsfield, Masachusettes in 1791. To prevent damages to the newly built meeting house, a law, now refered to as the, *'Broken Window Bylaw'* was implemented. Games such as wicket, cricket, baseball, batball, football etc. were prohibited from being played within 80 yards of the structure. Games involving bat and ball was commonly played on the town green, town square or commons as these were open areas and this is where people generally gathered in numbers. This provides the earliest written reference to cricket and baseball on the same document in North America and was discovered by Baseball historian John Thorn which states:

"Preservation of the Windows in the New Meeting House . . . no Person or Inhabitant of said town, shall be permitted to play at any game called Wicket, Cricket, Baseball, Football, Cat, Fives or any other game or games with balls, within the Distance of Eighty Yards from said Meeting House."

We find more instances of laws being passed to curb the enthusiasm for ball playing in the vicinity of town halls, and as the Church had influence – playing or merrymaking on Sabbath was strictly against the Lord's wishes. At a meeting held at Frederic Mennert's Inn on 27th March, 1837 an ordinance was passed in Canton, Illinois.

"Section 36 - Any person who shall on the Sabbath day play at bandy, cricket, cat, town-ball, corner-ball, over-ball, fives, or any other game of ball, within the limits of the corporation, or shall engage in pitching dollars or quarters, or any other game, in any public place, shall, on conviction thereof, be fined the sum of one dollar."

A similar ordinance was also passed by Indianapolis during the same year.[44]

Until now, cricket history and timeline was congregated from diaries, newspaper advertisements, laws and articles, but in 1793, for the first time we 'see' cricket being played on the grounds of Dartmouth College in Hanover, New Hampshire! Here we see a group of students or men playing cricket applying the earlier method of underarm bowling, the use of the long curved bat and an early version of the stumps. According to the Dartmouth College Library Bulletin, *"this is the earliest known portrayal of the college in an engraving which appeared in the Massachusetts Magazine in February of 1793. The copper engraving is signed by J. Dunham, delineator and S. Hill, sculpt (the engraver). Dunham, we believe, was Josiah Dunham 1789, a preceptor at Moor's Indian Charity School, and later editor of The Eagle or, Dartmouth Centinel, a Hanover newspaper, and The Washingtonian in Windsor, Vermont. Samuel Hill of Boston was active there between 1789 and 1803. He made engravings for journal and book publishers."*[45] Two years later in 1795 we see a similar cricket scene, this time in front of the Colleges at Cambridge in a watercolor done by Houdin-Dorgemont. It depicts an identical cricket scene to the Dartmouth engraving except for a missing fielder.

It is generally accepted that the Dartmouth Cricket print of 1793 is the oldest visually documented evidence/reference to cricket in America, until I came across this 1954 advertisement for Philadelphia Whisky depicting a game of cricket being played in the 'Northern Liberties' around 1773! Could this be *the* earliest view of a cricket game in America? Was this taken from an original painting, and if so, where is it? This was too good to be true, for after conferring with Philadelphia Museum authorities and historical societies in that area, this is generally accepted as an artist's rendition of colonial scenes commissioned by the company, as the advertisements carried more than 45 different images of life in that era. (Still, I would like to find the original.)

CRICKET MATCH IN NORTHERN LIBERTIES, PHILADELPHIA, ABOUT 1773

Philadelphia Whisky was one of the brands under Continental Distilling Corporation of Publicker Industries in South Philadelphia, located on Snyder Avenue and Swanson Street which closed in the 1980's.[46] Publicker's main business was in chemicals and it was a huge one at that, later the company offices were located in Old Greenwich, Connecticut. The caption under the print reads, "Cricket Match in Northern Liberties, Philadelphia, about 1773." Present day Philadelphia was originally settled by the Swedes, and Northern Liberties was one of the counties till a "Consolidated Act" was passed in 1854 transferring all property to the consolidated city of Philadelphia under one municipal government.[47] Philadelphia was chartered as a city on October 28th 1701 and incorporated on March 11th

MASSA s8 L 779

S. Hill, sc.

J. Dunham del.

A front View of BROWNIAN UNIVERSITY

View of the Colleges, at Cambridge, Massachusetts. Dorgemont
1795.
E.B.O.LANE

1789 and Northern Liberties on March 9th 1803.[48] Hans de Nyce, a Mennonite preacher of Germantown was the founder of Northern Liberties later known as Nicetown.[49] The cricketers depicted above could very well have utilized the services of Star Tavern which was a favorite resort for early cricketers as it was run by an Englishmen, a predictably enthusiastic supporter and advocate of the game. *The tavern was located on the west side of Main Street, a short distance below Manheim Street in Germantown.*[50]

While the English may have been engrossed in a cricket match in Philadelphia, Boston would be having a 'Tea Party' in December of 1773, where 342 chests of tea from India were thrown overboard by the, *'Sons of Liberty'* as a protest against the tax policies of the British government and the East India Company, that controlled the import of tea into the American colonies.

Cricket was being gradually organized and we see here, quite possibly, *the earliest printed* 'Rules and Regulation' of a Cricket Club in the young United States of America! This document of the Virginia Cricket Club in Richmond also contains the, 'Laws of Cricket', and is dated June 16, 1795! Boston's Crescent Cricket Club was not far behind, as their by-laws appeared in 1809, after the Club was established in 1808.[51] (A copy of the 1860 revised bylaws and constitution containing 11 handwritten pages, is housed in the Lynn Museum and Historical Society near Boston). In 1839 the Laws of the Game were printed on page 324 of the 'Gentleman's Magazine and American Monthly Review', edited by William Evans Burton in Volume V - was this the first instance of the 'Laws of Cricket' appearing in commercial print in America?

WE the Subscribers, desirous of establishing a CRICKET CLUB, *and also Rules and Regulations that appear to us best calculated to render it permanent, have agreed to the following*

RULES.

I. THAT we pay into the hands of Joseph Jackson, who for the time present is appointed Treasurer and Secretary, one dollar each, to be applied as he and William Mewburn shall judge necessary in preparing the Play Ground, procuring Batts, Balls, Wickets, &c.

II. AS soon as our number exceeds twelve, and a majority of the Club wish an encrease, the following mode of election shall be established, viz. Any member desirous of introducing a friend, shall propose the same on any play day to the Secretary or his substitute, and on the next play day he shall be ballotted for, which ballot shall be taken in a hat by one of the bowlers, who with the other bowler shall examine the same; and if three fourths of the members present vote for his admission, he becomes a member on paying one dollar, which with the fines shall go into the General Fund As soon as every necessary to the game shall be procured, the said Fund shall be subject to the appropriation of the majority.

III. THE play days to be on Tuesdays and Saturdays each week, when the Club is to meet on the ground at half past five in the evening; absent members at that time to pay nine pence, and if not present at the choosing of partners, nine pence more.

IV. ANY member absent four successive play days, and in town any one of them, to pay a quarter dollar extra.

V. ANY member may withdraw on paying a dollar.

VI. THE Treasurer and Secretary to be chosen for the season: He may appoint a substitute (being a member of the Club.) It shall be his duty to prepare lists of the members, which he shall call over at the times appointed for attendance in the third rule, and shall receive all money arising to the General Fund; he shall also provide spirits, &c. for the Club, the cost of which, and every other necessary to be paid out of the Fund.

VII. THE Treasurer and Secretary (or his substitute) not appearing on the ground at half past five o'clock, P. M. on every Tuesday and Saturday during the season, with every necessary for playing the game, &c. shall pay a fine of half a dollar.

VIII. ANY dispute arising in consequence of different constructions of the above Rules and Fines, shall be determined by a majority of members on the ground.

John Hopkins, paid one Dollar.	
Nelson Berkeley,	ditto.
Samuel Shepard,	ditto.
Augustine Davis,	ditto.
William Richardson,	ditto.
Charles Grymes,	ditto.
William Wiseham,	ditto.
Stephen Crouch,	ditto.
William Dabney,	ditto.
John Carter,	ditto.
Joseph Jackson,	ditto.
William Mewburn,	ditto.
George Laughlin,	ditto.
William Berkely,	ditto.

Richmond, Tuesday evening, June 16, 1795.

1795 Virginia Cricket Club, Richmond, Courtesy: Library of Virginia.

Constitution & By Laws of the
Crescent Cricket Club
as revised by the committee of A.D. 1860

Preamble

We the undersigned considering the game of Cricket to be a harmless and innocent amusement tending to the promotion of our health have resolved to organize ourselves into an association for the purpose of enjoying said game and do hereby adopt the following Constitution & By Laws for our mutual benefit and control

Constitution

Article I   Name

This association shall be known as the Crescent Cricket Club

Article II   Officers

Section 1st. The officers of this Club shall consist of a President, Vice President, Secretary, and Treasurer in addition to which three (3) other members shall be chosen who with the Vice President Secretary and Treasurer shall constitute a board of Directors of which the Vice President shall be chairman.

1860 Crescent Cricket Club Constitution and Bylaws. Courtesy: Lynn Museum and Historical Society.

GROWTH AND DEVELOPMENT

Was cricket played mainly by the British? It would be foolish to think so, for we see the locals or the natives like Sheftall in Georgia and other places engaged in different recreational activities, with cricket being one of them. The Dartmouth engraving throws light on the game spreading to schools and enjoying a prominent place as an outdoor activity. The game was not only practiced in populous areas or where the English were concentrated, but also in other areas if we were to read the writings of Edward Oliphant's *History of America*, published in Edinborough in 1800. *The athletic and healthy diversion of cricket, football....are universally practiced in this country.*[1]

The War of 1812 heralded the industrial revolution in America (1820-1870) and as such society changed from a predominantly agricultural/subsistence farming model to urbanization with the advent of automation and mass production. The spinning and weaving process were combined and clothes were made in factories instead of homes, and the factories drew people towards urbanization which in turn led to communication, and developments of roads which led to transportation. River transport and railroads facilitated movement of goods and people alike. This domino effect further led to inventions and improvements throughout the 19th and 20th century. The increase in income and the influx of British immigrants from the industrial regions of Sheffield and Nottingham gave rise to semi organized leisure activities in team sports. A cricket match in Savannah between the natives and newcomers show the natives winning 57 to 25.[2] A New York paper copies a cricket challenge from a Savannah paper which notes, *'no legs before wicket.'*[3] Though the English took up residence in the two major cities at the time – Philadelphia and New York, other areas were also recipients of the new settlers, and as such, their lifestyle and habits followed.

A first cricket club of sorts or a group was formed in 1803, calling itself the, *'New York Cricket Club on July 3rd*, and in the pages of an old commercial advertiser appears a notice asking its members to attend a meeting on business of importance at Fryatt's on Nassau Street.[4] This *club is believed to have been located at, Bunch of Grapes Tavern, No. 11 Nassau St, and the club lasted for about a year. The information comes from Henry Chadwick's Scrapbook – "St.*

George Cricket Club was preceded in New York City by a club whose headquarters were at the old Shakespeare in Nassau St." The club meeting notices appeared in *Daily Advertiser, March 23rd 1803 p. 3 Col. 3. Another meeting notice was found* in *Commercial Advertiser on July 2nd, 7th & 8th. On February 10th, 1804, Evening Post carried a notice for a meeting at the same location.*[5] The first Cricket Club in Boston was taking shape and meeting notices would appear in newspapers for members to get together at mostly taverns or for drafting, '*Rules and Regulations for the Government*', as the Norfolk, Virginia Cricket Club would advertise for in 1816.[6]

With the movement of the new settlers to Midwest, recreational activities also followed. Transplanted from Surrey in England, new immigrants who were taking up residence in Illinois and indulged in cricket matches as early as 1818. In describing his daily life in the English Prairie in Illinois, John Woods writes on October 2nd, "*There was a game of Cricket played at Wanborough (Mr. Birkbeck's settlement) by the young men of the settlement, this they called keeping Catherine Hill Fair, (similar to the large pleasure-fair held in the vicinity of Guildford, Surrey) many of the players being from the neighborhood of Godalming and Guilford.*" Another entry, also on October 2nd the following year reads, "*This day was kept at Wanborough, as last year, instead of Catherine Hill Fair, but as some of the young men were gone to a county court at Palmyra, there was no cricket match as was intended, only a game of trap-ball. There have been several cricket matches this summer, both at Wanborough and Birk Prairie; the Americans seem much pleased at the sight of the game, as it is new to them.*"[7] (Just to give the readers an idea as to the time it took to travel in those days, Mr. Woods journey from Cowes, on the Isle of Wight in England to Baltimore in Maryland by sea took 58 days, another 16 days from Baltimore to Wheeling [280 miles] and another 38 days from Wheeling to Shawneetown [906 miles], and finally, 4 more days to reach the Prairie, not to mention the sickness or if there were no taverns on the way, one had to hunt for their meals!) At the time, Illinois was only about two years old and the 21st state to be admitted to the union. Cricket had been introduced to the 'Americans' in the mid-west as early as 1818 and it was played at Rincon Point in San Francisco during the Gold rush,[8] and the San Francisco Cricket Club was founded by the British Consul, George Aitken in March of 1852.[9]

Citing the *New York Evening Post* of June 16th 1820,[10] we see the first mention of a two day match between eleven New Yorkers and eleven Englishmen at Brooklyn, the location was most likely the Ferry House Tavern, a popular British stronghold at the time. It was during this time frame that we begin to see the first references to *organized clubs* being mentioned frequently. Who gets the distinction of being the first cricket club in America, is difficult to pinpoint. Lester mentions that around 1794, the New York Cricket Club was, "*meeting regularly, usually at 6 o'clock at Batten's Tavern.*" There were Cricket Clubs as early as 1790 when John Adams famously deplored naming the highest elected official in the country as 'President', "*even Fire Houses and Cricket Clubs have presidents.*" Was it the Union and Mechanic Cricket Club that played two matches on June 19, 1820 and the New York Daily Advertiser reported, "*this manly exercise excited astonishment in the spectators by their great dexterity*",[11] or were there other clubs that did not catch the attention of the print media? From the fragmented information we can safely concur that Cricket Clubs had been around since 1790's, albeit, not a formal organization (till evidence proves otherwise), but a club none the less. The boys at Haverford College organized the first native born American Cricket Club around 1834.[12] The 'Union Cricket Club' seemed to be a popular choice for a club name at the time; Philadelphia had one by 1832,[13] though Tom Melville's book talks about a Union Cricket Club being formed near George Tichnor's farm in West Philadelphia in 1843,[14] which later moved to Camden, after the sale of the Union Club Grounds.[15] William Rotch Wister also talks of playing cricket on the *Union Club Grounds* at Camden in 1843 and Cincinnati, Ohio had a 'Union Cricket Club' during the Civil War. The 'New York Cricket Club', was the first modern club founded on September 20th 1838, which was later changed to the, 'St. George Cricket Club', on April 23rd, 1839, on Saint George's Day in England.[16] It had moved to its' own grounds at the corner of Manhattan's Bloomingdale Road and 42nd St, an isolated location at the time.[17]

"In preparing this little work, it has been a principal part of my object to serve the cause of physical education by directing the attention of young persons to sports of a healthful and invigorating tendency... for some of my materials...I have been indebted to the English edition of the Boy's Own Book." [18]

Were cricket and other ball games promulgated by the availability of English sports books and local editions? It would seem so, and from the above statement by Robin Carver in putting together his *'Book of Sports'* in 1834, it *'directs the attention'* of the youth towards outdoor games. He also notes, *"The price (of the English Edition) of which work places it beyond the reach of most young people in this country."* A very interesting point is made here, which means, these were smaller and affordable books that could reach out to thousands more kids, than the English edition would, due to its prohibitive price, as they were more than 300 pages with fine binding and decorated covers. Besides, the *Boys Own Book,* not only provided instructions and rules/methods of the game on and off the field, but also stories and instructions in behavior on the playground. The expensive nature of the English books spawned American adaptions of the English publications and publishers from Philadelphia, New Haven, Connecticut, to Boston and New York etc. also came out with their own books. Some of these were:

1. *A Little Pretty Pocket-Book, Intended for the Instruction and Amusement of Master Tommy and Pretty Miss Polly, 1744.*
2. *The Book of Games; or, A History of the Juvenile Sports, Practised at the Kingston Academy. London: Printed by J. Adlard for Tabart and Co. at the Juvenile and School Library, 1805.*
3. *Sports and Pastimes for Children by F. Lucas Jr., 1824.*
4. *The Child's Own Book by Francis, Bowen, Hartwell, Anderson, Munroe & Francis, 1832.*
5. *Mary's Book of Sports, 1832.*
6. *The Book of Sports by Robin Carver, 1834.*
7. *The Schools Boy's Friend, 1835.*
8. *The Sports of Childhood by S. Babcock, 1840.*
9. *Newly Revised Eclectic First Reader, McGuffney, 1844.*

10. *Stories of School-Boys, American Sunday-School Union, Philadelphia, 1850.*
11. *The School Reader, First Book, Sanders. 1853.*

'Look and Learn' that's what we were always told to do as kids, and this applies to any situation. Watching others play, and wanting to join them is the most natural trait, so, it should not come as a surprise to see one participate in the excitement of a new sport. The Little Pretty Pocket-Book first printed for John Newbery in London in 1744 shows 32 different games and activities illustrated and accompanied by a poem as seen in the image below. American editions were reproduced and printed first in 1762 in New York and Philadelphia in 1786.[19] The Lilly Library copy shown below is a London edition which reads,

"A Little pretty pocket-book intended for the instruction and amusement of little Master Tommy and pretty Miss Polly, with two letters from Jack the Giant Killer, as also a ball and pincushion, the use of which will infallibly make Tommy a good boy and Polly a good girl ... to which is added a little song book, being a new attempt to teach children the use of the English alphabet, by way of diversion. 11th edition, Published in London, Printed for J. Newbery - 1763."

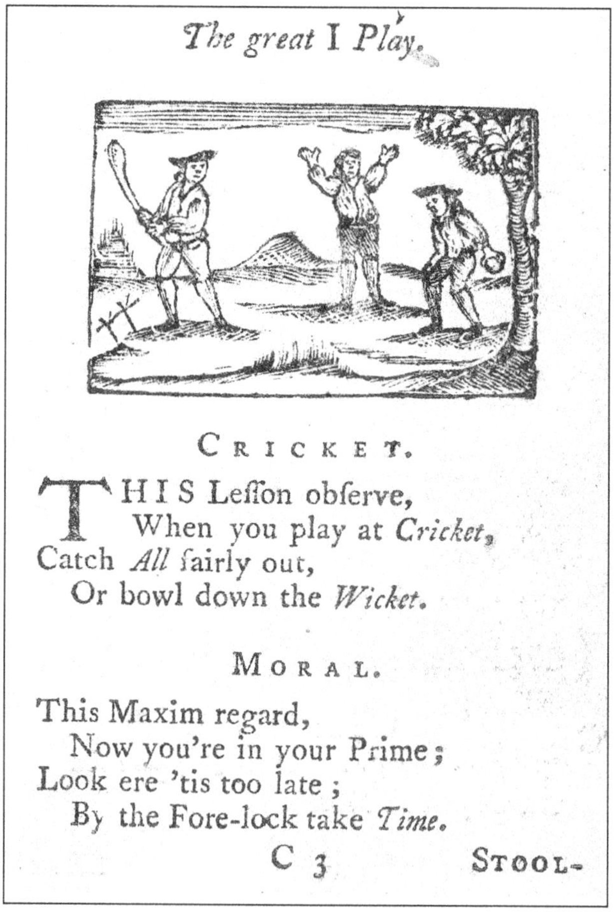

The great I Play.

CRICKET.

THIS Lesson observe,
    When you play at *Cricket*,
Catch *All* fairly out,
    Or bowl down the *Wicket*.

MORAL.

This Maxim regard,
    Now you're in your Prime;
Look ere 'tis too late;
    By the Fore-lock take *Time*.

C 3   STOOL-

Courtesy: The Lilly Library, Indiana University, Bloomington, Indiana.

THE PLAY-GROUND.

Cricket scene from 'The School Boy's Friend', by the author of 'The Young Man's Own Book.' Key & Biddle, Philadelphia 1835.

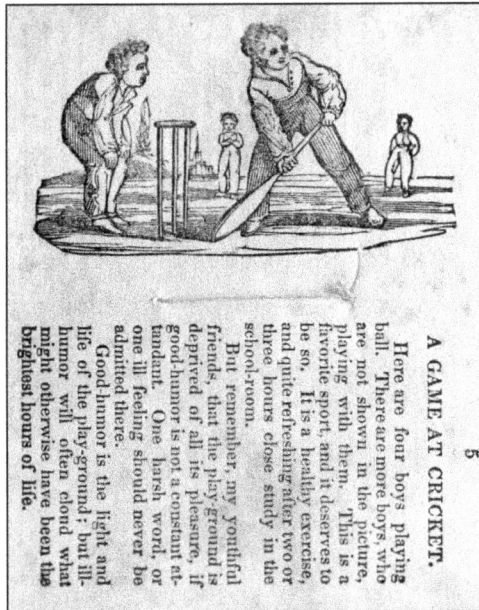

5

A GAME AT CRICKET.

Here are four boys playing ball. There are more boys, who are not shown in the picture, playing with them. This is a favorite sport, and it deserves to be so. It is a healthy exercise, and quite refreshing after two or three hours close study in the school-room.

But remember, my youthful friends, that the play-ground is deprived of all its pleasure, if good-humor is not a constant attendant. One harsh word, or one ill feeling should never be admitted there.

Good-humor is the light and life of the play-ground: but ill-humor will often cloud what might otherwise have been the brightest hours of life.

The Sports of Childhood, S. Babcock 1840. This same sketch appears in 'The Boy's Own Book' of 1829 by William Clark p. 56, which means the drawings/sketches from other books were freely borrowed/copied at the time. Another example is from, "The Book of Sports" by Robin Carver in 1834. The picture of boys running out of a school in the title page is taken from page 7 of, "The Boy's Own Book." The above sketch also appears in Robin Carver's book on page 49. (*I could have saved a lot of money, not paying for the copyright pictures!*)

107

One of my many finds on early American Cricket was this oil painting showing two players in a period dress typical of England in the mid-1800s. Initially looking at the windmill in the background, I did not realize that they were an integral part of the early American landscape, the knowhow which was brought over by the early settlers. The first windmill was at the Flowerdew Hundred Plantation built in 1612 [20] and the early windmill's were used for pumping water to make salt and grinding grain. In 1854 Daniel Halladay from Connecticut is credited with a design that automatically turned with the changing wind and controlled its' own speed. Later he moved his company, U.S. Wind Engine and Pump Company to Batavia, Illinois to take advantage of the developing western market. The frame and its' material, points towards the mid-1850s work by an unknown amateur artist, whether it's of American or English origin, is a toss-up, until it is evaluated.

"The first regular contest between two cricket elevens in New York, of which we have any record was that played on the vacant lots near Smith and Bergen Street, on the 20th of September, 1838," writes Henry Chadwick.[21] A little untoward incident by a Sheffield fielder who, while trying to catch a ball that slipped thru his fingers and onto his face giving him a black eye, kept the memory of the match fresh in Chadwick's mind. The team comprised of English born residents from Sheffield who scored 79 and 88 and Nottingham scoring, 21 and 23 thereby losing the $100 wager.[22] The second match was played at the same location. The ferry house tavern in Brooklyn is noteworthy for a couple of reasons as here, the first match between two instituted clubs in America was played between New York (St. George) and Long Island, *and,* the only match ever played for money in America (or so thought Henry), was played for a wager of $400 on October 22nd and 23rd 1838! The scores for the game are as follows:

NEW YORK

First Innings	Runs	Second Innings	Runs
J Wheatman lbw	10	b C Russell	5
Gill c C Russell	7	b Cordroy	0
G Stead b Cordroy	4	b Cordroy	4
S Wright b Cordroy	20	b C Russell	2
Ward b Cordroy	4	lbw	2
Taylor b C Russell	16	b Cordroy	11
Dodworth b W Russell	0	b C Russell	3
Barry b Cordroy	5	c C Russell	2
Andrews b C Russell	14	b Cordroy	1
Furniss run out	10	b Cordroy	11
Sloper not out	0	not out	1
Byes 4: wide ball 1	5	Byes	3
Total	95	Total	45

LONG ISLAND

First Innings	Runs	Second Innings	Runs
W Russell b Wheatman	3	c Stead	1
C Russell c Wright	0	b Sloper	12
H Russell not out	0	b Wheatman	10
Underwood b Gill	1	b Gill	2
Cordroy Lbw	0	c Wright	0
Nash Sr. b Wheatman	6	b Wheatman	0
R Nash c Wright	0	Lbw	1
G Nash b Andrews	4	b Wheatman	0
Wyvil Lbw	3	not out	0
Sneath c Taylor	0	b Gill	3
W H Parker b Wheatman	0	run out	17
Byes	2	Byes	2
Total	19	Total	48

Another interesting fact to note is that most of the Nottingham and Sheffield players were the same ones who played under the New York and Long Island banner, what brought that change in a months' time? Just two years earlier in 1836, Samuel Wright left Sheffield for America with his wife and then two year old Harry, who along with his brother George, would go on to become one of the famous names in Baseball history. In another oddity, Sam did not play for Sheffield in the September match, but we see him a month later scoring a high of 20 runs for New York in the first innings.

Lester in his book[23] brings our attention to an advertisement in the Philadelphia *Public Ledger* of November 1st 1841, from Wakefield Mills Cricket Club, challenging, *"the best eleven in the city to play two home-and-home games for from $50 to $100."* Challenges were a common feature in the early days, either it was for 'dinner and trimmings' as seen in the Wicket games in Connecticut, a simple 'treat' in colonial Georgia or later on for money, as disposable income and the question of prestige increased. In a Single wicket format which was popular at the time, a $100 wager between D. Winckworth of Toronto Club and H. Groom of St. George's was held in 1843 where the latter lost. In the 1844 engagement, Toronto Cricket Club on behalf of Canada, challenged any team in America for $1000, which was accepted by St George, but they could not win the money. Tom Senior, the coach to the eldest of the famous Newhall brothers, and also the landlord of Cricketer's Arms, who happened to be the best bowler in Philadelphia, challenged any two cricketers in America to play against Crossley and himself for $100 at single wicket. William Wilby of New York, and Hallis of Newark, two players who were to bowl against the first English team to visit America - George Parr's XI in 1859, accepted the challenge but lost the bet. Then there were others who encouraged competition in the true spirit go the game by presenting bats to younger players.[24] Not all challenges were accepted even when it involved money and the lack of interest shown by the public for the St. George matches was denounced by the *New York Morning News* as in the past few years they had played only a handful of matches.[25] American cricket was in its infancy and it was too early in its history to try and rationalize the issue. The catalyst may have been the contest between Canada and America which I am sure had some patriotic feeling mixed in, which resulted in popularizing the game, or at the least, generated interested in the sporting public, much more than a few individual clubs could achieve.

The first club comprising of local born youths, was formed at Haverford College around 1834 and the impetus was provided by an English born gardener, William Carvill[26] in much the same way Sam Morley did at St. Paul's School in Concord, New Hampshire. The Delina, Lycean and Dorian which had been formed by the college students in 1856 became part of the Haverford College Cricket Club in 1883 and to this day it would be the oldest continuously playing club. The English residents around 1831 would play cricket by underhand bowling on a level and prepared playing field and who were later known as the Union Cricket Club of Philadelphia, which was formed in 1842, (closed in 1846) under the leadership of Robert Waller an English importing merchant.[27] The printer for the *New York Spirit of the Times*, John Richards started the New York Cricket

Club on October 11th 1843.[28] Then there was the Star Club of Brooklyn, also founded in 1843, and a Junior Cricket Club was formed at the University of Pennsylvania in 1842. They played on the Union Club Grounds one afternoon a week for a fee of fifty dollars per year![29] The open pastures provided the ideal place to play cricket and Jones Wister, brother to William, formed the Germantown Cricket Club comprised of schoolboys from Germantown, the namesake to the famous club of later years (1854). According to George Newhall, the Germantown schoolboys were keen on doing something meaningful instead of, "*stoning birds, stealing fruits, fighting after school or licking the rowdies,*" (wonder what that means) and they happened to see the Englishmen playing Cricket, which led them to form the club.[30] Kensington players started the 'Washington Cricket Club' around 1852 and the 'Young America Cricket Club' in 1855. The heavyweights, Philadelphia Cricket Club was formed on February 10th 1854, and the Germantown Cricket Club on August 1st 1854,[31] provided the much needed impetus to the local cricket scene and galvanized the youth to take up the sport in larger numbers. Newspapers such as the New York Herald in 1845 were liberal in embellishing that the clubs were rapidly spreading to "*every city, town and hamlet.*" A club in Bedford, Long Island, was started by 16 to 18 year olds, and another club formed in Jamaica with mostly American players, then there was the Newark Club, Charleston in South Carolina, Rochester and Syracuse in New York State, Cincinnati in Ohio, Natchez on the banks of the Mississippi river in Mississippi and in Macon, Georgia as well as Chicago.[32]

This was the time when the underarm bowling gave way to round-arm bowling, the arm not going above the shoulder, more like a delivering a ball with one's arm extended at a 90° angle. Wister in his recollections, mentions that in the early days, when runs were scored, they were referred to as notches (runs were recorded on a stick), a Nottingham trait and English custom dating back to 1735.[33] The New York Cricket Club was formed on September 20th 1838 and renamed, 'St George's Cricket Club' on April 23rd 1839 [34] and their grounds were at the Red House on Second Avenue, about 110th Street, opposite Hell Gate. Samuel Wright from Sheffield was their cricket professional.[35] The Star Club of Brooklyn was also formed around 1843. The Union Cricket Club was formed in 1843 and a large tract of land was provided by 'The Camden and Amboy Railroad Company' at Camden. Mr. Robert Waller claimed that the name, Union Cricket Club was chosen to represent and bring together, Americans and Englishmen under one team, whereas William Wister recalls that the name was given because it was intended to bring in the English players from the Kensington district and there were also several Americans amongst its members.[36] Probably the first American club, comprising of local players was formed by William Rotch Wister and his friends at the University of Pennsylvania in the third quarter of 1842, "Junior Cricket Club."[37] Initial enthusiasms brought in more than 50 members and a coach, an instructor was hired for a moderate sum, and in winter, they practiced in a gymnasium. Some of these early members were instrumental in the formation of the 'Philadelphia Cricket Club' which is still in existence today.

Williams' youngest brother Jones mentions in his reminiscences that the 'Belfield Junior Cricket Club' was started by his brothers with the influence and guidance from a certain Mr. James Thorp, an old English Cricketer and a soldier. The impromptu club (1840-46) began with the pasture being flattened near their Belfield home and after the initial hurrah it was forgotten, till the summer of 1846 when Jones found the cricket implements in the loft. Jones being the youngest was busy with his games of marbles, tops, shinny and town ball (name at the time for baseball), till he came across the find in the attic and immediately set about gathering his friends and began playing near their house. This was short lived and ended as soon as it had begun, as they broke a window pane and the ball landed on the father's head. *"Both head pains and window panes were repaired,"* and they moved their grounds to a nearby orchard where they christened it the 'Germantown Cricket Club' in 1854.[38] Walter S. Newhall, another player from a family of Cricketers who lost his life during the Civil War, was a member of this early Cricket team. Their first challenge came from 'Delphian Circumferaneous' who beat them even though Newhall, their fast underhand bowler took five wickets in five deliveries! *"From this small beginning cricket grew like wild-fire in the fifties."*[39] With cricket clubs mushrooming all around, *"parties of small ragged boys, hardly out of petticoats, were to be seen with sticks for bats, and stones for balls, setting up their wickets on rough lots, covered with ashes and oyster shells."*[40] (Little boys wore petticoats - was this a unisex term used when describing clothing for little boys and girls during Mid-Victorian Philadelphia?)

Most of the clubs were started by English immigrants, such as the Newark Club, Washington Club and Syracuse Club as each has sizeable English composition. Jamaica was the only exception as it was organized with the help of the New York Club. In 1845 two clubs, Queen City and Union Club formed in Cincinnati, they had *Sheffield mechanics and immigrant English Jews,* such as the Moses brothers, Phineas and Elkin playing for the Union Club.[41] They were not the first English Jews to play cricket in America, the Sheftall families from Georgia were the earliest. The Union Star Cricket Club in Brooklyn, a largely Jewish club in New York was started by another English Jew, Henry Russell and his brother William, (both formerly of St. George Cricket Club) who is credited with introducing cricket to New York.[42] The ground was originally called Washington Park, today known as Fort Greene Park, located opposite Sharp's Hotel at the corner of Myrtle and Portland Avenues near Fort Greene. Philadelphia was one city where local born Americans were taking up cricket in large numbers, though the English mill workers were playing informally as early as 1841. Around the same time in 1843-44 a few youngsters in Germantown under the leadership of John Wister, formed the Germantown Cricket Club, they were young men from the schools and also included many English born lads.[43] A Junior Cricket Club was formed by William Wister and in 1846 the Union Club ceased to exist due to *"bickerings and want of money,"* and along with it the Junior Club also ceased to exist as they shared the ground with them.[44] Before the clubs demise, a match took place on September 27th 1845, between Wister's XI and Blight's XI, that was reported by the *New York Spirit of the Times* , a match considered to be played by all American players from the University of Pennsylvania.[45]

GROUNDS USED BY THE JUNIOR CRICKET CLUB IN CAMDEN, N. J., 1843. LEASED BY THE UNION
CLUB FROM THE CAMDEN AND AMBOY RAILROAD.

Archibald H. Graham, Jr. Cricket at the University of Pennsylvania, page 4 {UPS 83.2 Cr G738 (1930), University of Pennsylvania Archives, Philadelphia, PA}.

With the clubs disappearances, the desire to play still remained and members of the Junior Club, the Union Club and Germantown got together at Camden and played informally during 1852-53. In 1853 the first match between New York Club and Philadelphia was played resulting in New York's favor as they and St. George were the dominant teams at the time. As more 'cricketers' were generating interest in the game, it was felt that a formal organization was necessary to promote the game and having a proper ground was of the utmost importance. With that goal in mind 21 cricketers gathered in William Wister's office on February 10th 1854 (by the end of 1856 they had 106 members) and the Philadelphia Cricket Club was born with the President being J.D. Sergeant and William Rotch Wister as the vice-president, both attorneys.[46] Then there was the Washington Club organized by the Kensington players around 1852, against whom they played 3 matches and Philadelphia's first match against the New York was played on 17th and 18th October resulting in a win for Philadelphia. This first match had two 'Americans' Wister and Kuhn and as the frequency of games increased, so did the number of 'American' players. Trying to emulate the success of the Philadelphia Club, Germantown Cricket Club was formed on 1st August 1854, the precursor to the present Germantown Club.[47] This in turn led to the formation of the Young America Club on November 19th 1855 with younger members of the Newhall family and most of the players were under 16 years of age. For the first few years, they did not engage other clubs in matches, but soon they had three elevens and had it not been for them, who carried the cricket torch thru the Civil War, cricket might have not survived in Philadelphia. Later in 1890 they would merge with the Germantown Club.[48] As many of the club founders and members were owners/printers of the papers, articles and opinions were presented as we see in this *Cleason's Pictorial* of 1851.

"Little need be said of the fine engraving which we present to our readers below. It illustrates one of those fine field sports that modern times have not yet been able to obliterate from the taste and habits of lovers of manly games. Unlike archery, it still holds a respectable place upon the English and American turf, and has many an ardent and generous admirer. Scientifically played, it has many charms and pleasures that the casual observer would pass by unnoticed, but which have a firm hold on the feelings and prompting of the players. The scene below is an actual copy from life and the figures are likenesses, as many familiar with the club to which it refers, will at once bear testimony. Does not their healthful and jovial appearance almost convert you to love the game? The scene was drawn for us by Manning, from a large Lithograph by J. H. Bufford. We are beginning to realize the truth of the old adage — all work and no play, makes Jack a dull boy. Among the games now in vogue, none is more exciting, healthful and invigorating than the game of cricket. It is still one of the favorite games of England, and we are glad to find that it has imitators among ourselves. The St. George's Club, of New York and the New England Club, among us have created a taste for this manly sport, which fostered by a generous rivalry, will not be likely to meet with a premature decease. More than one match has already been played between these two societies, to the great interest of the sporting public, who have sought eagerly through the Spirit of the Times, and other sporting journals, the records of the game."

PETER LOW, Ground Keeper.   W. J. HOWELL.   J. R. WASLEY.   R. RESTIN.   B. B. TILT.
WM. CHADWICK, Scorer.   CHAS. TAYLOR.   THOS. JOHNSON.   CHAS. DRAPER.   THOS. MORGAN.   JOHN TUCKEY.   HENRY BENNETT.   WM. RUSSELL, Umpire.
JOHN LANG.   JAMES G. JOHNSON.   WILLIAM LUMB.
THE ELEVEN OF NEW ENGLAND.

Cleason's Pictorial Drawing-Room Companion, Boston, Saturday, August 2nd 1851.

CRICKET MATCH BETWEEN THE NEW ENGLAND AND ST. GEORGE CLUBS.

Cleason's Pictorial Drawing-Room Companion, Boston, Saturday, October 4th 1851.

Another cricket match was played between the New England and St. George Cricket Club. The match was played at Cambridge Crossing (Harlem, NY) and SGCC won by an innings and 31 runs. On Thursday NEC made 78 and SGCC followed in the afternoon and finished Friday afternoon with 180. NEC followed making only 71.

"The game was conducted throughout in the very best spirit, and all seemed highly delighted with the sport."

The first, 'All American' match engaged in by the *sons of the soil* was played in June or July 1854 as stated by the New York Times, and was played between New York and Newark with New York coming out victorious. *"This match being played exclusively by Americans… this ends the first match played in the United States between Americans, let us hope this will not be the last."* In the return match played on 21st August, the Newark team came out victorious. The exploits reached Philadelphia and they took on Newark at Camden in 1855 with Philadelphia winning by 8 wickets. Philadelphia's first match against St. George was played in Hoboken in 1855, with St. George winning by 81 runs. The frequency of matches between teams increased and so did their confidence and soon new clubs and renewed activity was coming up in Connecticut, Massachusetts, Milwaukee, Cincinnati, upstate New York etc. With improved performances 16 Americans (players from Philadelphia, New York and Newark) took on 11 Englishmen, but still lost by a wide margin. *"In looking over the records for the season, we find that we have published scores of nearly three hundred <u>bona fide</u> matches,"* wrote the New York Clipper for the 1857 season.[49] Three hundred matches - that was a threefold increase over the previous year and the *Clipper* further claimed that there were about five thousand cricketers in the United States, and in Canada, *"we have no doubt but there are quite as many."*

L to R: Geo. Wheatcroft (Umpire Newark), Barlow, Marsh, Sharpe, S. Wright, Gibbes, Highaw, Bingham, Cyup, Waller, Wilby & Senior.

1856 All United States Eleven, selected to contest against All Canada.
Courtesy: Harry T. Peters 'America on Stone' Collection, National Museum of American History, Smithsonian Institution.

CRICKET PLAYERS ON BOSTON COMMON.

Cricket Players on the Boston Common, by Winslow Homer (1836-1910).

"The spirited local picture was drawn expressly for us by Mr. Homer, and does credit to his artistic skill. The manly game of cricket, we are pleased to see, is enjoying great favor, as it deserves, for it brings into play physical energy and activity. We borrow it from our English ancestry, and the game itself dates from the sixteenth century, or even earlier. In England all classes unite in this game on the village green, and peer and peasant may be seen together striving for victory. There is no question that practice of athletic exercise has brought the English people to their fine physical condition, which every stranger observes with admiration; and on the other hand, that such out-of-door sports are needed to bring up us Americans to the mark. Exercise and amusement must be combined to develop the physique." BALLOU'S Pictorial, Drawing-Room Companion, Boston Saturday, June 4th 1859.

In a letter written to his friend 'Darby', Charles Collis, one of the English Eleven of N.Y. who took part in an 1857 match against eighteen Americans in New York on 10th and 11th June 1857, talks about the *"greatest cricketing times that ever happened in Yankee Land."* Charles made it to the first eleven under the tutelage of 'Senior' and his instructions in 'forward play', the same Tom Senior who was coach to Walter Newhall. He goes on to describe the local cricket scene where the Delphian Club were beaten by the Philadelphia Club and the Olympians beat the 2nd eleven of the Philadelphia Club which included John

118

Wister, and the boys from the Germantown Club beat the first American eleven for the 4th time. He opines that with the help of a professional bowler, they can take on any club in America save N.Y. Club (St. George). *"You could hardly believe the improvement that has taken place in these youngsters: they (can) certainly beat any of the University boys in England."*

A 4th of July match in Camden (1858) between 18 Americans and 11 Englishmen drew a crowd of five to six thousand and as William Wister put it, *"as usual the British were victorious,"* but the margin of victory were getting smaller. Sam Wright and his son Harry played the spoil sport, preventing the Americans from winning, though George Newhall, who was hardly 12 years old at the time and despite his three feet four inch height, was able to main a perfect 'line and length' and consistently bowled maiden overs to the amazement of all.[50] The *'Little Wonder'* drew *'applause and pistol fire'* from some of the six thousand spectators wrote the *Spirit*.[51] By this time regular fixtures were held with other clubs and in 1859 Young America played against the Germantown for the first time, only to be defeated by 8 wickets. On July 4th and 5th of 1860, eleven English met eighteen Americans, who in their 5th engagement emerged victorious for the first time with 8 wickets to spare at Camden.[52] In the same year, the Germantown Club had new playing ground at Nicetown and George Wright who was born in New York, made his debut for the 18 Americans versus the 11 Englishmen. According to the *Porter's Spirit* of 1860, (Vol. 9, November 6th, page 165), *"in November on the grounds of the St. George Club at Hoboken, Eighteen Americans were worsted by eleven English."* There were no players from Philadelphia in this match and the 'Americans' were made up of players from St. George and Long Island, *"as they were trying hard to induce the natives to take part in the game."*[53] These Americans versus the English matches were known as the 'Home International.'[54]

Hartford Daily Courant of October 6th 1859, reported on a cricket match between Hazardville Club and Hartford Club played on the South Meadows, where the latter lost by a combined two inning score of 101 to 60. As was the custom in those days, the ball was presented to the winning team and speeches were given. Another cricket club had opened on August 4th of the same year in Hartford and their grounds were on Van Dyke Avenue. Prior to the Civil War, there were 43 cricket clubs in Philadelphia, the leading clubs being, Philadelphia, Union Cricket Club and Germantown whose seven players took part in that war theatre. In 1859 the Philadelphia Clubs were invited to use the field across the Delaware River in Camden, and Bradshaw an English cricketer who lived nearby, allowed the use of his dwelling as a 'clubhouse' where they could change and store their gear and in the process Mrs. Bradshaw provided the lads with *'bread and butter and a kup of tay!'*[55] In the early period there were a lot of younger teams with healthy rivalry and after a few years for various reasons, they would merge or disband and the players would join rival factions. In 1859 when the English visited America, Jones Wister a young lad of twenty who worked for Reading Railroad, was one of the twenty two selected to play against them and scored the second highest score of 19 after being run out in the 1st innings. The match was played at Camac's Wood (St. George of Philadelphia played here),[56] a place for resort and picnics at the time which was converted to a cricket field with seating for spectators. Jones recalls that, had it not been for an incorrect umpiring, the outcome of the match may have been in the local teams favor instead of the visitors winning the match by seven wickets. When Carpenter was caught, Henry Sharp the umpire, called it a 'wide ball' in error, *"according to some of our best judges in England, he should have been given out,"* wrote Lillywhite.[57] Henry Sharp was the President of the New York Cricket Club and in 1856 he had tried unsuccessfully to organize the first English vs. American matches. *"This match was the beginning of scientific cricketing in Philadelphia,"* Bells Life, London.

PETTICOATS AND THE MANLY GAME OF CRICKET

Before Philadelphia's rise to prominence as the cradle of America Cricket, Georgia had an early start. We find from the journals maintained by William Stephens, the townsmen were playing cricket in the main square (Johnson) in Savannah as early as 1737. This was the first square to be established by the city's founder, James Edward Oglethorpe in 1733.[1] After the initial reports from the journals, we do not hear much on cricket, who played and where till 1801, when we read in the *Savannah Advertiser* (later merged with the Savannah Gazette in 1817) which reported on a match played on the south common on 13th of January 1801, after a challenge put out by 13 natives of Georgia to *"thirteen natives of any country to play a game of crichet for a treat."* The challenge was accepted by "Americans and Europeans" that resulted in a victory for the challengers by a score of 57 to 25.[2] The challenge was issued by Levi Sheftall, grandson of Benjamin Sheftall, one of the 42 original Jews that arrived in Savannah on 11th July, 1733, just 5 months after the colony of Georgia was established. These were mostly Portuguese Jews and two Jewish families from Germany. The earliest Jewish settlement would be New York in 1654, followed by Newport in 1695, Philadelphia in 1739 and Charleston in 1749.[3] Just before the match, Levi had an unfortunate mishap where he sprained his ankle and could not participate as a player, though he was chosen as a 'judges' on behalf of the natives of Georgia and David B. Mitchell 'judged' for the opposing team.

Though the notice issued to the newspaper show 'Cricket' as the game being played, the term 'Judges' were primarily used in the game of 'Wicket'. Cricket officials were referred to as umpires, so this raises a question – was this a game of wicket, it also had more than 11 players, though having a few extra players would not have mattered. The high scoring is also not atypical of cricket matches in those days, and also cricket is spelled with a slight variation. Wicket is reported to have been played as far south as New Orleans, could it have been played in Georgia, we cannot exclude the possibility as I have shown before, cricket and wicket were often transposed especially in New England when referring to those games.

One of the reasons for the paucity of cricket 'news' was the European war between England and Spain which had also reached American shores, known as the 'War of Jenkins' Ear,' which began in 1739 and merged with the War of the Austrian Succession that had started in 1740 and ended in 1748. On July 7th 1742, British forces engaged about 5000 Spanish soldiers at 'The Battle of Gully Hole Creek' on St. Simons Island, Georgia, where the Spaniards were pushed back to set the stage for the 'Battle of Bloody Marsh', which was fought in the afternoon of the same day, thus ending all hope for Spain in retaking Georgia.[4] Then there was the 'American Revolutionary War' (1775-1783) and it would have taken a few years for sports to have flourished back in the new independent young nation. During the Revolutionary War, Levi along with his father Mordecai (the highest ranking Jewish officer of the American Revolutionary forces) were imprisoned by the British in Antigua. Upon George Washington's election as the first President of the new nation, Levi wrote a congratulatory letter which was replied to and it is one of the many Presidential letters housed in the collection at Congregation Mickve Israel in Savannah, Georgia.

Levi believed there was no one equal to him when it came to cricket in Savannah.[5] Cricket matches or games did take place as such, a club may have also been organized though short lived.[6] In later years there was lack of coverage for team sports or the cricket matches may have been few and far between, so much so that in 1859, the *Daily Morning News* reported that introduction of cricket was a recent development for America.[7] Undoubtedly Levi Sheftall would have the distinction of being the first Jewish cricketer in America or rather, the world!

Translation from the copy (Language, spelling unchanged).

On Tuesday the 13th day of January 1801 a game of Crichet was played on the South Common by 13 natives of Georgia against 13 natives of America & Europiens, Viz-

Natives of Georgia	Americans & Europiens
1. Adam Cope	1. Mr. Durment
2. John Lang	2. Mr. Meggs
3. Peter Oates	3. Mr. Turnbull
4. Benjamin Sheftall	4. Mr. Williamson
5. Thos. Norton	5. Mr. Gunn
6. Saml. Spencer	6. Mr. Mace
7. Christopher Gugal	7. Mr. Wylly
8. Moses Sheftall	8. Mr. Marshal
9. David Gugal	9. Mr. White
10. Thos. Hais	10. Mr. Murray
11. Thomas Brown	11. Mr. Cannavan
12. Henry Anderson	12. Mr. Nailor
13. Thos. Gilbert	13. Mr. Willson

[Sunday the 13 day of ... ...]
Cricket was played on the South Common
vizt 13 Natives of Georgia Against 13 Natives of
America & Europeans — (Vizt)

Natives of Georgia	Americans & Europeans
1 Adam Ifie	1 Mr Dorminer
2 John Long	2 — Mr Jeffs
3 Peter Oates	3 — Mr Lambull
4 Benjn Sheftall	4 — Mr Williamson
5 Jno Norton	5 — Mr Gunn
6 Saml Spencer	6 — Mr Mace
7 Christopher Gugal	7 — Mr Wally
8 Moses Sheftall	8 — Mr Marshal
9 David Gugal	9 — Mr White
10 Fredk Hawes	10 — Mr Murry
11 Thomas Brown	11 — Mr Cannavan
12 Henry Anderson	12 — Mr Nailor
13 Th: Gibbry —	13 — Mr Willson

after the match was made up, 2 Judges was
chosen vizt Saml Sheftall in behalf of the Natives
of Georgia — and B: Mitchell in behalf of the others
the Game was Played, underneath is the
Statement of each partys Game
        the Natives of Georgia Got — — 57
        the other party got — — — — — — 25
                in favr of the Georgians (32)

Mr Hunter please to insert in your Gazzet,
that 13 Natives Americans & Europeans met
the 13 Natives of Georgia, at the Place appo-
=inted to play the Game of Cricket & underneath
is the Statement of the Game —
NB — an accident hapned to Levi Sheftall who was
the Instigator of the Challenge given, Just before
the Game was to have begun his foot turnd by
accident & Strained his Ancle & prevented his
Playing, 2 or 3 More good hands was not there
this memorandum is only done to shew what 13 Natives
of my Country Can do —

After the match was made up 2 Judges was chosen, Levi Sheftall on behalf of the Natives of Georgia and David B. Mitchell on behalf of the others. The game was played, underneath is the Statement of each party's game.

The Natives of Georgia got	57
The other party got	25
In favor of the Georgians	32

Messer. Printers please to insert in your Gazzet, that 13 Americans & Europiens met the 13 Natives of Georgia, at the place appointed to play the game of Crichet & underneath is the statement of the game---

N.B. An accident happened to Levi Sheftall who was the instigator of the challenge given. Just before the game was to have begun his foot turned & by accident sprained his ankle & prevented his playing, 2 or 3 more good hands were not there. This memorandum is only done to show what 13 Natives of my country can do.

The Savannah Cricket Club was formed in August of 1859 and just 18 months later Georgia would join a confederacy of 11 Southern Slave States in a historic Civil War (1861-1865) against the north. The war was fought over the secession of the Confederate States from the United States, which resulted in the surrender of the Confederacy and abolition of slavery. The *Savannah Republican* in their August 25th edition carried the news of the formation of the Club, as also did the *Daily Morning News* on the 29th and they also included an explanation of the rules for the game – the first paper to do so in the country?

After a few practice sessions the two elevens played their first match on September 24th 1859, and the second being played on October 8th with the Savannah Republican reporting that there was much improvement compared to the first match and the outlook for the club according to one member, *"was in a prosperous condition."* What happened then in the very next season? The paper was asking its' readers, *"what's become of the Savannah Cricket Club?"* [8] What brought about this sudden re-emergence of cricket and its 'clubs, was it the interested generated by the impending English tour of Cricket Professionals that year? *Spirit of the Times,* a New York newspaper, carried regularly cricket news and had readers as far as Savannah. The Savannah Republican had a correspondent based in New York City and he provided information on the pending cricket engagement by the first overseas team which was generating a lot of excitement. There were 25 clubs in southern cities at the time, Richmond, Virginia in 1857, Baltimore, Lexington in Kentucky and New Orleans all formed in 1859 and also Mobile, in 1860.[9]

A noted Massachusetts cricketer Rev. Thomas Higginson is credited with what is sometimes called, 'Muscular Christianity Movement', which promoted an ideology that a healthy body sustained a healthy mind. Cricket at the time proved to be the ideal choice, one that *"encouraged honorable behavior, sportsmanlike conduct and discipline – the ideal Christian game."*[10] Another reasoning was that, it would keep the youth's away from spending their idle time in drunken orgies and other un-social behaviors. Cricket was promoted as a 'noble and manly game,' a game which drew all classes on to the same field and were recognized by their prowess on the field irrespective of their social standings off the field. By organizing into an entity and following the rules of the game and club, it provided the young men of Savannah, a degree of respectability which otherwise may not have been achieved with informal games. Another advantage was that their manly exploits were covered in the newspaper and this would portray them in a positive light to the fairer sex, who were in attendance during various the matches.

Timothy Lockley's dissertation on "Cricket and Masculinity in Georgia" is based on the premise that Southern women were only spectators not participants in popular sports, for he writes, *"unlike in England, there is no report of women in the south playing Cricket. Southern women do seem to have been content to be spectators rather than players in the antebellum revival of team sports. For the players, the absence of female participation naturally made success on the field seem all the more manly."*[11]

It may not have been played in Georgia at the time, but, it was very much in evidence during the turn of the century in Staten Island and in Pennsylvania. An article from, *The Atlanta Constitution* of April 19th 1896, titled, "Cricket in Petticoats, Newest fad for Girls," provides two wonderful sketches (shown in the following text) along with the exploits of the women cricketers. 'Staten Island Cricket and Base Ball Club' in Livingston was the bastion for women with athletic proclivities during that era. The club was founded in 1872 and at the time the Ladies' Club was considered the oldest and the largest association of its kind for women in the country! The 'oldest' - it was only 24 years old, imagine what the paper would say today after 140 years of continuous existence!

Why did the Atlanta Constitution[12] carry articles about Women's cricket? Was it to promote and influence the ladies in the south to take up the sport which was in vogue, or merely to emulate their northern counterparts? There were two teams at Staten Island, 'Livingstons' captained by Miss Marion Bruce Heineken, and the 'Richmonds' captained by Miss McNamee. In Philadelphia the team was captained by Miss Agnes Morgan. Out of the 300 or so members of the ladies' club, twenty-four played cricket and their coach was the sibling of Lohmann of Surrey, England, who was regarded as being one of the best all-round cricketers in the world. The article extoled the abilities of the girls having attained remarkable degree of efficiency in throwing the ball, and an unwary batswoman venturing far from the wicket is bound to be caught napping by a well-directed and accurate throw-in of the ball by a fair fielder.[13]

GAME IN FULL SWING.

Courtesy: Allen County Public Library Foundation.
2 Sketches from, 'The Atlanta Constitution' April 19, 1896, Atlanta, Georgia.

126

The fair damsels of Staten Island had become so skillful in the game that, another eleven from Germantown, PA were challenged to a match, but no records have been found. Soon the girls found themselves playing against their brothers and cousins and the *'masculine cricketers were beaten'* for they had used baseball bats and even played left handed (a right hand bat would find it difficult to bat in the 'left' position), so they claimed. In another contest where the men again played 'lefty' they were handily defeated by 7 wickets. *"A word to the wise, just here, cricket is the coming game for young women, sooner or later, they are going to wield the willow and go in for fielding and bowling, so it is just as well to become familiarized at once with some of the technical terms,"* [14] for many a maiden overs would be bowled or were the fair maidens, bowled over by the manly players!

IN POSITION.

127

During mid to late 19th century, cricket was generally referred to as the 'manly game' and the young English youth *"were encouraged to think of sporting endeavor as a mode of expressing their manly prowess, and later they would take this interpretation of sport throughout the empire."*[15] London still wielded considerable cultural influence over its' former colony and the manliness was evident not only in cricket but other sports as well. Lockley rationalize the manliness was due to the fact that it enabled the youths to show off their skills to the fairer sex, more of a courtship ritual, as the matches were attended by a fair number of ladies. The other social engagement or avenues for courtship available were formal balls or church sponsored events, but being nimble on the dance floor would not be considered manly. An important point though put forth is that the people in power were either slave owners who were at their zenith of the social ladder or political power or those having *'patriarchal authority over women and children.'*[16] For the youth who could have neither, joining a club and demonstrating their manliness on the field could showcase their courage and character, *"punctuality, energy, quickness of perception and execution and good temper,"* as one supporter of the game put it. *"Success on the field brought public attention and acclaim to otherwise undistinguished young men."*[17] On the other hand in Philadelphia, a dozen years earlier, Wister lamented that, *"all field sports were looked down upon by our elders, and they neither aided nor abetted us in our cricketing endeavors, nor did the ladies smile upon our efforts."*[18]

The club disappeared as soon as it had appeared, one major cause was the conflict between the North and South that was headed towards an inevitable war, more so after the October 16th raid on an United States Arsenal at 'Harpers Ferry' in Virginia in 1859 by white abolitionist, John Brown who wanted to start an armed slave revolt, but was defeated by Robert E Lee, who was to lead the Confederate Army of Northern Virginia in the American Civil War when Virginia seceded from the Union in April of 1861.[19] The resulting raid and fear of losing their way of life were simmering in the Georgian minds and would set events in motion that would also lead Georgia to join Virginia in the war. Many of the manly youths joined the revolution and paid the ultimate sacrifice for their cause. There were a few games held during the winter months and the attendance was sparse as by the summer of 1860 they had all but disappeared, as the cricket matches were replaced by military parades by the same youths who had earlier wielded the willow were now skillful with rifles and what better way to show their manliness than by joining the military.

Was this the extent of women's cricket in America, no, by no means was this limited to a club or a school, there was a little known but thriving cricket community engaged by the girls at various preparatory schools and colleges. The most prominent rivalry was between Rosemary Hall and Pelham Hall. Boxwood School for Girls[20] in Old Lyme, Connecticut, advertised that the school had twenty acres devoted to, 'Cricket, Golf, Tennis, Basketball and other open air games,' and 'The Mason Collegiate School and The Castle Preparatory School, 'The Castle,' [21] at Tarrytown-on-Hudson in New York also has ample grounds and cricket featured prominently amongst their many outdoor exercise, including tennis, basketball, golf and hand ball. Their principal, Miss C.E. Mason said that the girls have plenty of open-air exercises, under a resident athletic and sports teacher.

Then there was Wellesley College in the town of Wellesley near Boston, Smith College in Northampton, Massachusetts and Mount Holyoke College in South Hadley, Massachusetts. Wellesley College had drawn up plans in 1893 for a 100 yard athletic field which would include running, jumping, base-ball, cricket, golf and football.[22] The 1904 Mount Holyoke College 'Student's Handbook' describes their 'field day' as, *"one of the most important events of the college year,"* and a May 23rd 1925 field day program lists the events beginning at 9 a.m., with cricket being one of them and references to cricket activities is documented till 1932![23] On the other hand, the girls at Vassar College in Poughkeepsie, New York, when given a choice where walking was cited as a game, they picked walking over cricket![24] Field hockey was popular with the girls at Vassar, Mount Holyoke, Smith, Radcliffe and Bryn Mawr though at some places they used cricket balls, which were painted white.[25] The girls at Smith College went a step further to make the game more interesting and made a few changes akin to base-ball plays.[26] The archives at Smith College have a wonderful 113 page *hand written* Criquet[27] 'Record Book from 1912-1923' which contains the following information.

1. Rules and Regulations of the game as played at Smith
2. General Information
    a. General Class
    b. Teams (how chosen)
    c. Captains (duties)
    d. Coaches (duties)
    e. Representatives (duties)
        i. College
        ii. Class
    f. Games
    g. All Smith Criquet team (method of choosing)
    h. List of Class Teams, Captain and representatives by seasons, beginning 1913.
    i. List of results of games since 1913
    j. List of all Smith Criquet teams since Spring of 1914

It contains detailed information and to be considered for the 'All Smith' team, a 20 point system was instituted for:

1. Play Ability – Team and Individual   10
2. Carriage   4
3. Attitude   4
4. Appearance   2

Interest was waning after 1923 and a table shows the points received by the players with the highest being 18.95 out of 20 for E. Rust and the last team members are listed for the year 1926.

Cricket as Played at Smith College

BY DOROTHY WOOSTER.

In order to adapt cricket for practical use, the following additions and changes have been made in the official rules, as published in the Spalding Athletic Library.

A. Additions:

1. Diagram of Field: Use center line,"*x*," drawn between wickets. Cross this line by another line, "*y*," drawn parallel to the popping crease.

2. There shall be 3 innings to a game, each inning consisting of 3 "outs" on a side.

3. There shall be a definite batting order.

4. If a batter touches the ball with the bat she must run, or take her "out."

B. Changes in Rules:

10. . . . and to be a good ball, the ball must hit the ground on or across the center line "*y*."

13. A "Bowling Over" shall consist of six "good balls," or four "wide balls," or four "no balls."

33A. . . . except in case of a "Caught Ball." The ball is then in play until it is settled in bowler's or wicket-keeper's hand. This change gives an opportunity to put two runners out on one play; i. e., "Caught Out" and "Run Out."

The scoring has been simplified. For practice games, when full teams are not present, an individual score is kept. Using these changes the game progresses rapidly and holds the interest of both players and spectators.

Rosemary Hall was named after the Atwater family farm and came into being in 1890 when Mary Atwater Choate hired Miss Caroline Ruutz-Rees, a scholar from England as headmistress to run a new school for girls in Wallingford, Connecticut. Ten years on she would move the school to Greenwich, Connecticut where it would remain for 71 years before being merged back with the Choate Boys School in Wallingford which was also founded by Mary along with her husband Judge William Choate in 1896.[28] Their on-field rivals, Pelham School in Pelham Manor in Westchester County New York, opened in 1889 under the leadership of Emily Hall Hazen,[29] and were the finest girls' schools till it closed after twenty-five years.[30] When Rosemary Hall moved to Greenwich in 1900, match records between the two schools are elusive to find, did the rivalry for the 'light blue banner' dissipate as soon as it had started, did the move to Greenwich, for whatever reason, put a damper of the competition? On the other hand the girls at Pelham were not going to be around for long as the school closed at the end of the 1915 school year.

'Girls at the Wickets,' the first detailed account of the November 14th 1896 match was carried by the *New York Times* issue the next day, though they have been reported to have started their interschool rivalry three years earlier. A year earlier in 1895, Rosemary Hall had defeated Pelham Hall at Wallingford and on this return match the times reported, *"the banner was won back, and joy reigned throughout Pelham Manor. Mrs. Hazen's excellent institution at Pelham Manor and Rosemary School, have come to settle their long secret rivalry on the Cricket field."* Though Pelham won, a dispute over a lost ball had arisen (almost derailed the game) and the Rosemary Girls had, *"openly vowed and declared a well-grounded distrust in the umpire!"*[31] These girls were serious!

Earlier in the year, the *New York Times* of May 24th reported that a cricket match was played on Prospect Hill between two teams from Pelham Hall just two weeks earlier. The winning team was captained by Miss Madeline Broun and was victorious by a solitary run. For her spoils she received cuff buttons and studs of gold set with carbuncles and her team mates received cuff links and silver studs with blue enamel, while the losers received – two bunches of American beauty Roses! The opposing team's captain was Miss Elva King daughter of the Vice President of the Baltimore and Ohio Railroads, and her teammates included her sister Miss Annie King who would feature prominently in the upcoming win against Rosemary Hall.

"Prospect Hill...a winter contest of a most unusual kind...arrayed against each other, were young athletic maidens."[32] The November cold did not seem to dampen the enthusiasm as they were intent on winning the rivalry, with uncovered heads and wearing sweaters and skirts, the Pelham girls were intent on winning the Light-Blue Banner back. They wore dark blue sweaters with light blue P.H. logo, while Rosemary girls had R.H. in dark blue on white sweaters. The girls from Connecticut had brought their own cheering section and the *'college cries would have done justice to Yale-Harvard football match.'*[33] Miss Annie King, would captain Pelham Hall (Elva King did not play) to a 69 run victory. *"A Baltimore Lass Distinguishes herself in a match game at Pelham Manor, New York,"* ran the article headline

in the Baltimore Morning Herald of November 16. *"Miss Annie King, daughter of Thomas M. King, former second vice-president of the Baltimore and Ohio Railroad, distinguished herself on Saturday in a game of Cricket played at Pelham Manor, an aristocratic suburb of New York City."* It goes on to say, *"Miss King was easily the heroine of the day, for, besides directing her players in a mastery way, both at the bat and with the ball, she surpassed all her companions. She displayed wonderful ability and some of the men cricketers present even had an envious glow in their eyes while she was up. She scored 15 runs in the first innings and 21 in the second. She bowled out 7 of the opposing team, all of whom managed to score but a total of six runs."* The Rosemary Girls, besides Miss Cromwell and Miss Hickory, were no match this time and returned home without the banner, though at the end of the match *cold cream was in great demand and a special manicure was sent for from New York!* [34] It is only fitting to provide the one match score that is available from the game.

PELHAM HALL

First Innings	Runs	Second Innings	Runs
Emily Gray c Hickory b Weston	2	c Hickory b Orius	5
Milldred du Bois c Hickory b Weston	0	b Orius	0
Annie King b Recneps	15	Run Out	21
Eleanor Emmet c Getson, b. Orius	2	c Salguod b Orius	9
Laura Haughton b Weston	2	b Recneps	2
Annie O'Kane c Hickory b Recneps	7	b Recneps	1
Helen Leland c Getson b Orius	13	c Getson b Orius	0
Alice Paintor b Recneps	1	c and b Orius	0
Stewart Simpson b Orius	4	b Orius	0
Bertha Fenessey b Recneps	0	c Salguod B Orius	0
Dorethea Day not out	12	not out	0
Wides	23	Wides	13
Total	81	Total	51

ROSEMARY HALL

First Innings	Runs	Second Innings	Runs
C Linton b King	0	b Paintor	0
R. Nator hit wicket, b King	0	not out	0
A Recneps run out	6	b King	0
A Hickory b King	0	b Paintor	2
E Weston b King	1	b King	6
B Getson run out	1	c Du Bois b Paintor	0
A Orius b Paintor	0	b Paintor	4
H Cromwell not out	10	c and b Day	13
J Sobs st. Emmet b Paintor	2	b King	6
Grace Salguod run out	0	b Day	0
M Dollerin b Paintor	0	b Paintor	0
Wides	6	Wides	6
Total	26	Total	37

"This afternoon the cricket team from Pelham Manor will play the Rosemary Hall team on Rosemary Hall Grounds," was the small blurb that appeared in, *'The Morning Record'* a Meriden (Connecticut) paper of Saturday May 14th, 1898. Looking at the ongoing rivalry, Rosemary Hall administrators thought it prudent to hire a cricket coach for the girls and a member of the Yale Alumni, Miss. F.W. Hulseberg was hired to coach the girls in the fall of 1898.[35] It turns out that she was not the first coach. In a Rosemary Newsletter from spring of 1965, 82 year old Elizabeth Richards Day narrates of her time spent at the school. *"I don't know whether the school still plays cricket, but in my day it was the only competitive sport, although Pelham Manor was the only girl's school available for competition."* She also remembered when Miss Ruutz-Rees called Yale looking for a cricket coach and Henry Canby was sent to coach the girls, he is pictured in a scrapbook that was kept by Alice Wood Schipper (class of 1898). The pictures in the scrapbook depict numerous cricket and other activities between 1897 and 1898. The girls overheard him telling a friend, *"These girls know so much more than we do, I am scared they will discover we are only a bluff."*[36] Lelia Caperton Stiles who died of typhoid fever at a very young age of twenty in 1895, studied at Rosemary Hall and in her book "After-Glow" she talks about the tribulations with the cricket game and describes how the girls initially were more akin to an obstinate goat, *"the old cricketers had resigned themselves to coaxing and encouraging the novices into something like enthusiasm, and went to the first game, looking and feeling like martyrs, but, with the first advent to the bat, what astonishment sized them."* All the players carried battle scars and were looking forward to the *"possible game with Pelham Manor girls, that is, if they accept our challenge."*[37]

The exploits of the two schools were recorded far and wide, *"A Series of Matches between the leading Schools for Girls"*, read the caption headline in, *The Evening Telegram* of St. John's, Newfoundland of Monday June 27th 1898. Plans were being made to include more schools near New York into the existing inter-school matches judging from the success of these 2 schools which had been going on for the last 4 years. *"Miss. Edith Cunningham Hazen was not only an expert player herself but also an author of, American Cricket Annual and Golf Guide,"* writes the correspondent,[38] whereas in fact, she only wrote a chapter, 'Cricket for Women' in the 1898 issue which was edited and compiled by Jerome Flannery.

"All men's athletics are the outgrowth of scholastic and colligate competitive sport, so the freedom in out of door sport which exists in a few of the more liberal out of town schools is the foundation of the growing interest among women in various forms of athletics as a means of physical development and healthful enjoyment, despite the disadvantageous petticoat." Regarding her partiality towards cricket, she said, *"It is a game that is not over severe for them, yet calls into play every muscle of the body. The play is so distributed as to give each player variety and interest and is simple enough for them to learn easily. With cricket, as with all similar games of ball and bat, the vigor of the play grows only with the vigor of the player, so that for a woman's game it is beyond criticism of being too severe. The quickness of the eye, of judgment and of movement, together with the free action in throwing a ball, in catching it and in running are forms of training every woman would be the gainer by having more frequently than in the past."*[39]

In her article, Miss Edith mentions that Pelham Manor hopes to *"open a series of competitive games with other schools it has taught Cricket."* Who were these other schools, were they in contact with Mount Holyoke, Smith or schools whose cricket program we are not aware of – quite possible. *"The difficulty of arranging games between schools and these outside clubs have lessened the opportunities to establish cricket as an accepted athletic sport for women."*[40] If there were only more like minded enthusiasts, girls cricket could have spread, though the closing of Pelham Hall did not help the cause. Even the *Parisian Illustrated Review* of 1900,[41] talks about the girls from the two schools playing cricket after many years. Did they stop for a while, as this would most likely allude to the move to Greenwich and they may have revived the annual competition only to end in 1915 or earlier? Incidentally, the 1900 Olympics in Paris saw cricket being played for the first and last time and now talks are afoot for the T20 format to be included in the 2024 Summer Olympics.

Women in Southern California had also taken up cricket in 1910 as the *Santa Monica Outlook* announced that, *'Women will form Cricket Club at the beach,'* and that the first match was to be played on August 13th on the old Polo grounds. Their captain and most famous player of all was May Sutton, the winner of the US Tennis Open in 1904 and in the following year (1905), beat the reigning Wimbledon champion, Dorothea Douglass Chambers, the first American women to do so. The Santa Monica Men's team, who were playing left handed, were defeated by the ladies by a small margin of 2 runs.[42] Many more untold cricket matches and teams would have taken place in different part of the country, but, without recorded evidence, we will never come to know.

"HURRAH FOR THE BAT, HURRAH FOR THE BALL, HURRAH FOR THE
CRICKET OF ROSEMARY HALL"

Pelham Hall girls at Rosemary Hall in Wallingford, Connecticut 1897-98.

These 'blue' pictures are called cyanotypes.

Girls at Cricket, Smith College 1890s.

Smith College Sophomore Cricket team of 1925.

Mt. Holyoke Cricket team of 1925.

Uniforms are similar at both colleges, but there are no records of them playing each other!

First Family of Cricket, Baseball –
The Wright Brothers

Samuel Wright and his wife Annie Tone Wright, emigrated to America from Sheffield, England, in the summer of 1836 when Harry was a year and a half old (his birth has not accurately recorded).[1] Sam Wright Sr. found work as a professional at St. George's Cricket Club (Dragon Slayers) New York in 1837. As per the *'Encyclopedia of ethnicity and sports in the United States,'*(George B Kirsch, Othello Harris and Claire Elaine Nolte) the club grounds were first located at East 31st Street, near 1st Avenue, and in 1846, they moved uptown to Red House field on 3rd Avenue in Harlem. Christopher Devine in his book, *"Harry Wright: the father of professional base ball"* puts the Red House grounds at 2nd Avenue and 106th Street in New York City. Another location for the Red House is given at the current site at 105th St, now cut through the Harlem River near 3rd Avenue. I believe the consensus would be in the vicinity of 2nd Ave and 106th and 3rd Ave and 105th street!

The encyclopedia further goes on to say that, *'five years later they relocated to Hoboken, New Jersey, where they remained until 1867, when they occupied a new field in Bergen Heights (Hudson City). In 1871 they moved back to Hoboken.'* Sam Wright would stay with the club for 33 years till his retirement in 1869.

William Henry 'Harry' Wright, (b. January 10, 1835) the eldest of the five siblings, was the first player manager of the Boston Red Stockings and George Wright (b. January 26, 1847) was a shortstop for the original Cincinnati Red Stockings. The fourth youngest sibling Sam Wright Jr. "Sammy" (b. November 25, 1848) also played baseball, but Dan (b. 1837) who was born after Harry, never played baseball. Sam Wright Sr. was one of the XI who took part in the first international cricket match that took place between America and Canada played at St. George's ground in 1844. The four brothers had a sister Mary, who was the youngest (b 1858).

Young Harry dropped out of school to apprentice as a jeweler at Tiffany's, when he was only 14 and the following year in 1850, joined St. George's cricket team. One day, while imparting the finer points of cricket to his little brother George in the Elysian fields, Harry noticed a game of base ball in progress, and later, adapting to the game, he joined the New York Knickerbockers Base Ball Club in 1857. In 1864, he joined the New York Gotham's as the Civil War had reduced the schedule of the Knickerbockers and other clubs. In the following year he started afresh as a cricketer in Cincinnati as he was tired of base ball. Interestingly enough, 1865 was the year when the game of base ball had been endorsed as the National Game of ball in America,[2] and the New York Clipper went on to say, *"Never did a season terminate leaving the public appetite so eager for a further supply of ball playing to feast on than this has done...1865 will be known as the year when base ball was first regularly established as the national game of America."* [3]

Harry was hired by the Union Cricket Club in Cincinnati for $1200 per year and in a short span the queen city had a promising club playing in the Lincoln Park Grounds (later known as Union Grounds). Just as he had taken up baseball in Hoboken, Harry in a similar way switched back to base ball with the Cincinnati Base Ball Club (Red Stockings) after an invitation from Aaron Champion, and took a number of Union Cricket Club players with him. In 1869, George joined his brother Harry to play with the Red Stockings, and at the time, he was one of the best base ball players in the country, and he also had one of his best seasons that year. A lot of 'plays' in baseball were pioneered by Harry - changing pitchers to upset batter's timing, batting practice, positioning fielders according to the batters hitting tendencies, fielders backing up one another, scorecards etc.,[4] does this all sound familiar to cricketers?

Harry was known for his honesty and ethical standards, *"there was no figure more creditable to the game than dear old Harry,"* opined *The Sporting News* (Dec 12, 1895). He stood for fair play and gentlemanly conduct and kept high standards for the advancement of the game. He was trusted enough to umpire within his own league in later years. During their September 1869 trip to San Francisco, the Red Stockings played some cricket matches against the Pacific Club and the Atlantic BBC, the latter match producing a score of 76-5 which prompted the *San Francisco Chronicle* to headline, 'Suicides Yesterday.'[5] Just a few months earlier on May 10, history was created when the presidents of Central Pacific Railroad and the Union Pacific Railroad met at Promontory, Utah, to drive in the last ceremonial spike which made transcontinental railroad travel possible for the first time in the country.

Boston was one city that did not have a club or the grounds for a professional team, the first club to form was the Elm Tree Club in 1855 and they played according to the New England Game. The Boston Common had level grounds and being a public place, permission was required to play there. In 1869 the Union Grounds were improved and to form a professional team, George Wright was approached who suggested that his brother Harry run and manage the team. The Boston Red Stockings were established on January 20, 1871, in the new National Association which was the first professional baseball league.

The Red Stocking name was changed to Boston Red Caps when Cincinnati entered the National League in 1876.[6]

In the summer of 1874, the Boston Red Stockings and Philadelphia Athletics went on a tour to England to showcase the 'American Game'. Harry was the driving force behind this endeavor and this was more of a personal desired to play in the country of his birth, but ended up receiving a 'frosty reception.'[7] (Though in 'Athletic Sports in America England and Australia,' by Palmer, Fynes, Richter & Harris published in 1889, the date is given as 1875. A few books and prints from Harpers Weekly give the date as 1874.) Their first exhibition game initially drew only 12 spectators, but increased to about 500 by the time the game started which saw a win in Philadelphia's favor.[8]

They also played cricket as the English were more interested in that than baseball. Later in 1888/89 Spalding embarked on his ambitious World Tour to spread baseball all over the world but ended with similar results as Harry did.

By 1881 he had moved to Providence and later to Philadelphia in 1884 and he is credited with the concept of 'spring training.' Henry would take his team on a 'southern trip' to give his player a six week head start in training over the others before the season began. His health was beginning to deteriorate and in 1890 he had catarrh of the eyes and was blinded. It took him ten months to recover partial eyesight. Two years later he was to lose his wife, but he remarried in January of 1894, a short marriage as he passed away on October 3rd, 1895 due to serious illness of the lungs.

George first played for St. George as early as 1861, except for 1865, when he played for Philadelphia Club, whose grounds at the time were in Camden, NJ. For the next twelve years from 1867 onwards, he played only international cricket matches as he had switched gears and was involved full time with playing baseball for Cincinnati, Boston and Providence. After his retirement from baseball in 1880, he went into partnership with H.A. Ditson, (Wright & Ditson) dealing in sports goods and returned to his roots - cricket, playing for the Longwood Cricket Club.[9] During the tour by Baseball players organized by Harry Wright to England in August of 1874, the Wright brothers did most of the bowling during the exhibition cricket matches. This baseball team would be the second international sides to tour England, the first visitors of any sport to England, were the 'Australian Aborigines' who in 1868, played a record 47 cricket matches.

The first Baseball game was played at the Lord's Cricket Ground on August 3rd, and the 18 American would win their first cricket match by a score of 107 to 105 against the twelve Gentlemen of MCC. In all, seven cricket matches would have been played by the American ballplayers before the end of the tour and winning all seven! This was not a regular match, the day started with a baseball warm-up and the cricket match commenced at noon, when play stopped for lunch around two, a diamond was marked and an exhibition baseball game commenced. The Boston Red Stockings won 24-7 against the

Athletics and the nine inning game was completed in a little over two hours. The cricket match resumed later in the day and concluded the following day under rainy conditions in America's favor. As the American won all their matches, the press back home was all praises in contrast to the British counterpart as the matches had not been played against the best of England's eleven.[10]

George had the best betting average on the trip and in a local match, scored 120 runs which was the highest individual score in New England in 1888 at Boston.[11] When the New England Cricket Association was organized, George was elected President. Here is a summary of his cricketing career as provided to the *American Cricketer* in his own words.

"I first commenced playing cricket when about ten years of age in the rear of the house where I lived at Hoboken, NJ. Under a long grape arbor my father first placed a cricket bat in my hands and taught me the way to handle it, as well as the way to bowl. The first match I played in was at the age of thirteen, as one of St. George's Junior eleven against the Newark Juniors, at Newark (I then being not much higher than the wicket). I bowled in this match taking five wickets, for which the president of St. George's club gave me a silver quarter dollar for each wicket captured. During that season I also played in several second eleven matches, after which I commenced to play on the first eleven at different times, and when sixteen years old I became a regular first eleven man. I visited Boston with the club, and no doubt many of the old cricket members of the Boston Club will remember me as 'little Georgie' (p. 154) as I was then called. In this match against the Boston Club I made double figures and bowled well, for which I was presented with a silver mug. After the match I threw a cricket ball one hundred and fifteen yards, which was considered a very long throw in those days. The Boston cricketers took my cap and placed in it many silver dollars.

In 1865 I went to Philadelphia, playing with the Philadelphia Club, which had its grounds at Camden, NJ. During the season I had a good bowling average. I made myself conspicuous in a very exciting match against the Young America Club of Philadelphia, bowling five of their men out for a very small score. During that season I made a score of 50 not out in a match, Philadelphia against New York, at Philadelphia, for which score I received a prize cup, presented to me by the Philadelphia cricketers. In this match my father and brother played against me.

I remained one season with the Philadelphia club and then I returned to my home and old club, the St. George, with which I played two or three seasons, when my base-ball career commenced, going to the Cincinnati Red Stockings. During the two seasons I was with the Cincinnati Reds, I played one cricket match that was when the club visited California, we played a picked eleven of San Francisco defeating the cricketers easily. I made 50 runs in this match. During the time I was a member of the Boston Baseball Club, the team played three or four matches a season, generally defeating all comers, owing to the good fielding of our ball players, and the bowling of my brother Harry and myself.

In 1872 I was selected as one of the Massachusetts twenty-two to play against Grace's eleven, which was played on the base-ball grounds. In this match I bowled a ball to Lord Harris, who hit it hard back at me about two feet above my head. It was hit so quick at me that many did not know where the ball had gone to, and were surprised when they found I had caught it. After retiring from baseball in 1880, I became a regular member of the Longwood Club of Boston, playing with them ever since. Cricket was my first game, and I always enjoyed playing it, and I look forward to continue playing it for a number of years to come."[12]

George was an outspoken critic when it came to baseball players using gloves, *'the players did not have gloves to protect their heads,'* New York Sun 1915. The great baseball winter tour of 1888-89 around the world organized by Spalding also included George, though retired, he umpired most of the baseball games. Spalding had deposited $30,000 in a Chicago bank and spared no expenses for the tour. He had no trouble in signing on ten of his Chicago White Stocking's most able members, but putting together an All American nine proved troublesome even though they had signed on initially. Billed as Spalding's Australian Base Ball Tour, it was expanded on route to include Egypt, a brief stop in Sri Lanka, Europe and England. Along the way George taught cricket as the distance from Honolulu to New Zealand was nearly 3900 miles and some form of activity was required, and as Anson put it, *"We shall all be as stiff as old women and as fat as Alderman by the time we reach Australia."[13]* They did indulge in a cricket match in Sydney, the outcome going in Australia's favor.

George was also instrumental in constructing America's first golf course at Boston's Franklin Park in 1890, though when he ordered a set of clubs from a Scottish distributor, he had no clue as to its' purpose and use! A Scottish gentleman helped him out with the intricacies of the game and forwarded him a copy of the rule book.[14] After suffering from inflammation of the heart for a year, George contacted pneumonia and passed away on August 21st, 1937 in Boston. Just a few weeks earlier, he had been inducted into the Baseball Hall of Fame.

Sam Wright Sr. on left, and his son, Harry Wright 1864. Photography Collection, Miriam and Ira D. Wallach Division of Art, Prints and Photographs, The New York Public Library, Astor, Lenox and Tilden Foundations.

Harry Wright, late in the career managing from the bench for Philadelphia.

1874 Boston Red Stockings. Back row (L to R): Cal McVey, Albert Spalding, Deacon White, and Ross Barnes. Middle Row: Jim O'Rourke, Andy Leonard, Harry Wright, Harry Schaefer, and Tommy Beals. Front row: George Wright and George Hall. Courtesy: Baseball Hall of Fame Library, Cooperstown, NY.

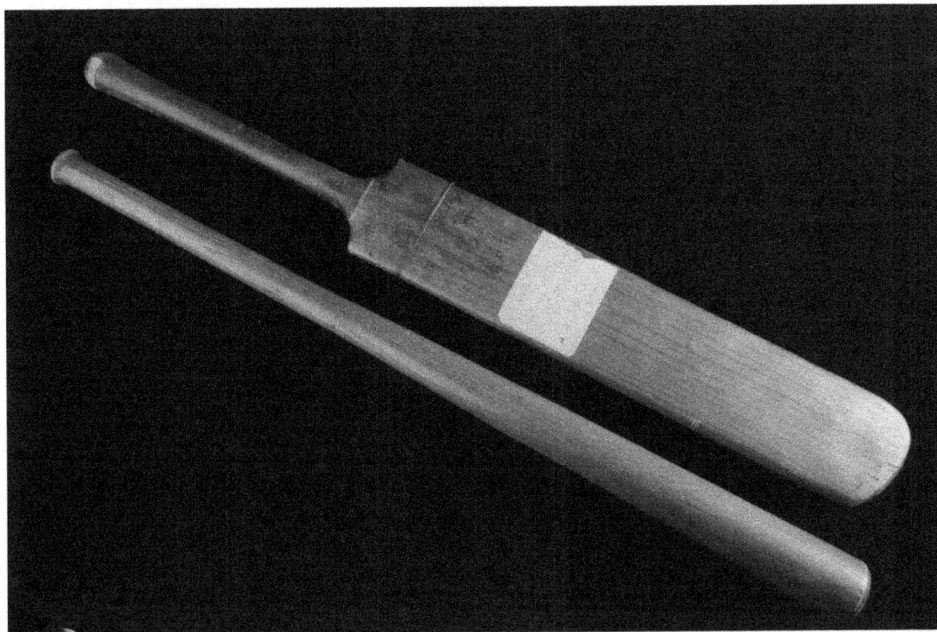

Cricket Bat signed by George Wright (L.C.C. - Longwood Cricket Club 1890) and his Baseball bat when he was with the Providence Grays, who won the Championship in 1879). Courtesy: Baseball Hall of Fame Library, Cooperstown, New York.

ANTEBELLUM CRICKET IN AMERICA AND THE CIVIL WAR

hiladelphia, not only was it the original Capital of the country, but it was also the Cricket Capital of America, and though the game may not have begun here, it did put down its roots and the city along with players from its neighboring states and took on the might of the English and Australian professionals at home and abroad. The seeds of cricket were sown by the Wister's and the Newhall's, the school elevens and the clubs of New York and New Jersey and with Philadelphia as the hub, formed the triumvirate of American Cricket and various factors contributed to the ebb and flow of the sport in the region and beyond. One such factor is focused upon in a study, *'Social Class and the Sport of Cricket in Philadelphia, 1850-1880,'* by J. Thomas Jable of William Paterson College in Wayne, New Jersey, whereupon he looks at the social fabric thru a single prism – cricket, and how that sport provides a glimpse into mid-Victorian Philadelphia. Granted, its' but one aspect, and one that nonetheless examines the role of cricket in, *"formation and maintenance of social classes thru club influences and relation to other urban clubs and the inculcation and transmission of social values to the youths."*[1] In his famous 1835 study of American society and institutions, *Democracy in America*, Alexis de Tocqueville noted that, one of the new nation's most striking features was the proliferation of "voluntary associations." He was struck by the *"proclivity of Americans to associate themselves with organized activities as a means of establishing identity."*[2] The urge to associate oneself with people of similar interest, views and social standings, was the driving force behind these diverse and varied organizations which in itself were like small communities, intimate enough to provide constancy and camaraderie outside of the home environment. Interestingly enough, when the Philadelphia Cricket Club was formed, there were a few middle class members and one from the lower class, Mr. W. M. Bradshaw – a wood turner,[3] as the clubs were started on the basis of all-inclusiveness, but with the passage of time, (after the Civil War) the elite controlled the membership and the clubs became exclusive.

Many historians believe that the Civil War was the turning point in baseball's favor as it was a popular ball game in the camps. It was easy to throw down four bags in an open area to make a base and play ball, also thousands of soldiers when they returned home, continued with the game they had learnt and that majority in numbers further propelled the game forward into the collective consciousness of the masses and media alike. Cricket on the other hand, had been around a lot longer and clubs were being organized in the 1840s and they did not reach their peak well into the fourth quarter of the nineteenth century! 1850s saw a growth in number of establishments across various American communities where thousands had taken up cricket, and before the war, cricket was played in at least twenty free states (slave free) in more than hundred cities and towns across America. An estimate by the *Porter's Spirit of the Times* mentions over a thousand clubs in the late 1850s. Also, how is it that the number of fixtures peaked at more than 375 in 1905 and for the school cricket scene in Philadelphia, it peaked with 45 matches between 10 schools in 1904?[4] Against this backdrop, I find it difficult to accept that notion, yes, before the war, all classes of society played on the same field just as they did in England. The working class diminished with the advent of industrialization and urbanization took the clubs away from the city for lack of space and moved to the leafy suburbs and the upper crust clubs became exclusive in nature. The common man did not have the time nor money, to indulge in leisure activities and cricket was promoted as an English Game suited for the rich with time on their hands. To add to that, *"Cricket with its trappings of white flannels, lush green lawns, scheduled tea breaks, and three-day matches has been understandably perceived as an upper class sport."*[5] It was around 1850s[6] that the concept of Baseball as 'Americas Game or National Game' was introduced and that nationalistic fervor gradually chipped away at Philadelphia Cricket scene and around the country in general. *"I have fought for years in the Cricket arena on behalf of American Cricket and in that time I have necessarily encountered considerable prejudice of a national character in my efforts to advance the popularity of the noble game in this country,"*[7] wrote Henry Chadwick. New York and New Jersey though continued well into the 1930s with cricket where Philadelphia had left off and the period after the second World War brought in a new dimension to cricket with the influx of immigrants from cricket playing nations and the hope is one day it will regain its' former glory. George Kirsch is also of the opinion that Civil War was not the demarcation for Cricket's decline and it revived from the 1870s to World War I.[8] I would further add that cricket has been played since the advent of the settlers and continues unabated till the present day. The period after World War II would be the lowest point of interest in American Cricket and the period from 1885 to 1912 were the undisputed glory days.

Judging by *Spirit of the Times,* more than 6000 cricketers lived in the triangle formed by Philadelphia, New York and New Jersey area with Philadelphia leading the way with 120 clubs, home to cricket in America! By 1860, an estimated 10,000 cricketers were engaged in the game of cricket and when Chicago hosted Milwaukee in 1859, Abraham Lincoln is said to have been among its spectators.[9] The civil war did take its toll on cricket as thousands of 'players' lost their lives on both sides, families were displaced and were on the move and patriotic fervor was high. In such a situation base ball became a popular ball game of choice as it was an 'American' game and very easily played by all and it soon began to be touted as 'Our National Game.' After the first ever visit by the English Eleven in 1859, the next one did not materialize until 1868, in my opinion, had the first tour taken place *after* the Civil War, the cricketing landscape in America just might have been a lot different and may have gone hand in hand with base ball! If the tour of 1868 had been the first one, more would have followed on a consistent basis and unbroken regular tours would have fostered more inter country tournaments which in turn would have generated new talent locally as there would have been more players and clubs, and as they say, timing is everything. Cricket, stubbornly continued and solidified its grip on the city of brotherly love at the turn of the century.

Cricket followed the English community wherever they settled, from Ohio, Indiana, Illinois (Chicago had 3 clubs by 1840), to Michigan and to small towns like Ripon, Wisconsin where it had become a community staple for 50 years.[10] The Jacksonian era saw an increase in cricketing activity, mostly in the Whiggish centers of business. It spread westward as the irresistible gold rush of 1848 pulled cricketers to California and it yielded not only nuggets, but Cricket Clubs too. A Sports Historian, Roberta J Park's work on, *"British Sports and Pastimes in San Francisco, 1848-1900,"* throws light on the Cricket scene in San Francisco during the 1850s. The original members of a group disbanded in 1852 formed the Pioneer Cricket Club in 1857 and the California Cricket Club was also formed in June of 1857. Their President, William Booker also served as President of Occident Cricket Club which was later founded in 1874. Then there was the San Francisco Club of 1864 which later changed its name to St. George Cricket Club in 1868. The Union Cricket Club and the Excelsior Baseball and Cricket Club were short lived, as was the case with countless other clubs. The majority of the clubs were run by white collar and affluent members, at the same time, the working class also set up clubs, though shot lived, they were none the less operative for a while such as the one started by the mechanics of the Ogdensburgh Railroad at Rouse's Point, New York in 1856, New Brighton Mechanics Club and United of Waltham, Massachusetts. Then there was the unique *'Shoemakers Cricket Club'* of Berlin, Massachusetts in 1859 and the one set up by newspaper printers in Philadelphia around 1858 and aptly named, *'Typographical Cricket Club.'* The blue collared New Brighton Mechanics club, not to be confused with their white collar brethren, changed their name to Staten Island Cricket Club in 1858.[11] *"The first ever game of cricket played in the State of Michigan came off on the Pontiac Cricket Ground, July 13, between the Detroit and Pontiac Clubs,"* wrote the *Spirit of the Times: A Chronicle of the Turf, Agriculture, Field Sports, Literature and the Stage,* of August 1st, 1857. The two-innings match went in Detroit's favor who won by eight wickets.[12]

Cambridge educated clergymen, Samuel Calthrop, taught cricket at a private boarding school in Bridgeport, Connecticut in 1856. It was done not because he wanted to institute English activities, but it grew out of need as the pupils did not know anything about outdoor activities.[13] Not only cricket, but hockey and boating was taught as well. A match played between Mr. Calthrop's boys and Mr. Wilson's school was reported in the *Hartford Daily Courant* of September 8th 1858. The match was played in East Bridgeport and Calthrop's boys scored 60 runs, while the opponents replied with 66. While the second innings did commence, play was stopped due to darkness and that it was to be continued next Saturday. It was at West Point during his first visit to America in 1851, that Calthrop met Colonel Robert E. Lee, who said he would be greatly obliged if he could teach cricket to his officers, but as there were no *'instruments and apparatus'* for the game, he could not teach them.[14] The beautiful green *sward*[15] that Calthrop had noticed at West Point, could not be used for the first cricket demonstration at the time, but which he later did. On his return to America, he ended up teaching at Mr. Such's school in Bridgeport, founded by members of the *"Four Hundred of New York City."*[16] At Marblehead, Massachusetts where he was ordained a Unitarian Minister and led the Unitarian Church, he started the first cricket club there in 1860.[17] Other schools where cricket was played were, Newtown in Massachusetts, Ohio's Miami College and New York's Clinton Institute.[18] With increased patronage and participation, cricket was being played in at least 22 states and over 125 cities and towns and the number of clubs were estimated to be around 1000 in 1859 per *Wilke's Spirit of the Times*, though a more realistic figure would have been between 300 to 400 according to Kirsch in antebellum America.[19] To inspire the game amongst the young lads, *The New York Clipper* encouraged them to send in the scores of even their street games for publication.[20]

"The streets in the vicinity of our factories are now full at noon and evening of apprentices and others engaged in the simpler game of ball, thus counteracting the injurious effects of the sedentary pursuits in which some of them are engaged," wrote the *Newark Daily Advertiser* of May 14th 1860. Factory workers, white collar workers, artisans, all took part in pick-up games and cricket was not only limited to Clubs, but was also played between employees of companies, such as Philadelphia's Landberger and Company against Germantown's Spencer and Company. Henry Sharp, the president of New York Cricket Club organized cricket outings for his workers and so did other employers who gave time off so that their workers could enjoy some outdoor activities.[21] There were famous cricketers at the time like William Tylee Ranney, an accomplished artist *and* cricketer who was born in Middletown, Connecticut in 1913, and was one of the founders of the New York Cricket Club. As an artist it is unfortunate that he did not paint any cricket scenes, or did he, as these would have been first-hand accounts of the game as envisaged thru his eyes for the antebellum era. An avid cricketer, he continued playing in his forties till he succumbed to tuberculosis at a young age of 44. Enterprising individuals including Politicians, Doctors, and Scientist in diverse cities formed their own organizations to promote the game or were part of it, whether it was in St. Louis, Missouri, Lancaster, Pennsylvania, Madison in Wisconsin, New Brunswick in New Jersey or Redwing in Minnesota, Cincinnati in Ohio and in New Orleans, Louisiana.[22] Cricket thrived in the textile towns of Shelbourne Falls, Lowell and Dorchester in Massachusetts. Benefit matches were already being held at the time and in a match to raise funds for the 'Relief for Sufferers from the Late Riots,' the Rensselaer Club of Troy, N.Y., sent their members to play a series of matches during the week of August 30th 1863, to play against St. George (2nd eleven, mostly American players), New York CC, and the Newark and Union Clubs of Newark, N.J. The New York eleven comprised

of players from New York, Queens County, Willow CC, Manhattan CC, and East New-York Clubs, while the Troy Eleven were from the Rensselaer Club only.[23] Cricket was played by teams from Albany, Troy and Schenectady in New York State as early as 1837.

Bostons, Bay States, Star and Thistle, Young Bostons, Mount Vernon and a few other clubs were formed in the late 1850's in the Boston area. James Lovett, a baseball player (claimed he would have remained loyal to cricket had it remained popular) belonged to 'Young Bostons' and in 1885 joined the Longwood Cricket Club which was founded in 1877, located near Fenway Park on the outskirts of Boston (now located in Chestnut Hill since 1922) and it is still in existence today, although, the cricket greens are now home to the tennis courts. A young lad of sixteen appeared in 1863 with the St. George Cricket Club of New York to play a match on the East Cambridge grounds - he was called 'Little Georgie.' George Wright went on to become the 'king' of the diamond in Baseball as well as a great cricket player and wrote the 'Cricket Guide' in 1894. In 1869 Boston was visited by the highly successful, Cincinnati 'Red Stockings' who were on a country wide trip playing 63 games and losing none.

The nine members of the baseball team included:

George Wright – short-stop.
Harry Wright – center field.
Douglas Allison – catcher.
Fred Waterman – third base.
Charlie Gould – first base.
Andy Leonard – left field.
Calvin McVey – right field.
Charlie Sweasy – second base.
Asa Brainard – pitcher.

George led the batting with a total of 339 runs, 304 base hits for a total of 614 bases and 49 clean home runs. He assisted 179 times and made 82 fly catches out of 86 chances, thus proving that he was rightly called the 'king of the diamond.'[24]

D. Wright Unknown   Unknown Vanderlip   Vincent   Betts
       Van Buren   Fuller   Pomeroy   Kendall
          Taylor Geo. Wright Ford   Haughton   Ayers

ST GEORGE CRICKET ELEVEN AND SUBSTITUTES, HOBOKEN, N. J. 1861

ST GEORGE CRICKET XI and SUBSTITUTES at Hoboken, New Jersey, 1861.

{Harry & George Wright played for the Dragon Slayers, Dan & Samuel Jr., the other 2 siblings did not play for the club, so the 'D Wright' pictured is in fact Harry and his beard and dress does confirm with the 1864 picture with Sam Sr. as shown earlier}
From 'Old Boston Boys and The Games They Played – James D'Wolf Lovett 1906.

To many, cricket was the most absorbing and fascinating game, the University of Michigan students became so obsessed with the game after the Civil War that they could not stay away from it.[25] The Detroit and Pontiac Clubs no doubt would have aided and abetted it, though the same could not be said for the overall sentiment for cricket after the war as these were not in the majority of the populace.

The United States Sanitary Commission listed Cricket and Baseball as approved ball games for the camps, though baseball turned out to be more popular.[26] Cricket suffered more as even the administrators of the Philadelphia clubs took up the national cause and joined the Union army, leaving clubs like Young America, to keep the flame alive. Baseball thrived during the conflict and according to Kirsch, baseball's ability to flourish in these tiring times occurred in 1862 when a select nine of Philadelphia took on teams from Newark, New York and Brooklyn. The victory over the New York nine *"did more to advance the interest and popularity of the game in the city than five ordinary seasons could."*[27] On the other hand, the annual convention for cricket did not attract any crowds and the National Organization disappeared after 1862 due to confusion and inaction and the clubs withered down to half a dozen or so in New York, Newark, Orange, Paterson and Trenton.[28] *"The locale of American Cricket, Philadelphia, has been occupied by the American National Game of Base Ball, nearly all of the young American Cricketers of Philadelphia having volunteered to defend the nation's stumps, at the expense of their own,"* wrote the *Clipper*. Walter S. Newhall, was one of the famous cricketers to lose his life in the Civil War on December 18, 1863, he was just 21 years old. He was present during the historic Battle of Gettysburg (June 1-3, 1863) and was severely injured when he led a cavalry charge on the third day.[29] Cricket Clubs contributed a lot of players for the war effort, from the first eleven of Philadelphia, seven went to war and from the first eleven of the Germantown Club, eight signed up for duty. From the Young Americans – all eleven took part, and at one time there were 5 Newhall's and 6 Wister's serving at the same time. So many have taken part from different clubs that there have been no matches played for the last three years![30] During the Canadian visit in 1859 and the All England Eleven's first visit, Walter scored 549 runs for the season and a high of 105 in one of the matches, a talented cricketer lost to the perils of war. The Civil War came to an end in 1865 and the unsung heroine of it all may have been one Anna Ella Carroll.

Walter Newhall

"We, the undersigned, agree to unite in a Cricket club to meet for play next spring at least once a week," thus began the life of the Merion Cricket Club in October of 1865. Fifteen young lads between 14 to 22 years of age, led by William Montgomery and Maskell Ewing signed their names below the statement. The first meeting was held on December 16, and the meeting was recorded by Rowland Evans (one of the founders) as, *"In the fall of 1865, a number of young gentlemen of Lower Merion, Montgomery County and Radnor, Delaware County met together and took preliminary steps for organizing a Cricket Club. After considerable discussion it was decided to call the club, The Merion Cricket Club."* The original grounds were near Wynne Wood Station where they played regularly twice a week and in December of 1873, they decided to lease new grounds in Ardmore. The club was chartered in 1874 when the constitution and by-laws were adopted.[31] Cricket made way for Tennis in 1879 and Golf in 1896, and on June 10-16, 2013 it hosted its fifth US Open for Golf, a record 18th United States Golf Association event after a gap of 32 years,

and the eventual winner was Justin Rose, the first Englishman to win America's National Championship in 43 years.

There were players and there were inventors, always looking for ways to improve the implements of their trade or play. One of them was Michael Doherty of Boston, whose "Improvements in Cricket Bats" was granted a patent - No. 23,017 on February 22nd 1859,[32] wherein he describes his improvements.[33] Did it make it to the cricketing field - we do not know, but what is interesting is that this was done before the excitement had built up over the first English visit later in the year. He called it the 'combination cricket bat,' where the idea was twofold as described in his letter to the patent office.

1. *Constructing the blade of the bat of a wooden shell with a filling of cork, or other elastic material, substantially as described.*
2. *Constructing the handle of the bat of a wooden tube with a central strip of whale bone, or other elastic material of similar character, running down into the blade, substantially as herein described.*

There were three main areas of improvements. One was to prevent the bat from being dented or bruised. Second was to prevent jarring to the hand when the ball hit certain spots on the bat and the third, enhancements in the handle. As the hollow of the bat was to be filled with cork or other material with elastic characteristics, this would make the bat lighter by four fifths and the impact would send the ball farther.

M. Doherty,

Cricket Bat,

Nº 23,017.

Patented Feb. 22, 1859.

Fig. 1.

Fig. 2.

Fig. 3.

Fig. 4.

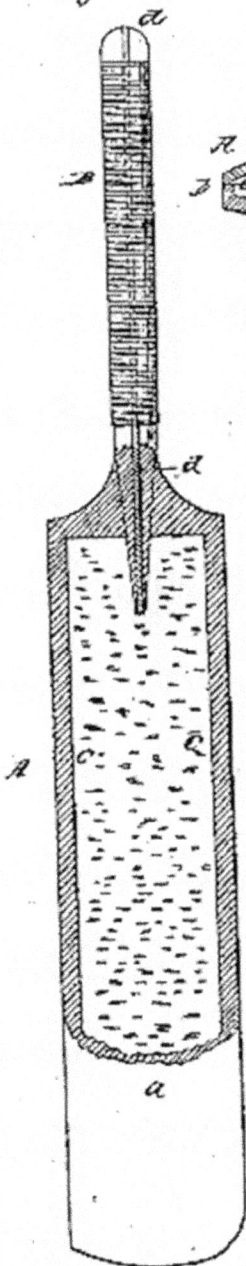

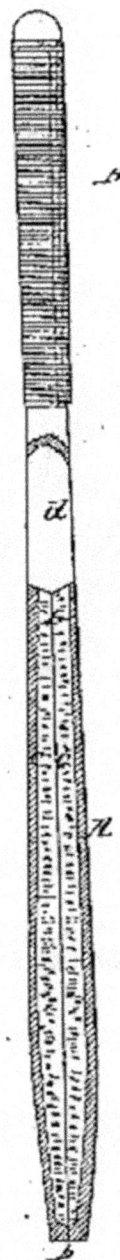

Witnesses:

Inventor

M. Doherty

The drawing, as registered with the patent office.

Doherty was not the only one to get a patent related to Cricket. The game touched different strata's of society, so, why was a trapeze artist interested in improving the design of the stumps even though there seems to be no record of him being an exponent of the game? Whatever the infatuation, it provided an invaluable and interesting insight into a time saving design for the wickets one that also received a patent – No. 32,869. (On checking with the patent office I was informed that, at the time working models would have been made before patents were given out, unfortunately, many of the inventions from the era were destroyed in a fire.)

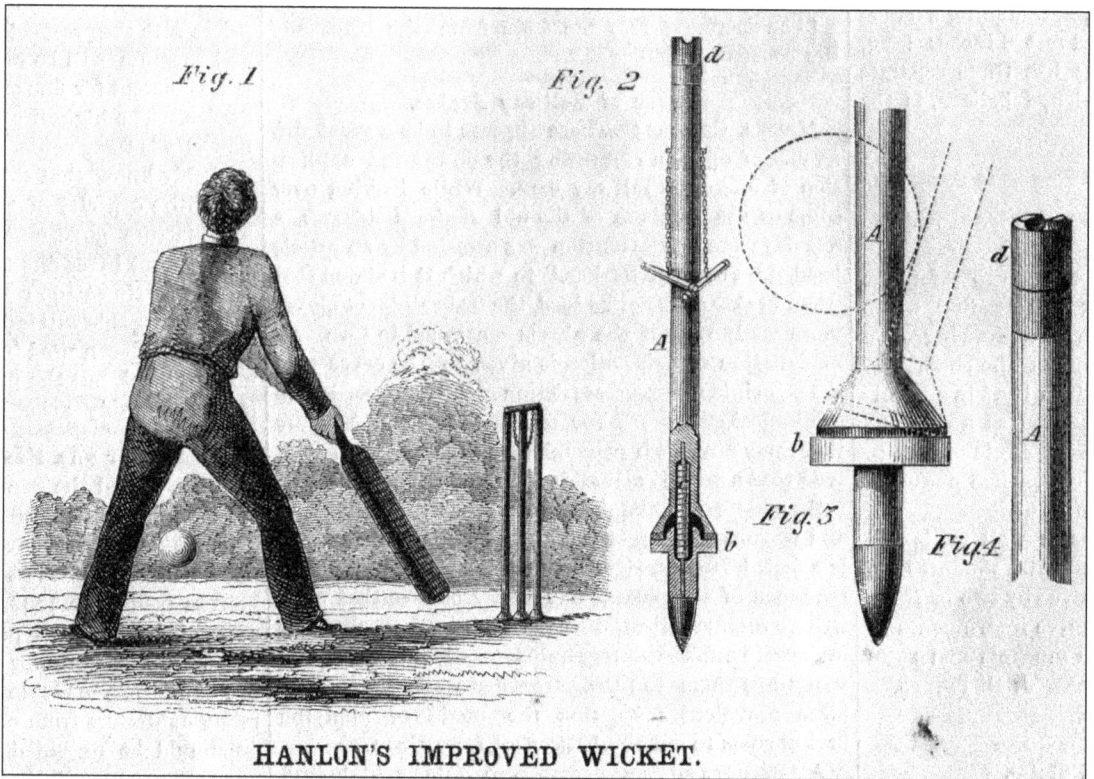

HANLON'S IMPROVED WICKET.

The Scientific American, August 10, 1861.

The stump, A, Figs. 2 and 3, is made with an elastic joint at the surface of the ground, so that when it is bent from the perpendicular it will immediately return to its proper position without breaking the ground. The joint is shown in section Fig. 2. The spike piece, b, which enters the ground has a shoulder to aid in supporting the stump, and is rounded at its upper end in the form of half a globe. The stump is enlarged at its lower end, and is hollowed out to fit over the semi-globular protuberance upon the upper end of the spike piece. The two parts are fastened together by an elastic tie, c, which may be either of India-rubber or of spiral steel wire. To make the joint soft and silent in its acting, a flat ring of India-rubber is interposed between the ends of the two pieces at the joint.

From this arrangement, it will be seen that when the stump is bent aside by the ball, as represented in dotted lines in Fig. 3. It will immediately resume its perpendicular position without demanding any attention from the players. As the bail will be thrown off whenever the wicket is hit, the labor of replacing them is facilitated by suspending them by chain to the side of the (middle) stump, as shown in Fig. 2: thus obviating the necessity of stooping to the ground whenever this frequently occurring task is to be performed.

To enable the notches for the bails to be arranged in line without changing the position of the stumps, each of the latter is crowned at its upper end with a brass cylinder, d, Fig. 4, which revolves freely on a spindle.[34]

This, *'convenient and elegant'* cricket stump was the invention of the William Hanlon, one of the six Hanlon brothers who were famous for their circus acts as the daredevil acrobats and pantomimes who performed regularly at Niblo's Garden in New York. Why was a well-known acrobatic athlete interested in improving the cricket stump? Nothing has been found to link the gentleman to the game of cricket, but I must agree, it's a very ingenious and practical invention, well before its time and even better compared to the modern flexible stumps. A patent was granted through the Scientific American Patent Agency on July 23rd, 1861; though it's unlikely it was ever produced commercially.

Patent No. 32,869 as described in the 'Annual report of the Commissioner of Patents"

William Hanlon of Philadelphia, PA. – Improvement in Cricket Wickets.

Patent dated July 23, 1861 – This invention consists in constructing the stump with spring joints near the bottom, which will permit them to yield and fall over sufficiently to displace the bails when struck by a ball, without disturbing their security in the ground, and to enable them to resume of themselves the upright position after the ball has passed them. The bails are attached to one or more of the stumps by chains or cords to prevent them from falling far from the top of the wickets. The upper ends of the stumps are provided with adjustable bail supporters, containing the grooves for the reception of the bails, to enable the grooves to be brought into line with each other to receive the bails.

Claim: The construction of wicket stumps with spring joints, substantially as and for the purpose set forth.

Second, the attachment of the bails to one or more of the stumps by chains or cords, substantially as and for the purpose specified.

Third, the adjustable bail supporters fitted to the heads of the stumps, substantially as and for the purpose described.[35]

The letter that was sent to the US Patent Office (Letter Patent No. 1865) was more detailed in its description and makes for interesting reading as to Mr. Hanlon's observation and the time and effort that went into creating the patent. If he did not play the game, then he must have been an aficionado and a keen and practical observer to come up with such an invention.

The Scientific American explains the premise behind the invention was that the stumps that were set in the ground had to be constantly driven in again and this breaks up the ground near the stump. The 'annoyance' of constantly picking up the bails and rearranging the wickets, slows down the game and tends to make it more laborious than a fun sport. To me as a bowler, the sight of seeing the stump cartwheeling after beating the batsman is a sight that never goes out of fashion and it provides that extra psychological satisfaction, not to mention, a certain smugness.

This was by no means the only patent for an efficient stump design, across the pond, another patent was obtained by Messrs. Fuller and Margaret in London around the same time frame I am guessing, was it a co-incidence? [36] An oblong metal plate with *three sunk collars of vulcanized rubber* to hold the stumps in place, were held in place by two long spikes. The collars provided the true position of the stumps and the wicket could be fixed in two minutes. This was a simple design but there was another called the 'Self-acting Regulation Wicket' more in line with William Hanlon's invention. A frame or 'shoe' was placed on the ground and the stumps when knocked down would regain the upright position with the spring action. Hanlon's design was by far the best as it incorporated the easy setup for the bails also, an all-encompassing design.

Octavius Valentine Catto was the most famous black cricketer in Philadelphia, he was also an educator and civil rights activist. Like most young boys at the time, he started with cricket as it was the dominant game and at one in which he also excelled at. Catto's high school was the prestigious Institute for Colored Youth in South Philadelphia from where he graduated in 1858. Today, it is known as Cheyney University of Pennsylvania, America's oldest historically black institution of higher education. Later, he went on to become the principal of the school in 1869.

There would be regular cricket matches between the boys at the Institute for Colored Youths and Lombard School. While stationed at camp William Penn outside Philadelphia during the Civil War he was introduced to baseball, a popular sport around the camps. In 1866 two ball clubs were formed, the Excelsior and the Pythians, under their captain and shortstop, Octavius Catto who was the founding member of the Pythian Base Ball Club which was composed of African American players. In 1867 they had an undefeated season, following which they applied for admission (later withdrew and the National Association of Base Ball Players ruled against admitting any clubs that included black members later that year) into the newly formed Pennsylvania Baseball Association with the backing of the white Athletic Base Ball Club. In 1869 they challenged different white teams and finally one team accepted the challenge – Olympic Base Ball Club – this is considered to be the first official match between a white and black baseball team and was played on September 3rd 1869. It would take 78 years (1947) before blacks (Jackie Robinson) could play alongside whites in the major leagues! The *New York Times* reported on it the following day:

BASEBALL – A Novel Game in Philadelphia – A Negro Club in the Field – The White Club Victorious, Philadelphia, Penn., Sept.4.

The Pythians Base-Ball Club, (colored), after challenging a number of white clubs of this city, who refused to play, succeeded in getting an acceptance from the Olympic, which defeated them by the score 44-23. The novelty of the affair drew an immense crowd of people, it being the first game played between a white and colored club. Umpire – Col. Fitzgerald, of this city.

Col. Thomas Fitzgerald was the founding president of the Athletics and the owner of the newspaper, *City Item*. Another match was played two weeks later where the Pythians did defeat the *City Item* ball club by 27-17.

The ladies were not far behind and of the two earliest known women's baseball team, one was an African American nine called, 'The Dolly Vardens' which was formed just one year after the first black men's team was organized. [37] Miss Porter's, an all-girls school in Farmington Connecticut, also started their first baseball team in 1867 called, 'Tunxises' but the distinction of being the first, belong to the girls at Vassar College for starting a baseball club in 1866. According to their website and the Journal of Sports History, it talks about Annie Glidden, a student in the spring of 1866 writing to her brother, *"They are getting up various clubs now for out-of-door exercise; they have a floral society, boat clubs, and base-ball clubs. I belong to one of the latter, and enjoy it hugely I can assure you."* There were two teams, 'Laurels' and the 'Abenakis' and in 1876 there were the 'Resolutes' of which there is a team picture of the girls in uniform, in the college archives. [38]

During the same time frame, Philadelphia also had three black cricket clubs. The Olives, Metamora and the Diligente which served as a practice team to the other two, who were fierce rivals. The vacant lot behind the music academy at 16th and Pine Street served as their match venue and though there were numerous white clubs in the city, who knew about them and had seen them play, they were never invited to a match, and it goes without saying that they would not have asked some of the good players to join their clubs. [39] Catto's life was cut short on Election Day, October 10th 1871, as he was shot and killed, one of the forgotten heroes of the era.

W. Hanlon,
Cricket Wicket.

Nº 32,869.

Patented July 23, 186_

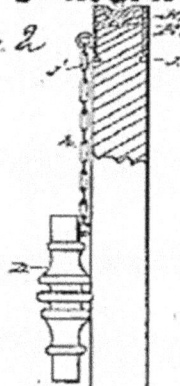

Fig. 2.

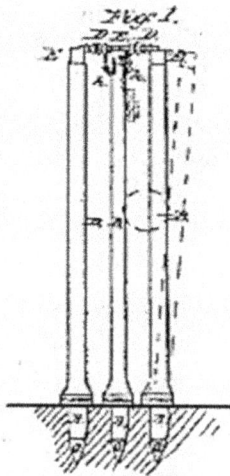

Fig. 1.

Fig. 3.

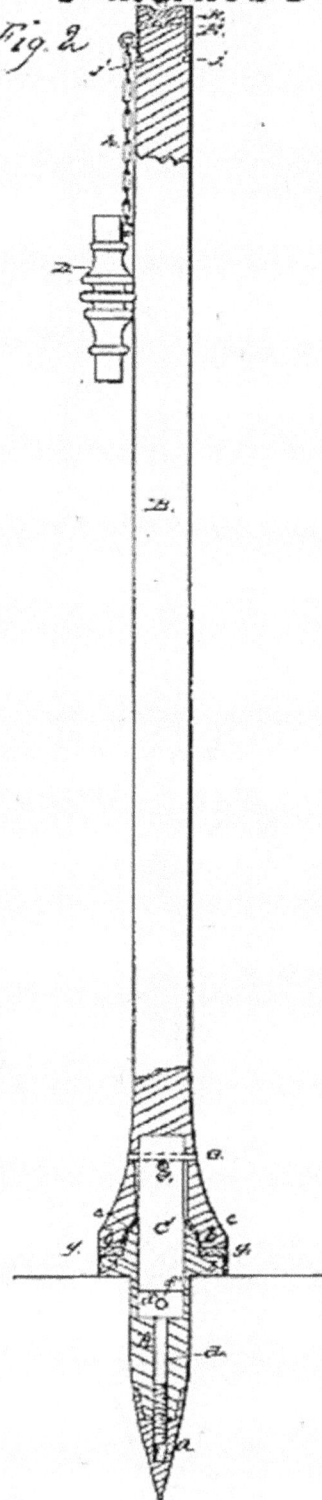

Witnesses.

Inventor:
W. Hanlon

The drawing, as registered with the patent office.

Octavius Valentine Catto

While the black cricketers were busy with their games, the Germantown and Young America cricketers being more affluent posed for a pictured after a match. Did they watch them from a distance and did the idea of challenging the black cricketers cross their mind, even if it did, I am sure it was quickly disapproved of. During the 1872 tour by R.A. Fitzgerald's English team to Canada and United States, would they have played the black cricketers from the Olives or Metamora? An exciting prospect and I am sure given the opportunity, they would have, just as surely as they did with the first Australian aborigines to visit England in 1868 for a series of cricket matches. Though in 1911, Haverford School cancelled a match against the visiting West Indies team when they learnt that there might be some 'black Americans' in the team![40]

CRICKET MATCH BETWEEN THE FIRST ELEVENS OF THE GERMANTOWN AND YOUNG AMERICA CLUBS, 1867.

Cricket Match Between the First Elevens of the Germantown and Young America Clubs 1867. Cadwalader Family Papers. Courtesy: Historical Society of Pennsylvania.

The 'Young America' team in 1864.
Standing: G.M. Newhall, W.M. Bayard, E.M. Davis Jr.,
W.C. Watson, C.A. Newhall, W.B. Johns Jr.
Sitting: R. Wister, D.S. Newhall, H.L. Newhall, Alfred Mellor, C.A. Vernou
CDV (carte de visite) albumen photograph by Brady's National Photographic Portrait
Galleries, Broadway & Tenth Street, New York.

The Intercollegiate Cricket Association (ICA) was founded on April 26, in 1881 to foster competitive matches between Ivy League colleges, such as University of Pennsylvania (U Penn), Harvard, Cornell, Columbia, Princeton and Trinity. There was no winner in 1881 as the schedule was not completed, but the honors went to U Penn in the second year and they won it a record 17 times till the intercollegiate competition ended in 1924. The first inter-college match may have been played between Dorian Club of Haverford and U Penn in 1864 where Dorian ended up beating the boys from the University. The ICA was championed by John B Thayer Jr. who was 19 at the time and three years later would join the Gentlemen of Philadelphia on their maiden cricket tour to England. He met an untimely death on the night of April 14-15, 1912 as he went down with the Titanic, he was born on April 21, 1862.

At the inaugural meeting, U Penn, Columbia, Princeton and Trinity College of Hartford were present and a $100 cup was to be presented to the winners of this annual competition (as seen in the picture below). During the first year in 1881, six teams played for the first and last time, they were: U Penn, Haverford, Harvard, Princeton, Columbia and Trinity. U Penn and Haverford were the only two constants from the beginning to the end of the tournament in 1924. Harvard joined in 1881 and played till 1905 (missed a few years) and Cornell joined in 1904 playing till 1911, except for 1908 and 1909.[41]

Cricket team of 1887 (photograph, ID Number 20050908007). Collection UPX 12, Box 71, Folder 12, University of Pennsylvania Archives, Philadelphia, PA.

"College Boys at Cricket, Princeton's players easily defeat Hartford's Trinitarians," read the head-lines in *The New York Times* of May 22, 1881. This was the only year they had participated and now it was captured in print for posterity. In 1882 both these teams withdrew from the association and never played again.[42] This was the first of the inter-collegiate match played on Staten Island and Trinity opened the innings, scoring 32 for the first 6 wickets before the rest crumpled and, *'for some time afterward "duck eggs" were the order.'*[43] The innings ended at 38 and in reply, Princeton put up a score of 57 runs which the Trinity boys began to target in the second innings which began at 3:15 pm. They scored 3 runs more than their first innings score, which was not enough to hold back Princeton who won by 7 wickets. After the Trinity class of 1881 graduated, cricket also declined at the college though it may have revived for a short time in 1888.[44] Haverford is one institution that has carried on its cricketing tradition till today.

Princeton vs. Trinity

Tompkinsville, Staten Island, May 21, 1881.

PRINCETON

First Innings	Runs	Second Innings	Runs
WJ Taylor lbw b Emery	4	c Bohlen b Grint	0
DP Morgan b Emery	7	b Grint	1
JB Shober b Grint	24	run out	10
R Norris b Emery	2	b Emery	0
JT Haxall b Grint	2	not out	5
FS Conover (Capt) b Grint	5	not out	3
EM Royale c Perkins b Grint	0		
W Tod not out	4		
RJ Hamilton run out	0		
L Riggs b Emery	0		
G Westervelt b Emery	0		
Extras (Byes 3, Leg Byes 5, Wide 1)	9	Extras (Byes 4, Wide Ball 1)	5
Total	57	Total	24

TRINITY

First Innings	Runs	Second Innings	Runs
WS Emery run out	10	b Shober	6
JL Purdy c Norris b Shober	3	c Shober b Haxall	9
AT Mason c Todd b Shober	2	c Royle b Haxall	0
DM Bohlen (Capt) c & b Shober	10	c Shober b Haxall	0
GE Perkins b Shober	2	c Hamilton b Haxall	0
LC Washburn b Shober	5	c Todd b Haxall	0
AP Grint c Norris b Shober	0	c Morgan b Shober	1
SBP Trowbridge c Conover b Haxall	0	not out	8
FC Gowan c Morgan b Shober	0	c Riggs b Haxall	7
J Brainard not out	1	b Shober	2
WC Sheldon b Haxall	0	run out	1
Extras (Byes 2, Leg Bes 1, Wide 2)	5	Extras (Byes 3, Wide 4)	7
Total	38	Total	41

Bowling	Balls	Runs	Maiden	Wickets	Balls	Runs	Maiden	Wickets
PRINCETON		First Innings				Second Innings		
JB Shober	78	11	4	7	84	10	7	3
JT Haxall	74	22	4	2	80	24	3	6
WS Emery	-	-	-	-	42	6	4	1
TRINITY		First Innings				Second Innings		
WS Emery	82	20	1	5	-	-	-	-
AP Grint	78	10	5	4	41	13	4	2

Umpires: Princeton – James Smith : Trinity - Cleverly
Princeton wins by 7 wickets.

Harvard Cricket Team, winners of the Inter-Collegiate Cup in 1899.

Princeton took up cricket in the fall of 1857 and initially it was feared that it would be stopped by the authorities as there was *'something wicket in it.'* Students hailing from Philadelphia formed the *Nassau Cricket Club* and officers were elected in 1858. Players were hard to come by in the beginning for various reasons and the earliest match on record is for a nine-a-side match between two Princeton teams, the score, 76-28. The situation improved in 1862-63 under the captaincy of S.B. Huey and they played several matches against Philadelphia teams, but no records are available as the diary containing the scores was lost. Base Ball was also started at the same time and the team was called, *Nassau Baseball Nine.*

After two years of practice, Nassau Cricketers challenged the University of Pennsylvania Eleven on May 12th 1866 at Princeton, and won the match by 6 runs! But, here is the interesting part, the match was decided on first innings basis, even Lester in *Century of Philadelphia Cricket* (p.379) only mentions a win for Princeton, but does not provide further detail. The match started at noon with the University of Pennsylvania batting first and scoring 34 to which the Princeton boys replied with 40 runs. In the second innings, University of Pennsylvania scored 106 runs and seeing this big total, the Nassau team felt a defeat was certain, so they played for a draw and succeeded in doing so, scoring only 21 runs with the loss of 4 wickets when the play was stopped!

Here are the scores from the match played on May 12, 1866.

NASSAU CRICKET CLUB vs. UNIVERSITY OF PENNSYLVANIA at PRINCETON

Nassau Eleven	How Out	Runs
WH Katzenbach	b Magee	1
WJ Lyon	b Magee	1
JR Phillips	b Magee	1
JT Newhall	run out	0
JA Cake	b Magee	1
WY Johnson	b Magee	1
RMJ Smith	c Evans b Hoffman	5
C Burnside	b Magee	0
FS Katzenbach	not out	8
SM Murphy	b Beasley	2
RW Parker	?	2
Byes		10
Leg Byes		1
Wide Balls		7
No Balls		0
Total		40

University of Pennsylvania	How Out	Runs
Hoffman	b Burnside	7
Ashbridge	b Cake	0
Hopkinson	c Cake b Burnside	4
Magee	c Phillips b Burnside	5
Morgan	run out	1
Evans	b Cake	0
Beasley	b Burnside	0
Simms	c and b Cake	1
Horace	c Lyon b Cake	1
Lex	not out	1
Fraley	b Cake	1
Byes		1
Leg Byes		2
Wide Balls		9
No Balls		1
Total		34

Nassau's next engagement was against Delaware Cricket Club at Lambertville in New Jersey on June 2nd 1866, which they lost, and that was followed by another defeat at the hands of the same club. Cricket was not able to put down its' roots at Princeton and they played intermittently, and matters did not help when just a few years into their existence, the Nassau Club was in debt and stopped playing for eight years! (No one thought of electing a finance major as a Treasurer to handle the money, besides eight years is a long time.) With new interest in cricket, the club was re-organized on September 11, 1874, and they were surprised with their victory over the second XI from Merion Cricket Club on October 24th, as they had little practice. The following year, they played against Staten Island Cricket Club which they won, but, there are no records of matches being played in 1876 even though they had surplus money! The next few years the interest waned again despite the offer of re-organization from none other than, St. George Cricket Club. In February of 1881, a meeting was held which again revitalized the club for the big inter-collegiate competition where they defeated Trinity College from Hartford. They played only 2 matches during the year! After defeating Trinity in May, they played Columbia at Hoboken on October 8th, where they lost by a score of 56 to 39. The last Cricket match to be played as a representative of Princeton was played on June 3rd 1882 at New York against the Manhattan Cricket Club which resulted in a win for the Nassau Cricket Club.

(From, 'Athletics at Princeton, a History.' Compiled and edited by Frank Presbrey and James Hugh Moffatt. 1901. p. 557-562)

1862 Princeton Cricket Team.

L-R: Oscar Keene, E. Vanderpool, H.A. Boardman, S.B. Huey, G. Kidd, H. Young, D.W. Guy, J.W. Patton, H.L. Sampson, L.W. Mudge, J.L. Munn.

CRICKET ELEVEN, 1867.

W. J. Lyon, '67.	F. S. Katzenbach, '67.
J. T. Newhall, '69.	S. M. Murphy, '67.
R. W. Parker, '67.	E. R. Miller, '67.
J. P. Polk, '68.	W. H. Katzenbach, '67.
W. M. Johnson, '67.	J. S. Young, '67.
J. R. Phillips, '67.	

1867 Princeton Cricket Eleven.

THE CRICKETING TOURISTS

The oldest continuing cricket rivalry in the world, or any sports for that matter, is the United States versus Canada under the aegis of the KA Auty Cricket Trophy which has been an on again off again relationship one that perpetrated from a hoax in 1840. No other sport in history can claim to have a team travel by sea in 1859 – just to play some games! Looking back on it today makes one wonder in amazement at their endurance and spirit to undertake such a venture. Even before the English could lay claim to being *the* 1st overseas 'athletes/sportsmen' a group of native Indians lead by their Chief, Mew-hu-she-kaw and his clan of Iowa Indians, became the first *Americans* to 'play' at the Lord's Cricket Ground in 1844, but, it wasn't cricket. They participated in an Indian Archery Fete and Festival organized by the Marylebone Cricket Club, (founded in 1787) and the London Summer Olympics of 2012 would bring archery back to the very same ground when it hosted the men's and women's competition after a gap of 168 years!

The English set sail on *Nova Scotian*, a steamship with sails, for Montreal on 6th September 1859. W.P. Pickering of Montreal and Robert Waller of St. George Club in New York, had communicated with Fred Lillywhite back in 1856[1] and as the terms could not be agreed upon, the trip had not come about earlier. Now, the English had reached Albany from Montreal on October 1st, and from there the 'New World' riverboat was to take them to New York which they reached Sunday morning. Unfortunately, there was no welcoming party due to the lack of arrival information! Now that the English cricketers were a reality, other cities like Cincinnati, Albany, Baltimore and St. Louis tried unsuccessfully to lure them to their cities. Astor House Hotel where they stayed was full of onlookers and there were more than two thousand people on the ground on Sunday afternoon when the team had gone to inspect the playing surface at Hoboken. [2] On Monday, there were more than 10,000 [3] people on the grounds (many of them were here for the novelty of it) and the 22 Americans were put in to bat after losing the toss. There were eight players from Philadelphia including Walter Newhall and his instructor Tom Senior, the best bowler at the time who dismissed Grundy, Stephenson and Lillywhite in consecutive deliveries – a hat trick. [4] That may have happened at the match played at Camac Estate where he did take 6 wickets and those of the players named. At Elysian Fields in Hoboken, the bowler was Hallis, who took 6 wickets and those of Grundy and Stephenson, but not Lillywhite as he umpired the match due to injury and we don't see Senior bowling for the 22 at all. The batting of the '22' was *scarcely tolerable* and the bowling, *reckless* wrote Lillywhite. It may have been jitters on the part of the Americans and some players were too old, as they were facing a much stronger and experienced opponent for the first time and a style which they were not accustomed to. For comparison, in the five matches against the Englishmen the American bowlers bowled 73 wide balls, as opposed to 3 by the English. George Parr's eleven played four matches on this inaugural tour winning all, the first in Montreal against Lower Canada, next at Hoboken, third in Philadelphia and the fourth against Canada at Hamilton. An extra match was played at Rochester which was snowed out! [5] The score from the first English match on American soil is as follows:

Match played at Elysian Fields, Hoboken on October 3rd 4th & 5th 1859.
All England vs. Twenty two of the Unites States.

22 *of* UNITED STATES

First Innings	Runs	Second Innings	Runs
Long b Parr	6	c Carpenter b Wisden	7
R. Waller run out	0	st. Lockyer b Caffyn	0
H. Sharp st. Lockyer b Jackson	1	c & b Caffyn	5
W. Hammond c Hayward b Parr	6	b Caffyn	0
A.H. Gibbes b Jackson	0	c Lockyer b Caffyn	0
J.W.S. Scarlett lbw Parr	4	c Carpenter b Caffyn	1
A. Marsh lbw Jackson	0	c Wisden b Caffyn	0
W. Wilby b Parr	3	b Caffyn	0
T. Senior hit wkt b Parr	3	c Carpenter b Caffyn	1
H. Wright c Lockyer b Parr	1	b Caffyn	5
J. Higham b Jackson	1	b Caffyn	0
Head b Jackson	0	c Lockyer b Caffyn	5
S. Wright st. Lockyer b Jackson	1	b Wisden	3
W. Newhall c Diver b Jackson	5	b Caffyn	6
Morgan c Jackson b Parr	0	c Lockyer b Caffyn	0
J. Walker b Jackson	2	b Wisden	0
W. Crossley b Parr	0	c Carpenter b Caffyn	4
W. Comery hit wkt b Parr	0	lbw Caffyn	5
R. Bage b Jackson	3	not out	0
Harry Lillywhite c Carpenter b Jackson	0	st. Lockyyer b Caffyn	0
F. Barclay run out	0	run out	1
H. Hallis not out	0	b Wisden	5
Extras	2	Extras	4
TOTAL	38	TOTAL	54

11 *of* ENGLAND

First Innings	Runs
Thomas. Hayward b Hallis	33
Robert. Carpenter c Senior b Hallis	26
T. Wisden run out	3
George. Parr b Gibbes	7
William. Caffyn b Gibbes	5
Tom. Lockyer c Lang b Hallis	12
Alfred. Diver c Hallis b Gibbes	1
H.H. Stephenson b Hallis	10
Julius Caesar b Hallis	6
James. Grundy b Hallis	20
John. Jackson not out	8
Extras	25
TOTAL	156

Bowling	Balls	Maiden	Runs	Wickets	Balls	Maiden	Run	Wickets
USA	First Innings				Second Innings			
S. Wright	56	7	20	0				
Crossley	4	0	1	0				
Comery	72	5	31	0				
Hallis	173	26	45	6				
Marsh	32	4	6	0				
Gibbes	84	9	28	3				
ENGLAND	First Innings				Second Innings			
G. Parr	116	12	26	9	-	-	-	-
Jackson	112	19	10	10	-	-	-	-
Wisden	-	-	-	-	136	22	24	4
Caffyn	-	-	-	-	136	25	26	16

England won by an innings and 64 runs.
Umpires: John Lillywhite and Charles Vinten.

This first match was a spectacle of sights and sounds both for the English visitors and the immense crowd of more than 20,000 that had gathered over the three days to witness this historic inaugural contest. Flags of both nations were displayed and arrangements were made for the public's comfort and convenience at the ground. The English batted to the backdrop of 'Rule Britannia' (interesting choice) being played by the band. A benefit match was played at the same location on the 6th 7th & 8th after the first game was over, a mix of English and American players between T. Lockyer's side and Stephenson's side with Lockyer's side winning by 74 runs. A grand dinner was held on Friday in their honor at Astor House and after the customary speeches and toast, the English were looking forward to the match at Philadelphia and left New York the night of October 8th. On reaching the city at midnight, they were met by the welcoming committee and Henry Chadwick at the Girard House Hotel and even at the late hour they had supper and retired to bed late as there was no play on Sunday.[6]

Rain had been falling all night and the match could not commence till 3.30 pm on Monday afternoon and that too after a couple of wagon loads of sawdust was spread around, and when the match ended at 5.30 p.m., the score stood at 41 runs for the loss of 9 wickets for the twenty-two of the United States. The American captain was W.R. Wister and there were nine New Yorkers and thirteen from Philadelphia who made up the twenty-two.[7] The match commenced again on Wednesday as Tuesday was an election day. Both Caffyn and Lillywhite were impressed by the ladies who turned up in their finest attire and Caffyn recalled that this was the match where Carpenter was caught off a wide ball but was not given out. Amidst the festive atmosphere the match ended in favor of the English who won by seven wickets, the score being 94 and 60 for the twenty-two Americans and 126 and 29 for the English. Another 'benefit match' and with the hope that *Cricket in Philadelphia has every prospect of becoming a national game,*[8] the visitors bid adieu and continued to Hamilton with a stop at Buffalo to see the Niagara falls. The journey was by no means pleasant and arriving late at Buffalo they learnt that the train to Niagara had left, leaving them to take carriages which took five hours to traverse a distance of 22 miles. The grandeur of the falls was worth the troubles and after spending time there, they crossed the suspension bridge and reached Hamilton to a huge waiting crowd. After engaging the twenty-two of Upper Canada and defeating them by 9 wickets on 17, 18 & 19 October, they left the same night for Rochester for the last outing as this match of combined Canadian and American twenty-two had been arranged while they were in New York.

Nearing the end of October the weather was cold now, and against this backdrop, one last match commenced on Friday the 21st October in front of a sizeable audience. The twenty-two were bundled out for only 39 runs, with the English putting up 35 runs for the loss of two wickets. We are very familiar with 'rain delays' but this was the first and probably the last time a cricket match was delayed due to snow, yes, it was snowing! The cricketers were also introduced to baseball at another ground a mile away. This was the time when the 'first bounce' rule was in effect and the English thought it was childish[9] and easy to have the batter caught out after the ball had hit the ground once. Saturday was snowed out and as there was no play on Sunday, this offered an opportunity for the visitors to make another trip to Niagara, and this time to the Canadian side of the falls. *"It is impossible to describe the delight with which the Eleven gazed upon the tumultuous crash of water,"* of the Horseshoe Falls wrote Lillywhite. The match resumed on Monday the 24th with the English concluding their innings scoring 171 runs and on the last day, the 25th, almost everyone had gloves and overcoats on and this frosty match concluded with the Eleven of All England being victorious by an innings and 68 runs. With the tour a success, they set sail on the *North Briton* and reached Liverpool on November the 11th and this trip netted each player about £90.

The cricket shower in the autumn brought about a new crop of clubs the following year. Places which were once devoid of the sound of leather against the willow, interest in the game was now blossoming in places like Maysville, Kentucky; Ripley, Ohio; Port Huron, Michigan and Grass Valley, California etc. and a match won by the Lincoln campaign workers against the Douglas campaign workers reflected the *sign of the times*. Clubs were springing up in Pittsburgh, Madison, Wisconsin; Lexington, Kentucky; St Louis and San Francisco. Philadelphia, which saw the biggest surge in cricket interest, the weekend would bring out a number of clubs to the Powelton Fair Grounds for matches.[10]

As we now know, the Civil War could not have commenced at a worse time, the first English team had concluded its maiden journey to foster a new sporting spirit which was derailed till the war ended and by the time Edgar 'Ned' Willsher's XI set foot in America in 1868, the early momentum had been lost to Baseball which now had a bigger footprint. June 10, 1864, saw the introduction of over arm bowling as M.C.C. adopted the new rule which changed the face of the game as we know it today and before 1806 all bowling was underhand. The change in bowling was brought about by Ned who in 1862 intentionally bowled overarm at the Oval and was no-balled on ever ball in the over by John Lillywhite the umpire, resulting in the team walking off the field. This incident led to the revision of the overarm bowling rules that were implemented four years before Ned led a team to America.

Again the English arrived late in the season as Edgar Willsher's XI left Liverpool in early September and the first match at Philadelphia was played from 3-6th October at the Germantown Cricket Grounds. Here, the English won by 2 wickets with the score being – 88 and 35 for the twenty-two Americans and 92 and 36 for the English XI, a close score when compared to the next match where the Americans lost by a bigger margin – 47 and 62 in reply to 117 and 64 (Charles Newhall took 6 wickets for 30 runs) by the English. Here the team was supposed to be the best at the time with a mix of amateurs and seven professionals.[11] A baseball game was also played between the English cricketers and the Union Base Ball Club of Morrisania to abridge the interest between cricket and baseball (also to increase the gate receipt) and the New York Times did not help by proclaiming that the, *"good old game of cricket has not been entirely given up in New York, and our old citizens still delight in this manly sport."*[12] In April of 1870, a letter was received by the New York City cricketers that Willsher would not be able to put a team together for a return visit later in the year.[13]

George Freeman a fast bowler with the English team who took 104 wickets out of which 74 were clean bowled, was happy to report back home in his letters to his uncle John

Freeman, that he had earned £100 plus presents on this trip.[14] In a match at Montreal he took 13 wickets for 12 runs as the home team of 22 players was all out for 22! *Clipper's* Frank Queen criticized the arrangement of paying professionals to visit America saying, *"Base Ball so greatly overshadows the game of Cricket in this country that we are surprised at their coming here for speculative purpose,"*[15] while Freeman observed after playing the game, *"it is a fool to Cricket, still the Yankees think otherwise."*[16]

Four years later on September 16th 1872, the indomitable W. G. Grace entered America after crossing over from Niagara on completion of their maiden engagement in Canada. The first match was against the twenty two of St. George's Club at Hoboken which they had to cross from New York on a ferry and Grace was surprised to see a car being driven on and off a ferry boat for the first time! [17] The English score of 249 was no match for St. George, who were bundled out for 66 and 44, despite the inclusion of the Wright brothers – Henry and George, the highest run getters and their fielding – *simply magnificent*, as Grace put it. This first match was 'captured' on paper as shown below in *Frank Leslie's Illustrated Newspaper* of September 18th 1872, the caption reads - *"A great catch by Appleby" Cricket match between the Eleven English Amateurs and the Twenty-Two American Amateurs, at the St. George's Club Grounds, Hoboken.* (Arthur Appleby was the only first class bowler in the English side).

The best match of the tour was against the twenty two of Philadelphia at Nicetown on September 21, 23 and 24, and was a very close one at that, one where the twenty two deserved a win according to Grace. Not only was there pomp and ceremony, there was a lot of excitement and wherever the English went, the Philadelphians went out of their way to make them feel welcome. An 'Official Handbook of the Cricket Fete,' was published for the occasion, a band was ready from the Navy Yard and match results would be ready to be telegraphed.[18] The Philadelphians managed to put up 63 runs and in reply the English scored 105 and W.G. heard the loudest roar he could remember when he was dismissed. Philadelphia scored a little better in the second innings scoring 74 runs which left the English with only 33 to win with a full days' play left. Cricket matches are known to turn on a dime and 33 looked easy enough to complete in an hour, alas, such was not the case. The English lost 2 wickets for eight runs and for the next hour the going was slow and they managed to move up to only 15 when another wicket was lost. Meanwhile Grace had managed a measly 7 runs after more than an hour and was finally caught in the slip as, *"hats and umbrellas were tossed in the air"* on his dismissal.[19] It was 4 for 18 and things looked dire till the score inched forward to 29 where another wicket fell, though only 4 runs were required. Another wicket at 29 and another, the score now read, 7 for 29!

The excitement of the crowds must have been palpable, every delivery would bring with it nervous anticipation and, *"they were in rhapsodies, and could scarcely keep still."*[20] At this point the English were prepared for the worst, Newhall's ball hit Lubbock on the legs resulting in a leg-bye and Appleby put the finishing touch by hitting a boundary, thus denying the Philadelphians a victory that was within easy reach. With another match in their favor, the English had to forgo the customary reception as they had to rush and catch the train to Boston which they missed anyway. The match was reduced to a day's play (26th) on the most extreme conditions as it had rained the night before and many players were standing *ankle deep in sawdust and slush*! It was a close match against the twenty-two of Boston and bad light prevented the innings from being completed and George Wright presented each of the English players with a baseball after the game. The successful visit drew to a close and they made their return trip on board the *Prussian* from Quebec on September 29th. This third tour by the English was initially opposed due to the *Alabama Claims* which were settled under the *'Treaty of Washington'* signed on March 8th 1871, and it would have been the first sporting casualty of political intervention.

The scores are taken from (Official Handbook of the International Cricket Fete) *Century of Philadelphia Cricket*, which differs slightly from Fitzgerald's *Wickets in the West*.

Match played at Germantown Cricket Club at Nicetown on September 21st 23rd & 24th 1872. Fitzgerald's 12 vs. 22 of Philadelphia.

22 *of* PHILADELPHIA

First Innings	Runs	Second Innings	Runs
F. Brewster b Appleby	4	c Rose b Grace	0
H.L. Newhall b Appleby	0	c Fitzgerald b Grace	0
W. Welsh b Appleby	0	b Appleby	1
R.S. Newhall b Appleby	4	c Hornby b Appleby	0
John Large hit wkt b Grace	13	c Appleby b Grace	7
Cadwalader hit wkt b Rose	2	b Grace	0
L. Baird c Harris b Rose	0	lbw Appleby	6
Geo. N. Newhall b Appleby	0	b Appleby	9
Joe. Hargraves b Appleby	2	b Grace	4
W. Morgan c Ottaway b Grace	7	c Hadow b Grace	1
Dan. S. Newhall b Grace	0	st. Ottaway b Grace	15
S. Law c Rose b Grace	2	not out	2
Chas. A. Newhall b Appleby	3	lbw Appleby	0
S. Meade c E. Lubbock b Grace	0	b Appleby	2
R. Pease hit wkt b Grace	0	hit wkt b Appleby	0
C. Baird run out	3	b Grace	1
T. Hargrave c Ottaway b Grace	0	st. Ottaway b Grace	3
R. W. Clay b Grace	4	c Hadow b Grace	11
John. Hargreaves run out	11	c and b Grace	7
G. Sanderson b Appleby	0	b Grace	0
H. Magee c Ottaway b Grace	3	b Appleby	1
S. Welsh not out	3	run out	0
Extras	2	Extras	4
TOTAL	63	TOTAL	74

12 *of* FITZGERALD

First Innings	Runs	Second Innings	Runs
Grace. b C. Newhall	14	c. J. Hargrave b C. Newhall	7
Ottaway run out	10	b C. Newhall	0
Hornby b Meade	9	c R. Newhall b Meade	4
A. Lubbock run out	9	c and b C. Newhall	3
Hadow c J. Hargrave b C. Newhall	29	b Meade	6
Harris c D. Newhall b C. Newhall	3	c J. Hargrave b Meade	8
Francis b Meade	5	b C. Newhall	0
Appleby c Magee b Meade	2	not out	4
E. Lubbock c J. Hargrave b C. Newhall	0	not out	0
Rose c J. Hargrave b C. Newhall	0		
Pickering b C. Newhall	7		
Fitzgerald not out	1		
Extras	16	Extras	2
TOTAL	105		34

Bowling	Overs	Maiden	Runs	Wickets	Overs	Maiden	Runs	Wickets
PHILADELPHIA	First Innings				Second Innings			
C.A. Newhall	53	26	45	6	18.1	8	24	4
Meade	51	28	44	3	18	13	8	3
FITZGERALD'S 12	First Innings				Second Innings			
Appleby	36.1	25	23	8	35.2	27	25	7
Grace	21	11	22	9	35	13	45	13
Rose	16	6	16	2				

England wins by 3 wickets.

When compared to the English, American Cricket provide a glimpse into the shortcomings as it still had a long way to go in terms of grounds, facilities, a central organization, clubs and players capabilities and we begin to see that take shape in the 1870s. These visits provided a good benchmark for American Cricket to improve upon and by 1884 we see progress in batting by Bob Newhall, Brockie and J.B. Thayer amongst others.[21] More clubs were being formed and grounds expanded, Belmont opened in 1874 and John. B. King would be amongst its' most famous members. The Halifax Cup was also started that year and it became one of the most recognized and premier tournaments from 1880 to 1926.

In the very first match the Philadelphia twelve beat the Canadians by an innings and 31 runs. The American Cricketer debuted on 28th June 1877 as a weekly magazine from May to November and monthly from November to May, with the editing committee headed by Dan Newhall and the magazine itself went thru changes and the last issue was printed in April of 1929. Along with the organization of clubs, the magazine provided a platform for news and happenings and on April 17 1878, the first National Convention of cricketers took place at the Penn Club in Philadelphia, thus ushering in a new era for cricket in America.[22] By September, this body was accepted and recognized enough to choose a team to face the Australians who were making their first trip to North America that year.

The Halifax Cup started with a letter from Capt. Wallace proposing a tournament between four teams: America vs. Canada / England vs. Canada / America vs. England / Halifax vs. All Comers. After the initial euphoria had died down, an 'American' team was chosen from the 'Philadelphia pool' as no other clubs submitted any names for inclusion, even though the news was widely circulated. The first match was played on 18th & 19th August, where Philadelphia emerged victorious over the Canadians and also over 'England' who were actually English Officers and this was played from 20, 21 & 22nd. The English Officers won against the Canadians and Halifax overcame the All Comers. The Americans brought home the inaugural silver trophy and in September of 1875, a return International tournament took place between Canada and the English Officers who were led again by Captain Wallace and Philadelphia again defeated the English by a score of 230 to 98 on a first inning basis.[23]

PHILADELPHIA XI. Winners of the International Tournament at HALIFAX in 1874.

Standing: William Welsh, Jr., (substitute), Edward Hopkinson, Farrand (*Umpire*), Daniel. S. Newhall (*Captain*), George Ashbridge, A.J.D. Dixon (*Scorer*), Robert. S. Newhall, Albert. A. Outerbridge (*Manager*), R. Nelson. Caldwell.
Second row, seated: R. Loper Baird, John. B. Large, Charles. A. Newhall, Richard Ashbridge.
Front row, on ground: Horace Magee, Francis. E. Brewster, Spencer Meade, William Hopkinson (substitute).

From 1880 to 1926 the silver cup became the premier Halifax Cup Tournament in Philadelphia and in its 47 year history; the cup was awarded 45 times, except for 1881 and 1918. The 1881 rules required the teams to play 10 games each and two each with the other five teams and as the teams did not fulfill the condition, the cup was not awarded that year. In 1918 there was no tournament held. The players with the best batting and bowling averages in the Halifax Cup were awarded the Childs Cup.[24] When the Nova Scotia Cricket Association was established in 1967 it took steps to introduce the Halifax competition again. John Marder's, 'The International Series, The Story of the United States versus Canada at Cricket,' describes in depth the rich American-Candaian cricket history.

PROGRAMME OF EVENTS
FOR THE
CENTENNIAL YEAR, JANUARY 1 TO DECEMBER 31, 1876.

THE CENTENNIAL EXHIBITION.
RECEPTION OF ARTICLES COMMENCES JANUARY 5.
RECEPTION OF ARTICLES ENDS APRIL 19.
UNOCCUPIED SPACE FORFEITED APRIL 26.
MAIN EXHIBITION OPENS MAY 10.
GRAND CEREMONIES ON EXHIBITION GROUNDS, JULY 4.
TRIALS OF HARVESTING MACHINES, JUNE AND JULY.
TRIALS OF STEAM-PLOWS AND TILLAGE IMPLEMENTS, SEPTEMBER
    AND OCTOBER.
EXHIBIT OF HORSES, MULES, AND ASSES, SEPTEMBER 1 TO SEP-
    TEMBER 15.
EXHIBIT OF HORNED CATTLE, SEPTEMBER 20 TO OCTOBER 5.
EXHIBIT OF SHEEP, SWINE, GOATS, AND DOGS, OCTOBER 10 TO
    OCTOBER 25.
EXHIBIT OF POULTRY, OCTOBER 28 TO NOVEMBER 10.
MAIN EXHIBITION CLOSES NOVEMBER 10.
EXHIBITS MUST BE REMOVED BY DECEMBER 31.

SOCIETY MEETINGS, PARADES, REGATTAS, ETC.
KNIGHTS TEMPLAR (MASONS), ANNUAL CONCLAVE, MAY 30.
KNIGHTS TEMPLAR (MASONS), GRAND PARADE, JUNE 1.
ORDER OF GOOD TEMPLARS, SPECIAL GATHERING, JUNE 13.
INTERNATIONAL REGATTA (NEW YORK HARBOR), JUNE 22.
YACHT REGATTA, DELAWARE RIVER, IN JUNE.
SONS OF TEMPERANCE, SPECIAL GATHERING, JUNE.
INTERNATIONAL SERIES OF CRICKET MATCHES, JUNE AND SEP-
    TEMBER.
CONGRESS OF AUTHORS IN INDEPENDENCE HALL, JULY 2.
PARADE OF IRISH SOCIETIES (DEDICATION OF FOUNTAIN), JULY 4.
PARADE OF MILITARY ORGANIZATIONS, JULY 4.
UNITED AMERICAN MECHANICS, PARADE, JULY 8.
KNIGHTS OF PYTHIAS, PARADE, AUGUST 22.
INTERNATIONAL ROWING REGATTA, AUGUST 20 TO SEPTEMBER 15.
INTERNATIONAL RIFLE MATCHES, IN SEPTEMBER.
INTERNATIONAL MEDICAL CONGRESS, SEPTEMBER 4.
INDEPENDENT ORDER OF ODD-FELLOWS, PARADE, SEPTEMBER 20.

A very interesting article from Macmillan's Magazine, 'Americans at Play,' talks about a cricket trip to America during the Centennial year in 1876 by a group of, *"absolutely useless, except to make up the number, and might without undue harshness be fairly described lay-figures."* The other four or five cricketers, who made up the team had been in *public school or college elevens* and were decent 'cricketers.' This candid article by one of the, shall we say, college cricketer, puts the touring English amateurs side in an unflattering perspective. Unfortunately the name of the contributor is not mentioned, nor was I, or the MCC Library at Lord's, able to find further information on this rag tag team.

The trip was organized with an aim to take in the sights of the 100 year celebrations and play three one day matches on the Germantown grounds against the three leading Philadelphia clubs which were arranged for them. With a confessed ignorance to the caliber of the Philadelphia teams and not having stepped on a cricket pitch for more than two years, they were relying on their trump card, Mr. Powys, the best amateur bowler in England to see them thru. At the last minute their ace fell ill and had to continue without him, *"In such plight, then, we started for the stronghold of American cricket."*[25] Once in Philadelphia, some of them went to the ground a day early to practice and noticing the well-worn pitch and a glance at the score book confirmed their worst fears, *"A Canadian XI ...had been here within the week to be routed with utter ignominy."*[26] Retiring for the night with a sense of trepidation and guilt, they faced their opponents the next day, but were surprise to put up a respectable 80 or so, *despite the procession from the pavilion to the wicket and back* by the lay-figures. The home team put up a little over two hundred runs losing most of their wickets at the end of days play, presumably ending in a draw. The lay-figures were substituted in the other two matches and they fared better there, thus closing the chapter on this hastily arranged trip, *"with but the vaguest notion as to the quality of Philadelphia Cricket."*[27]

The Australian cricket team at the Niagara Falls, 1878. Standing from left: H.F. Boyle, W. Murdoch, W.C.V. Gibbs (assistant-manager), Tom Garrett, D.W. Gregory (Captain), T. Horan, Frank E. Allan, G.H. Bailey.
Seated L to R: F.R. Spofforth, J. Conway (Manager), Alec Bannerman, J.M. Blackham.
Courtesy: Mitchell Library, State Library of NSW, Australia.

In 1878, the Australians set about making their maiden first class cricket tour to England by reciprocating an earlier visit made by the English during the previous year. The team sailed from Sydney to San Francisco and across the country to New York by train (I am sure the likes of Jesse James were on their mind) and from New York, they set sail for Liverpool. On finishing their successful English tour, the Australians left England aboard the *City of Richmond* on 18th September, and arrived in New York ten days later. They encountered the big seas of the Atlantic on the fourth day and were at the mercy of the Atlantic gale as the couplings on the shaft in the engine room had given away and they had to endure the fierce gale and seas for six hours, during which, young C. Bannerman inquired *"if they were getting the boats out!"* Once in New York, they had time to take in some sights, amongst them was the unfinished, *'monster suspension bridge'* in Brooklyn which would be completed in 1883. On October 1st & 2nd, they played against a New York eighteen at Hoboken and defeated them by 5 wickets before moving on to Philadelphia. Boyle and Allan were the only two players to go in double digits 19 and 13 respectively and the novel feature of the game was the introduction of baseball throwing, (as they called it) it was a quick sling, straight on the ground delivery by J. E. Sprague, and it reminded the Australians of the old style of bowling in New South Wales known as the 'Sydney Grubber.'[28]

This would be the first time that the Philadelphians were going to play a visiting team on equal terms – eleven men, and that too at a time when the Australians had defeated the English by nine wickets in under 5 hours at Lord's, a two innings match! Grace's strong MCC team was bowled out for a paltry 33 with a young Spofforth taking 6 wickets for 3 runs, including a hat trick! The Australians did not fare any better though scoring only 41 and if one thought things could not get any worse for M.C.C, it did, they added *only* 19 in the second innings, leaving the Australians 12 to win which they accomplished but not before losing Charles Bannerman. A most unusual and enthralling match for the record books.

Now they were ready to spread terror in the Philly camp, with the 'Demon' Spofforth opening the bowling. The teams had gathered on the 3rd 4th and 5th October at Nicetown grounds and on the last day when it looked like the *'cocky young Americans would beat the foreigners at the own game'* the crowds has swelled to 15,000 according to the American Cricketer.[29] Before the match would be over there was drama as this match was subjected to disputes and walk-offs before it was declared a draw.

Bob Newhall was the highest scorer with 84 on either team and Philadelphia ended their first innings total with a healthy 196. On the Australian side, Bannerman was the high scorer with 46 and their innings ended at 150 thus giving the home team – yes, the Philadelphians, a lead of 46 runs! Anticipation was running high on the last day and some of the local employers were forced to declare half day, as most of the employees who were keeping up with the proceedings of the match were not going to miss the exciting finale. The Australians had changed their fielding strategy for the second innings as the fielders were near the boundary, as opposed to the close field setting demonstrated in the first innings. The field was set to tempt the batsmen into hitting and even a seasoned player like Bob, the champion of the previous inning, succumbed to it. Spofforth's first delivery and Bob hit him high, Boyle who was on the boundary reached over to make a one hand catch! [30] As we still see today, a collapse always happens when the top orders is dismissed cheaply and here things took a turn for the worse as the Australians walked off the field when Dan, who missed a drive as he stepped out to hit and appeared to get back into the crease, was not declared stumped out by the umpire.

The antipodeans had already received a check for $2,500 in the morning towards the gate receipt, and now it was put on hold. It was explained to Captain Gregory that, they would not receive the money if they did not take to the field and also, an omnibus was arranged at the back of the ground to quietly whisk them away from the ground to avoid being lynched by the public, who had paid 25 cent admission fee. The Nottingham and Yorkshire dialects were getting vocal in their criticism as the game was further protracted and were close to over running the grounds, had the Australians not taken to the field again.[31] The Philadelphians could not capitalize on the break in action to regroup, and lost wickets cheaply to end the innings at only 53. The first innings results would have been the same, had it not been for Bob's 84 runs.

As the two captain's had previously decided to end the game every day at 5 p.m., there was less than an hour's play left in which the Australians were set a target of 100 runs. According to William B. Morgan whose eyewitness account is the basis of Lester's work, [32] recalls, how the match now becomes exciting in the last hour. Alec Bannerman was hit on both the elbows by rising deliveries from Charley Newhall and at one point the two umpires were massaging his elbows, but despite the personal attention, he retired hurt without scoring.[33] Charley then bowled Charles Bannerman with a yorker and next to go was Spofforth, his stump somersaulting away from him. I am sure as a bowler he did not like to see that spectacle. The eyewitness account goes on to state that Murdoch was the next one to go, bowled by another yorker from Charley, while the 2nd innings score shows him at 'zero' not out when play was stopped.[34] Charley ended up taking 3 wickets (not 4 as Morgan states) and the Australian innings ended at 56 for 4 in 35 overs, who knows, the outcome may very well have been in Philadelphians favor, had the game not been stopped for about an hour. A letter of apology sent later by the Australians ironed out whatever ill will that might have arisen. The scores of the 1st exciting and marginally controversial Australian visit to Philadelphia are given below:

Match played at Germantown Cricket Club Grounds at Nicetown on October 3rd, 4th & 5th 1878. Australian XI vs. Philadelphia XI.

PHILADELPHIA

First Innings	Runs	Second Innings	Runs
John. Hargrave c & b Spofforth	10	st. Blackham b Spofforth	7
F.E. Brewster c Murdoch b Allan	15	c & b Allan	0
C. A. Newhall b Allan	3	lbw b Spofforth	5
R.S. Newhall b Allan	84	c Bailey b Spofforth	0
G. M. Newhall c Spofforth b Horan	13	c Gregory b Allan	2
R.N. Caldwell st. Blackham b Boyle	22	b Allan	8
E. Hopkinson c Gregory b Bailey	0	c Bailey b Spofforth	5
D.S. Newhall not out	31	c Boyle b Spofforth	7
T. Hargrave b Allan	1	st. Blackham b Allan	9
E.T. Comfort b Allan	3	b Allan	4
S. Meade b Allan	0	not out	0
Extras	14	Extras	6
TOTAL	196	TOTAL	53

AUSTRALIA

First Innings	Runs	Second Innings	Runs
C. Bannerman c G Newhall b Meade	0	b C. Newhall	27
A. Bannerman c G Newhall b C Newhall	46	retired hurt	0
T. Horan run out	5	c R. Newhall b Meade	0
F. Spofforth c R Newhall b C Newhall	4	b C. Newhall	4
D.W. Gregory b C. Newhall	0		
W.L. Murdoch b D. Newhall	37	not out	0
G.H. Bailey c Meade b C Newhall	0	b C. Newhall	24
J. M. Blackham b D Newhall	20	not out	0
T.W. Garrett b C. Newhall	1		
H.F. Boyle c T. Hargrave b D. Newhall	30		
F.E. Allan not out	4		
Extras	3	Extras	1
TOTAL	150	TOTAL	56

187

Bowling	Overs	Maiden	Runs	Wickets	Overs	Maiden	Runs	Wickets
PHILADELPHIA	First Innings				Second Innings			
C.A. Newhall	52	28	67	5	18	9	29	3
S. Meade	26	12	36	1	7	4	16	1
D.S. Newhall	26.1	14	34	3	10	5	10	0
E.T. Comfort	3	0	7	0				
R.N. Caldwell	2	0	3	0				
AUSTRALIA	First Innings				Second Innings			
Spofforth	24	8	51	1	18.3	7	24	5
Allan	20	4	27	6	18	6	23	5
Boyle	19	6	39	1				
Garrett	13	5	26	0				
Horan	10	2	24	1				
Murdoch	10	2	10	0				
Bailey	4	1	5	1				

Match ended in a Draw. This was a 4 ball per over match and the boundary yielded 3 runs.

Before heading to California, they played two matches at Toronto (8th & 9th) and Montreal (10th & 11th) and one in St Louis against the nineteen of the Peninsular Cricket Club on the 14th and 15th October, where they won by an innings and 66 runs.[35] The last leg of the journey brought them to San Francisco where they played the twenty-two of California on October 24th, 25th & 26th at the Recreation Grounds. On winning the toss, they elected to bat and scored 302 in 134.1 overs (4 balls per over) in their first innings with a generous helping of 42 extras. In reply to this overwhelming score, the home team managed a measly 33 plus an *extra* 30, thanks to the Australians who were no less generous. The follow on brought about a respectable 105 (only 10 extras) but still fell short by 134 runs. Before departing for home after an eight month tour, a drawn match was played with mixed players from both sides on the 26th between Gregory's XI and Boyles XI. The Australians left San Francisco on 28 October and reached Sydney on November 25th. This impetus no doubt provided experience and incentive for the cricketers to continue for years to come and *The American Cricketer* reported of a Thanksgiving Day match between the Occident and the San Francisco Cricket Club within a week of their departure.

"The Australian Cricketers have followed up their success in England by some excellent play in America,"[36] wrote the *Inangahua Times* of the second Australian visit to America in 1882. Fresh from their maiden victory over the English at the Oval, later considered a test match *and* the birth of the *'ashes'* [37] the antipodeans played eighteen of New York on October 9th & 10th at the Hoboken grounds which was witnessed by a large turnout. The visitors easily won the game with Spofforth taking 10 wickets for only 12 runs and 7 for 25 in the second innings, though a reporter said, *"Spofforth's bowling, although only against moderate cricketers was marvelous."* This was the same bowler who, earlier in the summer had taken 7 for 46 in the first and 7 for 44 in the second innings when England needed only 85 to win.[38] Philadelphia was the next stop on October 11,12 & 13 at Nicetown for Murdoch's Australians who won by 9 wickets. Except for four new faces, these were the same players who had visited America the first time in 1878. The Americans who faced them with eleven players during their first visit now took to the field with eighteen and only the three Newhalls and Tom Hargrave, had played against them earlier.[39] On the last day, the Australians required 54 to win in 43 minutes in their second innings, which they achieved with 6 minutes to spare!

Just as the Canadian did some soul searching after their loss against the Australians, this defeat, which was worse off when compared to the first visit based on numbers, (in '78, eleven Philadelphians set a target of 100 for the Australians in their second innings and this time the target was only 53 set by eighteen) it was agreed that they needed proper batsmen, followed by a reliable wicket-keeper and finally, slow/spin bowlers and the principal requirement – new blood in the form of youth.

G.E. Palmer, H.F. Boyle, W.L. Murdoch, P.S. M'Donnell, F.R. Spofforth, T. Horan, S.P. Jones.
C.W. Beal, G. Giffen, A.C. Bannerman, T.W. Garrett, H.H. Massie, G.T. Bonner.
The 1882 Australians.

1879 was a busy year for cricket in Philadelphia as they were visited by three over-seas teams beginning in May (a very early start to the season), with Lord Harris's team en route home from a summer of cricket in Australia/New Zealand in 1878/79, the Irishmen gracing the American shores for the first time in September, and Richard Daft's Professional XI soon followed in quick succession. Lord Harris's team was scheduled to play in Philadelphia on May 6th & 7th but had to be postponed to 7th & 8th as a telegram was received by Mr. J.T. Soutter, Vice President of the Cricketer's Association of the United States saying they were going to be delayed from San Francisco.[40] It was a one sided affair at St. George Cricket Club at Hoboken where the match was held and, *"in one inning they beat the score of their opponents for two innings,"* as was so vividly described by the *New York Times* of May 9th. The combined strength of Philadelphia and New York could not hold off the opponents who were strong even though they were not professionals, by putting up a total of 253, (A.P. Lucas missed scoring a century by 2 runs) while the American XI could only muster 84 and 55 runs. The visitors were dined at Delmonico's after the match and left for England the next day.[41]

Richard Daft's professionals XII that toured Canada and America after the 1879 English season, were a strong contingent from Yorkshire and Nottinghamshire and played a total of twelve matches, none of which they lost. Daft observed that the American bowlers *"were superior, as a rule, to the batsmen."*[42] One match was played against a team comprising of all baseball players on 15th October at Brooklyn and the highest scorer was George Wright, who in the first innings scored 20, but joined the rest of the seventeen in scoring single digit in the second innings, and losing the game by an innings and 18 runs. They scored a decent 62 runs in the first innings, but managed only 27 in the second, and the fall of wickets kept up with the runs which fell at a steady clip, 1-1, 2-2, 3-4, 4-5, 5-6, 6-6, 7-8, 8-8, 9-8, 10-8, 11-13, 12-14, 13-16, 14-20, 15-25, 16-25, 17-27. The bowling honors also went to George who took 9 wickets for 38 runs in 24 overs.[43]

Lillywhite's Cricketers' Annual of 1880 contradicts the above scores and match information which was referenced from Arthur Haygarth's Cricket Scores and Biographies Vol. 16, and also from *'The American Cricketer.'* The Lillywhite Annual lists this as a <u>one inning match</u> played on October 16, 17 with the English XI scoring 109 and the eighteen Baseballers' scoring 62, giving the English a win by 47 runs.[44] According to Lillywhite, they played cricket against eighteen baseball players and a game of baseball the next day against the Providence Champion Nine. *"They gave us a pitcher and catcher to equalize matters at their own sport, but we were as much aboard at our old friend rounders revised and amplified as they were at Cricket."*[45] The Providence Grays baseball team won the National League pennant in 1879 and George Wright was their shortstop.[46] There were three future Hall of Famers in the Baseball Eighteen, George Wright, Jim O'Rourke and John M. Ward.

Daft's professionals comprised of, Arthur Shrewsbury, Alfred Shaw, John Selby, William Oscroft, William Barnes and Frederick Morley from Notts and Yorkshire was represented by 'Tom' Emmett, George Ulyett, Ephraim Lockwood, George Pinder and William Bates.[47] Alfred Shaw, a slow medium bowler was the highest wicket taker with 178 for 426 runs, Daft called him the 'Emperor of Bowlers', who was unplayable on 'sticky' wickets.[48] They were met with little resistance save for one worthy foemen and most of the matches ended in their favor by more than an innings. They left Liverpool on August 28th and on September 24th, they entered Detroit after concluding their engagement in Canada and for the next three days, they played against the eighteen of Peninsular Club. Rain on the third day saved the Peninsular from an inevitable innings defeat as they managed only 59 in reply to the first inning total of 191 and they were down by a wicket for 5 runs when the rain stopped play.[49] The New York Central Railway brought them from Niagara to Syracuse to play against a twenty-two of Central New York, on September 31st and October 1st, a one sided affair as, *"they all showed the propensity for cross-hitting, so common to baseball players,"*[50] in other words, they were swinging at every ball.

The match against the twenty-two of New York at Staten Island on October 3, 4 & 6 also ended in an easy win for the English by an innings and 27 runs. At Philadelphia they were expecting a better adversary but the batting of the fifteen did not meet their expectations. The match was played on the Germantown grounds on the 10, 11 & 13, and again the English won easily by 145 runs, the only double figures in the second innings of the Philadelphia fifteen came from the extras – 16! The visitors made up for the lost revenue at other matches as the 3 day crowd here was estimated at 25,000. The match against Young America on October 18th & 20th was the only one played on equal terms – 11 a side, but the outcome was worse as the English won by an innings and 60 runs. The last match against the twenty-two Merion Cricket Club fared no better but the English were robbed of another certain victory due to rain, resulting in a draw. The next morning, October 25th, they departed for New York with the hope that, *their visit will have the effect of encouraging cricket in a marked degree.*[51]

Richard Daft's 1879 English Cricketers
G. Pinder, W. Barnes, E. Lockwood, J.P. Ford Esq., R. Daft (Capt.), Capt. Holden, J. Selby
A. Shrewsbury, G. Ulyett, A. Shaw, (Hon. Sec. Notts C.C.) W. Oscroft
T. Emmett, W. Bates, F. Morley.

The details for Alfred Shaw's 30 match tour to America, Australia and New Zealand in 1881-82 are hard to come by, probably because the tour was privately arranged, and in all, 5 matches were played in America, 18 in Australia and 7 in New Zealand.[52] The players, besides Shaw were, R.G. Barlow, R. Pilling, W. Bates, W. Scotton, T. Emmett, J. Selby, James Lillywhite, W. Midwinter, A. Shrewsbury, E. Peate and G. Ulyett. Their highest score on the tour was against the 22 of San Francisco – no surprise there – 313 for the loss of two wickets, and here Ulyett scored 167 not out.[53]

The first match was played at Philadelphia on October 1, 2 & 3 with the Philadelphia XII scoring 126 and 47, and losing the match by an innings and 104 runs, though the eighteen of St. George's Club managed a draw on October 5, 6 & 7 which was played at New York. The English Eleven against the eighteen of America resulted in a win for the English by 32 runs in the match played at Milltown on October 7, 8 & 10. The next match at St. Louis is interesting for the fact that no reason is given as to why the twenty-two of St. Louis did not go in to bat. The English scored 5 for 144 including 3 byes, but no further detail are given and this was to be a two day match played on 12th & 13th. The statement or phrase, *the Twenty-two did not go in* implies a situation or an altercation that may have arisen which prevented the home team from taking the field, or maybe – it just rained out. The Recreation Grounds in San Francisco hosted the last match of Shaw's XI on October 20 and 21, which was officially called a draw, but should have been incomplete as the scores were one sided. Lillywhite did not play in the first innings where the English only put up 93 and the 22 of San Francisco scored only 44 runs. It was here in the second innings that the English scored 313 for two, their highest score, with Ulyett remaining not out at 167.[54]

An 'All Ireland Eleven' kicked off their maiden North America tour arriving aboard the 'Algeria' at New York City on September 9th with an assortment of about 80 *portmanteaus of various sizes and ages*, [55] to play a total of 13 matches in the United States and Canada. To record the successful outing, the team wished that a book be published which resulted in, *'The Irish Cricketers in the United States, 1879, by One of Them.'* (Henry Brougham). The bulk of the side was drawn from members of the famous Phoenix Club in Dublin, except for Brougham, who played at Oxford, England. Miller and David Trotter had earlier played against the Boston and Athletic Baseball eighteen when they had visited Dublin in 1874, a trip that had been organized by Harry Wright.

The team comprised of:

Captain - Nathaniel 'Nat' Hone.
William Hone, captain's brother – the 'General'. (Accompanied by his wife)
Charlie Barrington - the Crasher.
Young William Hone
Geoffrey Hone
Brother of the Lord Mayor of Dublin, Sir George Colhurst, surnamed Jackie.
David Trotter – the baby.
Hamilton.
Henry Brougham.
Nunn.
Dr. Arthur R.F. Exham.
Miller.
Casey.
Hugh Gore.

An uneventful voyage which initially started with sea sickness or as they called it, *"land sickness at sea,"* was soon forgotten and with appetites returning, attention was diverted to amusements to speed up time. Shuffleboard, quoits, spoiled five (an old Irish game) and of course cricket games were indulged in, and also gambling. The ships' log was the object of money changing hands, as bets were placed on the distance traversed by the ship in a 24 hour period from noon to noon and thirty miles are taken as margin in which the ship is likely to have run. The basic premise was, if the ship has travelled 300 miles, then

30 miles from 285 to 315 would be put up for auction. If the maximum was exceeded, the person buying the highest number wins and if the ship travelled less than the minimum, the buyer of the lowest number took the prize. Numbers were picked from the min/max and the money collected went towards the prize money.[56]

"All the men were thin and wore long moustachios and all the horses were thin and wore long tails." This is the first impression the Irish had of Americans, which changed with their advent further on. The initial impressions were innocent and straight forward observations which changed quickly. When they came across, as they put it, *'fine looking niggers,'* the Irish, call them naive, simpletons or ignorant, were afraid their dark color might rub off when they served food to them! It was a genuine concern initially because for a majority of them, this would be their first exposure to people from the African continent, but that feeling soon went away.

Before their first American debut match, the visitors set out in a convoy of carriages to check out the cricket grounds at Hoboken and later on dined at Martinelli's and afterwards headed to Niblo's Garden's, where the 'Pinafore' was being performed. This was the same Niblo's, where the daredevil acrobatic team of Hanlon brothers performed, and one of them, William Hanlon, had submitted a patent for an improved wicket design not too long ago in 1861. The following day some of the players were interviewed by the *New York Herald*.

The first match was approached with a little apprehension, as they feared defeat in their first match and its' moral consequences. Nat rejected St. George's wish for eighteen men on their team and they played against their XI. Their fears were soon misplaced, for they easily overcame Mr. Soutter's XI. The match umpire for St. George was none other than George Newhall, captain of the Philadelphia XI, the Irish felt he was spying on them and learning their strength and weaknesses! A sizeable crowd of about four hundred had shown up to witness the Irishmen and some were friends from 'Algeria.' A large tent had been pitched to accommodate 250 ladies and their admission was free. Arrangements were also made for four-in-hand, drags and carriages, so the occupants could watch the match without leaving their mode of transport.[57] The Irish scored 184 runs with 52 being contributed by the General, St George replied with 25 in the first innings and 35 in the second innings.

The next match was at Syracuse, which they reached by train at night and the local club delegation was there to take them to Globe Hotel where the team ordered dinner as they were famished. The servants had a little fun at their expense as the visitors had ordered dinner instead of asking for supper. They were patted on the shoulder encouragingly and were told 'supper' would be 'right up.' Young William was easily exasperated, they only laughed and as the author puts it, *"they probably thought what strange savages we were."*[58] Next morning they went for a little sightseeing in their horse drawn buggies and the ride was anything but smooth as the only level surface was the tram tracks and the railway lines. The match against the 'Eighteen of Central New York' did not begin till noon at Newell Park and on winning the toss, Nat put them to bat and Hamilton and Exham promptly sent them back to the 'tents', the score was 16 runs and 15 wickets down! (The New

Yorkers were three men short) "*Och Hone! – The Central New York cricketers fairly slaughtered by the Gentlemen of Ireland,*" read the *New York Daily Courier* of September 17th. The bowling and fielding on the other hand by the 'eighteen' was commendable as the team included several regular baseball players who restricted the Irish XI to a first inning total of only 57 runs, but the Central New Yorkers were unable to reach even the small total of 41, which left the Irish winning the match with an innings and 3 runs to spare. Hitting to the boundary fetched three runs as per the agreement between the two captains.

It was decide that another match should be played the next day and an interesting play on words by the reporter made the Irish look bad. The *New York Herald* reported, "*The Irish gentlemen did not arrive on the ground until a late hour. They had been dining at Major Davis's the night before.*" Henry Brougham agrees that was the case, but it was unfair of the reporter to *put the two statements in such close proximity.*[59] The match was a repeat performance of the previous day but with higher scores – 154 by the Irish in reply to 50 by the eighteen. "*The Irish Cricketers – They gave the Americans what Paddy gave the drum – A bad beating,*" *New York Daily Courier*, September 18th.

The Irish were observing the American curiosity and traits at work, as the author puts it, "*They had been imbued with the American 'go-ahead' principle.*" There was thirst for knowledge, to understand new things and improve upon the existing, also, asking questions to quell their curiosity and not take anything at face value. The visitors drew crowds where they went and the local Irish were not convinced that the visitors were from Ireland as their names were un-Irish. There were too many Hones and not one was O'hone, but after interacting and hearing them talk they were convinced as to their Irish origins. One of the spectators wanted to see their cricket boots and see if there were any improvements he could make and adapt (the modification to the bat and stump design comes to mind).

Pavilion Hotel was their next abode in Staten Island where they encountered the eighteen of the Staten Island Cricket Club and this time the Irish were playing with XII members. On winning the toss, the SICC elected to bat but only managed 34 runs as it may have been the reputation of Hamilton and Exham, that had preceded them after the Syracuse outing. They recovered in the second innings to make 102 runs surpassing their Irish total by just one run, thus putting the Irish to bat again to score 2 runs for victory, but they continued playing for the spectators and the runs remained unrecorded. To the spectators, surpassing the Irish score was more akin to winning than savings an innings defeat, none the less, they were the first team to make the Irish bat again.

It wasn't all games for the visitors as many evenings were spent dancing in the company of pretty maidens and at times there was jealousy shown towards Tommy Turbett's choice, as she was a tall, lithe young lady. Boys being boys, they fought over one pretty lass in particular as she was light and graceful in her movements. They were learning the 'Hop', 'Boston', 'German', and the Hop ended with the 'Virginia reel' which is the American for 'Sir Roger.' "*It was a very pleasant evening: and, though we had to blame it for sowing the seeds of a gloom which possessed many of us on leaving the Island, still the sovereign antidote against the wounds inflicted by one lady was never far away – the presence of another."[60]*

INTERNATIONAL MATCHES. 1879.
NICETOWN GROUND.

IRISH GENTLEMEN ELEVEN,
Thursday, Friday & Saturday, Sept. 25, 26 & 27.

ENGLISH PROFESSIONAL ELEVEN,
Friday, Saturday & Monday, Oct. 10, 11 & 13.

Admit One. **SEASON TICKET.** Five Dollars.

Section **B.** *No.* **73**

The fifteen of United New York were pitted against 'the Knights of the Willow,' as the *Herald* so appositely described them. They went in to bat first but managed only 119 runs and were it not for Nat's 34 and Jeff's 31, the total could have been any two numbers. At stumps, the 'fifteen' had scored 40 runs for the loss of 9 wickets. The ladies from the dance were spotted at the games and our boys were able to pick them out from the crowd and another fun evening awaited them. A plan of attack was put in place for the second day, first, to get the remaining tail-enders out, second, to put up a decent total and finish their innings (197) and lastly to bowl out the New Yorker's again. Only half an hour was left to accomplish the last task which they had no difficulty in doing so. As Casey had positioned himself near the ladies section and prevented any ball from falling in their enclosure, he was christened, 'Knight of the Willow' by the *Herald*. At Philadelphia, Casey was shedding himself of his garments, his green tie finding a new delicate neck, his sash was wrapped around the shoulders of another and one lady was the recipient of his cap though owing to the cool air he did not part from his Phoenix club coat.

It was interesting to note that, besides being excellent dance partners; a sizeable number of ladies were present at the Philadelphia match and not just as pretty faces in the grand stand. Match cards were given with the names printed and the ladies came prepared with pencils to record each ball of the match, and they did. Many of them kept complete analysis which showed their understanding of the proceedings and were able to converse on equal terms. This, the visitors found refreshing and hoped that someday Philadelphia would occupy the highest place in the cricketing world and compete on equal footing with the English.

The Germantown grounds proved fatal and the Irish were bundled out for 58 after electing to bat. At the fall of every wicket, a carrier pigeon was sent out of the scoring tent carrying the good news for Philadelphia. Their main folly was their habit of playing on back foot as they were accustomed to, on the wet Irish soil. In reply at stumps, Philadelphia had scored 115 runs and the following day brought a bigger crowd in anticipation of a victory. Philadelphia ended their inning at 149 and no sooner had the Irish started, their wickets began to fall, and at lunch they were down 6 wickets for 26 runs and at the end, the combined total of two innings was 9 short of the Philadelphia first inning score – a first decisive victory for the home team. The papers were eloquent in their praise of the Irish, *"Just as elsewhere they bore success modestly, here they bore defeat gracefully. It would have been no disgrace for our team to have been beaten by a picked team of All Ireland. It was a great honour to beat them."*[61]

A return match was to be played the next day and the play promptly started at 11 am. The Irish had learnt their lesson from the previous two days and improved on their bowling accordingly by delivering short pitched balls. This proved effective and as the ground was 'hard as iron' and the Philadelphians did not feel inclined to play forward strokes. There was also a chance of the ball bouncing up to the face, nor did they want to leave the safety of the crease. The visitors were given a target of 108 runs and time was short. They started off well with the opening pair of Geoffrey and Miller putting in double figures, but then, Nat and Brougham were out for a duck. It looked bleak till Casey stepped onto the crease and runs started coming easily again.

The excitement was building around the grounds as the regulation time for ending the match at 5 o'clock was fast approaching. They had just crossed 100 and 8 more runs were required in about 5 minutes, the excitement was definitely palpable. 2 more were added and 105 runs appeared on the scoreboard at which point, Hamilton lofted one to deep long on. There was dead silence, everyone held their breath as the ball raced back towards the ground so too did the fielder who fell forward and rolled with the ball in his hands. *"How's that?"* was the appeal and all appeared tense as they waited for the verdict, which went against the fielder. This of course would be debated for days to come, but when two runs were left to score, the stumps were drawn. This was more than the spectators could bear at the undecided results and a groan could be heard, *"Go on! Finish! was shouted all around the ground."*[62]

The two captains agreed and play was resumed with the Irish finishing at 122 and ending up victorious. This was the most exciting match of the tour and in Philadelphia they had found a worthy opponent. Two days later, they were playing fifteen Americans at Merion where the ladies associated with the club were to present a silver cup to the highest scorer of his side. The Irish scored 138 in reply to Merion's 81 and in their second innings the Merion boys score 130 but still lost the match by 97 runs. The last Merion wicket fell with a minute to spare and they could have easily wasted time to take the match to a draw but the sportsmanship spirit was alive and well and they did not stoop to it. The sliver cup went to Trotter for the Irish and Law for the Americans.

Briefly, the scores are as follows:

1. September 12th & 13th defeated St. George's eleven at Hoboken, N.J. in one innings with 124 runs to spare.
2. September 16th & 17th defeated "Eighteen of Central New York" at Syracuse, N.Y. This was taken as two defeats for the Syracuse team as they were defeated by an innings and 3 runs in the first match and again by 104 runs the next day.
3. September 19th & 20th defeated Staten Island's eighteen at Staten Island, N.Y. with 10 wickets to spare.
4. September 22nd & 23rd defeated Fifteen of United New York at Hoboken by 212 runs.
5. September 25th & 26th lost to American eleven at Philadelphia by an innings and 9 runs.
6. September 27th defeated the American eleven at Philadelphia, 108 to 122.
7. September 30th & October 1st defeated the Merion fifteen at Ardmore, PA. by 97 runs.
8. October 22nd & 23rd defeated the Peninsular eleven at Detroit, Michigan in one innings with 107 runs to spare.

By the early 1880s, sixty two percent of the players in the National Baseball League were of Irish or German descent as this was one quick way of gaining acceptance and respect in their newly adopted society. The Irish professionals found fame and fortune more so in baseball then other sports, as by the turn of the century most of the teams had an Irish captain, Kelly in Brooklyn, Collins in Boston, Gleason in Detroit and Delehanty in Philadelphia to name a few. As expected, a lot of Irish clubs were set up due to the interest in cricket and baseball, 'Shamrock' being *the* most popular name for a club in the New England area (Boston, Holyoke and Woburn in Massachusetts, Concord in New Hampshire and Galt in Ontario). Then there was the 'Fenian' in Augusta and New Orleans and 'Emerald' in Savannah, Georgia.[63]

When the Irish visited Philadelphia for the second time in 1888, it was their third meeting (they had played against Philadelphia on their home turf in 1884) with the Philadelphians at Nicetown on September 20, 21 and 22nd where they lost by a narrow margin of 7 runs and again by 39 during the next match played on 27, 28 & 29th.[64]

Before playing Philadelphia, the Irish paid a visit to St. Paul's School in New Hampshire to play against the school boys as they were making a name for themselves, no other international team had visited them before or after. On Monday September 17th, the school was gearing up for the big match against the visiting Irish Cricketers and the match commenced at 11 a.m. On winning the toss the school elected to bat and one of the players, Mr. Dole, thinking he was playing the 'national game' made a sacrifice hit on his first ball, and was run out, the school managed a modest total of 88 runs. The Irish went in to bat after lunch and put up a total of 109. JW Hynes was the high scorer with 41 including a few boundaries.

This time a boundary fetched 4 runs and unlike their maiden visit which yielded just 3 runs. J Weldon was the only one out for a 'duck', or as they called it 'goose egg.' The school called them the most "gentlemanly and jolly cricketers."[65] Next stop, Boston.

I was wondering as to how the Irish ended up in New Hampshire to play against St. Paul's. No other International team had done that and then I found out that during their first tour in 1879 one of the players on St. George's team was Mr. P.J. Condin, a graduate of the school, which would explain their interest in taking up the lads at SPS.[66]

"Imagine a matchless square lawn of velvety grass upon which the picked champions of the two countries have met to defend the dignity of their national cricket. Around this arena are congregated several thousand of eager, enthusiastic spectators, comprising people from almost every walk and rank of life, from the native-born millionaire on his perfectly appointed coach to the humble British artisan who has sacrificed a day's wages in order to witness his favorite game."[67] Charles Blancke in writing for Harper's Weekly espouses the pleasure and benefits of witnessing an 'International Cricket Match' during the visit by the Gentlemen of Ireland on their third tour to America in 1892.

In 1889 when Philadelphia toured England for the 2nd time, they played against Ireland in Dublin, their 4th engagement, on July 2nd and 3rd which resulted in a draw and so did the follow up match on July 4th & 5th. On average, the matches generally have been in Philadelphia's favor so far, but during the 3rd Irish visit to America, "the last meeting at Manheim, Philadelphia was compelled to lower her colors to the doughty willow-wielders from over the seas."[68] A certain Mr. Whitney commenting on Philadelphia's play writes to Harpers Weekly, which was re-produced in the American Cricketer, "the Gentlemen of Philadelphia played like duffers last year against Lord Hawke's second-rate team, and they again played like duffers lately against the Irishmen." He goes on to point out that the team should have been selected at least a month in advance to give them a chance to practice together, the result, lots of dropped catches unworthy of a team, "purporting to represent the native amateur strength of our country." Another one of the numerous reasons why cricket did not progress to a higher standard and a recurring theme was the time taken to finish a match. Another astute observation was, "when cricketers are chosen for their ability rather than for their pedigree, Philadelphian cricket will be in a healthier condition than it is today." The American Cricketer responded to the criticism stating that Lord Hawkes team was not second rate and they did not see an advantage in selecting a team in advance when they play together all summer long. The first match against Philadelphia was played on September 23, 24, 26 & 27th which the Irish won by 127 runs and the second was played on September 30th, October 1st & 3rd and was won by Philadelphia by a narrow margin of 3 runs.[69]

The Irish would be making their last tour to Philadelphia under the captaincy of F.H. Browning in 1909; he was ambushed and killed in Dublin by the Sinn Fein along with four others who were returning from a route march by the Veterans' Corps of the General Reserve in 1915. At the time, he was the president of the Irish Rugby Football Union.[70] The Irish arrived in Canada playing two matches there on the 5th and 7th September against Ottawa and

Ontario, and then moving down to play against the All New York team on 11th September and against Baltimore on the 14th. The Irish lost against the Gentlemen of Philadelphia by an innings and 168 runs with King taking 10 wickets for 53 runs in the first innings! The match was played on September 17, 18 and 19 and they drew against the Philadelphia Colts in their next match. Their second and last match against the GOP also ended in a loss by an innings and 66 runs, thus bringing to a close a chapter on the Irish visits to North America.

A SECTION OF THE GRAND STAND.

...ND IN AMERICA AT THE MANHEIM CRICKET-GROUNDS, PHILADELPHIA—FROM PHOTOGRAPHS BY RAU.—[SEE PAGE 991.]

Section showing the spectators at a match between the visiting Gentlemen of Ireland and the Gentlemen of Philadelphia, played on the Germantown Cricket Club Grounds in Manheim, Philadelphia. Harper's Weekly October 15, 1892.

The Tour of the "Gentlemen of Philadelphia" in Great Britain in 1884 by One of the Committee - John Pugh Green AND a sterling silver tray presented by the Ladies of the "Philadelphia, Germantown, Young America, Merion and Belmont Cricket Clubs" in appreciation of their performance on the English tour.

The architects of this maiden venture were, W.W. Montgomery of Merion, Daniel S. Newhall of Young America, F.M. Bissell of Germantown, John C. Sims of Philadelphia and John P. Green of Belmont Cricket Club. It's the, *"voluntary enthusiasts who are always ready to do the hardest work, and whose general reward is scant appreciation and liberal criticism."*[71] *The impetus of the tour of 1884 on our Cricket was direct and powerful,* [72] the Philadelphians winning 8 matches but lost and drew 5 matches, a most encouraging first step in the International arena far away from their home base, granted the teams were not the strongest save for the M.C.C. XI at Lord's one that included, C.T. Studd, G.F. Vernon, Russell, Maude, A.J. Webbe, I.D. Walker and H.M. Rotherham, one of the fastest amateur bowlers at the time in England. The weakest teams were the amateurs from Cheshire and Northumberland.

At Lord's the GOP lost by an innings and 171 runs. The London *Sportsman* wrote, *"Both Scott and Thayer, especially Scott, played the bowling of Rotherham and Studd in a thoroughly masterly manner. I have not seen a finer or sounder bat than Scott for a long time. His cutting is brilliant, his defense is sure and easy, and he hits on and off with equal vigor. Thayer is also a skillful wielder of the willow. He in fact plays the game with finished skill, and he hits hard. The Philadelphians are woefully weak in bowling,* [73] *but their fielding, were the field properly bestowed, would leave little or nothing to be desired. The pick-up is swift and clean, the return rapid and accurate, and the backing up excellent. But they do not save runs. If the ball comes to them, all right, they take it, but if it does not, they are all abroad."*

The Philadelphians were surprised that the English found their bowling to be weak, whereas they were of the opinion that their batting was letting them down, which in fact was praised by the English.[74] The 1885 edition of Lillywhite's Cricketer's Companion also wrote, *"Their principal weaknesses were in bowling and wicket-keeping."* The 'improved' batting performance was credited to Bob Newhall's *diligence and foresight.* In spring, the team was put through their paces against two bowlers, Handford and George Lane - the best professional bowler in America at the time. George 'The Crab' Lane had taken 7 for 35 against the Philadelphians at Hoboken when he filled in for Lord Harris in 1879.[75]

In the fall of 1883 they set about selecting a team of fourteen for their first tour, an idea that had manifested for almost 10 years was finally taking shape with representatives from each of the five chief clubs putting together a fund that reached $8200.[76] The final team composition was made up of:

Young America Cricket Club:
R.S. 'Bob' Newhall (Captain) – one of Philadelphia's greatest batsmen
Charles A Newhall, *'Grand Old Man'* – fast bowler
Francis 'Frank' E. Brewster, (University of Pennsylvania) brilliant opening bat and slow bowler
Hazen Brown (Pittsburgh Cricket Club) – Wicket Keeper
E. Walter Clark Jr. (University of Pennsylvania) – Fast and medium pace bowler
Howard MacNutt – medium pacer

Germantown Cricket Club:
William. C. Morgan Jr. *'the stone-waller'* developed as a wicket-keeper during the trip
William. Brockie Jr. (University of Pennsylvania) – attractive onside batsman and brilliant fielder, favorite field position - silly point

Merion Cricket Club:
Joe M. Fox, (Haverford College) All-rounder.
Sutherland *'Sud'* Law, (University of Pennsylvania) fast bowler, good at fine point and also a good bat
William. C. Lowry (Haverford College), slow bowler (took 110 wickets on the tour for an average of 12.72)
John Borland. Thayer Jr. (University of Pennsylvania) excellent bat and fielder

Belmont Cricket Club:
J. Allison Scott, (University of Pennsylvania) the baby of the team only17 years old (by the time the book was written in 1897 he was Dr. Scott)
David P. Stoever. (University of Pennsylvania) Best leg hitter in Philadelphia and medium round arm bowler

Guide philosopher and friend, Mr. Thomas also the teams' official historian/scorer of the trip, Messrs. Montgomery & Greene of the committee and Messrs. Morton McMichael 3rd, Andrew L. Green, Mr. Samuel Welsh 3rd and other friends. Henry Perkins, Secretary of the Marylebone Club had arranged the fixtures and there were to be 18 matches played from June 2nd to August 2[nd.]

1. Trinity College, Dublin University 2nd & 3rd June - Drawn
2. Gentlemen of Ireland in Dublin 4th & 5th June – <u>GOP won by 6 wickets</u>
3. Gentlemen of Scotland at Edinburgh 7th June – Gentlemen of Scotland won by 5 wickets
4. Scarborough Club 13th June - Drawn
5. Gentlemen of England at Lord's 16th & 17th June – MCC won by an innings and 171 runs!
   a. Australians at Cambridge University – 16th June
6. Gentlemen of Cheshire at Cale Green Park, Stockport 21st & 22nd June – <u>GOP won by an innings and 292 runs!</u>
7. Gentlemen of Leicestershire 23rd & 24th June – <u>GOP won by an innings and 108 runs!</u>
   a. Australians at Liverpool – 23rd June
8. Gentlemen of Hampshire 27th June – Gentlemen of Hampshire won by 5 wickets
9. Gentlemen of Gloucestershire at Cheltenham 30th June & 1st July – <u>GOP won by 168 runs</u>
   a. Australians at Sheffield – 30th June
10. Gentlemen of Somersetshire at Lansdowne Club, Bath 2nd & 3rd July – Drawn

     a. Australians at Huddersfield – 3rd July

11. 4th of July match Castleton at Rochdale – <u>GOP won by an innings and 16 runs</u>

12. Gentlemen of Liverpool at Aigburth 7th & 8th July – <u>GOP won by 4 runs</u>

13. Gentlemen of Northumberland at Newcastle 11th & 12th July – <u>GOP won by 96 runs</u>

     a. 1st test at Old Trafford – July 10, 11 & 12th. [151 miles from Newcastle]

14. Gentlemen of Derbyshire 14th & 15th July - Drawn

15. Gentlemen of Surrey at The Oval 17th & 18th July – <u>GOP won by 3 wickets</u>

     a. Australians at Lord's – 17th July

16. Gentlemen of Sussex at Brighton 21st & 22nd July – Gentlemen of Sussex won by 10 wickets

     a. 2nd test at Lord's – July 21, 22 & 23rd. [58 miles from Brighton]

17. Gentlemen of Kent at Maidstone 24th & 25th July – Gentlemen of Kent won by 6 wickets

     a. Australians at Sussex, Hove – 24th July

18. United Service at Portsmouth 1st & 2nd August – Drawn

     a. 3rd test at The Oval – August 11, 12 & 13th. [82 miles from Portsmouth]

Before the team left for the tour, two matches were arranged as 'practice' matches against a New York XII captained by Cyril Wilson of Staten Island Cricket Club. Philadelphia won both matches, the first by 9 wickets and the second by 66 runs on the basis of the first innings score. The team left New York on May 17th 1884 aboard the 'City of Rome,' and reached Liverpool on 25th May after an eight day journey. In an earlier reference to travel by sea of an English Gentleman from Illinois around 1810, it would take him about 45 to 50 days to travel from Isle of Wight to Baltimore, advancements in steamship travel had certainly reduced the time taken for travel.

The Gentlemen of Philadelphia (GOP) had an inauspicious start as Charles Newhall sprained his back during their practice session at the Aigburth grounds and could only play a few matches during the tour. Wherever they went, extreme hospitality was extended to them – the Royal Irish Yacht Club extending the privilege of their homes, Lady Mayoress of Dublin hosting a ball to which they were invited, the team including the ladies were invited to lunch and the Irish were excellent dancers when compared to the English. The first match on the tour with Trinity College ended in a draw with Trinity scoring 181 and 218 runs; the GOP tied the 1st inning score and added 23 runs in the 2nd innings before time ran out.

The one ground that they all looked forward to playing on was at the Lord's - all these years they had heard about it and now they would be stepping on the perfect turf and to think at one time sheep were used to 'trim' the grass! As far as the match was concerned, the GOP met with the strongest team on the tour and were soundly beaten and they hoped that this would spur them to improve their skills in all areas of the game. This tour after all, was a learning experience and the idea was to play the game in the country of origin and experience the variety of Gentlemen and amateur players on expansive grounds. One of the traits that endeared the Philadelphians and created goodwill amongst fellow proponents of the game happened during the match at Lord's. JB Thayer Jr. was at third man and caught a very low ball from G.F. Vernon and thinking he was caught started walking off the field. Thayer was the only one who knew that he had caught the ball very close to the bounce so as to look like a catch. After informing the umpire the batsman was called back, this display of sportsmanship commended the Philadelphians wherever they went.[77] Despite three players scoring a duck, MCC put up a total of 406 runs to which the GOP replied with 174 in their first innings, though the second was an absolute disaster where they were able to muster a measly 61 runs. When asked of an old Philadelphian cricketer in the pavilion on their second inning performance, *"What do I think of it? I think it is hardly worthwhile to come 3000 miles to get scared. We can do that at home."*[78] The absence of Charles Newhall was greatly felt here, the runs would not have flowed so freely and the outcome could have been a lot more tolerable, though the very next match the GOP defeated the Gentlemen of Cheshire by an innings and 292 runs!

A total of four centuries were scored by the GOP, two by Stoever and one each by Brockie and Bob Newhall, and these came about in only two matches, one can safely infer that these would have been against two easier teams.[79] The most brilliant catch of the series was brought about by Thayer off W.G. Grace in the match against Gloucestershire. As John Green put it, *"where the champion put over two hundred pounds clean behind the ball, and where the stroke of the bat against the ball and of the ball against the fielder's hands were simultaneous,"* and everyone was looking towards the ropes! Grace *"threw his bat to Thayer, only asking that he be allowed to retain it in one or two matches, and afterwards formally presented it to him."* This was one of the heirlooms that were unfortunately lost when the club house at Merion in Haverford was burnt down on January 4th 1896.[80] Grace practically bowled unchanged throughout the two innings and in the process taking 7 wickets in each. Mr. C.W. Alcock, secretary of the Surrey Cricket Club and editor of *Cricketer*, sent a note to John Green after the defeat of Gloucestershire,

"Yankee Doodle came to town, for Cricket not for races,
Knocked the Gloucester wickets down, and out go both the Graces."[81]

Against Liverpool, Thayer also made three great running catches in the 2nd innings off Lowry's bowling when Liverpool had 4 wickets on hand and required only 8 runs to win. Lowry was brought back in when the scoreboard read 111 for 6 and 12 minutes of play was left, but were bundled out for 114 runs and Lowry would have had an hat-trick had E.E. Steel been caught at short-leg, thus giving the GOP a win by only 4 runs. Playing for Sussex was a young chap, Charles Aubrey Smith (debut 1882) who in 1888/89 captained the first English team to South Africa and later went on to become a Hollywood actor and, the Hollywood Cricket Club started by him in 1932 is still in existence today.

The exploits of the GOP reached the ears of Henry Chadwick who, *"never dreamed that an eleven of American players, from one city only, would be able to beat an English county eleven on its own ground."*[82] Though the GOP did not face any professional bowlers or a full strength county team, still, the very idea that a team from 'one city' was able to put up a decent show was commendable, what if there were pool of talent all over the country to choose from? What if cricket had developed alongside baseball, then the United States would have had an formidable team and it would have been a daunting task of picking just eleven players from all over the country and with bowlers like Bart King incorporating the curve pitches of baseball into bowling, the rest of world would have had a rough time adjusting to the American style of bowling.

Before the Derbyshire match, John Green had an opportunity to witness the American Lawn Tennis champions, James Dwight, the father of American Tennis and his cousin Richard Dudley 'Dick' Sears, the winner of the first seven national championship, playing doubles at the Wimbledon tournament in 1884, a first for them.[83] This was also the year when the first Ladies Championship were held and 19 year old Maud Watson winning it in three sets, and as John put it, *"the playing in the Ladies Championship was especially fine."*[84] He was also able to take in the races at Ascot where, *"a number of ladies as charmingly dressed as at our tennis tournaments at Newport."*[85] A snapshot of tour reveals Lowry to be the best bowler of the side capturing 110 wickets for an average of 12.72 as compared to 176 combined wickets taken by eight other players. The other two bowlers to cross the century mark in bowling from Philadelphia cricket were Herbert Vivian 'Ranji' Hordern, an Australian studying at the University of Pennsylvania in 1907. He took 115 wickets against public schools [86] and the following year, Bart King took 120, the same year when he topped the English bowling average. Thayer was considered the best all-rounder, Clark and MacNutt adding to the all-round effectiveness and the baby of the team, Scott, displaying remarkable batting aptitude. As far as batting averages were concerned, Scott came out ahead of Newhall, followed by Thayer and in bowling the honors went to Lowry, Fox and MacNutt. [87] The committee in charge put out the following numbers:

Philadelphia – Aggregate runs scored 5880 for 283 wickets at an average of 20.78 per wicket.
Opponents – 5085 runs for 298 wickets at an average of 17.06 runs per wicket.

At the conclusion of their successful tour, they were invited for dinner by the Royal Albert Yacht Squadron aboard *Nelson's old flagship, the 'Victory'* at Portsmouth[88] and on the teams return, a dinner was hosted in their honor at the Union League Club on 4th October and in attendance was none other than Mr. William Rotch Wister, one of the stalwarts of American Cricket in Philadelphia who presided over the function. The treasurer, W.W. Montgomery provided the details of the expenditure for the tour[89] and it was interesting to go thru the accounts. The total receipts were $9577.39 and expenses were

$7319.21 and after paying .25 cent dividend, they were left with a balance of $208.18! The gate receipts provide an interesting insight. The net proceeds on the match against the New York XI played on May 9th & 10th before their departure, yielded $348.50 and a match against the United States on their return played on October 4th 6th & 7th netted $347.15, and when this is compared to the net balance of receipts from ten venues in Great Britain, only $658.62 was realized. Dan Newhall blamed this on the Australians who were in town, *it is but proper to say that the presence of the Australian team in England interfered seriously with the attendance at county matches and that this accounts for the comparative smallness of gate receipts abroad.*[90] Looking at the distance and match fixtures (shown in red within the GOP schedule), the Australians were nowhere near and were miles apart and could not have divided the public into choosing a game. The only match of consequence was the 17th July match, where the Australians were at Lord's while GOP were playing at the Oval, a distance of 5 miles. Granted there were 32 matches on this 4th Australian tour, conveyance was not, shall we say, urbanized to enable travel to great distance just to watch a match. Given below are the scores from the GOP's first victory on a foreign soil against the Gentlemen of Ireland, this was their second match of the tour in which they were victorious by 6 wickets. In the bowling analysis, notice the number of overs are not given, but the total number of balls bowled is shown, which were four per over.

GENTLEMEN OF PHILADELPHIA

FIRST INNINGS	RUNS	SECOND INNINGS	RUNS
J.A. Scott, b Nunn	19	c Nunn, b Penny	1
H. Brown, b Hamilton	43	b Nunn	8
J.B. Thayer, b Penny	42	b Nunn	0
R.S. Newhall, b Hamilton	8	not out	27
E.W. Clark, c Haynes, b Penny	16	not out	3
S. Law, c Haynes, b Nunn	19		
J. M. Fox, c Hone, b Nunn	19		
D.P. Stoever, c Trotter, b Nunn	8		
C.W. Morgan, b Penny	12	c Nunn, b Penny	4
H. MacNutt, b Hamilton	10		
W.C. Lowry, not out	3		
Extras	20	Extras	4
Total	219	Total	47

GENTLEMEN OF IRELAND

FIRST INNINGS	RUNS	SECOND INNNINGS	RUNS
J.W. Hynes, C Fox. B Lowry	0	st. Brown, b Lowry	27
J.R. Maxwell, c Thayer, b Lowry	16	lbw, b Lowry	23
J.H. Nunn, c Scott, b Lowry	9	b Law	0
D.N. Trotter, c Clark, b Lowry	7	not out	42
D.Cronin, lbw, b Fox	27	c Law, b Lowry	18
J.A.C. Penny, c Brown, b Lowry	16	c Scott, b Lowry	30
N. Hone, b Fox	3	c Fox, b Lowry	0
J. Bayley, b Fox	3	b Thayer	16
H. Hamilton, b Lowry	2	c Brown, b Fox	7
G.D. Casey, not out	4	c Clark, b Lowry	7
H. Hemsworth, c Newhall, b Lowry	0	c Scott, b Fox	1
		Extras	6
TOTAL	88	TOTAL	177

Bowling	B.	R.	M.	W.		B.	R.	M.	W.
GENTLEMEN OF PHILADELPHIA									
		First Innings				Second Innings			
Clark	64	29	6	0	Fox	82	22	12	2
Lowry	92	55	4	7	Lowry	204	84	13	6
Fox	24	4	4	3	MacNutt	36	16	3	0
					Clark	28	5	5	0
					Thayer	40	25	3	1
					Law	76	19	9	1
GENTLEMEN OF IRELAND									
		First Innings				Second Innings			
	B.	R.	M.	W.		B.	R.	M.	W.
Hamilton	136	35	17	3	Hamilton	26	13	3	0
Hemsworth	20	20	0	0	Penny	56	22	9	2
Nunn	152	51	20	5	Nunn	32	8	5	2
Bayley	16	12	1	0					
Casey	24	25	0	0					
Penny	140	56	16	3					

An abridgment to the Australian tour of England that year put forth by an 'Observer' in, *'The Argus'* (a Melbourne, Victoria paper) dated September 16th 1884, provides a lively but telling perceptiveness into the underlying acrimony between the two. Under an *"utterly absurd arrangement three representative test matches were to have decided the supremacy between the two with England winning one and the other two drawn in favor of the Australians,"* (this would imply a win, but two matches ended in a draw even though the Australians had an advantage). This was the first year of the 'ashes' and the beginning of the 'test' series. The writer was also critical of the Australian performance and internal bickering. *The attitude of the English press towards the Australians has not been at all generous*, as they were accused of being interested only in money. As this was a self-funded tour, it <u>was about money</u> and as, *"Australia is a working community, and young men with their own future to mould, cannot afford the time and expense of an English tour without some return."*

He further goes on to say that the *"comparison between the Australian and American cricketers' was another little device of the shallow type. Had the Australians been less ambitious they would have been more welcome. Had they been content to give and take with amateur elevens from third-rate counties instead of ruffling British conceit and hurting British dignity by throwing out a challenge to the United Kingdom and maintaining it in the field, there would have been less trenchant criticism. We have been constantly reminded this season that the Australians take gate money and the Americans do not, but it has yet to be insinuated that they obtained any of that money under false pretenses, by not giving full value for it in a cricketing sense, the position of the American team in this respect is apt. The one comforting reflection is that, if the position of the Australians is to be successfully assailed, it will be done by good cricket only, and not by bad criticism."* I wonder how Dan Newhall would have reacted to that.

"There is also every probability that the Australian eleven, who are to visit England this Spring, will return via this continent at the same time that Shaw's eleven comes here. Should such be the case, the lovers of the game will have an opportunity of witnessing a game on neutral ground, between two of the greatest teams the world has ever seen," wrote the *New York Times* in their March 5th edition, unfortunately that was not meant to be, though the English spectators were treated to much more than cricket with the three teams converging during the same time period on the English soil.

John Borland Thayer (seen here when he was the second Vice-President of the Pennsylvania Railroad) was returning from Europe where he had been the guest of the American Consul General in Berlin.[91] He was on board the Titanic with his wife and son 'Jack' Thayer, when it was struck by an iceberg on that ill-fated April night in 1912, he did not survive, but his wife and son did.

According to the 30 page booklet, *'The Sinking of the S.S. Titanic, April 14-15, 1912,'* that was published by John 'Jack' Borland Jr. in memory of his father in 1940, he describes the events that took place on that fateful night. Jack had been separated from his parents and when he finally jumped in the water with his friend Milton, his watch had stopped at 2.22 AM. He witnessed the ship break up and sink, the second funnel fell about 15 yards in front of him which sucked him underwater (he was to learn later that his father was last seen standing under the second funnel) and when he resurfaced, he was next to an upside-down collapsible lifeboat with men on it. Later there would be 28 of them and at daybreak they were picked up by two lifeboats from the Titanic, number 4 and 12, Jack's mother was in one of the life boats manning one of the oars! They reunited on board the Carpathia. Whether the sketches were done by the *Carpathia* passenger L.D. Skidmore to whom Jack had narrated the incident[92] or by Jack himself which[93] showed the Titanic breaking up in two, was not accepted as fact till the actual discover that showed the ocean liner laying on the sea bed in two pieces.

The obituary in the 1913 edition of Wisden described him thus:

MR. JOHN B. THAYER, for some years one of Philadelphia's leading cricketers, went down in the Titanic on April 15th. He was born on April 21st, 1862, and was only fourteen when he played his first match for Merion. When he visited England as a member of the first Philadelphian team, in 1884, Lillywhite said of him :-- "Bats in finished style, and, with more patience, would be the best in the team in that department. Can hit hard, and is a dangerous man when once well in. Bowls medium round-arm with good command of the ball and a break both ways. Is a splendid mid-off, and shows fine fielding whenever he is placed either at the boundary or close to the wicket." During that tour he made 817 runs with an average of 28, his highest score being 93 v. Gentlemen of Derby-shire, and took 22 wickets for 21 runs each. Owing to business claims, he was seldom seen in the cricket-field in later years, but to the end he took the greatest interest in the game.[94]

In 1885 Philadelphia achieved their maiden first-class win over a touring side, when they beat EJ Sander's XI by 109 runs at Germantown Cricket Club Ground. This was played from September 17 to 19th, with Philadelphia scoring 200 and 178 and the visitors replied with 147 and 122. A match against Staten Island earlier in the month had ended in a draw. Compared to the 1884 team that visited England, the 1889 Philadelphians were better equipped to take on their English amateur counterparts as evidenced when comparing the results. On June 19th they set sail aboard the '*City of Chicago*' and after sightseeing around Dublin, played their first match on July 2, 3 against Trinity College, which started roughly for the Philadelphians but recovered well enough to end in a draw. July 4th saw them taking on the Gentlemen of Ireland who left them a target of 294 in the second innings with not much time remaining and the score at the end read 196 for 6 - another draw.[95] An interesting match against the Gentlemen of Scotland at Edinburgh saw them scoring only 66 in the first innings and 340 in the second, leaving the Philadelphians 99 to win in a very short time, which was accomplished by Stoever and R.D. Brown in half an hour, a first win for Philadelphia on this tour followed by a win over Liverpool in their next match.

If they were looking for three wins in a row, it was not meant to be, as their next opponents were Gloucestershire captained by none other than W.G. Grace. Chasing a score of 311, the Philadelphians were soon reeling from the loss of Stoever, R.D. Brown, Clark and Etting for only 3 runs but managed to put up a total of 173. During the follow on, they scored 249 runs which the opponents easily surpassed winning the match by 8 wickets. Against Surrey, the visitors recorded one of their highest scores of 458 runs, but even that was not enough to secure another win and the match ended in a draw.[96] They lost the next two matches against MCC and Kent, but then against the Gentlemen of Hampshire played at Southampton on July 29th 30th and 31st, it was a close one where they won by only 2 runs. Two more matches ended in a draw, one against United Services at Portsmouth and the other against Sussex, while the last match of the tour against Cambridge Long Vacation Club went in Philadelphia's favor, as most of the Cambridge players were away (an aptly named club). The tally for the 1889 endeavor – won 4, lost 3 and drew 5.[97] "*The visit of the Gentlemen of Philadelphia was an agreeable and welcome episode in the English season.*"[98]

"Cricket has never been popular here as a field sport. It is too slow for the average American, but Philadelphians like it" – New York Herald's message to the team before it sailed – a sweeping statement with the same sentiments time and again. While on the other hand, 'A Secretary' writing on Philadelphians visit to England in the 1898 issue of Lillywhite, writes that *"Cricket in the United States has had to make its way in the face of every possible difficulty...with limited support confined to one or two districts, it speaks volumes for the energy of the Cricket fathers in America that the game has been able to maintain its ground as it has."*

The third visit by the Gentlemen of Philadelphia to England in 1897 was different for one major reason, for the first time they were facing the full strength of the English county and all the matches that were played by the GOP till the advent of the First World War were considered first class matches. They won 2 matches, one against Sussex and the other against Warwickshire, while losing 9 and drawing 4 (3 of the 4 matches showed Philadelphia at an advantage) and despite this, the tour was considered fairly successful. The match and individual player statistics were now regularly printed in the local papers.[99] Patterson and Baily were the only two players from the 1889 trip, and this time one of the newcomers was J.B. King, who would become the best all-round cricketer in America. On this trip he lead the bowling averages taking a total of 72 wickets, while Lester with a total of 891 runs, an average of 37.12 per innings, led in the batting department while King contributed 440 runs on this occasion. The services of Noble, E.W. Clark and Walter Scott, three of the best all-rounders at the time were sorely lacking as they could not make the trip.

The match against Sussex was played at Brighton on June 17 and 18, one which resulted in a win for the GOP by 8 wickets. The architects for this win were Lester who scored 92 and 34, while King's analysis showed his bowling prowess – 10 overs, 5 maiden, 7 wickets for only 13 runs.[100] Keep in mind these were first class players and in the first innings, Sussex who were able to put up only 46 (at one point they were 7 for 13), put up 252 in the second innings, a bit too late to make a difference though. One of the best players at the time – Ranjitsinhji, was bowled by King on the first delivery he faced and this would lead to a lasting friendship between the two and spur Ranji to bring the strongest team to America in 1899, his only tour as a captain and he was taking no chances! The other win was over Warwickshire by five wickets and the GOP would also have won against Notts at Trent Bridge, had it not been played to a draw, Woods (100) and Patterson (162), both scoring centuries. This proved the Philadelphians were capable of playing with the best and the future engagements beginning with the 1903 tour were played against first class teams and on this tour GOP's record was 7 wins, lost 6, and drew 3,[101] a marked improvement indeed. Following are the scores of the match against Sussex.

Gentlemen of Philadelphia vs. Sussex

Brighton, June 17 and 18, 1897.

PHILADELPHIA

First Innings	RUNS	Second Innings	RUNS
GS Patterson c Butt b Bland	4	b Bland	4
AM Wood b Tate	10	b Tate	42
JA Lester b Tate	92	not out	34
L Biddle c Butt b Tate	21	not out	1
JB King c Ranjitsinhji b Tate	58		
C Coates Jr. b Tate	4		
FW Ralston b Tate	13		
HL Clark lbw b Bland	1		
HP Baily c Bean b Tate	9		
EM Cregar c Butt b Bland	0		
PH Clark not out	0		
Extras (Leg Byes)	4	Extras (Leg Byes)	2
TOTAL	216	TOTAL	83

SUSSEX

First Innings	Runs	Second Innings	Runs
WL Murdoch b King	3	c substitute b King	1
Marlow c P Clark b King	6	b Baily	19
KS Ranjitsinhji b King	0	c H. b P Clark	74
G Brann b King	10	c Wood b King	41
W Newham c Biddle b P Clark*	0	b King	67
Vine b King	4	c Patterson b Cregar	8
Killick c Ralston b Cregar	7	c King b Cregar	4
Bean not out	8	b King	29
Butt b King	4	b King	1
Tate b King	0	b King	2
Bland c Biddle b Cregar	1	not out	0
Extras	3	Extras	6
TOTAL	46	TOTAL	252

Bowling	Overs	Maiden	Runs	Wickets	Overs	Maiden	Runs	Wickets
PHILADELPHIA	First Innings				Second Innings			
King	10	5	13	7	38.1	11	102	6
Cregar	10	2	30	3	13	2	41	2
Baily					17	6	37	1
P Clark					16	1	53	1
Patterson					5	0	12	0
Coates					1	0	1	0
SUSSEX	First Innings				Second Innings			
Bland	32	14	53	3	13	2	37	1
Tate	38	12	84	7	17.1	10	21	1
Killick	12	4	30	0	9	2	23	0
Ranjitsinhji	5	2	22	0				
Bean	7	2	23	0				

Philadelphia wins by 8 wickets.

* The actual score book used in the match which resides with the CC Morris Library, shows Newham being bowled by Cregar, not Clark as shown in Lillywhite, though the bowling analysis show the correct number of wickets by Cregar, therefore a typographical error. There have been numerous occasions where I have come across discrepancies with names, dates and scores when comparing Lillywhite's Annuals and records in the books written about the tour.

Fourteen members, who made up the Gentlemen of Philadelphia, set out from New York on their fourth tour of England on May 27th 1903 aboard the 'Majestic,' Morris and Sharpless travelled shortly later by another ship. G. S. Patterson their captain and anchor was not available for this tour and Lester took on the reins of Captaincy. Also missing was the slow left arm bowler, Cope Morton whose present was felt in the first match against Cambridge. Six new players were hoping to make their mark on the tour, they were, Graves, Haines, Jordan, LeRoy, Morris and Sharpless. The first match was lost to the boys at Cambridge University by six wickets and a draw ensued at Oxford due to rain. Bart was beginning to show his skills by taking 8 wickets for 39 runs in Oxford's first innings, [102] and the combination of King and Clark would end up taking 157 out of the 217 first-class wickets on the tour, more than 72% between the two! [103] Their first victory on the tour came against Gloucester on June 16 and 17, who were defeated by an innings and 26 runs.

Against Nottingham the newcomers proved that they deserved to be included in the team, Chris Morris scored an almost flawless 164, while Graves demonstrated of things to come with his 62 not out. Sharpless turned out to be a dependable and permanent member of the eleven.[104] This was a high scoring match where Lester declared the innings at 400 and in reply Notts fell short by 165 runs.[105] M.C.C. won the next match at Lord's by 5 wickets and included in the team were their best bowlers, J.T. Hearne, Mead and A.E. Trott, who played havoc with the Philadelphia batting lineup and they scored their lowest total on the tour – 65. King and Clark again kept the batsmen in check with King taking 7 wickets for 51 runs in the first innings.[106] Against Kent they won by 62 runs and Kent would pay them a visit in Philadelphia later in the year winning all four matches there.[107] They would lose to Somerset by 10 wickets even though they were not a strong team compared to Kent or Surrey. The July 6th to 8th match at Old Trafford against Lancashire ended in a win for Philadelphia by 9 wickets due to Kings bowling and partly due to the absence of MacLaren, Tyldesley and Brearley in the Lancashire lineup. Here King was at his best, in three overs he took 5 wickets for only 6 runs and ended the innings at 9 wickets for 62 runs. At Edgbaston against Warwickshire, Philadelphia lost by 7 wickets and also lost to Worcestershire by 215 runs; here Percy Clark was filling in for Lester. They had few injuries on their roster, Lester had a split finger, and King was nursing a strained leg while Bates and Scattergood had injured their hands. The match against Hampshire played at Southampton ended in a draw due to frequent rain.[108]

On July 23rd, 24th and 25th Philadelphia took on an old friend, P.F. Warner's XI at The Oval and lost to them by 196 runs. *"American Cricketers badly beaten"* read the New York Times of 25th July. In both the innings even though Philadelphia had an upper hand, they could not capitalize on it as the tail-enders added triple digits in both the innings. In the first innings, Warner's team was 98 for the loss of 8 wickets but the stragglers took the score to 187. Philadelphia could not reply to Bosanquets' googlies, who took 5 wickets for 33 runs and the team folded at only 82. In the second innings the home team again had lost half the players for 70 runs, but then Bosanquet steps in to rescue, this time with the willow, adding 150 between himself (63) and T.A.D. Bevington (91) setting a target of 381 for the visitors. Philadelphia could only score 183 runs with Bosanquet again adding to the misery by taking 7 wickets for only 46 runs.[109] *"The Philadelphians' next match will be on Monday at Brighton against Sussex, where they will encounter the crack bats, Ranjitsinhji and C.B. Fry."*[110] Unfortunately, not a single ball was bowled as it was rained out completely and they could not experience the exhibition of the two fine batsmen.

Top Row from left: E.M. Dowson, F.C. Sharpless, P.N. LeRoy, R.W. Nichols
Second Row: A.G. Archer, J.C. Hartley, T.A.D. Bevington, P.H. Clark, F.H. Bohlen, Tarrant.
Third Row: J.B. King, J. Stanning, P.F. Warner, J.A. Lester, B.J.T. Bosanquet, H.J.
Stevenson, E.M. Cregar.
Bottom Row: H.A. Haines, C.C. Morris, F.W. Orr, T.C. Jordan, N.Z. Graves.
P.F. Warner's XI & GOP at the Oval on July 23, 24 & 25, 1903.

Another match was played at The Oval on August 6th 7th & 8th, this time the opponents were Surrey and this turned out to be the most exciting match of the tour. The weather was a non-issue on all three days and it was played on a perfect wicket till the end when ten minutes before the end of allotted time Bart, the man of the match, took the last wicket and handed Philadelphia a win by 110 runs. More about the match is detailed in the following chapter, 'A Prince and the King.' The tour ended with two drawn matches, one against the Scottish Eleven at Edinburgh and a match at Grantham where King in a free hitting match scored 178, the highest by an American. The marked improvement in Philadelphia's' performance was noticed by a prominent English write going by the initials, 'W.A.B.' who said, *"this year the bowling has made a great advance, and there are very few counties who have a better pair than King and Clark…both understanding the art of variation and concealment of pace. As regards batting, Dr. Lester is unquestionably the best batsman in the team…if King and Lester were living in England it would indeed be a surprising thing if they were not asked to play at Lord's for the Gentlemen."*[111]

In 1907 an M.C.C. XI had visited Philadelphia in September led by HV Hesketh-Prichard playing four matches beginning with an All New York team on 17th & 18th at Staten Island which ended in a draw due to rain. The next engagement was at Germantown Cricket Club against the GOP on 20, 21 & 23 which also ended in a draw and a four day match, also against the GOP played on the 27, 28, 30 and 1st October at the Merion Club Grounds, also ending in a draw. The only match MCC won was against the Philadelphia Colts played on 24 & 25 winning by an innings and 173 runs.[112] When the Gentlemen of Philadelphia visited England for the fifth and last time in 1908, they would defeat MCC by 26 runs. This trip would also coincide with the **Games of the IV Olympiad** held in London for the first time.

This tour was marred by rain and wet pitches wherever they went, it seems rain followed them from Philadelphia since they left on June 20th. As we know, wet pitches were not conducive to them in England whether it was the batting or the bowling, but despite that Bart King would create history by being the first and last American to lead the English bowling averages that year! Once they reached Liverpool they moved to London staying at the Imperial Hotel but they would normally be based at the Victoria Hotel. The first match against South Wales at Cardiff was an easy victory by 36 runs, followed by a win against Worcestershire by 95 runs in a rain affected match. In another rain affected match against Hampshire, the visitors lost by an innings and 36 runs, the loss mainly attributed to the slipshod fielding.[113] Rain completely washed out the Folkestone match and they were looking forward to some dry patch of spell before playing Middlesex at Lord's. This turned out to be a memorable match for a different reason, Philadelphia scored their lowest in both innings here – 58 & 55 and the architects for this debacle were Tarrant and Trott each taking 10 & 9 wickets in both innings respectively, there was one run out! [114] A three day match ended up being played out in one day with Middlesex winning by seven wickets!

With frequent trips and exchanges, friends were made and they reciprocated the hospitality by entertaining them in the best possible manner. Sir Arthur Priestley, who had visited with Ranji's XI in 1899, dined them at the House of Commons and some of the veteran cricketers took them out for a dinner and theater. Similar treatment was meted out to them wherever they went and after the Northamptonshire match was over in two days with a win for the home team by 5 wickets, *'the VP of the County Club, Mr. Wentworth Vernon, 'a descendant of a friend of George Washington after whom Mt. Vernon was named,'* took them to his estate for lunch and tea.[115] After losing to Surrey by 122 runs at the Oval, the GOP travelled to Dublin to play an All Ireland team where they won by an innings and 7 runs. Here also they were entertained by a Captain Ruttledge, who had managed the Irish tour of Philadelphia in 1892, invited them for dinner, and the following evening they were guest of the Irish teams that had visited America. They were also guests to the Gaiety and Royal Theater and the different clubs. After defeating the Ulster team at Belfast by an innings and 114 runs, they were invited by the American Vice-Consul and taken to the Palace Theater and Hippodrome.[116]

Back in London they played MCC on a drier wicket and beat them narrowly by 25 runs. The evening dinner at Lord's on the first day was one of the things they looked forward to and the next day they were taken to the Imperial Restaurant on Regent Street. Bart King not only spun the ball, but also tales at various gatherings and it was difficult to ascertain whether he was factual or embellishing them. At Derbyshire they won by 9 wickets and as they had one day to spare, they were taken on a coach trip to the valley of Derwent to Matlock Bath by the manager of the Bell Hotel, Mr. Phillips.[117] Rain was again an issue at the Trent Bridge grounds where Nottinghamshire won by 130 runs but GOP won against Durham by 106 runs. Kent won the last official match by 4 wickets even though there was heavy rain. Arthur Priestley, Member of Parliament from Grantham, who earlier had dined the team at the House of Commons, now invited the team to his home and play against a Grantham XI, which was played when the rain allowed. They stayed there for two nights and received the royal treatment,[118] unfortunately, all good things comes to an end and on September 2nd they left for Southampton to board the 'Majestic' which also had some of the 1908 Olympians on board for company. Originally the host country for the Olympics was Rome, but after the eruption of Mount Vesuvius in 1906, the venue was moved to London.

The first cricket tour from the island nations of the Caribbean to North America, took place in 1886 under the captaincy of Laurie. R. Fyfe of Jamaica, and had it not been for his 'journal keeping' on the tour, the details would not have been known. It was published by Argo press in 1887 titled, *"The Tour of the West Indian Cricketers; August and September, 1886, A Memory, by One of Them."* Fourteen amateurs from three territories formed the "West Indies" team - Demerara (British Guiana), Barbados and Jamaica.[119] Guy. N. Wyatt from Guiana (Captain of Georgetown Cricket Club) a hard hitting batsman was behind this promotional tour and people were skeptical till the foray into international cricket turned out to be a success.[120] *"These West Indians...were wined and dined as equal partners within the context of a sporting enterprise that valued the importance of human dignity and mutual respect"* writes Professor Beckles, [121] but, would that 'human dignity and mutual respect' have been the same had the team included all or a few black players, after all 'color' *was* an issue, this team comprised of British expats, sugar planters and businessman only. In 1911, Haverford College was to cancel a match against the visiting 'West Indians' when they learnt there might be a black player in the team!

After receiving a favorable response from Montreal C.C., teams from the three colonies would travel independently to North America due to lack of accommodations on a steamship in Jamaica. They had planned to rendezvous there for practice before embarking on their maiden international cricket voyage. The Jamaican group arrived in Boston on the 9th of August and as the first match at Montreal was scheduled for the 16th, they practiced at Longwood C.C. which was at their disposal. As the rest of the team could not arrive before the 19th, local substitutes were used for the first two games played on the Montreal C.C. grounds. Six matches were played in Canada where they won 4 lost 1 and drew 1, the Canadian leg of the tour was a success when compared to their American outing.

1. Montreal C.C. on August 16th & 17th where the visitors were victorious.
2. The Halifax Wanderers on 18th & 19[th,] here the West Indians won by an innings and 42 runs. Rests of the matches were played with a full West Indian squad.
3. Ottawa C. C. on August 22nd, West Indians win by 26 runs.
4. Toronto C. C. on 24th August, West Indians win by an innings and 39 runs.
5. Ontario Cricket Association XI on 25th & 26th, here the tourists win by 16 runs.
6. Hamilton C.C. on 28th & 29th, where Hamilton defeated the touring team by seven wickets.

The team members were:

Jamaica

Laurence R. Fyfe – Captain
J. Lees – all-rounder
E.N. Marshall - batsman
W.H. Farquharson - bowler
J.M. Burke – all-rounder and youngest player on the team
Percy Isaacs – wicket-keeper
Leo Isaacs – left-hand batsman

British Guiana (Demerara)

G.N. Wyatt – batsman
R.H. Stewart – spin bowler (reached Boston from England)
A.W. Swain - bowler
Louis Kerr – batsman & wicket-keeper

Barbados

E. M. Skeete - batsman
T.S. Skeete – defensive player
W.O Collymore

Four of their best players, E.F. Wright - P.J.T. Henery - A.J. Goodridge - R. Garnett, all from Demerara (one of the three Dutch colonies), could not make it due to business engagements.

The first official cricketers to visit the Caribbean Islands were the Americans, who in the 1887-88 season paid them a return visit, and in 1895 the islands received their first English team captained by R. S. Lucas, followed by two teams from England under the captaincy of Lord Hawke and Arthur Priestley in 1898. Interestingly, Sir Pelham Warner who was born in Trinidad in October of 1873, toured under Lord Hawke's side and his brother, R. S. A. Warner, was captain of the first West Indies team to tour England in 1900.

In America they played 7 matches, winning 2, lost 4 and drew 1 and from a tour total of thirteen matches, they won 6 and lost 5 and 2 were drawn. On August 30th, the islanders reached Philadelphia late in the night and were met by representatives of different clubs and their first match was going to be against Merion C.C. at Ardmore. It was a low scoring match as the visitors put on 54 runs in their first innings and Merion replied with an equally low total of 86 runs. The score seemed within reach as, at the close of play in their second innings, the West Indians had scored 11 for the loss of a wicket. But the morning brought about ill tidings and they were all out for 36 only, leaving Merion 5 runs to win, and since the match ended early, a single inning re-match was suggested which the islander's ended up winning this time by putting up 111 in response to Merion's score of 107 runs.[122] The score of their first engagement on American soil is given below, the match was played on August 31 and September 1.

WEST INDIANS

FIRST INNINGS	RUNS	SECOND INNINGS	RUNS
J. Lees, c Morley, b Bates	0	c Haines, b Morley	3
E. M. Skeete, c Bates, b Morley	13	b Lowry	7
E. N. Marshall, b Bates	4	b Morley	2
W. H. Farquharson, run out	4	c Haines, b Morley	11
G. Wayatt, b Morley	0	c Law, b Morley	0
R. H. Stewart, b Morley	6	c Haines, b Lowry	3
L. L. Kerr, c Etting, b Morley	1	not out	1
L. Fyfe, c Haines, b Morley	0	c Lowry, b Morle	0
J. M. Burke, not out	10	b Law	2
L. Isaacs, c Philler, b Lowry	5	c Philler, b Lowry	1
A. Swain, c Haines, b Morley	4	b Lowry	5
Extras	7	Extras	1
Total	54	Total	36

MERION CRICKET CLUB

FIRST INNINGS	RUNS	SECOND INNINGS	RUNS
W. E. Bates, c Kerr, b Farquharson	0	C. S. Edwards, not out	2
C. S. Edwards, c Kerr, b Burke	2	A. C. Craig, not out	0
N. Etting, run out	3	Extras	4
Morley, c Issacs, b Burke	13		
A. G. Thompson, c Kerr, b Farquharson	2		
S. Law, b Farquharson	7		
A. C. Craig, b Farquharson	14		
B. Henry, c Kerr, b Burke	2		
G. S. Philler, not out	26		
C. E. Haines, b Farquharson	0		
W. C. Lowry, b Burke	13		
Extras	4		
Total	86	Total	6

On August 31st 1886, a most damaging intraplate earthquake struck Charleston, South Carolina at 9.51 p.m. and the tremors were felt as far as Boston. Whether it was the tremors or a coincidental accident, the 'wagon' in which our cricketers were travelling, suddenly stopped and collapsed, and the visitors were thrown to the ground. As they walked towards the station, many of them felt the *upheavals of mother earth*.[123] The islanders lost the next match to the Belmont C. C. by an innings and 32 runs. They observed that the club grounds were newer and a peculiar fact was that there were about 300 lady members belonging to the club, for there were, 27 Lawn Tennis Courts. Against Germantown C.C. they fared no better and could only muster 74 and 148 against their first innings score of 310 runs. The Philadelphia segment came to an end with the last match against Young America C.C. at Stenton played on 7th and 8th September, again coming up short by more than an innings but the match ended up being declared a draw as time ran out. The Philadelphia papers attributed the defeat of the West Indians to a few principal reasons, the first being that, the captain did not know the individual strength of his players till they got together at Montreal and second, the visitors were not familiar with the American wickets and conditions as they were used to harder and faster pitches.

On 10th and 11th September, the West Indians found themselves locking horns against the Longwood C.C. hoping to leave the bitter Philadelphia taste behind and end the maiden tour on a happier note. It turned out to be a close match as Longwood required just 42 runs to win in the second innings, but were bundled out for only 23 runs, a second win for the West Indians in America. The last match against Staten Island C.C. was played and lost at Livingston with twelve men on both sides on the 13th and 14th, the defeat for the visitors was attributed to dropped catches, or as Captain Fyfe put it, '*dropped in the most unaccountable manner,*'[124] they lost by 9 wickets. With the trip coming to a successful conclusion the team departed from New York and Captain Fyfe hoped that the new found friends from Canada and America would be *'seen on the Cricket grounds of our fair isles of the West.'* The Americans took up on that offer, with a tour the very next year playing twelve matches in the winter of 1887-88.

Were it not for Henry R. Holmes, whose desire to paint a complete picture of *'The American Cricketers in the West Indies 1887-88,'* the cricketing world would not have known the exploits as there were no records or memoirs kept by any teams, besides the brief mention of the match results in *Wisden, Cricket* and *American Cricketer*. It was not the strongest of teams that departed for St. Kitts on December 12th 1887 aboard the S.S. *Barracouta*. Incidentally, the ship's departure and arrival from the different islands dictated the match schedule. They reached Basseterre on the 24th and played on the same day, but, the match had to be abandoned, as the ship was set to sail for Barbados that evening! Gentlemen of USA scored 91 and St. Kitts replied with 51 for 6, a drawn match.[125] The Gentlemen of U.S.A. were made up of:

C. L. Bixby – Captain - Longwood C.C.
J. T. Carter – Montreal C.C. Canada was the 12th man.
Carl. C. Champion – Young America C.C.
Crawford Coates – Belmont C.C.
W. J. Duhring – Germantown C.C.
Newbold Etting – Merion C.C.
J. Mercer. Garnett – Seabright C.C. of New York.
J. de S. Hamilton – Staten Island C. C.
William Cole Morgan – Germantown C.C.
Charles R. Palmer – Young America C.C.
E. W. Sadler – Seabright C.C.
S. M. Waln – played at Merion and Germantown C.C.

The next match was played on the 27th against the Barbados Garrison after they had arrived in the morning and before the day was over they left for Grenada. USA won by 3 wickets, the score was 103 for 8 wickets in reply to Garrison's 102 runs, it was a twelve-a-side match. On reaching Grenada next morning, they went straight to the ground for another match and the score was a measly 44, maybe the frequent travel and tight schedule was reflecting on their performance now. The Grenadians fared 'one' better scoring 45 and winning the match on that basis as the Americans went in to bat again scoring 107 for the loss of 4 wickets, before running off to the catch the boat to Trinidad late in the day.[126] By now the tourist must have acclimatized to a routine of playing during the day, catching the boat in the night and next morning, on the ground again, as this happened on four consecutive engagements. In British Guiana, they got a break from the daily grind as January 1st was a Sunday and they were to play on the 2nd which was a public holiday, but, the *Barracouta* which was 'their' ship for the past week did not reach Georgetown till the 4 p.m. disappointing a large gathering which had turned up from the countryside.

December 30th and 31st saw the visitors engaging Trinidad at Queen's Park, a full two day match with Trinidad winning by 20 runs. These were the rainy months and when Trinidad opened the first innings they were able to put up only 51 runs due to a wet pitch as it had rained earlier on. The Americans had a drier pitch and fared a little better scoring 82 runs, though they started with the loss of 2 wickets for 2 runs! Trinidad replied with 110 on the second day, leaving a target of 79 runs for the Americans to chase, again, the start was disastrous and they were down by 3 wickets for a solitary run. Bixby who had opened the innings was still at the crease when the score reached 55 for 5, the target, within reach. The tail-enders however, emulated the opening batsmen and the last 5 wickets fell for only 4 runs, leaving Bixby the captain not out at 13 who lasted thru the whole innings. The next match at Guiana brought out the lowest score for both the teams, weather being the main enabler of the low scores. December and January are the wettest months in Georgetown, and the 80° F heat adds to the uncertainty, especially for players from Philadelphia who are not used to such conditions.[127] The Gentlemen of U.S.A. played British Guiana at Bourda on January 3rd 1888, and the visitors went in to bat after winning the toss and within 40 minutes, the 12 men team was able to put up only 18 on the scoreboard! A local reporter wrote, *"we should say it is unprecedented, at any rate it is phenomenal."* In a low scoring match where the Americans scored 18 and 43, the home team won by an innings and 25 runs, having scored 86 runs. Another match was played on the same grounds on the 5th against a combined 'West Indies' with the roles being reversed as far as low scoring was concerned. Captain E. F. Wright of the home team on winning the toss, elected to bat, hopeful that the pitch would be more conducive to batting than it did in the previous match. The second delivery of the inning saw Skeete send the ball to the ropes for 4 and that turned out to be the highest individual score of the match which tied with the 4 extras, and the eleven put up a grand total of 19! I wonder what the local scribe had to say this time. Final score for the home team, 19 and 55, and the Americans replied with 64 and 11, thus winning the match by 9 wickets.

January 5th 1888, match played at Bourda, British Guiana.

WEST INDIES

FIRST INNINGS	RUNS	SECOND INNINGS	RUNS
W.H. Robinson c and b Coates	2	c Carter b Duhring	5
E. Murray Skeete st. Morgan b Waln	4	c and b Palmer	11
L.L. Kerr b Waln	0	b Palmer	5
T. Warner c Palmer b Coates	0	run out	3
E.F. Wright b Waln	3	b Palmer	3
R.B. Butts b Waln	0	b Palmer	19
D.M. McAulay b Waln	2	b Waln	6
C. McLean lbw b Coates	0	c Morgan b Palmer	0
W.A. Harrison c Hamilton b Coates	0	b Palmer	0
A.G. Hughes b Waln	1	c Bixby b Palmer	2
F.W. Griffith not out	3	not out	1
Extras B 2, lb 2,	4		
TOTAL	19	TOTAL	55

UNITED STATES OF AMERICA

FIRST INNINGS	RUNS	SECOND INNINGS	RUNS
C.L. Bixby B Hughes	2	not out	4
W.J. Duhring b McLean	5	b Harrison	1
C. Coates b Harrison	9	not out	6
C.R. Palmer run out	14		
W.C. Morgan Jr. not out	10		
N. Etting b Harrison	7		
C.C. Champion c Butts b Harrison	0		
S.M. Waln c and b Harrison	0		
J.T. Carter b Wright	9		
J. de S. Hamilton c McAulay b Wright	3		
J.M. Garnet c Wright b Harrison	3		
Leg Byes 1 nb 1	2		
TOTAL	64	TOTAL	11

Bowling	Overs	Maiden	Runs	Wickets	Overs	Maiden	Runs	Wickets
USA	First Innings				Second Innings			
S.M. Waln	9.3	8	8	6	6	3	18	1
C. Coates	9	5	8	4	3	-	8	-
W.J. Duhring	-	-	-	-	10	5	19	1
C.R. Palmer	-	-	-	-	12.3	9	10	7
WEST INDIES	First Innings				Second Innings			
C. McLean	8	4	12	1	-	-	-	-
A.G. Hughes	8	2	13	1	-	-	-	-
W.A. Harrison	28	17	19	5	-	-	-	1
D.M. McAuly	7	5	4	-	-	-	-	-
E.F. Wright	10	13	14	2	-	-	-	-

USA won by 9 wickets.

Returning to Barbados from the British Guiana colony on the South American continent, the Americans played the Barbadians on January 9, 10 & 11 at Wanderer's Bay Estate. Wanderers was one of the most exclusive of all West Indian clubs founded in 1877, [128] here the weather being an issue, the Barbadians managed a score of 171 in their 2nd innings. After the captains had agreed to continue the match on the third day with the Americans chasing 185 and having scored only 33 for 2, another downpour flooded the grounds leading them to abandon the match.

Their transient home on the water, the *Barracouta,* gave way to *R.M.S. Nile,* which took them to Jamaica where they were met by L. R. Fyfe, captain of the Kingston C.C. who had earlier brought a team to America in 1886. After playing St. Elizabeth C.C. and winning by 4 wickets, a high scoring match awaited them at Sabina Park on the 19th and 20th against Kingston C.C. The Kingston team included some familiar players from the earlier tour and the Kingston team put up the highest score against the Americans – 196 in the second innings with Lees and Moon putting up the 100 run partnership. The Americans were dismissed for 106, well short of the 210 runs required for victory. Against the Jamaica Garrison, the visitors fared a little better winning by 9 wickets. The last one day match on the tour was played against a local team at Port Antonio on 26th January which turned out to be a delightful sendoff match in the sense that the Gentlemen of U.S.A. scored 356 with Coates scoring 134 and the opposition were bowled out for 69! Were it not for Mr.

Holmes and a certain Mr. Wagg who intensified the search for the scores, we would not have known the details and scores on this tour, two of which are included here.[129]

January 19th and 20th 1888 at Sabina Park, Jamaica.

KINGSTON

FIRST INNINGS	RUNS	SECOND INNINGS	RUNS
Lt. J. Lees b Coates	28	c Duhring b Waln	61
J.A. Gibb b Waln	5	b Waln	5
G.E.R. Pearce b Waln	0	b Waln	0
W.H. Farquharson b Palmer	5	c Morgan b Palmer	8
L.R. Fyfe b Palmer	0	b Waln	10
Lt. A.W. Moon b Coates	6	run out	48
E.N. Marshall c Coates b Waln	20	b Champion	38
Lt. S. Walter b Palmer	14	not out	0
J.M. Burke c Champion b Palmer	9	run out	1
F.L. Pearce c Champion b Palmer	2	b Waln	1
G.H. Pearce not out	1	c Morgan b Palmer	0
Extras B 12, lb 2	14	Extras b 18, lb 6	24
TOTAL	104	TOTAL	196

GENTLEMEN OF USA

FIRST INNINGS	RUNS	SECOND INNINGS	RUNS
C.L. Bixby b Farquharson	4	lbw b Pearce	8
W.J. Duhring b Burke	20	b Farquharson	3
W.C. Morgan b Farquharson	16	b Burke	9
C.R. Palmer b Farquharson	5	not out	39
C. Coates b Lees	25	b Burke	14
S.M. Waln b Lees	4	b Farquharson	0
C.C. Champion c Lees b Pearce	3	b Farquharson	1
N. Etting b Pearce	5	b Farquharson	24
E.W. Sadler c Burke b Lees	1	b Farquharson	0
J.M. Garnett not out	0	b Burke	0
J. de S. Hamilton c Walter b Lees	5	b Burke	0
Extras	3	Extras	8
TOTAL	91	TOTAL	106

Bowling	Overs	Maiden	Runs	Wickets	Overs	Maiden	Runs	Wickets
Gentlemen of U.S.A.	First Innings				Second Innings			
W.J. Duhring	10	2	15	-	10	5	17	-
S.M. Waln	20	9	22	3	27.1	10	55	5
C.R. Palmer	18.4	8	29	5	14	2	41	2
C. Coates	6	2	13	2	6	2	13	-
C.L. Bixby	4		11		11	4	23	-
C.C. Champion	-	-	-	-	10	2	23	1
Kingston	First Innings				Second Innings			
J.M. Burke	15	7	27	1	16	3	36	4
W.H. Farquharson	17	7	24	3	5.2	-	16	5
Lt. J. Lees	11.1	3	23	4	7	2	15	-
G.E.R. Pearce	9	4	14	2	2	-	15	-
F.L. Pearce	-	-	-	-	4	1	16	-

This was a 5 ball over match which Kingston won by 103 runs.

Pelham Warner in an 1898 Wisden article compares WI and American Cricket and opined that Philadelphia was better at batting while the bowling strength lay with the West Indians.[130] Was this premature as Pelham was certainly aware of Bart King, Percy Clark, Lester and even the *Manchester Guardian* acknowledged, *"with him (King) they may beat any of the counties,"* or was it because of the loss against his team in 1898 that made Warner compare the two teams, whatever the reason behind it, King was to top the English bowling average in 1908. At the end of 1903 P.F. Warner himself believed that King would have been an automatic choice for England, had he been eligible![131] The West Indians exposure to international teams/tours when compared against the Americans' at this juncture was minimal to warrant such a comparison.

Edward James Sanders who was a partner in Exeter bank and Exeter Club and a keen proponent of the game, embarked on a tour to America and Canada in 1885. They played two matches in Canada and six in America. Though educated at Harrow and Cambridge, he was not part of the cricket eleven at either. The two matches at Philadelphia drew great crowds numbering eight to nine thousand and the honors were divided equally.[132] Sanders decide to revisit North America the following year encouraged by his first visit. This tour was documented by William Clulow Sim, who went under the nom de plume, 'Old Un.' He was born in Madras, India, in 1832 and joined the Indian Civil Service, but had to retire early due to ill health and lived near Exeter. He was the Honorary Secretary of the Devonshire County Club and it was later learnt that for a few years he had financed the club out of his own funds.

When approached by Ned Sanders, the Manager of the XI, he readily agreed to accompany the party in the unofficial capacity as the scorer and his underlying desire was to meet his son in California. They set sail aboard the White Star Line "Adriatic" from Liverpool on August 19th and reached New York on the 29th. After a couple of days of sightseeing, the first match was played on the 1st and 2nd September against Staten Island. Included in the roster for the Staten Island Club were two professionals who had played first class cricket for Nottinghamshire. Fred Butler, nephew to George Parr, played for Staten Island in 1885 and 86 and returned back to England the following year after disagreeing on the terms. In 1900, he emigrated back to Staten Island till his death in 1923. The other was George Lane who first played for them in 1879, the best left arm bowler in America, taking 65 wickets in 1883. He passed away in 1917 at Haverford College where he set up, Sports Outfitters, the same college which today houses the CC Morris Cricket Library. Cyril Wilson had played for Somerset as an amateur.[133] Butler scored 0 and 28 and Lane contributed 1 and 5 and the English Amateurs easily won by an innings and 49 runs.[134]

One of the 'go ahead' peculiarities of their American cousins observed by the visitors was that, just three months earlier, the cricket ground was an apple orchard! 'Old Un' goes on to say that in England it would have taken them three months just to think about it and another three to enter into an arrangement with a woodcutter! The Staten Island grounds were previously located on the "Flats" or old camp Washington Terminal (near the Staten Island Ferry). In January of 1886 they moved to a part of the Delafield estate, later naming it Walker Park in memory of a young resident of the area, Randolph St. George Walker Jr., a World War I hero. Also of historical significance is the fact that the first Davis Cup tournament was held here in 1880 as Lawn Tennis had found a home on the Staten Island Club grounds. This club has been playing cricket continuously since its inception in 1872, though initially, the club was named, "Staten Island Cricket and Baseball Club!" [135] *"The new grounds and clubhouses of the Staten Island Cricket Club were thronged yesterday by cricket enthusiasts and members of the Ladies' Outdoor Amusement Club. The occasion was the annual match between the American and English members of the club,"* reported *The New York Times of July 6, 1886,* on the first cricket match to be played at the new Walker Park a day earlier. Sander's XI would be the first International team to play on the new grounds.

Their next engagement took them across the border into Canada, playing against an amateur Ontario Association Club on 7th September, whom they defeated by 8 wickets. Here ended the scorers' duties and he parted ways with the team to continue his onward journey west to meet up with his son in California. Meanwhile, Sander's XI steamrolled through the next team Montreal Cricket Club, and crossed back into the American territory for its next engagement at Boston. Here they played against the fifteen of Longwood Cricket Club on September 15, 16 & 17 which according to Lillywhite was the most exciting match of the tour due to weather (rain on the second day and hot temperatures on the third) were not conducive to the batsmen. The last twelve of the home team scored only 25 runs in the second innings and the English lost 7 wickets in quest for the 63 runs required to win.[136] Chambers, another Nottingham professional, was on the Boston team and despite taking ten wickets, he could not prevent Sander's team from winning by three wickets. The previous year also, Chambers had taken six wickets for 34 runs and Sander's team had won narrowly by 16 runs.[137]

According to the Englishmen, Baltimore had one of the best grounds though their eighteen were easily defeated by an innings and 58 runs. Their final games was in Philadelphia, and here the crowds numbered around five thousand even on the second and third days, compared to smaller crowds in other cities. The English won the first match by an innings and sixteen runs[138] and the second by six wickets.

Peter Wynne-Thomas in his introduction to the book, 'Log of the Old Un,' opines that since the two matches against Philadelphia are considered 'first-class' matches and if *America were granted Test Match status prior to 1914, then it is not too far-fetched to say that these matches would now be regarded as Test Matches*. He considers these to be of a higher standard than the 1888-89 English tour to South Africa captained by Charles Aubrey Smith which were later granted 'test' status.

It's only fitting then, to present the scores of the *first two* 'Test Matches' in America.[139]

All Philadelphia vs. English Team played on September 24th, 25th & 26th, 1886.

(1887 Lillywhite gives the dates as 23, 24 & 25-also-Philadelphia player in Lillywhite is named as **H.I. Brown**, the book mentions H.J. Brown)

GENTLEMEN OF PHILADELPHIA

FIRST INNINGS	RUNS	SECOND INNINGS	RUNS
JA Scott, c Welman, b Buckland	18	c and b Buckland	31
GS Patterson, b Buckland	32	run out	19
WC Morgan Jr. b Buckland	27	c Welman, b Buckland	3
RS Newhall, c Welman, b Buckland	11	c Sanders, b Roller	25
W. Brockie Jr., c&b Buckland	0	b Buckland	1
EW Clarke Jr. b Turner	9	b Buckland	0
CA Newhall, b Turner	18	b Hine-Haycock	15
W. Scott, b Rotherham	6	c Roller, b Buckland	5
FW Ralston Jr. c&b Buckland	7	c Cottrell, b Roller	32
FE Brewster, not out	15	not out	1
HI Brown, b Cottrell	9	c Sanders, b Buckland	0
Extras	16	Extras	7
TOTAL	168	TOTAL	139

ENGLISH AMATEURS

FIRST INNINGS	RUNS
J.A. Turner, b C.A. Newhall	11
H.W. Bainbridge, c Brewster, b W. Scott	10
K.J. Key, c W. Scott, b H.I. Brown	109
W.E. Roller, c Clark, b H.I. Brown	75
T.R. Hine-Haycock, b H.I. Brown	5
E.H. Buckland, c Brewster, b C.A. Newhall	19
A.R. Cobb, c R.S. Newhall, b H.I. Brown	14
Rev. A.T. Fortescue, c C.A. Newhall, b H.I. Brown	31
C.E. Cottrell, c Morgan, b C.A. Newhall	2
H. Rotherham, c Morgan, b C.A. Newhall	27
F.T. Welman, not out	7
Extras	13
Total	323

The English won by an innings and 16 runs.
All Philadelphia Vs. English Team, played on October 1st, 2nd and 4th, 1886.

ALL PHILADELPHIA

FIRST INNINGS	RUNS	SECOND INNINGS	RUNS
JA Scott, c Buckland, b Cottrell	9	b Buckland	25
GS Patterson, b Cottrell	12	b Rotherham	40
JB Thayer, c Turner, b Cottrell	6	b Rotherham	13
WC Morgan, not out	45	c Cottrell, b Buckland	1
FW Clark, b Cottrell	0	c Bainbridge, b Roller	8
RS Newhall, b Cottrell	0	c sub, b Buckland	23
CA Newhall, hw, b Buckland	16	c Fortescue, b Buckland	3
FW Ralston, b Roller	11	b Buckland	15
ET Conefort, c Rotherham, b Roller	12	not out	0
HI Brown, c and b Brown	3	c Cobb, b Buckland	5
WC Lowry, b Roller	5	c Turner, b Buckland	2
Extras	9	Extras	11
TOTAL	128	TOTAL	146

ENGLISH TEAM

FIRST INNINGS	RUNS	SECOND INNINGS	RUNS
WE Roller, b Clark	28	b Clark	2
HW Bainbridge, lbw, b Brown	8	c Morgan b Clark	12
KJ Key, c Scott, b Lowry	30	b Clark	0
JA Turner, b Clark	0	c and b Brown	7
EH Buckland, c Rolston, b Lowry	82	not out	15
TR Hine-Haycock, b Clark	0	not out	3
AR Cobb, b CA Newhall	51		
Rev. AT Fortescue, c Morgan, b Lowry	12		
CE Cottrell, c CA Newhall, b Lowry	7		
H. Rotherham, not out	5		
FT Welman, run out	6		
Extras	6	Extras	1
TOTAL	235	TOTAL	40

English team won by 6 wickets.[140]

In April of 1889, Young America and Germantown Club had merged which resulted in the purchase of the Manheim grounds along with the Price and Littell mansions which had existed from the colonial times. The Price mansion was converted into the main clubhouse while the Littell mansion was turned over to the ladies for their use.[141] It was here on September 25, 26 and 28, 1891, Philadelphia had defeated Lord Hawke's XI on equal terms, that is, eleven players who not only were native born, but also belonged to the local clubs only. The visiting team of English amateurs lost by eight wickets, the scores being: England, 259 and 171; and Philadelphia, 248 and 183 for the loss of two wickets. The visitors won the second match by 4 wickets and Sammy Woods was the highest wicket taker on the tour. The first 'Yankee' victory was against Sander's XI in 1885 that were defeated by a Philadelphia XI, the feat was also repeated against the West Indies and Ireland by the same number of players.[142]

Lord Hawke was the Yorkshire captain when he toured America, and the victory over the tourist gave a boost to local cricket and a crowd of 15,000 watched on the second day and those who could not be at the ground, would gather at the newspaper offices to catch the latest news.[143] Overall, more than 30,000 watched the match over 3 days, they came *four-in-hands, tally-hos, T-carts, dog-carts, buckboards and they were lined three or four deep behind the fence.*[144] Other matches were played against an All New York team, Baltimore, Boston Athletic Association, Chicago and two in Canada against Western and Eastern Ontario. Hawke's XI were the strongest amateurs to have visited America since 1872 which included W.G. Grace. Lord Hawke, understandably taken aback by their defeat, commented, *"There is no telling what you Americans can do. I suppose the next time an English professional XI comes here, you will want to teach them to play cricket!"* In 1892-93 Lord Hawke took his team to India and the following year in 1894 when he revisited America, it was generally accepted that the main attraction for foreign teams was to match wits against Philadelphia. This time though the weather did not help the home team and they lost both matches, the first played on September 21 & 23 where Philadelphia lost by 131 runs and the other was played on 28 and 29, here again losing by an innings and 40 runs.[145]

The 1897 visit by Pelham Warner was the thirteenth in a series of English expeditions to America by teams of various strengths which included both amateurs and professionals and otherwise, such as the team that came over for the 1876 Centennial Year celebrations of which there is no mention.[146] The teams in order are as follows:

1859 – George Parr (Professionals)
1868 – Willsher's XI (Professionals)
1872 – Grace under Edgar 'Ned' Willsher's XI (Amateurs)
1876 – Unknown College & amateurs participated in the Centennial Year Celebrations.
1879 – Richard Daft's XII (Professionals)
1879 – Lord Harris's XI (Amateurs)
1881 – Shaw's XI (Professionals)
1885 – E. J. Sander's XI (Amateurs)
1886 – E. J. Sander's XI (Amateurs)
1891 – Lord Hawke's XI (Amateurs)
1894 – Lord Hawke's XI (Amateurs)
1895 – F. Mitchell's XI (Amateurs)
1897 – P.F. Warner's XI (Amateurs)
1898 – P.F. Warner's XI (Amateurs)

1899 – Ranjitsinhji's XI (Strongest Amateur Team)

Warner's XI lost one match to the Gentlemen of Philadelphia which was played on September 24, 25 & 27th by 4 wickets with the GOP having scored 242 and 194 for 6, while Warner's XI scored 63 and 372 runs. In the first innings, Warner's team lost the first 4 wickets for a 'duck' and the highest scorer was J. R. Head with 14 and Bart King ended up taking 9 wickets for 25 runs.[147] The other matches played were against New York where they won by 244 runs, a draw resulted against the twenty-two Colts of Philadelphia and a win by 74 runs against the sixteen of Baltimore. The fifth match against the GOP XI played on October 1, 2 and 4th resulted in a loss for Philadelphia by the same margin that they had won a few days ago - by 4 wickets. The Oxford and Cambridge players under Frank Mitchell's XI in 1895 had the worst record of any English XI in America; they won only 2 of the 5 matches played. Their first match against an XI comprised of past and present University of Pennsylvania players who won the match by 100 runs. At one point, they were 150 runs behind in their second innings but scored 307 runs and bowled out the English for a mere 61 runs. In the second match at Manheim, the visitors won by two wickets in an evenly contested match, and at Haverford, Philadelphia won by an innings and 39 runs.[148]

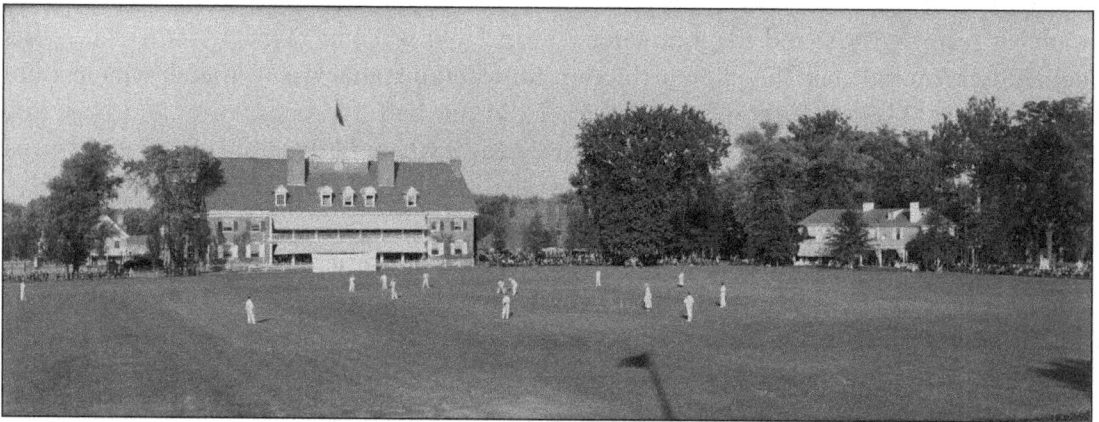

1898 PF Warner's XI v Philadelphia (fielding) at Merion Cricket Grounds. Haverford College Archives, Haverford PA.

It was in 1891-92, that the Australians had won the Ashes series by 2-1 for the very first time after losing to England on the previous eight occasions. The summer of 1893 saw the Australians embark on another quest for the Ashes led by Jack Blackham hoping that they would win the away-series by defeating England on their home turf. There was twice the burden and pressure on the home team to reclaim the Ashes and not lose on the home turf!

The English managed to retain the Ashes and keep the home record intact by winning the series 1-0. The Australians in their eight month journey crossed the Atlantic on their way home played six matches in North America, five in USA and one in Canada. This leg of the tour was not without controversy and it was objected to back in Australia as shown by the letter that was sent to the Cricket Council in opposition to the American Tour.

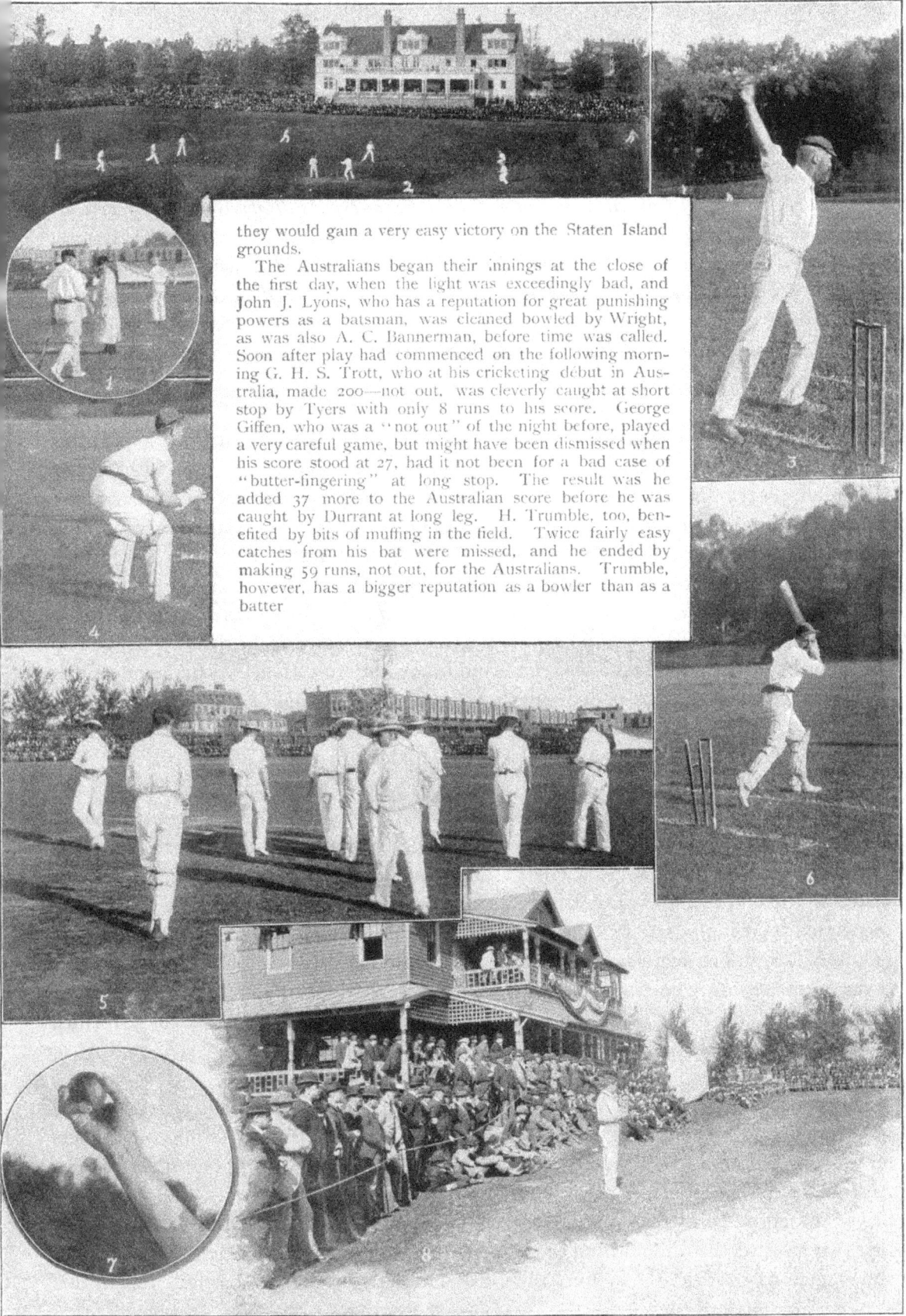

they would gain a very easy victory on the Staten Island grounds.

The Australians began their innings at the close of the first day, when the light was exceedingly bad, and John J. Lyons, who has a reputation for great punishing powers as a batsman, was cleaned bowled by Wright, as was also A. C. Bannerman, before time was called. Soon after play had commenced on the following morning G. H. S. Trott, who at his cricketing début in Australia, made 200—not out, was cleverly caught at short stop by Tyers with only 8 runs to his score. George Giffen, who was a "not out" of the night before, played a very careful game, but might have been dismissed when his score stood at 27, had it not been for a bad case of "butter-fingering" at long stop. The result was he added 37 more to the Australian score before he was caught by Durrant at long leg. H. Trumble, too, benefited by bits of muffing in the field. Twice fairly easy catches from his bat were missed, and he ended by making 59 runs, not out, for the Australians. Trumble, however, has a bigger reputation as a bowler than as a batter

VISITING AUSTRALIAN CRICKETERS: ALL PHILADELPHIA VS. AUSTRALIA.

1. Going in to bat.
2. The match—Philadelphia in the field.
3. A mighty bowler.
4. The wicket keeper.
5. All Philadelphia going into the field.
6. Bowled.
7. How the ball is held.
8. Watching the match.

Mr. H. Y. Sparks has written to, Mr. John Portus, secretary of the Australasian Cricket Council, as follows: "Adelaide, September 10, English telegrams which appeared in the daily papers this week report that the Australian Eleven is proceeding to America to play a series of matches, but that certain members of the team do not approve of certain fixtures, and that Messrs. Bannerman and Turner intend returning home this month, and will not go to America. If these statements are true, I think the Cricket Council should at once interfere, or express disapproval. So far as I am aware, the Eleven is in no sense justified in entering into any such engagements without the consent of the Cricket Council, and it is establishing an exceedingly dangerous precedent if the council does not object. The Eleven is practically under the auspices of the council, and the council is responsible for the team in so far as it represents as a whole Australian cricket." Mr. Sparks says he did not think when the team left Australia that it was intended that they should go to America and such an arrangement ought to have the approval of the council."[149]

It did not help matters when the Australians lost the first match against Philadelphia in a big way - an innings and 68 runs; the GOP posted a record score of 525 runs with Francis H Bohlen, contributing 118 in four hours. There was no doubt that the Australians were tired after a long voyage and were rushed onto Captain Green's private railroad car (number 30) in New York and straight onto the ground without any rest at all, [150] the players protested as they needed rest, but captain Blackham consented to play. *"You have better players here than we have been led to believe, they class with England's best,"* Blackham commented after the drubbing. A day's rest would definitely have worked wonders for the visitors, but no excuses were made and the other matches would show the Australians worth. Large crowds witnessed the match played at Belmont on September 29, 30 and October 2nd 1893.

George Patterson opened the innings for Philadelphia with a score of 56 while the other opening bat, Reynolds Brown, made 23 when the first wicket fell at 46 due to poor running between the wickets. At the end of first days play, Bohlen was not out on 82 and Noble was not out on 73 (Bohlen would go on to score a century). Australia at the end of day two were 125 for 4 wickets and at this point, all indications were that this match would end in a draw. Day three quickly turned in Philadelphia's favor, as the visitors ended their innings at 199, losing 4 quick wickets between 146 and 160, now they required 326 runs to avoid an innings defeat. It could have still ended in a draw, but the home team sensing victory, gave it everything and even with Bannerman's 79 not out in three hours and 58 by Trott, it was not enough as they were bowled out for 258 runs, handing Philadelphia their biggest victory over the Australians.[151]

The second match against the New York Eighteen which was played on October 4th, ended in a draw. New Yorkers were dismissed for 101 runs with Trumble taking 10 wickets for 41 runs and M'Leod 3 for 44.[152] For the home team, George Wright ensured that the Australians did not put up a big score by taking 5 wickets, incidentally, this match was played in Central Park! The Australians were looking to better their performance after the first two matches that did nothing to improve their standing and they required a stronger showing in their 2nd match against the GOP. Hugh Trumble was instrumental in this

Australian six wicket victory over the GOP played from October 6, 7 & 9th with Australia scoring 153 and 4 for 70, while the GOP scored 116 and 106.[153] At Boston they defeated the local team by 7 wickets, but at one point after the Australians had disposed off the eighteen for only 88 runs in the first innings, they themselves were faced with a similar situation. Playing with twelve men, the Australians put up an even smaller score of only 65 runs! The score: Boston Eighteen – 88 & 27, the visitors – 65 and 3 for 52. After playing in Toronto, they engaged the eighteen of Detroit where they easily won by an innings and 157 runs, [154] the match was played at Detroit Athletic Club Ground on 18, & 19th October and on their way to San Francisco, they stopped at the World's Fair in Chicago.

The 4th tour by an Australian XI happened under GHS Trott who visited Philadelphia in 1896 playing six matches in all including three against the GOP. Philadelphia lost the first two but won the third by an innings and 99 runs, thus the first-class matches ended 2-1 in Australia's favor. This team also included five members of the 1893 team, Trott, now the Captain of the team, George Giffen, Graham, S.E. Gregory and Trumble. The matches against the GOP started on 18th September at the Germantown club grounds in Manheim where the home team lost by 123 runs. The Australians scored 192 and 180 while the GOP scored 123 and 126. Giffen contributed with both the bat and ball for the Australians, scoring 69 and 42 runs while taking 5 and 2 wickets in each innings. For the GOP, E.W. Clark remained not out in both innings with 38 and 35 respectively.[155]

On 23rd September, they played against New Jersey at Bergen Point, a one sided affair with the host losing by an innings and 99 runs. At the match played at Elmwood on 25th, the Australians handed the GOP another defeat by an innings and 71 runs. Australia put up a formidable 422 runs with Giffen again contributing an individual high score of 96, kept in check by Bart King's 5 wicket haul for 90 runs. The Philadelphia batting could not muster enough runs, scoring 144 and 207. For the third match however, the tide turned and the GOP was able to defeat the Australians by an innings and 60 runs! [156] The match was played on 2, 3 and 5th October at the Merion Cricket Club ground in Haverford. Just eight days earlier on September 24th, the Clubhouse had caught fire again for the 2nd time that year (the January 4th fire had completely destroyed the old structure), partially damaging it. Australia lost wickets at a steady pace and that too at the hands of P.H. Clark who substituted for an injured Patterson, by removing Darling, Giffen and Hill, three of their best bats and ended the innings with a haul of 5 wickets for 49 runs, sharing honors with King, who also took 5 wickets for 43 runs. Philadelphia replied with a solid knock of 282 and this time the man of the hour was bowler E.W. Clark, who took 6 wickets for only 24 runs (PH Clark took only 1 wicket) and shutting out the tourist for 101 runs. The other two matches were against a Chicago team on 8, 9 October, where the Australians easily won and against a California team in San Francisco on 14 and 15 resulting in a draw.

1896 Australians.

On 30th September 1912, Philadelphia beat Australia in a thrilling 2 run victory in the most exciting match against an Australian team, though not an official one. The previous visits were from the official team stopping on their way home from a summer of cricket in England, this was not. Due to a dispute with the Australian Board of Control, seven of their best players, including Victor Trumper did not go to England and the ones that did make the tour, Bardsley, Macartney, Minnett, Hazlitt and Jennings did not travel with the rest of the team to Philadelphia. The rest arrived here only after an agreement was signed stating that these matches are not to be considered 'official' Australian matches. The home team was captained by P.H. Clark who in 1896 had taken out the three best Australian bats during his debut match, now the home team had amassed a decent 185 in the first innings with a high of 57 contributed by W. Newhall. Jimmy Matthews took 5 wickets for 65 runs which included a hat-trick. The Australians replied with a meager 122 as King nearing 40 years, was still in his elements taking 5 wickets for 40 runs.

No to be outdone, Whitty with 4 wickets and Emery with 5, wreaked havoc as the home team folded for only 74 runs, the only double figure of 17 was contributed by S.W. Mifflin, and oh, the extras contributed to the double figures too – 13. This left the Australians with an easy target of 137 runs, but lost 3 quick wickets for 7 runs. With the middle order steading the innings they were only 3 runs away from victory when Bart coming to the rescue again, bowled Whitty, thereby robbing the Australians of a nail biting victory.[157] The scores from this very exciting match are given below and the autographs of the Philadelphia players in Edgar Mayne's album are from this very same match!

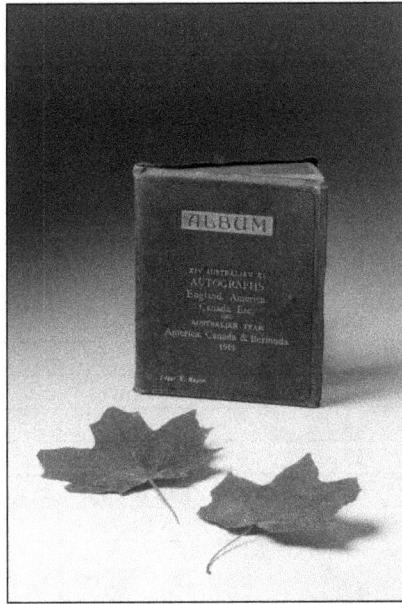

Cover - Edgar Mayne's Album that covered the 1912-1913 tour. (The 2 maple leaves were inside the album, probably from Canada or America) Photo Courtesy: George Serras, National Museum of Australia.

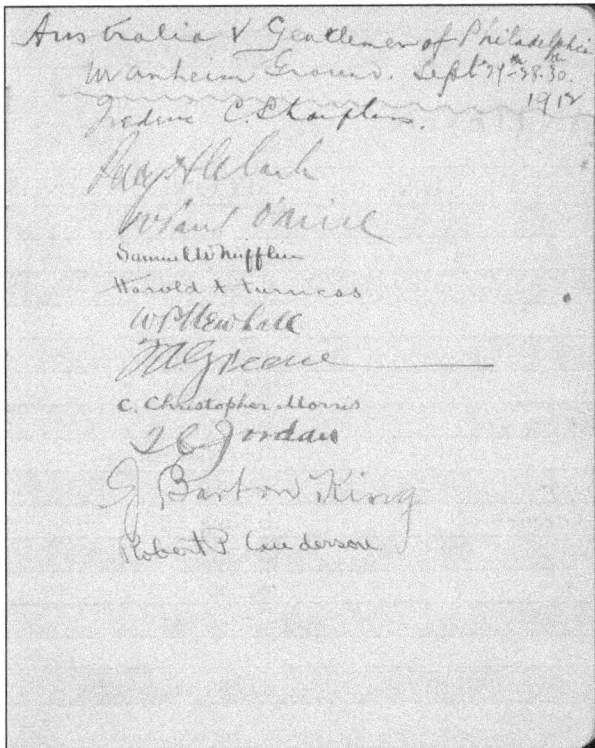

Signatures of the Philadelphia Cricket Team in 1912.
Photo Courtesy: George Serras, National Museum of Australia.

PHILADELPHIANS vs. AN AUSTRALIAN ELEVEN
Match played at Manheim, September 27, 28 and 30, 1912.
<u>Philadelphia wins by 2 runs</u>

PHILADELPHIA

FIRST INNINGS	RUNS	SECOND INNINGS	RUNS
JB King b Whitty	13	b Emery	8
FC Sharpless b Whitty	20	b Whitty	9
HA Furness b Matthews	0	b Emery	8
SW Mifflin c&b Matthews	14	run out	17
WP Newhall b MacLaren	57	b Whitty	1
RP Anderson c Whitty b Matthews	0	b Whitty	9
CC Morris c Whitty b Matthews	0	b Emery	7
PH Clark stumped Carkeek b Matthews	7	lbw Whitty	0
WP O'Neill b Emery	36	lbw Emery	0
TC Jordan not out	24	not out	2
FA Greene c Matthews b Emery	0	b Emery	0
Extras	14	Extras	13
TOTAL	185	TOTAL	74

AN AUSTRALIAN ELEVEN

FIRST INNINGS	RUNS	SECOND INNINGS	RUNS
CE Kelleway c&b Clark	4	b King	2
SH Emery b King	4	c King b Clark	3
TJ Matthews b King	3	b Clark	2
ER Mayne c Clark b King	13	c Newhall b King	20
SE Gregory b King	33	b Newhall	10
D Smith c Newhall b King	11	b Clark	0
H Webster b Greene	16	lbw Newhall	54
JW MacLaren c King b Greene	6	run out	0
WJ Whitty c Anderson b Greene	1	b King	23
W Carkeek not out	28	b King	4
E Penfold b Greene	0	not out	0
Extras	3	Extras	17
TOTAL	122	TOTAL	135

Bowling	Overs	Maiden	Runs	Wickets	Overs	Maiden	Runs	Wickets
PHILADELPHIA	First Innings				Second Innings			
King	22	8	40	5	20	7	38	4
Clark	13	1	32	1	17	4	40	3
Greene	7.3	0	27	4	5	3	10	0
O'Neill	6	1	20	0	-	-	-	-
Newhall	-	-	-	-	7	0	30	2
AN AUSTRALIAN XI	First Innings				Second Innings			
Whitty	20	7	49	2	13	3	23	4
Emery	2.2	1	6	2	12.5	1	38	5
Matthews	20	6	65	5	-	-	-	-
MacLaren	11	3	39	1	-	-	-	-
Kelleway	5	1	12	0	-	-	-	-

One hundred years ago in May, when an Australian team sailed for the American shores, little did anyone realize that it would be making its last trip to America, that this would be the last vestige of Victorian cricket in Philadelphia. They departed Sydney on board the R.M.S. Niagara on May 9th 1913 for Suva, Fiji on the invitation of the Governor to play a match there, en-route to Vancouver. The dozen Australians ended up playing 52 matches on the tour, winning 48, three ended in a draw and lost the only match to the Germantown Club XII.[158] This was one extensive tour to North America which began with a match against Victoria (Canada) on 28th May ending with the British Columbia Colts on September 26th. [159] Similar to the 1912 Australian tour, this was also a privately funded tour arranged by Edgar. R. Mayne who was on last year's roster too. A last minute effort to include Victor Trumper who was on board the Niagara just before it sailed, did not materialize. The team comprised of, W. Bardsley, C. G Macartney, A. Diamond, H. L. Collins, A. A. Mailey, S. H. Emery, P. S. Arnott, and L. A. Cody, from New South Wales; E. R. Mayne, J. N. Crawford, G. C. Campbell, and G. S. Down, represented South Australia.[160]

The first match against the GOP was played on June 20th at Manheim where Australia scored a massive 521 in reply to GOP's 124. There was no recovering from this and they added 219 in the second innings (106 being contributed by Furness) coming up short and losing by an innings and 178 runs. After playing two matches in Schenectady, the visitors returned on June 27th to play another match against the GOP and win it by 10 wickets. Due to an early end to the previous match another one was played on 28th & 30th which ended in a technical draw. Here again the Australians put up a big total – 412 for the loss of only 5 wickets with Macartney and Bardsley both scoring 109 and 101 respectively and a 97 by Cody. A three day match on the 4th 5th & 7th of July saw a combined Canadian and American team of players took on the Australians at Manheim. Same story different players, the combined strength lost by 409 runs. After playing in Canada and teams in Pittsburgh, Rhode Island and New York, the Australians were back in Philadelphia to play one last match against the Germantown Cricket Club XII on August 6th and 7th. *"The story of first-class cricket in Philadelphia ends with this extraordinary match."*[161]

This was a twelve-a-side match, and Australia fielded one man short as their fast bowler Crawford was ill, but the Germantown Club was allowed to play with twelve men. The Australians were put into bat and scored a comparatively small total of 144 with F.A. Greene and J.H. Savage keeping them in check with a haul of 4 wickets each. In reply, Germantown scored 190 runs with P.H. Clark contributing 82 with the bat and took 6 wickets for 38 runs. Australia in their second inning, were all out for a measly 126 of which 64 runs were contributed by Bardsley, which left the home team with a 81 run target. After a very shaky start where Germantown lost 4 quick wickets for only 14 runs, Clark and Newhall took the score to 41, when Clark was run out. Newhall was joined by W.P. O'Neill who contributed 13 and Newhall remained not out at 31 thus winning the match by 4 wickets.[162] According to the players, this match was won by excellent fielding. Next, they played the West Indian Colored XI in Brooklyn and three matches in Chicago, (August 27, 28 & 29) before heading north west to play in Canada (Winnipeg, Saskatchewan, Edmonton, Calgary and British Columbia) till end of September, before returning home. It would be 1932 before such an extensive tour would be undertaken by an Australian team again and that too during the depression era nonetheless, and this time it would include the legendary, Don Bradman.

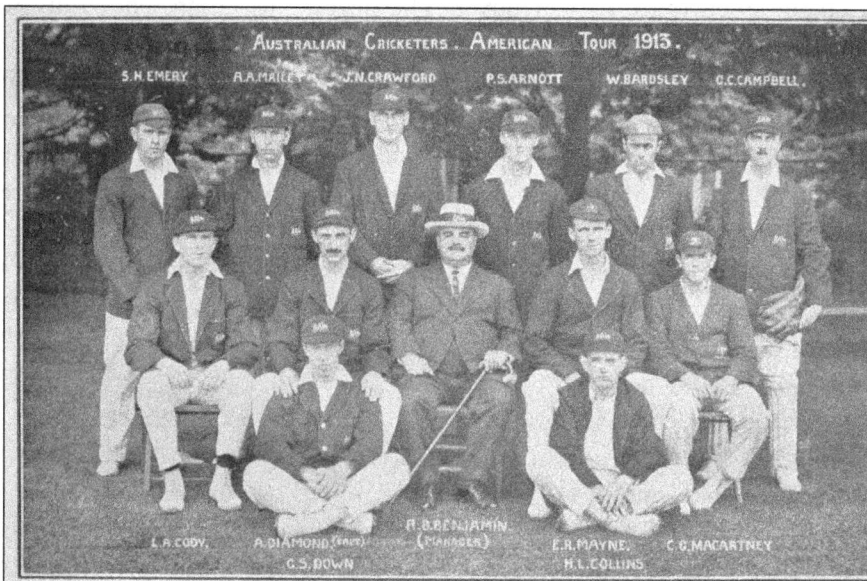

A Prince and the King

On a windy day in June, John 'Bart' Barton King was on his first tour of England with the Gentlemen of Philadelphia in 1897. On winning the toss they elected to bat and scored 216 in their first innings with the help of a 4th wicket partnership of 109 between J.A. Lester and King.[1] The Sussex batting lineup included their regular full strength team who came out to bat hoping to chase an easy target, but instead, in less than an hour on a perfect wicket, they were bowled out for a paltry 46 runs!

Taking advantage of a strong breeze blowing across the ground, Bart chose the bowling end where the wind was over his left shoulder and when he was done, the Sussex team was in shambles. His first inning bowling analysis read, 10 overs, 5 maidens and 7 wickets for only 13 runs! K.S. 'Ranji' Ranjitsinhji, one of the greatest batsmen of the era, was clean bowled, losing his middle stump in the very first delivery and later described how the ball, *"sprang in at him like a tiger, a good foot from the off and yorked him."*[2] Prince Ranji was bowled by Bart's special delivery, the 'angler.'

Sussex went into bat again and they were 12 for 1 at the close of play on the first day. They put up 252 runs with Ranji contributing 74, but that did not stop the Philadelphians from winning by eight wickets. By the end of the match the respect between King and Ranji was mutual, and Bart later admitted that once Ranji started scoring he had no idea how to bowl to him. *"One ball may be pitched up and hit for four between cover-point and extra cover, and the next, pitching in exactly the same place, may go for four between square and fine leg."*[3]

Ranji's only overseas tour as captain, to North America finally materialized in 1899, though he nearly visited Philadelphia on two previous occasions. One was with the Cambridge University team in 1895-96, and two years later, with C.B. Fry and Lord Hawke, but all three withdrew and instead Ranji went to Australia during the winter of 1897-98 with Andrew Stoddart's team.[4] This would have been one hectic year for Ranji had the tour materialized, as they had played against the Gentlemen of Philadelphia at home then going over to play in America and on return embark on the Australian tour.

Instead, Pelham 'Plum' Warner set out on a return tour by bringing a team over in September of that year and also in 1898.

These two cricketers came from two very different backgrounds.

October 19, 1873, Bart was born into a working class family and unlike most of his team mates, who were born into wealthy aristocratic families; he came from a humble background. His early working years were spent in his fathers' linen and yard goods trade, and later into insurance, which was created for him by his extended cricketing fraternity. This way he could devote time to the game and not worry about his source of income. Here we realize why baseball had spread to every corner of the country and became the game of choice and means for the masses as they could participate in the game as spectators and players alike for a few short hours. As with any other kid in the neighborhood, Bart started with baseball where he learnt the basics of pitching a curve ball, but the heavens had other plans for him and guided him towards cricket, for he was to be (one of) the brightest cricket star in the firmament.

It is a mystery then, rather sad in fact, that his name has been omitted from the galaxy of cricketers from the Golden Age of Cricket. Growing up, one read of the folklore of the cricket greats and would look up to for inspiration, but nowhere is Kings' name to be found (save a few books) in the popular culture. The majority of the names were English with a few Australians — why was Kings' name, a rarity? I can understand the American print media had nothing on cricket in the 20th century as it was off their radar as far as they were concerned, but the English cricketing world — they knew about Philadelphia cricket first hand, and by extension, the astounding achievements of J.B. King! In 1888 at the age of 15 he turned to cricket with the Tioga Cricket Club playing for the juniors.[5] Tioga was one of the principal clubs which participated in the Halifax Cup and his first recorded match was found in the following year where he played against the Germantown juniors on June 27th.[6] That year he ended the season with 37 wickets for 99 runs,[7] a sign of an approaching genius cricketer and a gentleman that was to evolve. Speaking of which, Bart enjoyed recounting an amusing incident that happened on a London street with an English professional cricketer.

"Hello, Mr. King," said the professional.
"Hello, call me Bart," said King.
"But you're a gentleman cricketer."
"Aren't you a gentleman too?"
"Oh no, sir, I'm a professional."

Ranjitsinhji or Ranji on the other hand was born a farmers' son in Sarodar, a remote village in Nawanagar state (comes under present day Gujarat state) in Kathiawar province. He was born on September 10th 1872, and was related to the ruling family of the state through his grandfather. At an early age he was sent to stay with his uncle due to his fathers' troubled behavior and as was the custom in those days, he was selected as an heir apparent, in case the Jam Sahib of Nawanagar did not produce an heir. Due to his father's continued troubles, the ruler delayed adopting Ranji and in the meantime he had a son of his own, which brought the matters to an end. At age six, Ranji had come so close to being the heir to the Nawanagar throne one which he would ultimately get at the age of 34 in 1906.[8] Though he was not a prince, he was always portrayed as one while in England, and with no less help from Ranji himself. The story of Ranji and his cricket exploits may have been very different if the 'image' had not been created. In the meantime, he was sent to the Rajkumar College for Princes and the desire to excel and be a worthy choice for the throne made him good at both studies and sports which ultimately caught the attention of Chester Macnaghten, the principal, who arranged for him to go to Cambridge University to complete his education.

Ranji not only excelled at studies, but also at tennis, gymnastics and cricket. He was sent to Cambridge where he was allowed admission into Trinity College as, 'youth of position' after he had failed the entrance exam. He was getting more and more interested in cricket and never graduated as he did not study more then was necessary. He made his debut for Trinity in 1892, however due to prejudice he was ignored by the other players and this made him work harder at the nets and improve his batting techniques. He made his first class debut on May 8th 1893 playing for Cambridge and scored 18 runs batting at number 9. At the end of the season his batting average stood at 29.9 the 3rd best in the team. His cricketing prowess made him more acceptable at Trinity and initially he was called Smith, and finally Ranji as they found it difficult to pronounce his name.[9] Ranji's debut for Sussex came against the MCC in 1895 where he scored 77 not out in the first innings and also took six wickets. His maiden century for first class cricket came in the second innings, scoring 150 runs in 155 minutes! He ended the season with an average of 49.31 which placed him 4th in the national averages scoring 1,775 runs. He finally made his test debut against Australia, on July 16th 1896, scoring a century (154 not out) in the second innings after being denied a spot on the team by the MCC selection committee during the first test.[10]

"The famous young Indian fairly rose to the occasion, playing an innings that could, without exaggeration, be fairly described as marvelous. He punished the Australian bowlers in a style that, up to that period of the season, no other English batsman had approached. He repeatedly brought off his wonderful strokes on the leg side, and for a while had the Australian bowlers quite at his mercy."[11]

Standing(L-R): R.A. Studd, K.S. Ranjitsinhji, R.C. Norman, W.G. Druce, Edwin Field.
Seated: C.M. Wells, C.G. Pope, A.R. Hoare, Frank Stanley Jackson, M.G. Tollemache.
Sitting on the ground – T.T. Phelps. 1893 Trinity College, Cambridge XI.

These were time of prejudice and not everyone was pleased at Ranji's success. A cricket journalist and statistician, Sir Home Gordon, made the mistake of praising Ranjitsinhji in conversation to a member of the MCC who angrily threatened to have him expelled from the MCC, for *"having the disgusting degeneracy to praise a dirty black."* Other MCC members were heard complaining about *"a nigger showing us how to play the game of cricket."*[12] It was no different in America, when in 1899 under these same conditions, Ranji captained the English team. I am trying to picture a dark skinned individual on the streets or hotels in Philadelphia, the expressions on the patrons would have been captured by a Norman Rockwell-*esque* painting, similar to the one showing a little black girl being escorted by the feds, to a school in the segregated south. Being a 'prince' had its perks and I am sure he was well received where ever he went. He was named one of the Wisden Cricketers of the year in 1896 and in August of 1897, released a book, *'The Jubilee Book of Cricket,'* with the help of his good friend, C.B. Fry.

The winter of 1897-98 saw Ranji in Australia under Stoddart's captaincy, his only Test tour where he scored 457 runs at an average of 50.77. [13] He missed the 1898 season as he was in India for most of the year to stake his claim to the Nawanagar throne and after being unsuccessful for the time being, returned to England in March of 1899. In June and August of the same season, he scored 1000 runs, a feat not achieved previously. In all, he scored 3,159 runs at an average of 63.18. He became the first batsman to pass 3000 runs in a season in first class cricket. This feat was repeated during the 1900 season where he scored 3,065 runs for an average of 87.57, placing him at the top of the national average. [14]

In June of 1899, he was appointed captain of Sussex and the following year, kept on producing great scores. The highest score was 275 runs against Leicestershire and he ended the season with 3,065 runs, averaging 87.57, thus placing him at the top of the table. Unfortunately, this exhibition of masterful scoring did not continue as his financial woes were getting the better of him, his inability to secure financial support almost caused him to declare bankruptcy. The inventor of the leg glance, could not get his house in order and it reflected on the field. 1902 was his final year where he played for England, he had played 15 test matches, all against Australia, scoring 989 runs. The following season he again managed a second place in the batting averages and this was to be his last year as captain of Sussex. In 1904 he returned to India after leading the batting averages for the 4th time scoring 2,077 runs at an average of 74.17. [15] His career had effectively ended that year though he continued to play when he returned to England in 1908 and for the last time in 1912.

In 1906 his luck had finally changed as the current Jam Sahib to the throne died unexpectedly without an heir, and Ranji was chosen by the Government as the new Jam Sahib of Nawanagar till his passing away in April of 1933. In his cricketing career, he had scored 24,692 runs at an average of 56.37, the highest career average of a batsman based in England.

The Prince of Cricket – K.S. 'Ranji' Ranjitsinhji, Sussex Cricket Museum.

Across the pond in Philadelphia, King was beginning to show his mettle from an early age where he had joined the Tioga club which was one of the principal cricket clubs in Philadelphia. The record of his first match shows up for the club in 1889, where he played for the juniors against Germantown juniors scoring 39 in his first innings and his season ended with a haul of 37 wickets for 99 runs. His first international exposure was against the Gentlemen of Ireland in 1892 after he had become a permanent member of the senior team. He remained with Tioga till the club disbanded in 1896 joining another Philadelphia club, Belmont , with whom he played most of his career matches till the Belmont grounds were sold and the club disbanded after the 1912 season. He eventually ended his career with the Philadelphia Cricket Club retiring in 1916. While at Belmont, Bart toured England on three occasions with the Philadelphia team, it is here where he produced his best performance.

Belmont Cricket Club

Indoors and Out, a Monthly Magazine from 1907.

Another cricket great of Philadelphia, John A. Lester introduces Bart in 'Century of Philadelphia Cricket, *"Bart King was without question the finest all-round cricketer ever produced in America."* Not only was he good with the bat & ball, he had a *"warm heart, ready wit, and ever-renewed stock of cricket stories, factual and fictional, he had a host of friends on both sides of the Atlantic, and was the best-known cricket figure in our history."*[16]

Confidence in one's ability is perhaps the key requisite for success in any endeavor, and Bart always experimented with different bowling techniques before adopting them and once he was settled on the method, *"he used them with that supreme confidence that was his outstanding characteristic."*[17] At six foot one inch, Bart was in top physical shape, and his strength lay not in his broad powerful shoulders but in his wrist and fingers which was maintained by his own special exercise. Lester writes that, *"with his wrist held tight Bart could send a new cricket ball to the second story window with a snip of two fingers and a thumb."*[18] His physical conditioning enabled him to have great endurance, which in turn aided him in extending his career as a fast bowler for nearly 25 years. *"The career of the greatest of all American cricketers, one whose achievements may be said to demand a place for him amongst the immortals,"* was none other than, John Barton King! [19]

To illustrate the confidence Bart had in his ability, this story has made the rounds in several versions and at times dismissed as fable, but none the less, it's true.

George Edward "Rube" Waddell was an eccentric power pitcher who led the Baseball major leagues in strikeouts, six years in a row and won twenty-two games for the Philadelphia Athletics.[20] In an exhibition game around 1901, Bart watched him send all the outfielders to the sidelines and then proceed to strike out the batter. He toyed with a similar idea and an opportunity arose during a match against Trenton at Elmwood in the Halifax Cup. King had just bowled out the ninth man and the captain of the Trenton team arrived late as he had missed the train. The captain remarked that his team would not have been in such a sorry state had he arrived on time. One knew better than to make such a statement in Kings' presence, for he was not the one to let anyone off the hook so easily and here was his opportunity to put that 'baseball play' in practice.

King called his fielders together as the Trenton captain was taking guard and sent them back to the clubhouse. He walked back to start his run up and noticed the Belmont wicket-keeper Edward Leech still in position behind the stump.

"Why Eddie, Eddie, whatever are you doing there? I won't need you, Eddie, join the rest."

After Eddie had left, the remaining people on the field were the two Trenton batsmen, the two umpires and of course, the ever exuberant, King. Surely the Trenton captain had numerous thoughts run thru his mind, was King hinting that he was not capable of scoring, nay, a single run in an empty field? He appealed to the umpires stating that the laws of the game called for eleven players on the fielding side and this was not to be allowed. A situation such as this had never arisen before and the two umpires after an informal deliberation concluded that, *"Mr King was well within the law so long as he did not have more than eleven men on the field."*[21]

The Trenton captain was in a no win situation and prepared to face the bowler, but, the King was not done with his theatrics yet. He paused, savouring the moment and sensed that his prey was cornered and ready for the kill. Before taking his run up, he said he may require another fielder after all, and called for one from the pavilion. Bart placed him exactly twenty yards behind the wicket and four paces to the leg side of the wicket.

"For heaven's sake, if you don't need a wicket-keeper, what on earth is that man doing there?"

"He's not a wicket-keeper" said King. *"He's is not even a fielder." You see, I have given the umpires enough trouble already, that man is there for one purpose only, which is to pick up the ball after the game is over and return it to the umpires."*

King bowled out the captain hitting the leg wicket with his potent weapon, the 'Angler.' Bart, in recollecting to Lester mentions, *"You know, what pleased me best was not to see the bails jumping, but that I grazed the leg peg just fine enough to take the ball to the man I meant to get it. He didn't have to move a step."*[22]

In the *Ten Great Bowlers*, Ralph Barker carries the version where the *bails* fall at the feet of the strategically placed fielder who then hands them over to the umpires. I would tend to go with the version given by Lester as that would have come straight from the man himself, Mr JB King.

In later years a third version was apparently narrated by 'the Captain' of the day, where he claims to be the only person to have hit King for 4 sixes in 4 consecutive deliveries during that fateful day. He further goes on to say that King may have been a great bowler, but he would have to take second place to him in one respect – telling lies, implying that King was apt to tell tall tales too.[23]

King, who grew up with baseball, learnt to swerve the ball while pitching and that soon followed him into cricket, though his final bowling action just before delivery was similar to a baseball pitch, where he held the ball with both hands above his head before the final delivery. He was never accused of 'throwing' the ball due to his run-up action, it was always a smooth delivery. Because of this early initiation to 'swing or curve ball,' he practiced different variations till he found one that was most effective and kept on improving on it. Another salient feature was that he used his special deliveries sparingly, so as not to render them ineffective.

"We must always remember that the ball that curves is just an adjunct to the stock in trade of a good bowler."[24] In describing how he bowled the angler in his own words, King observed that what worked for one bowler may not work for another. If the bowler always curves, a good batsman will find it just as easy to play as he would with a straight delivery. *"Every seasoned bowler will understand that I arrived at my methods by experiment – by finding out through a longish process of trial and error what worked best for me."*[25] Bart was a pitcher before he became a bowler and he learned a good deal from his baseball experience. 'Roundhouse' or 'outcurve' pitching was like an out swinger in cricket but this uniform curve was not effective as the batter could gauge its direction early on. This was replaced with the 'hook' a pitch that travelled with very little curve till the last 10-15 feet when it shoots out for the right hand pitcher and curves in for the left hander.

Bart began to experiment as this was difficult to achieve with a smooth bowling action. By the time he was eighteen he was genuinely fast and discovered he could swerve the ball. *"Finding that under certain unpredictable conditions the ball would respond, and suddenly swing in at an angle or tangent to the flat trajectory of my fast ball, I christened this infant my "angler."*[26]

To achieve this, *"I held the ball consistently with the seam just between the first and second fingers, with the thumb opposed. The third finger was just in contact with the ball and the fourth finger idle."*[27] Bart realised that it required a slight adjustment of the grip to make the ball go straight or impart enough spin to create a slight off-break. His flexible wrist and powerful fingers were instrumental in delivering the ball with lethal accuracy. He found out that a new ball was more apt to a sharp hook but not necessary, as he could produce similar results with a used ball if conditions were favourable. Next, from practice he concentrated on the ones that favoured him and weather was one condition he had no control of, but, it could be studied, and the conditions that suited him, he used them to his advantage.

John Barton King
Courtesy: C.C. Morris Cricket Library Association, Haverford, PA.

"When I began bowling I liked best a following wind just strong enough to flutter the left corner of my shirt collar. Although later, when I felt completely coordinated and physically fit, I could swing the ball with a wind coming from any quarter, I preferred it coming from the batsman's off, and if I could make it to order, I would have a gusty wind sweeping up the gully to the right of the second slip."[28] These are the hallmarks of a great bowler, one who studies, practices and implements, and on top of that, is constantly refining on the already improved technique.

On focusing on his body movements, he realised that a complete relaxation – absence of any tension in arms, legs, or shoulders was necessary for a whole-souled follow-through that gave him the feeling that he was hurtling after the ball towards the wicket. Another salient feature was the height of the action and the grip that he used, it was delivered straight from above the head and at times over the left shoulder. The control though lay in his wrist and fingers, and the tip of the first two fingers would be the last point of contact before the ball was released and the flight depended on the final pressure. This came about from a sharp downward flick of the wrist.[29]

"This principal of surprise and variety of attack applies to the sum total of the side's available bowling. My effectiveness was to a large extent conditioned on what was coming down from the other end. What success I had against English and Australian batsmen with my in-swinger was due in good measure to the bowling of Percy. H. Clark and H.V. Hordern (an Australian studying

at Pennsylvania State University) at the other end: Clark's sharp outcurve and Horderns googlies were both excellent foils for my angler."[30] He not only perfected his technique taking into account the physical state of his body, the weather conditions, the delivery, but another very important element – teamwork – was also incorporated to the maximum advantage. He was a brilliant strategist, a true genius, and it's no wonder one of cricket's finest historians, Rowland Bowen wrote, *"certainly one of the six leading bowlers in the world of all time, and arguably the best."*

Here is a blue print for all aspiring bowlers of the future, if you want to be the best in the world, there is no better person to emulate than the sultan of swing – John Barton King. The year he became a permanent member of the Tiago senior eleven in 1892, he was selected to play in an international match for the Gentlemen of Philadelphia against the visiting Gentlemen of Ireland and also against the Canadians in the annual USA, Canada match. He was off to a flying start capturing 3 for 6 and 2 for 15 against Canada and all this before his 19th birthday. In 1893 the Australian team played against the Gentlemen of Philadelphian on their way home from England. After a long tour the Australians, it is understood, unwisely agreed to play the very same day following their arrival after a rough crossing of the Atlantic. On winning the toss, the Gentlemen put up an impressive total of 525, Bart a newcomer batting last, scored a quick 36 to help top the 500 mark. The Australians were rusty, dropping catches, misfielding and the only hope of a wicket, was from a run-out, in fact three of them did get out in that fashion. The leading Australian bowlers of the day George Giffen finished at 0 for 114 and Hugh Trumble, 2 for 104! The tourists were in for more surprises as nineteen year old Bart, the new weapon in Philadelphia's arsenal, took 5 for 78, scalping the wickets of Bannerman, Giffen, Harry Trott and W. Bruce, the very same players who had topped the Australian Test averages in batting earlier in the summer in England.

The Australians were bowled out for 199, and then shut out again for 258 after being forced to follow on. Australia had been beaten by an innings and 68 runs. Gentlemen of Philadelphian, a team from a single American city had beaten the full strength of Australia! The return match was won by Australia by six wickets and Blackham the captain commented, *"You have better players here, then we have been led to believe. They class with England's best and reflect great credit on your country. With some improvement, you should soon be able to beat England at her own game."*[31] Defeating the English at their own game would have been the sweetest revenge of all, but alas, instead of embracing cricket and using it to defeat them, America in its misplaced patriotic zeal with the help of Spalding, decided baseball was *their* de-facto game (as it turns out, Baseball is of English origin) and let cricket wither away like an overgrown field that once so proudly embraced the running feet of their pioneering sons. If only, if only had the Americans, or at least the Philadelphians continued with cricket, this may have been the start of the first ever triangular series, between America, England and Australia!

"The Philadelphians really have some high-class players, but it was the fact of their bowlers ply-ing us with baseball curves that upset our batsmen," wrote George Giffen, providing evidence that American swing bowlers were original and the Australians were genuinely beaten.[32]

Here we have American bowlers incorporating the nuance of the swing from baseball and blending it effectively into cricket, and King, who perfected the art, to become the premier exponent of swing and in the process, became the best bowler in the world. We have Baseball and Bart to thank for the development of 'swing' which till now had mostly relied on sheer pace. What if there were more pockets of 'Philadelphia' across America and each with its' own 'Bart,' wouldn't be too far-fetched to say that American cricketers would have been one of the best in the world, would it? Unfortunately for the game, the chapter on American Cricket was more or less closed after WW1 with the exploits of an earlier generation left behind inked in memoirs, magazines and books. Who knows, American cricketers may have dominated the world stage for a while and it would have provided a different 'angle' to the sport of cricket. King is often credited as being the father of swing and Ranji for introducing the leg glance. Two distinct styles, two distinct individuals, both self-taught with a desire for perfection – a sign of greatness.

In 1896 Bart joined Belmont Cricket Club, his home for the next 17 years and it was here that his best performance of his career was showcased. Bart toured England for the first time with the Gentlemen of Philadelphian in 1897. They played fifteen first class matches against county teams. As described in the beginning of the chapter, the two greats met for the first time and King was so fast on this tour that a telegram was sent asking for a replacement wicket-keeper as, *"Mr. Ralston's hands are quite used up."* Against Warwickshire where Philadelphia won, King took 5 wickets for 95 and 7 for 72. On this tour Bart bowled 655.4 overs, took 72 wickets at an average of 24.02, and scored 441 runs for an average of 20.1. King's performance on and off the field did not go un-noticed, and there were several offers to join a county team where he would be provided 'clerkship' which would take care of his finances outside of the game. One county, lacking fast bowlers, sweetened the deal with an offer to marry a rich woman. They said there is a widow with an income of £7000 a year and that would leave him to play cricket all summer and hunt in the winter! [33]

A return visit was made by P.F. Warner the same year where they played two matches against the Philadelphians, losing the first and winning the second. King finished with 9 for 25 in the match which they won. Later, Warner was to opine that *'King at his best never had an equal.'* In 1901, an English team led by the famous spinner B.J.T. Bosanquet, played two matches against the Gentlemen of Philadelphia where Bart took 23 wickets in four innings at an average of 10.3. His bowling figures were: 8 for 78, 6 for 57, 6 for 74 & 3 for 28! The ability to 'hook' the ball combined with lethal speed and accuracy made him the king of swing. The next tour of England for the Gentlemen of Philadelphia came about in 1903 where they won seven out of the sixteen first class matches played against the English counties. They achieved their highest standard as an all-round team on this tour.[34] They lost six and drew two matches. The highlights of this tour were Gentlemen of Philadelphia's exceptional wins against Lancashire at Old Trafford and against Surrey at the Oval. Bart finished the tour with 78 wickets averaging 16.06 and scored 614 runs for an average of 29.23, all this coming from just 13 first-class matches, imagine what his averages would be for a complete season and this too at a time when both Australian and English teams were strong.

"King is so strong at all points that one would like to see him pitted at single wicket against one of our men such as Hirst or Jackson or Jessop," wrote one critic.

"Is there is a greater bowler today, I cannot think of him" - 'Short Leg' of the Wakefield (Yorkshire) Express.[35]

The 1903 tour began with Cambridge University where Bart finished with 5 for 136 and 4 for 28 and in a rained out match against Oxford. He ended the first innings with 8 for 39, and at one point his bowling figures read, 12 overs, 3 maidens, 6 wickets for 15 runs! [36] Against Gloucestershire, he took 2 for 26 in a match that Philadelphia won by an innings and 26 runs.[37] Then it was 4 for 44 and 3 for 661 against Nottingham, 7 for 51 and 2 for 28 against M.C.C. at Lord's. Against Kent at Beckenham, it was 5 for 58 and 4 for 73, and 2 for 75 and 0 for 28 against Somerset at Taunton.

The next match was against Lancashire at Old Trafford, where despite the absence of MacLaren, Tyldesley and Brearley, they were one of the strongest county sides, but were handily beaten by nine wickets. Batting first, they scored 158 runs and Bart bowled throughout the innings taking 5 wickets for 46 runs in 27 overs. The visitors in reply, ended the day with 103 runs for the loss of 5 wickets and finished their innings the next morning with 187, a 29 run lead. Lancashire in their second innings easily surpassed the lead without any loss of wicket, but that was to change drastically after lunch. It was a cold day with intermittent rain and the wind blowing over Bart's left shoulder, just the way the wizard of swing preferred it in those early days. As Lester put it, *"Bart on the prance, with a nice little quarter-gale fluttering up the flannel on his left shoulder, was always a sweet sight."* Later on in his career and with experience, Bart preferred the wind coming in from the gully to the right of the second slip.

The very first over after lunch, he sent the opener back to the pavilion with a yorker, and the replacement met with the same fate in the very next delivery! Bart's next over claimed two more victims whom he cleaned bowled. The third over from Bart saw Sharp's leg stump being uprooted, the tally after lunch – 5 wickets for only 7 runs! After being rested, King took the last 4 wickets, three in five deliveries finishing the match with 9 for 62, 8 of them clean bowled and Bart himself, *'ran out or rather ran down the tenth man.'*[38] Philadelphia was left with a target of 141 after bowling out Lancashire for 171 and ended up winning the match the next day by nine wickets.

Percy Clark on his comments on the tour ruminates on the run out incident which was amusing. Bart referred to sitters and tail-enders as 'rabbits' and having already taken nine wickets, the last man to come in was the new wicket-keeper for Lancashire, Worsley, who was making his first-class match debut. He walked on to the pitch dragging his bat behind him, a sign of anguish and futility, Bart said, *"Boys, look what's coming! A rabbit and I hate to take the money."* A fast yorker was delivered and to Bart's wonder and amazement it was played with ease so the same delivery was repeated. This time it was driven to Fred Sharpless at cover and Radcliffe the non-striker shouted to Worsley to take a run, "Go back!" he replied, and then sensing there might be a chance for a run Worsley said, "Come on!" The batsmen ended up in the middle of the pitch together and seeing Fred throw the ball to Bart both ran back safely to the bowlers end. Now, the two batsmen, and Bart with the ball in his hands, all were on the same side. Fearing a misthrow and not wanting to take a chance, Bart ran towards the open wicket with the two batsmen in pursuit (that must have been quite a sight!). He reached first hitting the wicket and appealed to see who would be given out as none of the batsmen had reached the crease, the umpire said Worsley. Amidst laughter from his team mates, Bart threw down the ball saying, *"just my luck,"* the rabbit had escaped! [39]

Bart had to sit out the next two matches as he had strained his side in a throwing demonstration but he was ready to play against Warner's XI, where he again showed his bowling skills, taking 4 for 64 and 1 for 51, and against Glamorgan, he took 7 for 38 and 2 for 30 and 4 for 72 and 1 for 27 against Leicestershire. [40]

"The finest exhibition of skill and endurance which ever came from an American in first-class cricket." This praise was heaped on Bart by Lester after one of the most memorable match against a full strength Surrey side played on 6th 7th and 8th August at the Oval. Philadelphians went into bat first, scoring 348 for 7 at day's end, with everyone scoring in double digits and ending the innings at 387 against the bowling of Dowson, Tom Richardson, Hayward, Lees and Hayes. It was Richardson, the great fast bowler's last full season for Surrey and he captured his hundredth wicket in this match. The match saw Bart wielding the willow to score a chanceless innings of 98 till he was unfortunately run-out by his club mate Wood. Surrey replied with only 241, Bart's partner in crime Clark, took 5 for 102 and King took 3 for 89. This gave them a lead of 146 but lost 2 early wickets for only 23 runs till Bart bating at No. 4, took the score to 81 at days' end, and ultimately scoring a century that had evaded him in the first innings. In a free hitting game, he scored 113 not out, (including 18 hits to the ropes) when the Philadelphia innings was declared at 251 for 5.

With just under four hours of play left, Surrey were left chasing a target of 398 on a still good wicket, an impossible task even for the best of teams. At the same time, for Philadelphia the task was insuperable, as they could not hope to get their opponents out in such a short time. But by four o'clock, an outcome no one expected was beginning to unfold, Surrey had unraveled to 117 for 7 when wicketkeeper Stedman came in to lend support to Hayward. Again, another unexpected but welcome outcome for Surrey, as the pair put on 134 runs in ninety minutes and in the process Hayward reaching his century. Soon Stedman was out along with the number 10 player leaving Tom Richardson the last man in and Hayward with still half an hour's play left. Tom was ordered to stay with Hayward for the duration and he almost pulled it off. The crowd on their feet and the minutes ticking away to six-ten, six-twenty and Hayward had managed to keep Richardson at the non-strikers end, away from facing the bowlers for another twenty minutes. When King finally did get his chance, he clean bowled Richardson on the third delivery, [41] thus giving the Philadelphians a thumping win by 110 runs with about ten minutes to spare. Tom remained not out at 156, his finest of the season and he had gone in first and lasted the whole innings. As for the bowlers, Clark took 5 for 112 and King taking 3 for 98. At a banquet after the match, tired and exhausted from all the play and excitement, King fell asleep during the speech given by the Lord Chief Justice. [42] 1903 ended on a high personal note for two Philadelphians' in English first-class averages – King was tenth in bowling and Lester was thirteenth in batting! [43]

W.A. Bettesworth wrote, *"This year the bowling has made a great advance, and there are a few counties who have a better pair than King and Clark, both of them fast, both having some sort of swerve, and both understanding the art of variation and concealment of pace."* [44] *"The success of the two men as bowlers came to be a thing so naturally anticipated as to obscure the splendid and consistent effort behind it."* [45]

Without any overseas trip or visits from foreign team, besides the Canadians, Bart's first class career was on hold for the next five years. Though he was confined to inter-club cricket he reigned supreme in them with both the bat and ball and won the Batting Cup and the Bowling Cup three and four times respectively between 1904 and 1908. On two occasions he exceeded 300 runs in an innings, first against Germantown and against Merion. The play-off for the Halifax Cup in 1905 brought out one of his best performances, where Belmont and Merion having tied in the play-off, Merion won the toss and were bowled out for a meager 56 runs, King taking 6 wickets for 30 runs. He opened the innings and hit 18 off the first over with Belmont winning the match by 9 wickets.

The year 1908 saw Bart tour England for the third and final time, but on this occasion, he was without his counterpart Percy Clark, but was ably assisted by an Australian leg-spinner studying at the University of Pennsylvania, H.V. Hordern, who bowled googlies. Bart was in his mid-thirties, still, he produced his best bowling performance in English first-class cricket taking 87 wickets in only ten first class matches at an average of only 11.01. It was to remain unbeaten for fifty years before Les Jackson in 1958 averaged it at 10.99. [46] The biggest handicap Philadelphian's faced on this tour was the weather, wet pitches greeted them wherever they went as they have never been comfortable playing on soft wickets.

The batsmen could not adjust to these conditions and would end up playing forward too soon, the bowlers would get the opponents out cheaply only to see their efforts wasted and when the batting did come thru, they would win the match.[47] Out of the ten first-class matches played, they won only four and on a number of occasions despite getting an upper hand, even against a stronger opponent, the advantage was squandered away. An example of their fluctuating fortune, like the ebb and swell of the tide was evident against Nottingham at Trent Bridge. The Notts on winning the toss elected to bat, but could only score 139 runs because of King, who in his customary fashion took 7 wickets for 76 runs (14 for 130 in both innings).[48] In reply, the Philadelphians could only do 'one' better, scoring 140 runs. Nottingham fared a little better in their second innings putting up a total of 206. They had left Derbyshire in the morning amidst drizzling rain for a fifteen mile drive to Tent Bridge and now the wicket was in the process of drying up making for a soft wicket, and they could only score 75 runs, thus *the Philadelphians got much the worse of the weather* a sympathetic *Wisden* noted.[49]

The weather was one unstable element of the matches, whereas King with his rock steady and unwavering bowling performance received heaps of praises and adulations.

"No one probably knows more than he of the art of the swinging ball," The Times.

At a dinner hosted by the Surrey Club for the Philadelphians, H.D.G. Leveson-Gower commented how England had picked up the finer points of the game from the different touring teams. Field placing and wicket-keeping from the Australians, perfecting the googly bowling from the South Africans and the art of swing bowling from the Americans! [50] It sounds so outlandish in the 21st century that the Americans were credited with taking the swing bowling to a higher level, but, all due credit to 'the King' for his mastery of the ball and making it turn where he wanted and when he wanted.

"When we knew him first, more than a dozen years ago, he was a very fast bowler, with a very pronounced swerve – a more pronounced swerve than that possessed by any other living cricketer, and very little artifice. He still has that very pronounced swerve, but he is no longer a fast bowler. He is a 'pace' bowler with many tricks up his sleeve. He has modified speed and developed cunning. He can still bowl a very fast ball, but he keeps it in reserve. It comes out suddenly and unexpectedly. Often it is a yorker, delivered at once to a new batsman, frequently with disastrous results. Then there are slight, well-disguised changes of pace and well controlled break and a ready eye for a batsman's weakness. And with it all there is a perplexing swerve and the sudden very fast ball. A great bowler." 'Long Leg' in the *Sporting Life*.

"It was a matter of general comment that season that the manner in which King swerved, broke, disguised his pace and arranged his leg—trap was an education in the art of getting batsmen out." Ralph Barker.[51]

The visiting Irish Gentlemen in 1909 were shown no mercy, as King took all 10 wickets in the first innings and the King proceeded to do a hat-trick in the second innings. On the local front, King had no equal and his Belmont Club dominated the Halifax Cup winning it seven times from 1901 to 1912 and Bart capturing the bowling and batting cup in the same season on four different occasions.[52] As late as September of 1912, Philadelphia beat an Australian test team at Manheim by two runs. King, even though he was 39 by then, took 9 wickets for 78 runs, after two decades, he still remained the 'King of Swing.'[53] This was a very close game, Philadelphia having batted first were only able to put up 185, and the Australians scored only 122 runs with King taking five of the first six wickets for only 40 runs!. The second innings score was even worse than the first as Philadelphia was bundled out for only 74 runs, handing the visitors an easy target of only 138 runs. This was a low scoring but exciting game and the master of ceremonies was not yet done, when Australia were 131 for nine, King probably on his last over started bowling to the tail-ender. The fifth delivery of the over, beat both the batsman and the wicketkeeper sending the ball towards the ropes for four byes and inching up the total to 135 – 3 more to win. I cannot imagine the crowds sitting at this point, everyone must have been on their feet holding their breath as King takes his final run up and clean bowls the last man clinching the match for Philadelphia by a narrow margin of 2 runs!.

H.V. Hordern in his autobiography, *"Googlies: coals from a test-cricketer's fireplace,"* introduces different cricketers in phases as a 'coal' glowing in the fireplace and contemplating on them writes…

My third bright coal is not one little bit like anyone you have ever seen on our Australian cricket fields. As a matter of fact you have never seen him here. It represents the great American cricketer, John Barton King. It is rather remarkable that the United States of America should have produced such a phenomenal player considering the small amount of cricket played in that country; still there it is.

A magnificent physical specimen, some 6ft 2 ins; still full of vigor of youth with a matured experience and brainy knowledge of the game sums up somewhat the JB King I first met in 1906. He is, or was, generally known for his extraordinary bowling ability but believe me he was a magnificent all-rounder; a first class batsman without being an actual champion, a splendid fieldsman, and as a bowler almost unique. Surely a wonderful combination. If I had been given the selection of a World Team in the years that I knew him, 1906-19010, he would have been almost my first choice, which is wonderful considering the galaxy of players at that time. (This was the Golden Age of Cricket)

He took a long bounding run up to the wicket, and just before actual delivery, the ball was gripped in both hands, high up over the head, a la baseball pitcher, and then followed the most perfect arm and body swing possible to imagine. The ball itself came along a shade faster than what is known as fast-medium, and in the last yard or so, swung in sharply from the off side - in other words an in-swinger! I have not only seen but experienced the very unpleasant sensation of a perfectly length ball from him pitched outside the off stump, and missing the leg stump by inches. Of course it was his sharp swerve at the last minute that did it; but what a devilish difficult ball to play at his pace!

This ball was his stock in trade but he had, as a variation, a really fast straight one, more often than not a yorker, and occasionally used the out-swing, which, however, had not the sharp late curve of his regular ball and was effective only as contrast.

Quite a wonderful repertoire. He had one other extraordinary peculiarity (which I have seen only once in another cricketer, the late aboriginal bowler, Jack Marsh), that was that he made the ball, occasionally, wobble in the air.

The first time I batted against King, after having been badly beaten by the first two or three balls, I turned to the wicket keeper and said:

"I must be bilious today; those balls all looked 'wobbly' to me."

The keeper replied with a smile on his face:

"You need not worry about your liver, young fellow, you will always be bilious when Bart King is bowling." A truly great bowler.

Though twenty years later he was to write, *"Barnes, in my opinion, was the greatest bowler of all time."*

The strongest English batting side ever to visit America, was led by Ranji in his only overseas tour as captain in 1899,[54] though, *"the amateur team personally conducted by K. S. Ranjitsinhji to the states should have returned with an unbeaten certificate could hardly have been a surprise to anyone at all conversant with cricket. The American Cricketer claimed for it that it was the strongest aggregation of cricketers that had ever visited America. By this, presumably, it meant the strongest amateur aggregation."[55]* The Red Lillywhite further goes on to say that the side was far too strong even for the Philadelphia XI.

"I think we have a pretty fair team, and, of course, we shall try to win all our games, but no one can tell how things will turn out at cricket, you know," answered Ranji on being questioned by *The New York Times*[56] about the prospect of winning all the matches, an understatement to say the least, the Prince was just being a thorough gentleman. Ranji's American tour was to, *"renew his friendship with "Demon" King, in fact the tour had originated from their first meeting, when the great Philadelphian had bowled him out on the first ball."[57]*

The team comprised of:

K.S. Ranjitsinhji of Sussex (captain).
G.L. Jessop – Gloucestershire.
A.E. Stoddart - Middlesex.
A.C. MacLaren - Lancashire.
B.J.T. Bosanquet – Middlesex and Oxford University.

C.L. Townsend - Gloucestershire.

G. Brann - Sussex.

C.B. Llewellyn – originally from Pietermaritzburg in South Africa.

A. Priestley – Marylebone Cricket Club.

C. Robson - Hampshire.

W.P. Robertson – Cambridge University. (NY Times reports it as J. Robertson)

S.M.J. Woods - Somersetshire.

Barton, the Hampshire professional, *"has been brought over only to look after the bats and so forth,"* reported the New York Times. I am sure he was not happy with such an introduction.

"English Cricketers Here – Prince Ranjitsinhji and his team will play their first game to-day at Philadelphia," read the New York Times article headline in their September 25th issue. They had arrived the previous day aboard the Cunard steamship, Etruria, from Liverpool. As was customary, they were met by a committee representing the Associated Cricket Clubs of Philadelphia comprising of J.B. Colohan of Belmont Cricket Club, E.S. Sayres from the Merion Cricket Club and George Stuart Patterson of the Germantown Cricket Club. The tour was funded by the Associated Clubs of Philadelphia, which was founded in 1895 to ensure schedules did not conflict with the visiting international teams at a time when such engagements of an 'international' nature drew large crowds and made a lot of money for the clubs.[58] Looking back on this statement today, it seems so estranged in the sporting landscape of today's America.

PRINCE RANJITSINHJI
and the
GENTLEMEN of ENGLAND
ELEVEN.
October the Eleventh
1899.

'Jungle Book' had just been published by Rudyard Kipling so India was seen as an 'exotic' land and the arrival of this exotic 'Prince of Hindoo' in America aroused a lot of curiosity. Soon the rumor mills announced that Ranji was looking to marry an American heiress and there was even talk about how the Prince's 'royal father' sacrificed two slaves every time a century was scored as offering to the gods.[59] On this trip at least, the 'slaves' were safe as 68 was the highest score Ranji was able to make against Philadelphia at Germantown.

Out of the five matches that were crammed in from September 25th to October 13th , Ranji played three. Against Philadelphia while scoring 57, I am sure Ranji's mind must have wandered back to the time he was bowled by King for naught. As for King he was not in form with either the bat or ball, scoring 0 and 11 and the bowling numbers were equally disappointing – 30 overs, seven maidens and managed only one wicket for 100 runs. Even the greats have a day off, Ranji's XI winning by an innings and 173 runs! At Manheim, Germantown, the results were almost similar, the visitors winning by an innings and 131 runs! Here Ranji had his highest score of 68, while King again scoring 0 in the first innings and managed 40 in the second innings, which was the highest for the team! As Lester points out, it was the bowlers that they were already familiar with that gave them the most trouble, Jessop and Bosanquet.[60] King took 3 wickets for 90 runs.

To the end of his days, King remained the tall, thin, erect man who blew English county batting line-ups apart in the Golden Age. But there were few to remember him. One of the exceptions, although in the nick of time, was the Marylebone Cricket Club. In 1962, a mere 54 years after King last bowled on an English wicket, he was made an honorary life member of the MCC - the <u>first and only American cricketer</u> ever to be granted the accolade.[61]

King died on 17th October, 1965, just two days short of his 92nd birthday, in the City of Brotherly Love where he was born. He died just two months after his contemporary and bowling partner, P. H. Clark had passed away. *"Let us remember that the career of one admirable American has played a part in the development of our game."*[62]

"At least the equal of the greatest of them all."

"Undoubtedly one of the finest bowlers of all time."

"King on his day is the most difficult bowler we have seen this season" – Warner.

"The best swerver I ever saw in my life was J. Barton King of Philadelphia" – C.B. Fry.

"Mr. King was a magnificent bowler, very fast, very accurate, and we remember at Philadelphia in 1901 being bowled by an unexpected in swinger which we left alone," wrote Eric Wilson, the Yorkshire and England batsman.

"Without question the finest all-round cricketer ever produced in America," wrote his contemporary, John Lester.

One of cricket's finest historians, Rowland Bowen, went even further: "Certainly one of the six leading bowlers in the world of all time, and arguably the best."

"The greatest of all American Cricketers, one whose achievements may be said to demand a place for him amongst the immortals" - Ralph Barker.

Wisden said his greatness was "beyond question."

The Cricket Quarterly called him "one of the greatest cricketers of all time."

Donald Bradman called him "America's greatest cricketing son."

"...in J B King (they) possessed a fine all-round player and a first class bowler who knew of the baseball pitchers art of swerving. He is probably the best fast swerving bowler who has ever been seen in England, and had he been of English birth would certainly have secured a place on the English side." A. E. Knight in his coaching manual 'The Complete Cricketer' (1906).

Just to show that I am not solo in my admiration of King: once upon a time, Prince Ranjitsinhji, then at the pinnacle of his fame, was clean bowled by Bart King in his first over. 'Ranji' in his charming way, walked up the wicket and said:

"That was a wonderful ball Mr. King and I wish you accept my bat as a momento."

A most sporting tribute from a very great batsman to a very great bowler. Have I said enough to enable you to realize that J B King was one of the greatest cricketers the world has ever seen! [63]

John Barton King
Courtesy: C.C. Morris Cricket Library Association, Haverford, PA.

262

Ranjitsinhji
Courtesy: Sussex Cricket Museum.

WANING PROSPECTS ON THE GREEN, THE 20TH CENTURY.

The peak period for Cricket, was reached around 1905 going by the table of fixtures as recorded by the American Cricketer (1877-1929), with almost 380 matches taking place that year.[1] Yet, ominous signs were there of things to come as the new crop of players were weaning away from the game of their parents into organized baseball with their ball parks and regularly scheduled seasons. There was still plenty of cricket no doubt, and would continue throughout the 1900s in localized spurts, but the talent and volume required to sustain the interest was waning. 'The Philadelphia Pilgrims' cricket club was conceived at Edinburgh at the end of Gentlemen of Philadelphia's 1903 tour to England, and membership would comprise of players who had competed against the foreign team at home and abroad. With this, they hoped to, *"encourage the game by electing to honorary membership, leading cricketers in other parts of the United States and Canada, and sending them on tours,"* a true representation of team America and Canada.[2] Lester goes on to say that the 'Pilgrims' were kept alive by three prominent cricketers who did their best to stem the waning popularity of cricket in the 1900s, they were Percy H Clark, C.C. Morris and W.P. O'Neill who continued with 'Cricket' till the present day (1950).[3] On the other hand, the initial rite of passage, from father to son whether it was attending the same exclusive schools or becoming a member of the club, the willow was passed down to the next generation of flannels on the sward. With the passage of time, the clubs were finding it difficult to recruit more youths into the game. A batting cup was instituted in 1907 for boys under 15, a form of incentive to generate interest in the game. The *American Cricketer* suggested the inclusion of Baltimore and New York Knickerbocker Athletic Club to increase competition in the Halifax Cup and the major clubs also instituted the Club Record Cup, which later became the Philadelphia Cup in 1900.[4] Percy Clark, who complimented King on the other end in bowling, had a daughter named Mary Todhunter Clark Rockefeller, the first Lady of New York. She was the first wife of Nelson Aldrich Rockefeller, the Governor of New York, who after their divorce went on to become the 41st Vice President of the United States during the term of President Gerald Ford.

1907 D.S. Newhall's Philadelphia Pilgrim XI Vs. All New York.
Photography Collection, Miriam and Ira D. Wallach Division of Art, Prints and
Photographs, The New York Public Library, Astor, Lenox and Tilden Foundations.
King is sitting on the ground on the left and Lester is standing on the right, E.M. Cregar is
sitting in front of him, others are not identified..

In 1901, Bernard Bosanquet who invented the 'googly' brought a team over to America where, two first-class matches against Philadelphia ended in a 1-1 draw. 1903 saw the first English county team Kent, visit America and it wasn't until 1964 that Yorkshire, another county team, paid a visit to the old and new cricketing haunts in America playing matches in New York, Washington DC, Hollywood, Canada and Bermuda. They set out on their tour after winning the county cricket championship that year. In 1904, Haverford College paid another visit to the English schools, and this was the most successful of the six tours and was captained by C.C. Morris.[5] This was also the year when Germantown Cricket Club celebrated its' 50th anniversary and in one match, 28 veterans were captained by William Rotch Wister and another 28 were captained by none other than George M Newhall, some had not played since the Civil War!

T. PAWLEY, *Manager*. BLYTHE. H. Z. BAKER. W. M. BRADLEY. K. L. HUTCHINGS. HUISH.
H. C. STEWART. E. M. DILLON. C. J. BURNUP, *Captain*. J. R. MASON. C. J. V. WIEGALL.
SEYMOUR. HEARNE (A.)

Kent County XI in Philadelphia, American Cricketer, October 15th, 1903.
Standing L-R: T. Pawley (Manager), Blythe, H.Z. Baker, W.M. Bradley, K.L. Hutchings,
Huish. Sitting L-R: H.C. Stewart, E.M. Dillon, C.J. Burnup (captain), J.R. Mason, C.J.V.
Wiegall. On the ground L-R: Seymour and Hearne (A.)

There was no dearth of cricket visitors in the northeast region, Hamilton Club from Bermuda paid a visit to Philadelphia in 1905 and one of their players was a young Australian by the name of B. Kortlang, who would become prominent in the New York cricket scene in the 1920s. M.C.C. XI made their maiden visit the same year, playing three matches and losing one to Philadelphia at Haverford. The exchanges with the Canadian teams continued, so also were the engagement with the Halifax Cup. In the same cup in July of 1906, John B. King scored 344 at Elmwood against the B team from Merion, a score that remains unbroken till today and will remain so till the foreseeable future. A new student by the name of H.V. Hordern arrived at the University of Pennsylvania that year, and in the following year took 213 wickets - a record. Playing for the University in 1908 against Radnor, Hordern took all 10 wickets, eight being clean bowled, for only 8 runs! The master of googly was perfecting his craft and became an exponent when later playing for Australia. University of Pennsylvania XI won 8, lost only 2 and drew 6 of the sixteen games when they played against the English public schools in 1907 on their home turf. This was the most successful trip by *any Cricket team* from America. Hesketh-Prichard's XI led M.C.C. made the second visit that year, both matches could not be finished due to rain. Philadelphia made a second visit to Bermuda in early 1908 losing the first match but redeeming themselves by winning against an All Bermuda team.

University of Pennsylvania and Haverford College both sent teams into Canada in 1909 with the former winning 4 out of the 5 matches while the latter only won 2 out of the 5 games and en route they played in Pittsburgh also. Philadelphia was also on the move, visiting Jamaica where they won 4 matches with the other two being a loss and a draw.[6] The Irish would be making their 4th and last trip to the American continent, and the Australians in 1913, the last visage of the old order with WWI providing the demarcation point of Victorian Cricket and forever change the landscape in America, as these were the last gasp of the 'International' visits for some time to come. King, the consummate performer and showman, took all 10 or rather 11 Irish wickets in the 1st innings! Morrow, who remained not out at 50, was cleaned bowled on a no ball, oh, and King had a hat trick to his name in the second innings. American Cricket received a one-two punch with the advent of WWI and the crippling blow would come from the British themselves with the formation of Imperial Cricket Conference in June of 1909 with members of the British colony, Australia and South Africa, thus excluding United States, who, otherwise would have had greater exposure to new cricketing climes and talents from nations like South Africa, New Zealand, India and Pakistan. United States was finally admitted as an Associate member in 1964.[7] In 1965 the name was changed to International Cricket Conference and from 1989 it is now known as the 'International Cricket Council.'

After all the 'Cricketing' exchanges and all the camaraderie and goodwill built up over the years with the former colony, why did England abruptly turn their back on America and leave them out of ICC and further competition – were they afraid? Just the previous summer, Bart had shown them that he was the best bowler in the world by topping the English bowling averages, and the Australians were matching wits and beating them at their own game. Bart King, a Philadelphia native was able to confront the English at their own game, what if the rest of the country had taken up cricket after being included in the ICC. South Africa, a relative newcomer was granted a 'Test' status in 1888-89 and there was no comparison to Philadelphia who would have beaten them hands down! Other countries, like toddlers, were just learning to pick up the bat and it would be a while before the English faced real competition, meantime, the only real threat was Australia, and that too they tried to take them down with the 'Bodyline' bowling, while South Africa and New Zealand were relative novices. Growing up, one heard a lot about the exploits of the English players followed by Australia, but America, its' as if they had never played cricket and had dropped off the radar! They did not want to start losing to the Yankees now, and that too at their own game, just as they did not want Ranjitsinhji teaching them the finer 'glances' of cricket.

1912 The All-New York cricket team played a two day match with the Australian cricket-ers at the Staten Island Cricket and Tennis Club, Livingston, S. I., and were defeated by the Antipodeans by nine wickets.

As there was no visit by foreign teams till 1912, the locals toured far and the Frankford Club in 1911(by 1927 they had ceased to exist) had the distinction of covering 11,000 land miles during August and September on their trip west to the Pacific! [8] In the same year, a first for Philadelphia Cricket, only XI from Germantown Club toured England and the following year, the same was done by an XI from Philadelphia Cricket Club. According to the *American Cricketer*, there were only 52 fixtures for 1913 and this was the year of the last hurrah, for after the Australian visit, cricket in Philadelphia would never be the same and came to an undeserving end but with a fitting finale. This unofficial Australian 52 match tour of Canada, Philadelphia and Bermuda was the longest in which they won 48 matches, losing one and three ended in a draw. Having won seven games in Canada easily, they won another four matches in Philadelphia in June and lost the sole match of the tour to the Germantown XII by three wickets on August 6th and 7th played at Manheim.

"If it was time for a finale, this was a fitting one. The old club of the Newhalls, the Pattersons, and the Clarks was playing through the last act and ringing down the curtain." [9] The 'cricketing families' the pillars of Philadelphia Cricket, the old guard were on their last number on the dance card, this was their swan song. In 1914 with the approaching war, Haverford and Merion did manage the last tour to England and besides the onset of WWI, the other factor that contributed towards the decline of cricket, were the loss of playing ground for Frankford Club. Belmont also lost its grounds which were sold to the city of Philadelphia, the home of the greatest American cricketer - J. B. King would now be a distant memory. The dearth of cricketing families left a bigger void, one that could not arrest the slide and relegate cricket to the confines of a few pages in history. The Wisters had started the ball rolling, the Newhalls had strength in numbers and playing abili-ty, while the Pattersons, Clarks, Morgans, Hargraves, Thayers, Scotts, Browns, Bailys,

Morrisses, Grahams and the Crosmans greatly contributed to Philadelphia Cricket.[10] From 1915, no worthwhile matches were reported and after the signing of a ceasefire in 1918, (WWI) George Newhall proposed a tournament to be held in Philadelphia in 1920 between Australia, Canada, England and Philadelphia[11] but the *'ashes'* between Australia and England took precedence and that became a staple between the two countries. These two countries were never to be seen again in America except for another Australian tour with a young Don Bradman in 1932 and by M.C.C. (Marylebone Cricket Club) in 1959.

In 1905 there were at least 90 interschool cricket matches in the two leagues and by 1923 *American Cricketer* records one appearance by Penn Charter against the juniors of the Philadelphia Club. When the Australians first visited in 1878 there were about fifteen thousand spectators and in 1913, *"ridiculously small"* according to a reporter.[12] From 1908 to 1913 there was an average of 250 fixtures during the season and by 1926 there were forty two and there is no record in *American Cricketer* from 1928 onwards. The post war tour started with the 'pilgrims' visiting England in 1921 and they were still able to compete on even terms with the county teams, though it's interesting to note that it was the stalwarts who carried the team, the young blood was getting thinned out and the writing was on the wall. The spirit of cricket was kept alive by the old order, by the likes of Morris, Taylor, Evans, O'Neill, Newhall, Clark[13] and once they left the green, cricket would be on a downhill spiral and the torch would now be passed on to the New York Cricketers. B. Kortlang, J.L. Poyer, Leslie Miller, J. H. Briggs and Lawrence DeMotte were some of the prominent players from 1915 to about 1930. Kortlang, an Australian first appeared on the scene against Philadelphia when he toured with the Bermuda team in 1905, and now he lived in New York and was a director of the cricket department at the A. G. Spalding store. He won the annual batting cup in 1915, 1916 and 1919 and in June of that year and he scored two centuries against Merion.[14]

B. Kortlang.

The rise of New York cricket can be seen when they defeated Philadelphia in two out of the three matches played in 1918, and the fixtures in general were being played more in the New York, New Jersey leagues. The Incogniti's were school or university cricketers who visited Philadelphia in 1920, and during their last visit in 1913, they were defeated at Manheim. On this tour, they won all seven – five against the Philadelphia teams and two against a combined XI of the best players, clearly Philadelphia was losing its touch. In 1921 for the first time a Canadian College XI paid a visit to Philadelphia, these were young colts between 15 to 18 years of age, representing Ridley College of St. Catherine's, Ontario. This was the very same college where in 1932, an Australian team with Don Bradman in the ranks played a match there. The school was also the recipient of an amazing Cricket memorabilia collection that was donated by K.A. Auty, President of Chicago Cricket Association. He was also an editor and publisher of the Illinois Cricket and Rugby Annual, that was published ten times from1935 to 1944 under different titles. Exchanges were ongoing with Bermuda, and Philadelphia visited them in March of 1922 and they returned the visit in June, followed by the 'Free Foresters' from England in September. The Foresters comprised of players from Universities, Public Schools, the Army and the Navy and they were reciprocating Norman Seagram's Canadian Cricketers who visited England earlier in the year and managed to play two games in Philadelphia.[15]

Haverford College was the last bastion for cricket talent in the region in 1924, though the best cricket still came from the veterans, again pointing to the dearth of new talent which was required to sustain the future of cricket in Philadelphia and beyond. The Incogniti's were on their last visit to Philadelphia after drawing a match with the New Yorkers where, the only century to be made against an English team was scored by J. L. Poyers who made 101, [16] also a good bowler and an opening bat for the Brooklyn Cricket Club.

J.L. Poyer, Brooklyn Cricket Club 1926.

Tom Garrett's XI from Haverford College made its' sixth and last trip to England in 1925 winning only 1 of the 14 games played, while the eleven 'Vandals' from Cambridge University would be the last team from England to play in Philadelphia in 1933. The Australians on the other hand were making their 18th tour to England in 1934, the days of going thru American and Canada were clearly over. The curtains were coming down rapidly on the Philadelphia cricket scene, and in August 1927 the last of the famous Newhalls, the great fast bowler, Charles A. Newhall passed away. The cup competition ceased as neither the Germantown nor Philadelphia sent a team and the 'American Cricketer' printed its' last issue in April 1929, the voice of Cricket in America, had fallen silent. [17]

THE CAMBRIDGE UNIVERSITY

VANDALS

CRICKET AND RUGBY FOOTBALL CLUB
OF ENGLAND

V

ON TOUR

U. S. A. AND CANADA

Season 1933

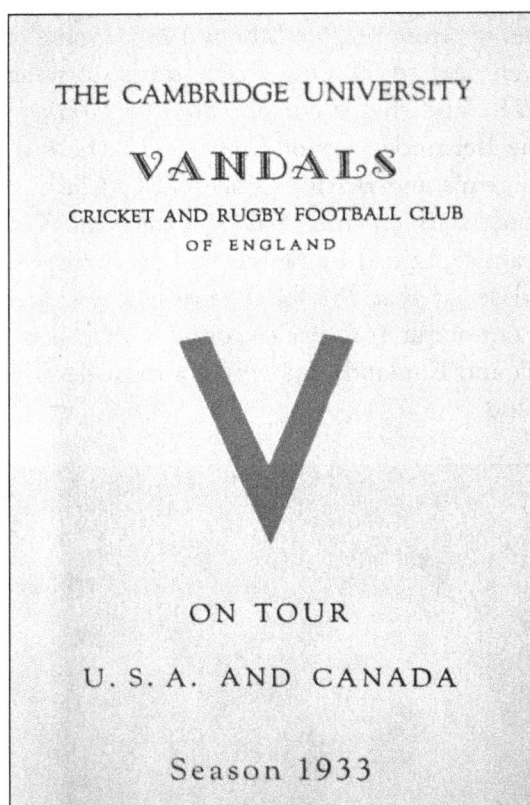

With urban sprawl, the available fields that until now hosted many a cricket matches were now being used for industrial or residential purposes and cricket at the major clubs was now becoming a distant memory. One may be led to believe that 'Philadelphia Cricket' had ended, far from it. It continued with players from disbanded clubs getting together forming the Ardmore Club and in 1929, G. B. Lacey who was from Schenectady (there was a H.A. Lacey at Schenectady C.C.) started the General Electric Cricket Club which was not limited to the employees and these two together with the Philadelphia Archery Club formed the 'Philadelphia Cricket and Archery Association' in 1938. The Ardmore had transferred its home ground to the Fairmount Park in 1937, which was also home to GECC and changed its name to Fairmount Cricket Club.[18] A new association building was completed in 1942 with W. J. Hole as its first president, and all this was happening during WWII. In 1949, there were 69 engagements scheduled, so cricket clearly continued to be patronized in Philadelphia and New York region, though not as prevalently as before. The scorebook of the British Commonwealth Cricket Club of Washington DC, records their frequent visits to Fairmount Park playing against GECC, Fairmount, and Prior CC well into the 1970s.

In an 86 page scrap book that once belonged to Arthur W. Norris captain of the Fordham C.C., various newspaper cuttings and photographs provide a wonderful glimpse of cricket in the New York, New Jersey region, the crucible for cricket in the early 1900s. Unfortunately, none of the clippings show the year, but, going into records and cross checking, the timeframe, it's from 1925 to about 1935. (Some of the photographs have the names and year given next to it). One article reads, '*Bermuda Cricketers Win, defeat Ardmore Club, 194 to 128,*' and this is corroborated in '*Century of Philadelphia Cricket*' wherein it mentions the Bermuda tour of June 1927, where they also played against the Philadelphia XI, Pilgrims and British Officers. F.C. Clark, a sprightly 73 year old, scored 12 runs for Ardmore! [19] In one match against the local West Indian XI at the New York Oval, the white team captained by Norris was easily disposed off for only 76 runs, while the opponents had declared at 252 for the loss of 1 wicket. The high scorer was A. Simpson who remained not out at 160. It also contains articles on the infamous '*Bodyline Series*' between Australia and England, one which almost derailed the '*ashes*' due to the bowling tactics of England.

AW Norris sitting front row on right with unidentified players.

While the Australians were on a tour of Canada and America in the summer of 1932 with a newly married Don Bradman along with his wife on a sort of extended honeymoon trip, Douglas Jardine, the Bombay born captain of the English team, was busy hatching plans to neutralize 'Don' the run scoring machine at the Piccadilly Grill Rooms in August of that year. According to Simon Briggs, four men sat down for lunch, Jardine and Arthur Carr along with Bill Voce and Larwood the pacer, who was asked by Jardine if he could bowl on the leg stump and make the ball rise to the body all the time, as they surmised

Bradman flinched every time a ball was bowled towards the leg.[20] The honeymoon was to come to an end and little did they realize what lay ahead of them when they returned home to Australia that winter. *"It's better to rely on speed and accuracy than anything else when bowling to Bradman because he murders any loose stuff,"* said Larwood, thus began the series with that singular focus in mind.

"The high feeling which has been aroused in Australian cricket circles by the 'leg theory' tactics of the English bowler, Harold Larwood, in the test match series, has culminated in official protest," reads one of the clippings dated January 18th 1933. *"In our opinion it is unsportsmanlike and unless it is stopped immediately, it is likely to upset the friendly relations existing between Australian and English Cricket,"* was the cable message relayed to the M.C.C. by the Australian Board of Control. When Jardine was appointed captain of the English team in the summer of 1931, a reporter had asked his cricket master at Winchester College regarding his prospects, *"he might well win us the Ashes, but he might lose us a Dominion."*[21]

The Australians on their 1932 tour did not play a single match in Philadelphia despite playing 6 matches in New York, a total of 18 matches were played in America and 33 in Canada. The scrap book shows the scores of various clubs and matches, and not just the local leagues but the visits by Bermuda, British West Indians etc. and judging by that one would not say that cricket had disappeared from the American landscape. These clubs were part of the Metropolitan District Cricket League and New York and New Jersey Cricket Association, some of them were:

Newark CC
Crescent AC
Columbia Oval CC
Fordham CC
Panama CC
Brooklyn CC
Staten Island CC
Union County CC
Brooklyn Sons of St. George
Paterson CC
Cameron CC
Plainfield CC
Kings County CC
Manor Field CC
Schenectady CC

Amongst the numerous clippings, one shows the 16 British West Indian Cricketers arriving to play 25 games in Boston, New York and Philadelphia. The New York & New Jersey Cricket Association played their matches at Manor Field, West New Brighton, Watessing Park in Newark, Bay Ridge, Livingston in Staten Island, Prospect Park Parade

Grounds, East Side Park at Paterson, N.J. and Fordham University Grounds. Another clipping espouses the exploits of the Brooklyn C.C. who won *both* the Metropolitan District Cricket League AND New York & New Jersey Cricket Association League. In one low scoring match of the Metropolitan District Cricket League played at Fordham University Grounds between Paterson CC and Brooklyn CC, Brooklyn beat Paterson 34 to 29! An intriguing incident is mentioned in the 1938 Illinois Cricket and Rugby Annual published by K.A. Auty, which provides the final match score of the United States Cricket Association (USCA) Challenge Cup played between General Electric of Philadelphia and Brooklyn CC at Haverford played on September 6th 1937. It shows Brooklyn defeating GE 152 to 60 but the trophy was not awarded. The text reads, *"this was supposedly the final for the USCA Cup in the East, however, the fact that one of the finalist, Brooklyn, had not played its semi-final round game with Union County, left matters sufficiently involved that there was no presentation of the Cup at the end of this game."*[22] So how did Brooklyn become the *finalist* if it skipped the semi-final and why were they allowed to play at all? Lot of questions but we will never know why, but it was fascinating. Even during the World War II, cricket continued in the Chicago area and the players that answered the call of duty were replaced by veteran cricketers in order to complete a team and the season, even though they were reduce to 5 clubs. Chicago C.C. became the first team to win the Championship for the 5th time and Lake Forest C.C. took home the K.A. Auty Knock-Out Cup.[23]

Newark Cricket Club 1924

In 1958, Pakistan on their way home from their Caribbean tour, made stops in Bermuda, USA and Canada. They played in New York, Philadelphia and Massachusetts and against Canada at the Varsity Stadium in Toronto. A.H. Kardar who captained the team captured the cricket memories in *'Green Shadows.'* In 1959 M.C.C. celebrated the 100th anniversary of the pioneering visit of George Parr's XI by playing a total of 23 matches mostly in Canada, winning 19, losing none and drawing 4, though only 2 matches were played in America – one against Philadelphia where they won by 217 runs and the other against the British Commonwealth Cricket Club (BCCC) in Washington DC at West Potomac Park on 13th September, who were also defeated by 214 runs.[24] Canada and America rekindled their cricket affair in 1963 with Canada emerging victorious by an innings at Toronto and in the following year, Yorkshire becomes the second county to visit America following their win in the English County Championships in 1963, touring Canada, American and Bermuda. Richard White, who played for the BCCC in the 60's and 70's, provided some recollections of his time on the field.

```
BRITISH COMMONWEALTH C.C.
        v YORKSHIRE C.C.C.
  at W. Potomac Park, Washington D.C.
           21st September, 1964
Yorkshire
G. Boycott b Bowen ..      ..     ..     ..      23
J. Hampshire c Williams b Scott ..     ..      18
D. Padgett c Darwent b White     ..     ..       7
B. Close c Stollmeyer b Scott    ..     ..      19
P. Sharpe c & b Bowen      ..     ..     ..       3
R. Illingworth c Rawlings b Bowen   ..  ..     103
J. Binks b Darwent ..      ..     ..     ..      69
F. Trueman c & b Shah      ..     ..     ..      20
D. Wilson c Scott b Shah   ..     ..     ..      62
R. Hutton c Rawlings b Bowen     ..     ..      21
M. Ryan not out     ..     ..     ..     ..       3
Extras  ..     ..     ..     ..    ..     ..      2
                                              ____
        Total (all out)    ..     ..     ..    350
Bowling Analysis
A. G. Scott 14-3-50-2; B. Darwent 10-0-48-1;
B. K. Bowen 24-2-0-119-4; R. White 9-0-52-1;
H. William 3-0-20-0; P. Shah 7-0-58-2.
British Commonwealth
M. Stollmeyer b Trueman    ..     ..     ..       0
B. Krishana b Wilson       ..     ..     ..       4
R. White c Hutton b Trueman      ..     ..       0
P. Shah c Ryan b Trueman   ..     ..     ..       2
H. William b Trueman       ..     ..     ..       4
B. Bowen st Binks b Wilson ..     ..     ..      22
B. Darwent c Illingworth b Wilson ..    ..      12
L. Rawlings st Binks b Wilson    ..     ..       0
W. Fraser c Wilson b Close ..     ..     ..       2
Y. Patel not out    ..     ..     ..     ..       0
A. Scott b Close ·  ..     ..     ..     ..       0
                                              ____
        Total (all out)    ..     ..     ..     46
Bowling Analysis
F. Trueman 5-2-4-4; M. Ryan 6-3-4-0; D. Wilson
9-2-31-4; B. Close 7·1-5-7-2.
YORKSHIRE WON by 304 runs.
```

The match was played at West Potomac Park, near the Jefferson Memorial and with the Potomac River being so close, Fred Trueman stated he would hit the ball into the river, which did not happen. It was a full strength Yorkshire contingent and at one point they were down 96 for 6 until Ray Illingworth scored 103 and with Binks adding 69, Yorkshire's total moved up to 350. In reply, BCCC were bundled out for only 46 as they were no match for Fred Trueman, who's bowling figures read, 5 overs 2 maidens 4 runs and 4 wickets! Besides the Captain Brian Close, some of the other were, D. Padgett, P. Sharpe, J. Binks, R. Hutton and a young Geoff Boycott. This match was played on 21st September and from here they went to Toronto, British Columbia, Southern California and Bermuda. During the 1960s and 70's, the clubs' single largest item purchase was the cricket mat which was stored in a wooden box and placed amid the cherry blossom trees that surrounded the Tidal Basin. The mat was cut up to provide for make shift tents on two occasions, once in 1963 during Martin Luther King's famous speech at the Lincoln memorial and in 1971 when protestors camped out in West Potomac Park during the Vietnam War and used it as a tent!

Another unusual incident happened to a team from Hamilton, Ontario, who arrived at midnight on June 16th 1972, being lost and new to the area, they were looking for the Howard Johnson Motel. This was the night when the biggest scandal hit Washington, the Watergate building where the offices of the Democratic National Committee (DNC) were located, several burglars' were arrested inside the office as they tried to re-bug the phone lines, and as the motel was located across from it, several players were picked up for questioning but later released. The infamous Watergate scandal led to the resignation of President Richard Nixon on August 8th 1974, after his role in the incident had come to light, the first President to do so. For a brief period the BCCC played on the Oval, a field across from the White House which provided the backdrop. 1964 was the year when the United States was finally admitted to the ICC as an Associate member.

Here we are in the 1960 and I don't see any sign of cricket abating, granted it was not on the same scale as the Major League Baseball with their stadiums and regular seasons etc. but matches, visits were still ongoing. Worcestershire after winning the county championship two years in a row, 1964 and 1965, sets out on a World Tour in 1964-65 and played their last two matches of the tour in Hawaii (30th March 1965) and Southern California (3rd April 1965). Against the Honolulu CC, they won by 139 runs (WCCC 185 for 6 declared & HCC 46) and the match with the Southern California Cricket Association at Hollywood was rained out.[25]

The BCCC's scorebook details all the matches played in the Washington D.C. region from 1958 to 1972 and they show a very robust cricket scene such as the mini league, which included teams like the Nondescripts, Windies, Academicals, Potomacs and the Maryland CC in Baltimore. Matches were played against Philadelphia, New York, Hartford, Connecticut, Mecklenburg and Charlotte in North Carolina and Atlanta and Savannah in Georgia on a home and away basis. Matches would also be arranged between teams from the United Nations in New York and the World Bank/International Monetary Fund in Washington, DC. Canada was frequently visited and only one tour was organized to Bermuda and the Prior CC of Philadelphia organized a tour of London and Devon, England in 1977 which included four members of BCCC. Universities were also active in the cricket scene as matches were also arranged with George Washington in Washington, DC, University of North Carolina, Yale, Penn State, Harvard, Howard University, William and Mary, Princeton and Pittsburg. Haverford College is the only varsity in the country where cricket has continuously been played on Cope field. BCCC had new grounds for the 1959 season on the East Potomac Park, which saw most of the action on the turf.

During the 1967 visit, MCC stops by in New York, Philadelphia and Washington DC, where they take on the BCCC on 30th August to win comfortably by 67 runs, and the next day they play against the USCA Southern Zone who only managed to put up a paltry 34 in reply to MCC's 177 for 5 declared.

*Standing L to R: R. Honda, W.F. Severn, S. Thackurdhin, M.A. Stollmeyer, H.A. Durity,
P.A. Merrett, A.W. Brook, R.C.S. Severn, A.F.P. Hollick, S.D. Dyal
Sitting L to R: L.C. Mullings, A.W.M. Cooper (Captain) Dr. M.A. Verity (Manager) J.I.
Marder (President U.S.C.A.) J.R. Gardiner (U.K. Rep) A. Lashkari, L.F. Fernandes.
1968 United States Cricket Team on tour to England.*

A USA National team, yes, a national team went over to England in 1968! According to USACA, *"there are over 25,000 active players who are members of more than fifty leagues and 1,100 clubs spread across the United States with more than 600 playing fields."*

1979 USA play in their first ICC Trophy in England where they beat Israel and Wales. USA were in Group C with Sri Lanka, Wales, Netherlands and Israel. On 22nd May, US played Israel defeating them by 126 to 85 and the other victory was achieved over Wales by a score of 190 to 182, a close match which was played on 4th June. On another ground on the same day, Sri Lanka refused to play Israel who were declared winners by a walkover. Sri Lanka ended winning the tournament with their strong batting and the two finalists, Sri Lanka and Canada, qualified for the 2nd edition of the World Cup that year which began on 9th June, with the West Indians emerging champions and they were the ones who had also won the inaugural cup also in 1975. West Indies would also have won the world cup for the 3rd time in 1983, had it not been for India, who staged a major upset by winning the Prudential Cup. India would have to wait till 2011 before claiming the 2nd World Champions title again in one day internationals.

This was the beginning of the modern day cricket under the ICC umbrella and USA continued to participate as we see more engagements taking place. As of 2013, team USA, an Associate Member is in Division 3 of the World Cricket League (WCL) and the other associate members are Argentina, Bermuda, Canada, Cayman Islands and Suriname. In the recently concluded World Cup Qualifiers in the WCL Division 3 held in Bermuda, USA missed securing a place in the World Cup Qualifier by losing to Nepal and they were helped by Bermuda who managed to beat USA. In the fight for the third place though, USA did beat Bermuda by 30 runs and Nepal who clinched the Division 3 Title by beating Uganda who will compete at next year's World Cup Qualifiers. They hope to advance further and play in the big league - the World Cup to be held in Australia and New Zealand in early 2015. As regards to the future, only time will tell and cricket will hopefully develop just as Major League Soccer did and become an accepted sport and once again create the future 'Kings' of America and the world.

DEMISE OF CRICKET IN AMERICA, A VICTIM OF *PROPAGANDA*?

"**D**isruptive effects of the Civil War, class or ethnic differences, or the emergence of American sporting nationalism," are according to Tom Melville, 'macro analytic interpretations'[1] one that does not adequately explain the Demise of Cricket in America, or its relegation to the pages of the history books. "*Cricket failed in America, because it never established an American character*" he goes on to say, so then, why did it germinate in every nook and corner of the Indian subcontinent? It never established an individualized character or color in the countries where it became popular, in fact, India established an identity for cricket in the country, a second religion so to speak, was this then an Indian character that made cricket popular there?

What then is an American character or American temperament, as Lester was frequently reminded and was trying to unravel its enigma? "*The facet of the American temperament which Cornelius Weygandt fixes upon as intolerant of cricket is impatience.*"[2] Melville provides views by two other authorities, Melvin Adelman and George Kirsch. He goes on to say that, while Kirsch opined that cricket failed due to "*inadequate coaching, playing grounds and promotion,*" while Adelman recognized cricket's failure as an American sport lies in its "*understanding of the more subtle interplay between culturally conditioned behavior and its expressions thru specific sporting structures.*" Based on this premise, he believed that baseball with its, "*shorter, rapid transition structure, and alternating periods of excitement*" gave the Americans their "*cultural expression that cricket with its advanced technique and culturally unmalleable status which was prematurely modern, could not*"[3] or was Cornelius right in saying, "*Americans do not like a game in which proficiency can be attained only with labor and patience.*"[4] Was this then *the* American temperament?

Why then, did it become so popular in the Indian sub-continent, India's un-official national game is field hockey, but this British import successfully assimilated throughout the region. What were the factors that attributed to it growth, whereas in reality, there were so many against it in context to the American 'conditions and temperament.'

In describing temperament against the backdrop of personal liberty, Lester rightly points out that there is no difference between the temperament of the Americans or the Australians, noticeable enough to rationally explain why cricket decline in one place and took off in the other. The same can be argued for India which I have alluded to time and again, as the majority of the arguments are not viable when taken in that context. One thing was certain, cricket was not on the same growth path as baseball with its stadiums, national league structure, seasons etc. and where one could hope to make it up the leagues to play for the majors and money, whereas cricket was more like a Sunday game in comparison. Even the British press observed that when the Philadelphians came over, they played continuously for a couple of months as compared to playing on weekends at home. Ancillary industries spring up around baseball, equipment makers, apparel, folklore, legends, myths, gambling etc. that build up on baseball's popularity and generating interest in the public's eye. *"I don't think you could have had the rise of baseball without gambling. It was not worthy of press coverage. What made baseball seem important was when gamblers figured out a way to spur interest in it. ... In the beginning, there were people who turned their noses up at gambling but they recognized the necessity of it. You would not have had a box score. You would not have had an assessment of individual skills. You would not have had one player of skill moving to another club if there were not gambling in it,"* writes baseball historian, John Thorn.[5] The money potential was there for a baseball player to turn professional but not so for a cricketer, a major factor in the games attrition! Baseball was promoted as being equal for all classes which provided an opportunity on the ball field and also for the recent immigrants, a means to assimilate into their new surroundings and community by joining the locals on the diamond.

As baseball flourished *"owners schemed to turn the national pastime into a profitable business,"*[6] and for that to happen a viable nexus between the sport and political entities grew which provided the owners with new ball parks in prime locations which had access to public transportations, civic amenities and the law enforcement. It established itself as a powerful force culturally and socially in America.[7] There is no dearth of arguments/opinions as to why cricket could not conciliate the American psyche.

New York Herald in 1859 writes, *"Cricket is too slow, intricate and plodding a game for our go-ahead people. In cricket a very smooth ground is wanted on account of the bowling as the ball must strike the ground before it reaches the batsman or strikes the wicket. In baseball very smooth ground is not required, but a rather larger space is necessary for cricket. It occupies on an average about two hours to play a game of baseball – two days to play a game of cricket."* Fast forward to the year 2013, both games require a level playing field, and with cricket's new "Twenty20" or 'T20' format, both games are over in less than four hours! Slowly but surely, cricket is making a comeback and with the first stadium built in Florida and new grounds coming up in Indianapolis, things can only get better from here. The five day Test Matches and One Day International's still remain popular in the cricketing world and should remain so.

Cricket not only has to start at an early age, but one should also be surrounded by images of the game in the form of live matches or TV/Internet, so that not only are the sensory receptors active while playing or watching, but the audio/visual is ingrained in the sub conscious memory bank for quick reference later on. Once a child develops an interest in the game and yearns to learn more as he grows older, he takes the initiative to get better at it by practicing, reading up on the game and then starts to idolize professional players who become their role model and try to emulate them in the hope of reaching their status someday. Who has not been awed by a player whom you have always idolizes and if seeing them up close and personal, and getting an autograph or a few encouraging words were spoken to…there is no better elixir than that.

In general, baseball was an outgrowth of bat and ball games and it owes a debt to cricket. Comparing the two in 1859, Harper's suggested that baseball was at last crowding out cricket. But if cricket was shunted into a few fashionable enclaves of American Society, it left its mark on baseball. The umpire is common to both, and early baseball writers drew expressions from cricket, such as, 'excellent field' 'batsman' 'punish loose bowling' and 'playing for the side.' Further pioneers like Chadwick and Harry Wright, former cricket players themselves, introduced innovations into baseball.[8] Though Spalding brushed aside such dissent and argued that baseball, like America, must be *"free from the trammels of English traditions, customs, conventionalities."*[9]

Baseball came generally to be called by that name early in the 1830s, following the publication in 1834 of rules referring to it by that name, those rules being otherwise identical with an earlier edition in 1829 in which the game had been called rounders, which, of course, it basically still is![10] Later researchers have found baseball to be of English origin also. *If early baseball is related to the free spirited, democratic, and somewhat coarse religion of the time, then its parentage, like that of Christianity, is a more reserved and refined European figure: Cricket.* English born journalist Henry Chadwick, an early baseball supporter and player, represents this American 'conversion' from cricket to baseball. As a former cricket player he found baseball's pace more suited to the American psyche, *"Americans do not care to dawdle over a sleep-inspiring game all through the heat of June or July day. What they do, they want to do in a hurry. In baseball, all is lightning, every action is swift as a seabird's flight."*

George M Newhall – A Visionary

"At the hour appointed to begin (alas, what a sarcasm!)"…

In describing the rules of the game in, *"How to Play Cricket, A Manual for American Cricketers,"* (George M Newhall, 1881) the author could hardly contain his disdain, as this was one of the principal reasons why cricket could not hold the spectators interest. It goes on to say, *"To gain favor among a people who are not wedded to it by education and traditions, this game should be suited to the character and natural feelings of the populace. The English rules were made for the leisure class of England, they naturally do not fully provide for America, where we have no such class, numerous and active enough, to maintain the English custom in playing matches."* This was a very astute observation, which aptly describes the fabric of America during the period. Most of the matches in America were played on a two day basis, and it was foregone conclusion that four innings could not be completed, and the match was settled on the verdict of the first inning scores. Suggestions were made to decide the game based on the team showing the best record by the score book, in completing the play from the beginning to the end. If the matches were complete in all respects, this would add to the popularity of the game in America, as both the player and spectators would feel the best team had won, and without spectators there would be no cricket.

During that time three prominent matches ended in a draw, Australia vs. Philadelphia, Canada vs. Philadelphia and Resident English vs. Americans. This of course did not bode well for the game as the spectators were not happy and *'The Cricketers Association of the United States'* at their April 17th meeting in 1878, offered some recommendations of 'The Average System" for adoption by the clubs. (The Association was formed on April 17th itself and out of the nearly 150 recognized clubs, 17 principal clubs are members of the association). [11] We don't see any evidence of it being implemented though.

The Average System is based on the following conviction:

> *First – The Americans are not in a position to play 'two day' matches, but are destined, for years, to confine their game to a single day.*
>
> *Second – Unless the play of the day be not recorded in full, justice will, frequently, not be done that side having shown the best record, therefore making the result a matter quite so much of chance as of skill.*
>
> *Third – The people cannot afford to take an afternoon to attend a match which may be finished, virtually, before 3 o'clock in the day. If the spectators be wanting, our game is killed. The American public wish to see the result secured. The scrub game which follows the first innings is in no way entertaining, as a rule. So, it is contended, by the present system both players and public are dissatisfied.*

> 1) *No match shall be decided on the average system unless each side have played one full innings, and ten wickets shall be counted in said innings, whether a full eleven plays or not.*
> 2) *To get the average, the total score of the play of each side shall be divided by the total number of batsmen, less one. Thus the score of two full innings will be divided by twenty-one.*
> 3) *The striker carrying his bat out in the first innings shall go in first in the second innings.*
> 4) *The side going in second must play their full innings, unless when stumps are drawn their score shall exceed the score of their opponents; in that event they may win with wickets to spare.*

5) *Innings must be followed by a side according to the rules of a two days' match.*

6) *If a wicket be lost within two minutes of the time agreed upon to draw stumps, the captain of the batting side may send the next man in or not, as he chooses.*

COMMENTS AND EXPLANATION TO THE RULES

1) *Provides against the side going second to the bat winning with an incomplete innings, or, if the side be short, and the innings be played until all batsmen present have had a strike, the total score must be divide by as great a number as divides the score of those batting first. The principle is that one side should not need to divide their score by any higher number than the other side. Rule 5 explains how those second at bat win if they pass their opponent's score and still have wickets to fall.*

2) *The principle of calculating is very simple; if we consider that the batters of the second innings are different batters than those of the first innings. Suppose a side on their second innings have only fifteen minutes to play before 'time' is to be called, and the batters sent in first hold their own, consequently only thirteen batters of the side will have appeared at the wickets, and the total runs of the play of the two innings must be divided by twelve. The result is the average by which they win or lose.*

3) *The striker 'carrying his bat' who is apt to be one of the 'tail end' is thus compelled, as he should be, to face the music, otherwise the stronger players of the side would go in first to secure a high average, especially if the day were drawing to a close.*

4) *Require no comment*

5) *Require no comment*

6) *Is eminently a fair provision.*

Newhall, further goes on to explain and analyze what could have been the outcome of the drawn matches (he used the Australian match as an example), had the average method been applied versus the current system.

That was 1878, fast forward to the 1990's where two English statisticians, Frank Duckworth and Tony Lewis devised a system or a method based on mathematical calculation, now known as the Duckworth-Lewis method that calculates the revised target score for the team batting second in a one-day or Twenty20 Cricket match, which is affected by rain/weather or other circumstances. It was first used in the 1996-97 cricket season and officially adopted in 2001 by the ICC (International Cricket Council). To reach the match conclusion, it takes into account the situation of the game during rain stoppage, (overs played, runs scored, and wickets lost) and sets a target score that is up or down.

The basic premise of the D/L method takes into account two main resources in which to make as many runs as possible: (1) from the number of overs remaining and (2) number of wickets on hand. This system is based on the notion that a team's scoring ability depends on a combination of these two resources. Given the complexity of the math involved, the actual target or the par score is often a fractional number. Hence, the chasing team is set the next integer as the revised target.

The D/L formula is unique because it also takes into account when a stoppage has occurred in a match. For instance, if a match has been stopped during the first innings itself, the team batting second is set a higher total, since it has an abundance of both resources. However, if a match is stopped during the second innings--in the middle of a chase--the system automatically accounts for the overs remaining and wicket's lost, and sets a more reasonable target. This D/L method is far from perfect, but it's considered to be the best available method out there. It's used in ODIs (One Day Internationals) and T20s, and some have suggested that it should be tweaked for the latter format since T20s differ so much from ODIs as far as batting strike rates and strategy is concerned.

The one overwhelming reason for cricket's demise, and I would agree with George M Newhall's affirmation back in 1885 (Outing Vol. 5), *"It will never come to much until the school and colleges take to it, as no man can learn the science after his school days. It must be worked into a growing system."* Regrettably, his foresight held true of cricket, in America.

I have often wondered why the noble game of Cricket is not more popular as a pastime throughout the United States. It is my opinion the only reason is that its qualities are not sufficiently well known to be appreciated by the American people, who, although fond of out-of-door athletics, condemn this as an "old man's" game and not worthy of notice compared with our national game, base ball. [12] So much is observed here by George Wright.

"There is no doubt that the length of time required for a full two innings match (frequently two days) is a serious handicap for it in this country, and is at variance with the American temperament. The office boy can occasionally get a few hours off in the afternoon to see a baseball game, with the "grandmother's funeral" plea, but obviously this could not be worked two days running, for a cricket match." [13] On the other hand, *Spirit of the Times* asked, '*What can be done to naturalize the beautiful game (Cricket) in America?"* [14]

This common theme is being played over and over like a broken record. My first question is, 'Why did they have to play a two innings match?" Did you have to be part of a club and then only could you play? Didn't anyone play for a few hours in schools, at a park in the evening or for a few hours on a holiday? I never belonged to any club, we played anywhere with whatever equipment we had. It never crossed our minds, that to play, you must first belong to a club, no, we just played as much as we could in the park, schools and in local tournaments organized by ourselves when we were in college.

Trying to pinpoint *the main* cause for the games unceremonious relegation to the back benches is like trying to hit a moving target, there is no one easy answer, as there were a combination of factors that were responsible for Americans dwindling interest in cricket. The English blueprint of having clubs and playing two inning matches was followed to a tee, and a lot of emphasis was placed on the playing format. This would be one of the reasons for cricket losing out to baseball, not that it was difficult to understand the scientific play, as it was often referred to, but the length of play was not shortened. If this was true for every country, then cricket would have remained in England. Every author laments about the length of play and that the working class could not afford to spend two days to watch a match. In any country the working class *is* the spectator, then why is it that in countries like India, Sri Lanka, Pakistan, Australia and New Zealand, cricket took a firm grip? Take the Indian sub-continent, an agricultural country at the turn of the century, sent its first official team to England in 1932, a very late entrant when compared to the American, English encounters, though the Parsees were the first to take an amateur team to England as early as 1886.

Another noticeable reason was the patriotic card that was played against cricket. Again using India as an example, the National Game is Hockey (not officially), but did that prevent people from taking up a new English sport? Cricket could have thrived here had it not been for the impetus that baseball received as *the perceived* American ball game. When one looks in the content section of, *The book of American Pastimes, containing a History of the Principal Base Ball, Cricket, Rowing and Yachting Clubs of the United States*, by Charles Peverelly in 1866, Base Ball is arbitrarily headlined as The National Game, it had been decide for the masses that Base Ball is to be referred to as the National Game. This is too early in American Sports timeline for Base Ball to be christened *the* national game, but we see the underlying forces here and no doubt this would help in popularizing it in the collective consciousness.

"One of the greatest obstacles to the progress of Cricket is the tedious delays incident to the way of playing the game, customary with our English resident cricketers." The American psyche is governed

by, 'time is money,' whereas, the unemployed wealthy in England having time on their hand, try to absorb as much of their leisure time as possible. In America where the drones of society are in the minority and the busy bees of the community find little time for recreation, the game which economizes time will be popular.[15] *"Base-ball seems better to suit their national temperament."*[16] Baseball somehow, had escaped the 'English' tag.

Organized cricket began in America with the formation of the famous St. George Cricket Club in New York in 1839-40. Members of this club included English born, upper class businessman, professionals, diplomats, and military officers, as well as English immigrant craftsman and artisans. When the Union Cricket Club was founded in Philadelphia 1843, mechanics, including a saw maker, a frame smith, and a wood turner, were amongst its members. In 1848 more than 20% of St. George CC members were artisans. By 1865, however, that number had dropped to 5.7%.

The working class Americans who were playing cricket felt alienated from the English elite who governed the game and the clubs. Was the snobbishness of the English community in New York to blame for cricket's downfall, did the English exacerbate the situation by being aloof and thereby wielding the proverbial axe to their own feet? *"If conceit were as expansive as steam, the St. George of New York would have power enough to propel a frigate!"*[17] Wow, that sums it all up! The situation may have been further exacerbated by the fact that the recent English immigrants to America may not have been from the upper echelons of society in England, but here in America, they could emulate their counterparts, and none would be wiser.

Baseball increasingly became an integral fabric of American life making inroads into the economic, cultural, political and social life. Further impetus was provided when owners devised ways to make the national pastime into a profitable business venture.[18] While they struggled to make money, sports equipment manufacturers, especially Albert G Spalding, the consummate businessman and PR machine, made fortune in the manufacture of Spalding equipment and uniforms. Did he limit that to baseball only – no, of course not, after all, he was a savvy businessman. He also sold Cricket, Football, Tennis, Golf and other sporting goods, not to mention, the group also published books on almost all sports under, 'Spalding Athletic Library.' Spalding embarked on a World Tour in 1888-89 to showcase "Americas National Pastime" which provided for further impetus to the Americanization of baseball and in the process helped expand his business as well. Finally, a commission was set up by Spalding to find the origins of baseball and put an 'American Stamp' on the game once in for all after his friend Henry Chadwick wrote an article that claimed baseball grew out of the English game of Cricket and Rounders. Three years of search yielded a letter declaring Abner Doubleday as the originator of the game in Cooperstown, N.Y in 1839. A biased Spalding had commented, *"Our good old American game of baseball must have an American Dad."* He further went on to say, *"Baseball was purely of American origin and no other game or country has any right to claim its parentage."*[19]

Coming back to Melville espousing on the works of Melvin Adelman and George Kirsch who he notes restricted their works to a certain time frame and large metropolitan areas. *"The great strength of Adelman's analysis is the recognition that the rise of early American sports wasn't merely an inevitable, impersonal process, but a dynamic interplay between emerging sports structures and individual behavior, that involved human choice and cultural preference."*[20]

'Human choice and cultural preference,' I would argue that Baseball was not a democratic selection (though it should have been), the American psyche was psychologically corralled towards the 'National Game' or the 'National Pastime.' *"The publicist promoted the sport as a <u>democratic game</u> that offered all classes and ethnic groups an opportunity to play, immigrants immersed in the game as a way of joining the mainstream society."*[21] Baseballs became the game of masses as a wide gamut of society stepped on the mound and it was further solidified when in 1888, *"Ernest Lawrence Thayer dramatized in verse Mighty Casey striking out for the Mudville Nine. Thayer's piece was an early contribution to what became a vast body of baseball prose and poetry, as the <u>national pastime</u> generated its distinctive myths, legends, symbols and folklore."*[22] The aura created was too much even for George Kirsch, he opens with, *"This book grew out of two long term passions: sports-especially baseball-which I have loved since the age of five."*[23]

ST PAUL'S SCHOOL, CONCORD, NEW HAMPSHIRE.

"We can scarcely pass over the subject of college cricket without a word about the successful tour in 1889 of the St. Paul's school eleven from Concord, New Hampshire. This bright team won all its Canadian matches against our best clubs, and a more promising lot of young material we have yet to meet."[24] (Lost only to Upper Canada College by a solitary run!)

The following reference materials and photographs were provided by, St Paul's School Archives, Concord, New Hampshire.[25]

The cricket team of 1889 was the most successful and is shown here in the picture with cricket professional Samuel Morley on the far left (seated, holding a cricket ball), who had a very successful summer tour of Canada. Arthur Stanwood Pier, in his book, St. Paul's School 1855-1934, described it this way:

"In subsequent years the school eleven extended their itinerary, playing in Boston and in Philadelphia as well as in Hoboken and in New York. Their most ambitious expedition, undertaken when the game was enjoying the height of its prestige, was their tour of Canada in the summer of 1889, under the management of Mr. Charles A. Mitchell, a highly respected teacher of Greek. The eleven stayed at the school for a week after the end of the spring term in order to practice. Their professional, Morley, accompanied them on the tour, as did also two boys, not members of the team, who travelled, one in the capacity of special reporter, the other in that of scorer. Malcolm Kenneth Gordon was captain; the masters who played on the eleven were Rev. James P. Conover, Mr. William H. Foster, Mr. Godfrey M. Brinley, and Mr. James S. Hodges. The team arrived in Montreal on June 30, began

1889 St. Pauls's School Cricket Team

their first match there July 1, and played every day except Sunday until the 13th. . . Their trip, which cost about $1070, defrayed by subscription, was highly successful, as they won seven out of eight games, being beaten only by Upper Canada College."

If the rest of the country was taking up baseball, why was St. Paul's able to retain and produce such good cricketers in this little gem of a school in New England! Well, there are always exceptions to a rule, one such driving force behind the longetivity of cricket at SPS was Henry Augusts Coit, the first rector who presided over the school's first 39 years. The other was Samuel Morley a cricket professional whose retirement in 1902 virtually marked the end of cricket at SPS.

Cricket was first introduced to SPS in June of 1857 (1ˢᵗ match played on July 4ᵗʰ)[26] when cricket equipment was presented by Mr. George Brown who later went on to become the Mayor of Baltimore during the Civil War. Two clubs were soon formed in 1859, 'Isthmian' and the 'Old Hundred' the 'Delphians' were added in 1889, the year which saw 300 boys playing cricket. Henry Coit set the stamp of approval on cricket by offering a bat as a prize to the player making the best score for the season. Though he himself was indifferent to all sports, he favored cricket over baseball as it was a healthy form of exercise and one that gentlemen in Philadelphia played as it was clean and brought out no vulgar shouting. Baseball was always on the doorstep and once when the Kearsarge Baseball Club of Concord sent a letter for a friendly match, it ended up on Mr. Coit's desk.

He walked up to some boys playing a scrub game of ball and asked the captain, William Blair to reply to the letter stating that, *"there is no baseball nine at St Paul's School, that Cricket is the ball game of this school."* As baseball teams were being organised and games were played, Dr. Coit completely prohibited the playing of baseball at SPS! The constant threat from baseball took on a nationalistic tone and many resented the fact that encouragement was given to an English game, while schools in other cities were being American by taking up baseball. Why and how this turned 'nationalistic' after almost hundred years is interesting. Little did anyone know then and even today, that baseball originated in England and this was discovered by David Block from a book written in 1796 Germany describing the 'English game of Baseball.' *"Spiele zur Uebung und Erholung des Körpers und Geistes, für die Jugend, ihre Erzieher und alle Freunde unschuldiger Jugendfreuden,"* by Johann Christoph Friedrich Gutsmuths. (Games for the exercise and recreation of body and spirit for the youth and his educator and all friends of innocent joys of youth). Included is a chapter on: "Ball mit Freystaten (oder das englische Base-ball) which is 'ball with free station' or English Base-ball.[27] While Albert Spalding and America were trying to claim baseball as an American invention, it reached the ears of a 'Grandmother' in England and it got her mad enough to write to the editor of 'The London Times.'

August 13th 1874.
Sir,

Some American athletes are trying to introduce to us their game of base-ball, as if it were a novelty; whereas the fact is that it is an ancient English game, long ago discarded in favor of cricket.

In a letter of the celebrated Mary Lepel, Lady Hervey, written in 1748, the family of Frederick, Prince of Wales, are described as "diverting themselves with base-ball, a play all who are or have been schoolboys are well aquainted with."

Your obedient servant,
GRANDMOTHER.

(Lady Hervey was a maid of honor to Caroline, Princess of Wales.)[28]

As we all know well enough, grandmothers are always right, and in this case - never get her mad!

After complaints by the students in *Horae Scholasticae,* a magazine published by the students, the first professional cricketer named Brewster, was hired in 1876 to improve the game of cricket if it were to survive as *the* school sport at SPS. The first away game was played on June 25th 1876 against the second St. George XI at Hoboken. The first outing was a success and the next year the school eleven took on more teams including the Manhattan Club and Staten Island CC. In subsequent years the itenary included games in Boston, Philadelphia as well as Hoboken and New York. SPS also has the distinction of being the first school to have their cricket scores recorded in the *American Cricketer* when they played against Chestnut Hill in 1879.[29]

Mr Morley who was hired as a professional, arrived at SPS in 1882[30] and retired from the school in 1902. He was 50 years old when he came to Philadelphia from Nottinghamshire, England. Little is know how he ended up at SPS, but it may be due to the fact that Mr. H.P. McKean, then president of Germantown C.C. and a friend of SPS may have influenced his move to the school which would turn out beneficial for them. In a letter sent in by a certain G.G. Bonser of Sutton, who provided the early information regarding Mr. Samuel Morley states that Mr. Morley was a coach at Aston near Birmingham, at Sherbourne school and in the 1860/70's he captained the teams of Sutton and District Colts. His is remembered for his great feat of dismissing Richard Daft twice for a duck in one match, the same Daft who captained the English team to America and Canada in 1879. Under Mr. Morley's tutelage, the SPS XI reached it height with an impressive tour of Canada in 1889.

The SPS XI stayed at the school for another week after the spring term was over to practice for the up-coming Canada tour and on June 30th they reached Montreal. A total of eight matches were played which started on July 1st and continued everyday till the 13th, resulting in seven wins and one loss for SPS, an impressive feat indeed against the best Canadian players.

The results of the matches:

July 1 & 2	SPS	157
	Ottawa CC	44
July 3	SPS	84 - one innings
	Kingston CC	51 - two innings
July 4	SPS	78
	Napanee CC	27
July 5 & 6	SPS	154
	Toronto CC	119
July 8	SPS	187
	Peterborough CC	104
July 9 & 10	SPS	94 and 6 wickets
	Trinity College School	93
	(past & present)	
July 11	SPS	86
	Upper Canada College	
	(past & present)	87 & 8 wickets
July 12 & 13	SPS	141 – one innings
	Hamilton CC	112 – two innings

The matches against Trinity College School and Upper Canada School were tough as expected and according to SPS, the match against UCC was lost because of - overconfidence. Since these were two inning matches UCC scored 37 runs in reply to SPS score of 38 in the first innings. As there was an hour and a half left in regular time SPS went in to bat and were all out for 48 in the second innings, here according to them, is where they made the mistake of hitting all over the field instead of saving wickets. UCC had half an hour in which to score and they made 50 with minutes to spare. This was really a close match and had SPS won, they would have had an undefeated tour, even then, this was an astounding feat by school lads playing against a lot of seasoned Canadian team players. The boys were fortunate to play against George Wright who was on the Longwood team when SPS visited them on June 21 before their successful Canadian tour.

Mr. Morley's retirement in 1902 virtually marked the end of cricket at SPS, besides being a profesional cricket coach, he also looked after the cricket equipment and the playing turf, he also took coaching interest in racquet games, had the snow cleared off the pond in winter to create the first high-board rinks. He also laid out golf links and improved the running tracks, thus his love for sports created an inviting environment. During his time, there were as many as four elevens in each club. Cricket was played for another year by a few but no inter club games were held. Tennis and golf became popular and baseball that was kept at bay by the catalyst, Mr. Coit, finally took over the field that once hosted so many *pleasant spectacle of emerald green turf and white flanned youths.*

Team from the 1880's with the Isthmian and Old Hundred banners.
Courtesy: St. Paul's School Concord, New Hampshire.

This photograph is of the First Eleven Isthmian cricket team from the fall of 1880. Notations on this and other copies of the same photograph in the archives collection list the team members as:

Back Row (left to right):
Franklin Remington, Form of 1881
The Rev. Edward Melville Parker, Form of 1872 and faculty member from 1879-1906
Dr. James Milnor Coit, Form of 1860 and faculty member from 1877-1906
William Hamilton Foster, Form of 1881
[unknown]
Middle Row (left to right):
[unknown]
Lester Carrington Dole, faculty member from 1878-1918
Thomas Shoenberger Blair, Jr. Form of 1880 and team captain
Julius Tyler Andrews Doolittle, Form of 1880
James Gregory Mumford, Form of 1880
Joseph Howland Coit, Jr., Form of 1881
Front Row (reclining, left to right):
John Lawrence Pool, Form of 1881
The Rev. Thomas James Drumm, faculty member from 1874-1911

School XI at Manhattan Grounds

Members of the St. Paul's School Cricket Eleven at Germantown Cricket Club, Philadelphia, Pennsylvania. Initials under the photograph identify Malcolm Kenneth Gordon (Form of 1887 and faculty member from 1889-1917), William Hamilton Foster (Form of 1881 and faculty member from 1883–1928), and Joseph Howland Coit, Jr. (Form of 1881 and faculty member from 1883-1907).

Here we have a 'rag tag' team, in the overall scheme of things in a little corner of the country doing well against seasoned players who are exposed to international caliber cricketers and they were able to put up a spectacular performance against them. They proved, cricket could be played and competed against the best, if it had been allowed to grow unchecked, unfortunately the 'American' baseball sentiment was very strong which ultimately took over and relegated cricket to a sport the was played at one time with great élan.

St. Austin's in Staten Island was another school besides St. Paul, where baseball was prohibited.[31] It was founded in 1883 and located in New Brighton, Staten Island.[32] *St. Austin's School was housed in the Garner House (now called "The Villa" on the grounds of Richmond University Medical Center). In 1901, when neither Saint Mary's nor our Diocese of New York could afford to purchase the school it was sold to Sisters of Charity for the former St. Vincent's Hospital (now Richmond University Medical Center).*[33] The school then moved to Salisbury, Connecticut in 1901and was renamed the Salisbury School.[34] Unfortunately, neither the St. Mary's Episcopal Church in Staten Island, nor the Salisbury School has any history/ pictures of the St. Austin School boys in their cricketing glory days. The only mention of cricket that comes directly from the school is in the form of their Annual Register of

1887 which I have and the postcard shown below, which shows the boys playing cricket. The register talks about the school losing only one match at cricket and football that year. Hunt, a professional from the Staten Island Cricket Club provided his coaching services which helped improve the schools performance. The New York Times carried news of the local cricketers during the season and on May 26th 1895 the paper writes, *"The boys of St. Austin's School put up a very good game for the second eleven of the Staten Island Cricket Club."* The school tried to make cricket a year round endeavor by outfitting a part of their large greenhouse as a practice area for cricket during the winter months.[35] Before the school moved to Connecticut in 1901, cricket was very much part of the school activities as on April 30th 1899, *The New York Times* reported, *"the balmy weather of yesterday was an inducement for local cricketers to start the game."* St Austin kicked off their season with a visit from the Brooklyn Club who won by 99 runs. What happened to cricket once the school moved to Salisbury and why? What brought about this abrupt change? The boys could not have given up the game overnight, it must have been played, maybe not under the patronage of the school as they once did, but it must have continued for a while.

Cricket at St Austin's School in 1899.

Just as the Canadian's did some soul searching after their dismal performance against the visiting Australian team in 1878, so did the Americans, after Ranjitsinhji's visit to Philadelphia in 1899. Even twenty years earlier after similar defeats,[36] they had gone into an introspect mode (same time frame as Canada). 1880s though, was still an early development stage for cricket in the America continent when compared to England. From baseball's point of view/timeline, cricket was in decline or on its way out. An interesting conjunction of the two events, two different viewpoints which can be further expounded into a thesis of its own, but the point here is, do we look upon it as cricket in its infant stage – hence the growing pains or with baseballs advent, cricket - that was relegated to a few corners in the country, thereby a mature game in the eyes of the Americans that was past its prime?

To the Philadelphia cricketers, it was in its prime and comparable to the English and the Australians' and rightly so, as the 1890s to 1910s were their best years. *American Cricketer* called it, "deterioration of our cricket" and three areas of weakness/concern were identified.[37]

First and foremost were the dearth of younger players and the paucity of wickets to practice upon and hone their skills and also lack of regular playing pitches. Finding good slow spin bowlers was another and the third issue which showed up time and again and one of the major factors cited earlier in the chapter, which led to the decline was that, they never completed two full days of play.[38] The matches remained incomplete and ended without results (draw), which contributed to the lack of interest being shown by the spectators and this would spill over into the younger generation looking elsewhere for a game that was short and conclusive. Unfortunately for cricket, the public had a substitute in baseball, which was the right fit for the American way of life and one that was gaining ground rapidly.

The January 1900 issue of the *Sunday Times* ran a story, "The Decline of Cricket in Philadelphia," which set the events in motion to improve the game after an extensive opinion poll from active cricketers and replies to questionnaires. The outcome was to extend the Halifax Cup completion thru September and to encourage cricket within the schools and to support competition in the Inter-academic and Inter-scholastic Leagues with the help of the Associated Cricket Clubs. Three new clubs, Radnor, Frankford and Overbrook entered the Philadelphia Cup competition, and Cornell entered the Inter-Collegiate Cricket Association, but was all this viable in the long run or was it like a new year's resolution that would wear off eventually.[39] Cricket had almost become a vestigial part of American sports psyche.

No doubt there was that ebb and flow of cricket interest and it would be another 30 years before it would wane eventually, but for now, new batsmen and bowlers were being discovered though not of a consistent nature. The Haverford College XI embarked on their maiden tour of England in 1896 to play against the public schools and when the Haverfordians played Marylebone Cricket Club and they beat them by 204 runs, "the governors of Cricket" MCC[40] fielded a stronger side which included Stoddard and Warner – why would one field such players of caliber against a College team, doesn't that say a lot for Philadelphia Cricket? In 1902, *American Cricketer* printed 341 fixtures for cricket matches, was this a sign of decline, maybe not up to international standards and there was still a long way to go but definitely not a loss in interest, yet. Bart King, the greatest of bowlers was yet to reach his pinnacle and top the English bowling averages in 1908, but ominous clouds portending Philadelphia's demise as the once regal cricketing bastion, were visible on the horizon.

First Haverford XI in England 1896, Haverford College Archives, Haverford PA.

"It is a matter to be regretted by all true lovers of the manly <u>pastime</u> that this noble and invigorating game has never been <u>introduced</u> among us here in America, for it certainly never has been — at least to any extent or in a <u>proper spirit.</u>" By an experienced practitioner.[41]

'Introduced,' was this key to cricket's so called, failure in capturing a larger national audience, as it wasn't marketed properly? Some sort of a formal committee or an organization spreading and promoting the game — if so, it may have been premature even if it was 'introduced' for the society in general was beginning to get organized after the Civil War. Baseball, I believe, besides the National sentiment, was 'introduced' as an organized sport at the right time in Americas' history. Affluence, ability to organize, support, sponsor and sustain a paid professional team with regular season and ball fields and stadiums contributed immensely to baseballs rapid development across the nation, as an organised national ball game for all. Was cricket then considered, a pastime only?

I find that there's still enough cognitive dissonance even when the facts proves otherwise, one does not want to accept that cricket was and could have been *the* game of choice in America. *"Despite irrefutable evidence to the contrary, the media and the public, encouraged by the flag-waving bluster of the baseball industry, clung to the Doubleday Myth. It seemed they simply preferred the, "immaculate conception" of baseball by the war hero Abner Doubleday to the messy evolution that the historical evidence clearly indicated."*[42] When the collective conscience is coerced towards the nationalistic ideology with a myopic view, myth prevails over factual evidence. If baseball origins can still be mired in misconception, what chance does cricket have in re-establishing itself as *the* game of America?

First Cricket Stadium in United States, Central Broward Regional Park, Lauderhill, Florida

CRICKET IN HAWAII

Cricket in Hawaii may date from the early 1860's, when King Kamehameah IV reportedly expressed an interest in the sport. Honolulu Cricket Club was the first club formed in the isles in 1893 and the Maui Cricket Club was the first neighboring island club. In 1904, according to the Maui News, Honolulu's best players went to Maui and beat the team two games to one. Employees of the Big Island's Pepeekeo Sugar Company in 1939 formed a team to play monthly games against Hilo's best. They also played exhibition matches in Waimea and Kohala and all-star teams often competed against visiting British Cruise ship personnel.

In the early 1940's, Honolulu and Hilo teams played throughout the year. In November 1941, a thousand fans jammed the polo grounds of Kapiolani Park to watch Honolulu defeat Hilo, just two weeks later, Pearl Harbor was bombed!

In 1956 the Honolulu Cricket Club was reactivated and held weekly matches at Punahou School. The club has hosted touring teams from England and Australia. Cricket was added to the Aloha State Games in 1991 and in 1995 Hawaii sent a team to compete in the North American Cricket Tournament for the first time. There are two variations to the game offered in Hawaii, Cricket and Pacific Cricket. Pacific Cricket is more popular and the main difference is that the game is played with rubber balls and the matches are played at Keehi Lagoon Park. Hawaii's Samoan community enthusiastically supports Pacific Cricket and Cricket is Samoa's national sport! The Samoan Cricket League has over 30 teams, and preceding Samoan Flag Day in August, is the annual Hawaii-Samoan Championship game.

Information provided by Dan Cisco, courtesy Honolulu Cricket Club.

THE LATIN FLAVOR

MEXICO

C ricket has been played in México since the 1820's and the Mexican Union Cricket Club was formed in 1827. A document found at Lord's (Marylebone Cricket Club) provides details of the membership between 1827 and 1838 and one of the founding members may have been, Jr. Poinsset the first ambassador to México. Wherever the English went, cricket followed, so it should be of no surprise here that cricket was played by the expat community. Cornish miners came to Pachuca, and other industries following México's independence in 1821. It became popular enough to catch the attention of Emperor Maximilian (Ferdinand Maximilian Joseph, born in Austria and installed by the French at the behest of rich Mexicans) who briefly reigned for three years before being executed in 1867, is shown playing cricket at the Hacienda de Teji (now Colonia Cuauhtemoc). An unique and rare picture taken maybe around 1865 by François Aubert, [1] shows Maximilian (in white trousers) with the British Ambassador, Sir Charles Wyke (behind the stumps) [2] and other players.

In 1864-65, W.H. Bullock (Hall) [3] who travelled across México, writes about what he saw when he arrived at the village of Napoles.

"While croquet goes on at Tacubaya, the neighboring village of Napoles is the head-quarters of cricket. The district which it traverses consists of meadows as hard as iron, surrounded by hedges of cactus and maguey, or meadows as soft as a sponge, surrounded by ditches. On one of the meadows, as hard as iron, the cricket takes place. During the voyage out from England I had heard that cricket was played in the country, but supposed it would turn out to be cricket of that degenerate sort which one finds occasionally played by the English residents in different parts of Europe. So that when I got to the ground, and found an excellent pavilion, a scoring box, visitor's tent, the field marked out with flags, with the well-known letters M.C.C (México, not Marylebone, Cricket Club) marked upon them, and some eighteen or twenty players in flannels and cricket shoes, I was not a little astonished, and soon found out that I had to do with a very different sort of cricket to what I had expected.

303

Perhaps the most surprising part of the performance was that the best player on the ground was a Mexican, whose bowling and batting did infinite credit to the training which he received at Bruce Castle School. Among the English players were several gentlemen close upon sixty years of age, who all expressed to me their conviction that they owe much of the health and energy which they still possessed, in spite of forty years residence in México, to having stuck, through thick and thin, to their Sunday cricket. They assured me that they had never allowed political events to interfere with their game, which they had pursued unconcernedly, more than once, in view of the fighting going on in the hills around them. Being fully alive to the fact that cricket is nothing without beer, there is always a liberal supply on the ground, of a very excellent quality, supplied by the firm of Blackmore —a name revered, beyond all others, by Englishmen in México."[4]

MCC club members in the late 1860s divided the team into Red and Blue teams for their Sunday morning matches during the season, which began in November and lasted till March, and to increase participation, special trolley services were arranged from the capital to Napoles.[5] The only Mexican player and star of the team, M.J. Trigueros led his team to victory by scoring 64 runs in a match against the local British companies combined. He formed the Victoria Cricket Club along with his fellow students from the *Escuela de Artes y Oficios*. The Victoria Club did well winning matches in 1868, 1869, but lost the final rematch in 1870. For a while cricket had died down but was again revived in Pachuca, a town with English settlers who owned the Real del Monte silver mines. A cricket field was set up across the fashionable Paseo de la Reforma from the Chapultepec Park where the locals also took up the game which flourished for a few years. The game declined in Mexico City but remained popular in the British enclaves of Puebla, Pachuca and Monterrey till the turn of the century.[6]

In the 20th century, plenty of records for the 1900-1902 seasons show up in the Mexican Herald. The league at the time comprised of two teams in México City (RAC and MCC, both having their own grounds), and in Puebla, Orizaba and Pachuca. Leading in both the batting and bowling averages, was Claude Butlin, a 24 year old member of the Reforma Athletic Club, and this gifted sportsman went on to win the first ever point for México in the 1924 Davis Cup tennis at the age of 47. Understandably, during the revolution and the wars, there is no record of cricket being played in Mexico. In the late 1960's the game was revived at the RAC's new grounds in San Juan Totoltepec and now the México Cricket Association (MCA) is a newly elected affiliate member of the ICC.

The Mexico Cricket Club started from a former Mexican football team that played in the *Liga Mexicana de Football Amateur Association* prior to the professionalization and development of the Mexican first division. This club was founded in the small town of San Pedro de los Pinos, which now lie on the outskirts of Mexico City. From 1894 to 1903, Mexico Cricket Club played under the name of *Mexican National Cricket Club*, but later merged with *San Pedro Golf* (1905-06) and that changed to *Mexico City Country Club* (1906-08).[7] In an article published by Michael Costeloe, *"To Bowl a Mexican Maiden Over: Cricket in Mexico, 1827–1900"* he writes that the Mexico City Cricket Club was founded in 1827 by a *"mixed group of British and foreign nationals"* whereas the Mexico Cricket Association website names it the 'Mexican Union Cricket Club.'

Emperor Maximilian at a Sunday cricket match of the Mexico City Cricket Club.
© Royal Museum of the Army and of Military History, Nr Inv KLM-MRA: db-b-10215, Bruxelles.

Cricket in Mexico? Silly Point!

Stumped: The Case of Cricket in Porfirian Mexico, 1895-1911, by Craig White.

"The game of cricket is reputedly the oldest of the outdoor sports imported into Mexico."

- **The Mexican Herald**, 18 October 1903.[1]

"Wherever there is a score of sons of Britain one will discover a cricket team."

- **The Mexican Herald**, 28 February 1909.[2]

I. The Mexican Herald

In 1914 the distinguished George Harris, an administrator of British County Cricket and a founder of the Imperial Cricket Council, explained cricket was:

> more than a game. It is an institution, a passion, a religion. It has got into the blood of the nation, and wherever British men and women are gathered together there will the stumps be pitched.[3]

The estimated 2,485 Britons that resided in Mexico in 1900 shared this enthusiasm through establishing cricket clubs and participating_in matches against each other. One method of highlighting this is through consulting the archives of **The Mexican Herald** newspaper for information concerning cricket. Jerry Knudson notes that in 1895 F. Guernsey established **The Mexican Herald** in Ciúdad de México to encourage economic investment from New York and to provide American residents in the Capital with news from the United States. It did this until 1915 when the administration of Venustiano Carranza suppressed it because of the support it had given to the Victoriano Huerta inter-regnum.[4] The assistant editor was a Briton named L. C. Simmons and I suggest he was an enthusiast of cricket as **The Mexican Herald** provided sporting information and this included details of matches and incidents that occurred in Mexico and Britain. I noted in **Race before Wicket** the political and economic competition between the British and United States in Mexico, but in social occasions these allied because "after all" explained **The Mexican Herald**, despite all their differences, the Briton and the American stand for much that is common in the ideals of decency and progress. This is exemplified when they

---

1 *The Mexican Herald*, 18 October 1903, p. 9.

2 *The Mexican Herald*, 28 February 1909, p. 25.

3 A. Guttmann, *Games and Empires: Modern Sports and Cultural Imperialism*, (New York: Colombia University Press, 1994), p. 17.

4 Jerry W. Knudson, 'The Mexican Herald: Outpost of Empire, 1895-1915', *International Communication Gazette*, 63, 5 (2001), pp. 387-398.

are thrown together in a land foreign to both, where they will generally be found standing shoulder to shoulder in resisting the wrong and fighting for their innate conceptions of justice and fair play, which are so strongly implanted in the Anglo-Saxon character.[5]

In this regard **The Mexican Herald** is a crucial source of information for documenting the historical past of cricket in Mexico from 1895 to 1911 as it had a circulation of 10,000 which made it one of the most propitious publications of the time. This was due to it being government subsidised meaning it could be sold at five cents an issue which **The Two Republics** and the **Anglo-American** newspapers could not compete with.[6]

II. Mexican Cricket, 1895-1915.[7]

In 1894 British personnel of numerous industrial, financial and public enterprises in Ciúdad de México, such as the **London Bank of Mexico and South America**, established the Reforma Athletic Club with grounds on the fashionable Paseo de la Reforma.[8] The cricketing members in it "got up matches" with the neighbouring Mexico Cricket Club which was based on Lerdo and had grounds near a petrol station at La Piedad "where it is understood" commented **The Mexican Herald**, "the rivalry is about analogous to the state of feeling prevailing not so long ago between the Athletics and Photos in the baseball world" but it was fortunate "it is not one which at prevents the holding of some rousing good matches between the Clubs, rather it gives additional zest."[9] In one instance in 1896 "some prominent Germans" from the Capital made a daring "long cross country ride on horseback" to La Piedad grounds to provide lunch for the teams during the interval between innings.[10]

On occasions the Reforma Athletic Club and Mexico Cricket Club travelled on the Mexican railroad for matches against the Pachuca Cricket Club in the cool mountains of Hídalgo.[11] This team was comprised of British miners residing in the area as personnel for the **Sociedad Aviadora de Minas del Monte y Pachuca**.[12] The matches

---

5 *The Mexican Herald*, 10 July 1906, p. 5.

6 Knudson, 'The Mexican Herald: Outpost of Empire, 1895-1915', pp. 387-398.

7 See Michael P. Costeloe, 'To Bowl a Mexican Maiden Over: Cricket in Mexico, 1827-1900', *Bulletin of Latin American Research*, 26, 1 (2007), pp. 112-125 for a pioneering and excellent discussion on the introduction of cricket into Mexico and its precarious development from 1827 to 1876.

8 *Ibid*. p. 123.

9 *The Mexican Herald*, 9 October 1899, p. 8. *The Mexican Herald*, 30 August 1896, p. 2. *The Mexican Herald*, 21 September 1896, p. 7. *The Mexican Herald*, 14 November 1896, p. 8. *The Mexican Herald*, 1 January 1897, p. 8.

10 *The Mexican Herald*, 16 November 1896, p. 8.

11 *The Mexican Herald*, 21 June 1896, p. 11. *The Mexican Herald*, 30 June 1896, p. 7. *The Mexican Herald*, 9 September 1899, p. 11. *The Mexican Herald*, 20 August 1899, p. 2. Costeloe, 'To Bowl a Mexican Maiden Over: Cricket in Mexico, 1827-1900', p. 122.

12 These were descendants of the British who migrated to the area attracted to the home wage scheme to labour for the *Gentlemen Adventures in the Mines of Real del Monte* that operated the 116 silver mines in mountainous Hídalgo from 1824 until 1849 such as Santa Gertrudis, San Juan and Rosario. See A. C. Todd, *The Search for Silver: Cornish Miners in Mexico, 1827-1947*, (Padstow: The Lodenek Press, 1977)

occurred at **La Luz hacienda** near the suburb of Xochihuacan outside Pachuca and was "unrivalled in the world, whether for extent or picturesque surroundings"[13] claimed **The Two Republics**. On conclusion of these matches the miners treated the visiting teams from the Capital to delicious barbeques and even "sumptuous banquet[s] in the residence of the Governor [of Hídalgo]."[14] The Pachuca Cricket Club had "obtained a reputation of a superior team"[15] stated **The Daily Anglo-American** despite it being in a detrimental position in contrast to the Reforma Athletic Club and Mexico Cricket Club. Its members laboured in different silver mines to one another and at different times "so it was hard for them to practice together"[16] and "could make their practices on match days only"[17] with the teams of Ciúdad de México.

In addition the Reforma Athletic Club and Mexico Cricket Club often aventured to the humid tropical lowlands of Veracruz near San Andres on the Mexican railroad for matches against the San Cristobal Cricket Club which the British residing in the area had inaugurated "in a large dining room"[18] over a toast in 1889.[19] The team was comprised of a Chaplin and personnel from the **Pearson and Son** engineering concern which was in the midst of draining Lake Texcoco that surrounded the sprawling and industrialising Ciúdad de México.[20] **The Two Republics** noted the San Cristobal Cricket Club "was progressing without a hitch and in such a prosperous fashion"[21] even though it loaned cricket equipment from the teams it hosted for matches.[22]

Though more convenient for the Reforma Athletic Club and Mexico Cricket Club than visiting the Pachuca Cricket Club and San Cristobal Cricket Club, was travelling on the Azures tramline to Chapultepec outside Ciúdad de México near the suburbs of Cuauhtémoc, Condesa, Juárez and Roma for matches with the **Read and Campbell** engineering firm at **Condesa hacienda**.[23] The team had been established in 1892 and was comprised of the British and Canadian personnel from the **Read and Campbell**

13 *The Two Republics*, 8 May 1890, p. 4.

14 *The Daily Anglo-American*, 11ʰSeptember 1891, p. 2. *The Two Republics*, 8 May 1890, p. 4.

15 *The Daily Anglo-American*, 12 October 1891.

16 *The Mexican Herald*, 16 November 1896, p. 2.

17 *The Daily Anglo-American*, 12 October 1891.

18 *The Two Republics*, 29 November 1890, p. 1.

19 *The Two Republics*, 4 August 1892, p. 4. *The Two Republics*, 28 February 1892, p. 3. *The Two Republics*, 5 June 1892, p. 1.

20 The **Pearson and Son** engineering firm was awarded the contract to rebuild Veracruz in 1895 and competed this in 1902. Then the concern was commissioned to improve to Salina Cruz in Oaxaca and then construct the Tehuantepec railroad between 1896 and 1907. See A. Tischendorf, *Great Britain and Mexico in the Era of Porfirio Diaz*, (Durham: Duke University Press, 1961), pp. 46-53.

21 *The Two Republics*, 4 August 1891, p. 4.

22 *The Two Republics*, 28 February 1892, p. 3.

23 *The Daily Anglo-American*, 2 May 1892, p. 2. J. A. Garza, *The Imagined Underworld: Sex Crime and Vice in Porfirian Mexico City*, (Lincoln: University of Nebraska Press, 2007), p. 23. The **Read and Campbell** engineering concern was commissioned to aid the construction of the Interoceanic railroad between 1888 and 1889 and then build the 228 mile Mexican Southern railroad between 1888 and 11892. See Tischendorf, *Great Britain and Mexico in the Era of Porfirio Diaz*, pp. 46-52.

office on San Jose de Lesran in the Capital although persons not in the firm were "eligible for membership."[24]

There were other teams to augment the Reforma Athletic Club, Mexico Cricket Club, Pachuca Cricket Club, San Cristobal Cricket Club and **Read and Campbell** in Mexico as "wherever there are British colonies, no matter how small, there will also be a side for football, tennis and cricket"[25] stated **The Mexican Herald**. In windswept Coahuila the Sabinas and Ciúdad Porfirio Díaz Cricket Club had been established and there were teams at Saltillo and "cosmopolitan"[26] Monterrey in Nuevo León where "large numbers of Americans, British and Germans were settled."[27] But the Reforma Athletic Club, Mexico Cricket Club, Pachuca Cricket Club, San Cristobal Cricket Club and **Read and Campbell** were reluctant to travel to these areas on the Mexican railroad for matches however, because it was expensive due to the high rates on the route.[28] **The Mexican Herald** noted another reason in 1907 when it reported on the Monterrey Cricket Club's attempts to organise a match against the Reforma Athletic Club on the Paseo de la Reforma grounds in the Capital. It waded in with some advice,

> unless the circumstances were out of the usual run, it is hardly possible that a game could be arranged with the teams here [in Ciúdad de México] as the trip from Monterrey is so long that it would mean a considerable amount of time lost in making the journey. [...] Saltillo is convenient and games can be arranged there.[29]

But **The Mexican Herald** with its circulation of 10,000 might have reached most British households in Mexico which allowed them to read about developments in cricket throughout the nation.[30]

III. The Mexican Cricket League, 1900-1909.

To put cricket on a "firm basis" in Mexico representatives from the "most important clubs" founded the Mexican Cricket Committee in Ciúdad de México in 1900 with an office on the Paseo de la Reforma and established a league based on the British County Championship which the Mexican railroad would facilitate.[31] **The Mexican Herald** was confident this league would create "great interest" in cricket as each of the teams in it was scheduled to participate in two matches against each other during the season for

24 *The Daily Anglo-American*, 2 May 1892, p. 2.

25 *The Mexican Herald*, 10 September 1889, p. 10.

26 A. Tweedie, *Mexico as I saw it*, (London: Thomas Nelson and Sons, 1911), p. 71.

27 *Ibid.* p. 71. *The Mexican Herald*, 4 November 1896, p. 7. *The Mexican Herald*, 26 April 1906, p. 9. *The Mexican Herald*, 17 May 1903, p. 3. Costeloe, 'To Bowl a Mexican Maiden Over: Cricket in Mexico, 1827-1900', p. 122.

28 *The Mexican Herald*, 7 February 1897, p. 8.

29 *The Mexican Herald*, 15 November 1907, p. 7.

30 Knudson, 'The Mexican Herald: Outpost of Empire, 1895-1915', p. 389.

31 *The Mexican Herald*, 29 March 1900, p. 3. *The Mexican Herald*, 30 April 1900, p. 5.

points at home and away.[32] [See Figure One] The team with the most points at the end of the campaign would win the honours and prestigious Cricket Challenge Cup which was often exhibited in the window of the Camelia jewellery store on San Francisco near the zócalo area of the Capital.[33] The Reforma Athletic Club, Mexico Cricket Club, and the "invincible"[34] Pachuca Cricket Club were to be the teams in the inaugural season.[35]

One other team was invited to participate in the league and it was the not San Cristobal Cricket Club or **Read and Campbell** which had both disbanded, but the Puebla and District Cricket Club in the cool mountains of Puebla. The British residing in this area of "considerable commercial and industrial importance" had established it in "charming" Puebla with its "clean streets [...] and architectural charm"[36] on a "solid and firm basis" in 1899 with a ground at the **velodromo** which was "in good shape" near the suburb of Zochihuacan. One enthusiastic individual had even donated cricket equipment and cash to the team noted **The Mexican Herald**.[37]

The Mexican Cricket Committee structured the inaugural season so as to avoid the rains. The campaign was to open on 1 April with the Mexico Cricket Club visiting the **velodromo** ground for a match against the Puebla and District Cricket Club and closing on 29 July with the Reforma Athletic Club hosting the Puebla and District Cricket Club on the Paseo de la Reforma ground.[38] The championship matches were scheduled to occur on a Sunday as this was the "one day of the week members [of participant teams] set aside from business engagements" for cricket.[39]

---

32 *The Mexican Herald*, 29 March 1900, p. 3.

33 *The Mexican Herald*, 29 March 1900, p. 3. *The Two Republics*, 21 January 1897, p. 8. Garza, *The Imagined Underworld: Sex Crime and Vice in Porfirian Mexico City*, p. 111.

34 *The Daily Anglo-American*, 12 October 1891, p. 1.

35 *The Mexican Herald*, 29 March 1900, p. 3.

36 C. R. Enock, *Mexico: Its Ancient and Modern Civilization, History, Political Conditions, Topography, Natural Resources, Industries and General Development*, (New York: Charles Scribner's Sons, 1909), p. 207.

37 *The Mexican Herald*, 11 August 1899, p. 5.

38 *The Mexican Herald*, 1 April 1900, p. 1. *The Mexican Herald*, 29 July 1900, p. 8.

39 *The Mexican Herald*, 9 May 1908, p. 7.

A CRICKET LEAGUE

Means to Promote Interest in the Game Taken.

Championship Cup to Be the Object of the Contest.

Figure One: The Cricket Championship is announced in
The Mexican Herald on 29 March 1900.[40]

Article provided for inclusion by México Cricket Association.

---

40 *The Mexican Herald*, 29 March 1900, p. 3.

ARGENTINA

ricket stumps were pitched in Argentina as early as 1806 when Major Alexander Gillespie of the Royal Marines under the command of General Beresford on his way from Cape of Good Hope, sized 'Buenos Ayres' and he describes their life and stay in 'Gleanings and Remarks.' *"The village of St Antonio de Areca…became our resting place nearly three months, and yielded the pastime of fishing, cricket and horse riding."* Further on he writes, *"the arrears due being settled at Esquina, and a repose of some days being allowed us, full pockets and vacant time revived the national diversions of horse-racing, and cricket, for which we always carried the materials."*[1] It seems that cricket equipment was a standard issue for the English military, as we have seen before where Major General Edward Braddock also carried his gear with him when he set out to capture the French Fort Duquesne (modern day downtown Pittsburgh) in 1755. The siege was short lived as they were driven out by the locals who resisted another attack the following year.[2]

The next reference is provided by a locally published notice found in the weekly newspaper, *'British Packet'* of October 22nd, 1831. *"Perhaps, many of our readers are not aware that a cricket club has been formed in Buenos Aires, and that the members thereof have lately played some excellent games at that manly exercise…at present the club consists of about 25 persons; some matches are in anticipation. The members are uniformly attired in flannel jackets and straw hats, bound with straw colored ribband. Some of the best players are the "hijos del pais" (children of the country) who received their education in England."*[3] A match was played near the Socorro Church on November 1st 1831, where a few names are given but no scores were recorded. The next blurb in the news is from December 3rd, *"A Cricket Club, we hear, is about to be formed at Montevideo."* For the first time a match with scores but no names appeared on 23rd April, 1832, it was played between the Green and Pink teams and they were members of the Buenos Aires Cricket Club and it was played near the Socorro Church grounds. The Green team scored 135 in two innings while the Pink team fell short by 20 runs.[4] Between 1832 and 1839 cricket news is scarce except for a letter dated from 1835 which intimates that the BACC was no longer in existence.

During the dictatorship of Juan Manuel de Rosas, cricket notices were few and far between and appear only five times from 1840 to 1859. This was period of anti-British sentiments and the annexation of the Falkland Islands again on January 3rd 1833 under Commander Onslow[5] further added to those feelings. Rosas was overthrown in 1852 (fled to England and died there)[6] after a coalition under the new leadership of Justo José de Urquiza came to power bringing stability and English Railway engineers and along with the influx of people, the pastime also returned.[7]

The Buenos Aires Cricket Club came into existence again around 1860 as a score book dating from 1861 gives details of the 2nd match played on August 30th during the 1861/62 season. Unfortunately due to missing pages, partial information is provided on the early matches, one was played between Eleven married men and singles. The first complete record is found for an August 30th 1861 match between Mr. J.C. Simpson's Nine and Mr. H. Simpson's Nine where the latter team won by scoring 73 and 70 runs with the opponent contributing 55 and 77. The names of the players in the two teams were, J.C. Simpson, F. Parish, E. Darbyshire, W. Anderson, E. Forewinkle, C. Murray, J.H. Rostron, A. Hart and Joe Green. The other 9 were H. Simpson, H. Hinchcliffe, J.H. Green, J. Elliot, J. Brown, E. Kidd, H. Marshall, W. Cripps and E. Perry. The following year on January 6th 1862, the singles beat the married men by an innings and 26 runs. More matches followed and there is no entry for the 1863/64 season as they may have had difficulty in getting a ground.[8] Next entry is for the December 8th 1864 match against between BACC (Buenos Aires CC) and Bombay who managed a small total of 66 and 19 to which BACC scored 66 and 19 for the loss of a wicket. This match was played at Palermo Field. In a second match played the same day, this time Bombay beat their opponents.

During the next season in 1865/66, seven matches were played and this time BACC also played against the visiting sailors from the *H.M.S. Sharpshooter*. The following season of 1866/67 saw six games being played between various teams. More games were now being played and eight matches were played during the 1867/68 season which also ended with the first Argentinian visit to Montevideo on 9th and 10th April, where BACC scored 85 & 72, while Montevideo scored 54 & 70 in a twelve-a-side match. During this season also, T. Jackson scored 109 runs, a first century in Argentine cricket history. On September 8th 1869, team 'A to L' beat team 'M to Z', and other teams named in the old score book were the, 'United Railway Eleven', 'B.A. Railways' and 'Southern Railway'. The last entry in the score book shows a game in which 'Nine Members' scored 105 and 'Nine Committee' replied with 34! [9]

Argentina's first international cricket match was played against Uruguay in 1868 and contin-ued till the Second World War, where they played 29 times winning 21 and losing 6. In 1888 they played Brazil for the first time and to play against a team in Chile in 1893, they traveled to Valparaíso[10] (Santiago per ESPNcricinfo) by crossing the Andes on mules which took three and a half days to cross - talk about the desire to play. In 1891 the famous North v South series began with the advent of the railways. The formation of the Argentine Cricket Association in 1913 started with the formation of club championships that began in 1897-98 season.[11]

Argentina's first, first-class cricket took place during the 1911-12 season when M.C.C captained by Lord Hawke paid them a visit. Much to their credit, they won the first match played on February 18, 19 & 20, but lost the other two. The teams was made up of British expatriates, (similar to the 1886 West Indian team), who were mostly employed by the railways, or into business and farming. Between the wars, infrequent fixtures were played against Brazil. The second first-class matches were also played against M.C.C in 1926/27 captained by Pelham Warner, then against Sir Julien Cahn's XI in 1929-30 and Sir Theodore Brinckman's XI in 1937/38. In the four-match series against the M.C.C, Argentina lost 2 games to 1, with one being drawn. In the three-match series against Sir Julien Cahn's XI, two ended in draw with Cahn's XI winning the first game. The matches against Brinkman's XI were drawn 1-1.[12] Following are the scores from the first Argentinian win over MCC.

ARGENTINA vs. MARYLEBONE CRICKET CLUB

Match played at Hurlingham Club Grounds, Buenos Aires, February 18, 19 and 20, 1912.

<u>Argentina wins by 4 wickets.</u>

MCC

FIRST INNNINGS	RUNS	SECOND INNINGS	RUNS
W Findlay b Dorning	0	c Watson-Hutton b Foy	6
CE de Trafford c&b Foy	16	lbw b Dorning	2
MC Bird b Dorning	3	c Biedermann b Foy	29
HHC Baird c Garnett b Dorning	1	b Dorning	0
LHW Troughton b Dorning	5	not out	59
AC MacLaren b Dorning	0	b Foy	7
NC Tufnell c Dorning b Foy	5	c Garnett b Dorning	2
AJL Hill c Watson-Hutton b Dorning	17	c Biedermann b Toulmin	34
Lord Hawke lbw b Foy	27	b Foy	7
ER Wilson not out	67	lbw b Foy	1
CE Hatfeild c Biedermann b Foy	39	b Dorning	0
Extras	6	Extras	10
TOTAL	186	TOTAL	157

ARGENTINA

FIRST INNINGS	RUNS	SECOND INNINGS	RUNS
NW Jackson c Wilson b Baird	31	c Bird b Hill	49
EMO Toulmin C Tufnell b Hatfeild	59	c&b Hatfeild	27
SA Cowper c Hatfeild b Hill	8	did not bat	-
JA Campbell c MacLaren b Baird	0	st. Tufnell b Hatfeild	4
GA Simpson c&b Wilson	26	run out	10
H Dorning b Hatfeild	16	b Hatfeild	14
HEC Biedermann c Hill b Wilson	2	not out	8
CH Whaley not out	21	c Troughton b Hatfeild	0
PA Foy b Baird	15	did not bat	-
HG Garnett c Troughton b Baird	20	not out	19
AP Watson-Hutton b Bird	0	did not bat	-
Extras	11	Extras	5
TOTAL	209	TOTAL	136

Bowling	Overs	Maiden	Runs	Wickets	Overs	Maiden	Runs	Wickets
MCC	First Innings				Second Innings			
Bird	13.1	1	48	1	3	1	17	0
Wilson	16	4	32	2	3	0	12	0
Baird	24	10	47	4	4	0	16	0
Hill	9	0	27	1	10	2	37	1
Hatfeild	16	3	44	2	12.2	2	49	4
ARGENTINA	First Innings				Second Innings			
Dorning	17	1	65	6	18.1	3	60	4
Foy	17.1	3	65	4	17	2	49	5
Whaley	4	0	25	0	6	1	17	0
Toulmin	4	0	24	0	6	1	18	1
Cowper	1	0	1	0	2	1	3	0

NOTE: both teams changed their batting order in the second innings.[13]

Team "Argentinos", vencedor de "Brasil" en el match de cricket disputado los días sábado y domingo últimos en Hurlingham, constituído por los aficionados: Dorning, Foy, Gibson, Jacobs, Mold, Norris, Paul, Salmonson, Simpson, Smith y Scorey.

The Argentinos of 1921.

In 1932 a combined South American team toured England consisting of ten Argentinians, three Brazilians and two from Chile. They won two out of the six first class matches played and it also included other local fixtures. On the local front, fixtures between countries continued, as Argentina played ten matches against Chile from 1920 to 1939 and thirteen matches against Brazil from 1921 to 1929.[14] Argentinian cricket is not complete without the mention of the famous North v South series that began with the first one played at Palermo on November 11th & 12th 1891. 'North' were headquarters at Jujuy originally and later moved to Rosario in 1920 and then to the city of Buenos Aires itself, while the 'South' was always headquartered in the city. These matches were of high standard and were recorded as first-class, but have not been accepted as such. The 'North' comprised of San Isidro, Pacifico and Rosario Clubs while the 'South' was made up of Lomas, Buenos Aires and the Belgrano club. A publication called the *North v South by K.E. Bridger 1974,* provides the complete story on this series.

The two teams had their distinct colors and as they were rarely used, it is largely forgotten, however the colors were not attractive and plans are afoot to have them changed. The golden age of local cricket lasted till the early 1930s and the paucity of local talent and with less Englishmen coming over, the North South rivalry gradually ebbed. There was revival of cricket away from the cities between 1960 and 1990 in the colleges of St. Paul, Cruz Chica, Sierra de Cordoba under the leadership of A.H. 'Bob' Thurn. The A.C.A stepped in to reverse the trend by getting the youth involved and improving the quality of the North South matches. The current 'North' comprises of players from, Hurlingham

Club, Belgrano Athletic Club and the St. George College, while, the Lomas Athletic Club, St Alban's and St. George's College, Quilmes, make up the 'South.'[15]

The Banfield team pictured below was into its third season in 1897 and the Anderson brothers were already topping the batting averages. The club president, Daniel Kingsland was trying to recruit Yorkshire professional, Robert Peel, to train their team and also have an English team play against the club and gauge their resolve against seasoned cricketers.[16]

THE BANFIELD CRICKET TEAM, ARGENTINA.

1897 Banfield Cricket Team, Argentina.

BRAZIL

C ricket in Brazil began in the mid-1800s in Rio de Janeiro, during a period when a substantial portion of the city's population was British or of British descent. By the early 1860s, a number of cricket clubs were in operation, including the British CC, Artisan Amateurs CC, Rio British CC, Anglo-Brazilian CC and the British and American Club, although their playing facilities were limited to makeshift open spaces. Interestingly, Rio's Brazilian residents at the time had little or no interest in sport of any kind.

Beginning in 1860, as part of a much-needed beautification program for the city, Emperor Dom Pedro II created several new parks, including a large grassed area in front of his daughter's (Princess Isabel) house, on Rua Paysandu in the Laranjeiras district. Due to good relations between the British community and the Brazilian monarchy, this space eventually became the country's first proper cricket ground, and hosted cricket, tennis and bowls matches for many years. Princess Isabel and her father were frequent spectators, and often called upon to present trophies to the winners.

In 1872, George Cox formed the Rio Cricket Club, which soon began using the field as its home and in the early 1880s and George's son Oscar, organized Brazil's first football games on this same ground. When Brazil became a Republic in 1889, Princess Isabel was forced to move from her residence and the cricket ground was taken over by the new government, and although the sport was allowed to continue for a time, a permanent facility was now required. In 1897 the newly-renamed Rio Cricket and Athletic Association purchased a large property in Niterói, on the other side of Guanabara Bay. A cricket ground was built and hosted its first match on June 19, 1898. Cricket would continue to be played on this ground for the next 97 years. As the local British population declined steadily through the 1970s and 1980s, however, cricket at the club faded away, and today the Rio Cricket ground is used exclusively for football.

During those early days of cricket in Rio de Janeiro, the sport was also springing up at British sports clubs elsewhere in the country, including: the São Paulo Athletic Club in São Paulo (founded in 1888); the Santos Athletic Club in São Paulo (1899); Clube Internacional de Cricket in Salvador, Bahia (1899); the British Country Club in Recife, Pernambuco (1920); and the Clube de Cricket Vítoria in Espírito Santo (1899). Teams and grounds were also created at the British-owned Morro Velho mine just outside of Belo Horizonte in Minas Gerais (1887), and at the Frigorífico Anglo plant in Barretos, São Paulo (1913), where cricket was played until the mid-1990s. Cricket was also played in at the Fazenda dos Ingleses, Caraguatuba, on the coast of the state of São Paulo from 1927 until the Second World War.

It was in São Paulo, however, that the sport really took hold, and the São Paulo Athletic Club (SPAC) remains the country's centre of cricket to this day. In 1894, Charles Miller, the Brazilian-born son of British parents, returned from his studies in England with a football and some cricket equipment, which he immediately used to introduce these sports to the locals. In 1888 the São Paulo Athletic Club was formed, and Charles was a key member, organizing São Paulo's first football and cricket matches at the club's ground in the Consolação district. Football, as we all know, soon caught on, and Charles is known throughout the country as the father of Brazilian football. From 1928 to 1947, the club's cricket matches were held at a ground in Pirituba, before moving to the current site in Veleiros (Santo Amaro), which also houses the Brazil Cricket Museum. The Brazil Cricket Association was formed in 1922, with R.A. Brooking as its first President. The member clubs were Rio Cricket, the Pernambuco Athletic Club, Santos Athletic Club, São Paulo Athletic Club and the Paysandu Cricket Club. The BCA helped continue the series of matches that had been held between these clubs for many years, as well as inter-state and international games. In fact, matches between São Paulo and Rio began in 1878 and continued regularly until 1995.

As cricket in Rio de Janeiro faded from the scene, it was left to São Paulo to carry the torch until 1989, when the Brasília Cricket (BCC) was formed, which today fields three men's teams and two women's teams. In 1999 in Curitiba, Paraná, British bank HSBC built a cricket ground at its staff sports facility, which is now home to three men's teams, while São Paulo also has three men's teams.

To keep pace with this rejuvenation of cricket activity in Brazil, the national Associação Brasiliera de Cricket (ABC) was founded in 2001, and Brazil became an Affiliate Member of the International Cricket Council (ICC) in 2003. The ABC's continuing goal is to grow the sport throughout the country, particularly among Brazilians themselves. Since joining the ICC, cricket in Brazil has grown steadily, thanks primarily to financial and technical support from the ICC.

Matches between Brazil and Argentina began in 1888, while Rio Cricket began a series of matches with Clube Atlético River Plate from Montevideo, Uruguay in 1902. The old Brazil Cricket Association continued to stage matches with Argentina for many years, with Charles Miller playing for the Brazil team until the 1920s. Brazil also hosted the New Zealand XI in the mid-1970s and the MCC in 1978. Between 1921 and 1929 Brazil played thirteen matches against Argentina, though these were not considered first-class matches. With the creation of the South American Championships (SAC) in 1995, Brazilian cricket entered its modern era. The national team has since participated in all eight SACs, hosting the event for the first time in April 2009 (SAC8). In other non-ICC international matches, Brazil has hosted the Chilean team twice, the Mexican team once, and the MCC twice.

In 2006 Brazil qualified to join the ICC World League of Cricket, which is a pathway to the World up. Team Brazil competed in the inaugural ICC Americas Division 3 tournament in Suriname in 2006, as well as in Buenos Aires in 2008 and Santiago in 2009.

As of October 2009, the national men's team record is 17 wins and 26 losses in their 43 matches since 1995.

Brazil won its first ICC tournament at the Americas Division 3 championship in Santiago, Chile in October 2009. As a result of winning this event, Brazil has been promoted to Division 2 of the Americas WCL. Historically, the national team has consisted solely of expatriates, but this is changing. In recent years, the number of Brazilian cricketers representing their country has steadily increased. The winning Brazil squad in Santiago, for example, included six Brazilian-born players.

The Brazil national league is made up of nine teams, which compete for the Commonwealth Ambassador's Trophy. The teams are as follows: Candangos, Brasília and Pakistan Plus from the state of Distrito Federal, the São Paulo Indians, SPAC and São Paulo from São Paulo state, while the state of Paraná is represented by Swadisht, Gralha Azul and Paraná. Since 2000, São Paulo won five league titles, while Brasília won twice and Paraná once. Teams play 40-over a side matches from March to October. In November each year a Twenty20 tournament between the three state representative sides is held. This tournament rotates from year to year between the three major cities. In addition to this competition, Saquarembo CC is a São Paulo-based group of former Brazil players which plays just a few exhibition matches a year against Rest of the World (SP).

With Brazil's entry into the ICC came the creation of junior development programs in Brasília, São Paulo and Curitiba. In Brasília, a big breakthrough came when Cricket was offered as an accredited PE course at the national University of Brasília. This led to the formation of the Candangos team, made up wholly of Brazilians. It also created interest amongst female students and resulted in the beginnings of women's cricket in Brasilia. In terms of junior development, there are a growing number of boys participating in regular training sessions and games, giving us the core of a future Under 17 team. In São Paulo, progress is being made through a working relationship between St Paul's School and SPAC (the São Paulo Athletic Club). Enthusiastic people are in place to develop children's cricket further in São Paulo.

In Curitiba the focus has been on teaching children aged 8-12. The Associação Brasileira de Cricket employed a local junior development officer/coach for three years, and the success of the program, which works with about 300 kids at four schools, was recognized by the ICC through the Volunteer of the Year Award presented to Norman Baldwin and to the program itself for Best Junior Development Program. This ongoing program provided the platform for a very successful Under 13s tournament held in July 2009 in Curitiba, played between Argentina, the eventual winners, Chile and Brazil.

In addition to these three main centres of cricket, there are promising signs of life in the northern city of Fortaleza, and most recently, in Rio de Janeiro, the original home of Brazilian cricket. Development programs are planned for these cities with a view towards increasing the number of teams in the domestic competition in the near future. To help ensure the continuity and raise the level of our games, coaching, umpiring and scoring courses are being run throughout the year in all three cities, conducted by the coaches and umpires who have received ICC training. At present we have more than 20 level one umpires. In terms of facility development, Brazil is a little behind some of the other countries in the region. In Curitiba, the HSBC ground is very scenic and has a net, but is too small for ICC tournaments. In Brasília, there is still a need for a proper sized, permanent ground, though the club does have two permanent nets at the Australian embassy. In São Paulo, where SAC8 was held, there have been a number of improvements at the full-size SPAC ground, including two new nets and a resurfacing of the artificial pitch.

Since the success of the University of Brasília PE cricket course, women's cricket has grown steadily in Brasilia. In 2007 there was a three-match series in Curitiba against an Argentina XI. Then in late January 2009, the Brazil team visited Buenos Aires for a return series. While Brazil was able to win only one match, both series were closely contested. The improvement in the women's team was noted in Buenos Aires and led to their invitation to play in the ICC Americas Women's Championship in Miami in May 2009 and Cayman Islands in 2012. While unable to win any matches, the team was very competitive and earned the praise of all who witnessed how much they the players have achieved in such a short time.

Material provided for inclusion, courtesy of John Milton.

CHILE

ricket is recorded to have first been played in Chile in 1829, in the coastal city of Valparaíso between the officers and men of two Royal Navy vessels. The Valparaíso Cricket Club was founded in 1860, with regular matches scheduled between residents throughout the latter part of the 19th century. The growth of the Nitrate industry led to the foundation of Cricket clubs in Valparaíso and Iquique and they would have the 'Port v Pampas' matches in the port of Iquique. Although no official first-class games have ever taken place in Chile, the first international fixture between Chile and Argentina came in 1893 when it reportedly took the Argentine side 'three and a half days to reach Santiago, crossing the Andes by mule.'[1] Chile now possesses a rich history of international cricket, including visits by the MCC in 1927, 1960, 2001, and 2007 and a record in the South American Cricket Championship second only to Argentina. In 2006, Chile took part in its first ICC tournament, the ICC Americas Championship Division 3 held in Suriname, where it finished third to the hosts and behind the Turks and Caicos Islands. In 2008, promotion eluded them only on net run-rate, while in 2009-10 it finished with just one win in three matches, so the quest continues.

The game's heyday in Chile was during the 1926-27 season when Pelham 'Plum' Warner captained a touring side against a Valparaíso XI, though not considered a first-class match, it was an important match none the less. Regular matches were played between Valparaíso Cricket Club, the Prince of Wales Country Club as well as the Concepción Country Club, whilst the game was also played by St. Peter's and The Grange School as fiercely as any school in England. The standard of cricket in this era is highlighted by the success of one former St. Peter's student, Frederick 'Freddie' Brown who went on to successfully captain both Surrey and England in the 1950's. Between 1920 and 1939, Chile has played ten 'International Friendlies' against Argentina.[2]

However, as with in many parts of the world, interest in cricket waned following the Second World War as the British community in Chile dwindled and rugby began its rise to popularity amongst schools. By 1960, cricket was no longer played in Valparaíso, despite the cricket club continuing to function as a ladies hockey team. St. Peter's and The Grange played their final match in 1956 - with St. Peter's claiming the final honours. Nevertheless, cricket was kept alive by the Prince of Wales Country Club throughout the 1960's and in 2002, following the formation of the Asociación Chilena de Cricket (ACC), Chile was admitted as an affiliate member of the International Cricket Council and has since concentrated on junior development to ensure a healthy future for the game for years to come.

In 2006 Chile was awarded the ICC Development Award for having the best overall development program in the Americas region and this program instituted in 2001, emphasizes the importance of nurturing grassroots cricket. Since the inception, over 15 schools are now enrolled in the program and it's estimated that over 3,000 children have been introduced to cricket, several of whom have progressed to play senior cricket for one of the Metropolitan Cup sides. As a result, Chile can now boast of national sides at U13, U15 and U19 levels, all of which play regular fixtures against Associate members and neighbors, Argentina. An U15 Chilean team defeated the visiting Falkland CC team in 2009.

The senior national team plays in Division 3 of the ICC Americas Championship, finishing second in the 2008 tournament, ahead of Belize, Peru and Brazil. Chile's main domestic competition is the Metropolitan Cup, contested between six teams: Santiago, Las Condes, La Dehesa, La Reina, Estacion Central and Viña del Mar. It was first played in 2001-2002, and now it also has a Second Division of four teams. Chile also started an annual Beach Cricket competition which won the Spirit of Cricket award in 2009.

Cricket played near the Nitrate plants, North of Chile near Iquique in 1912. Picture courtesy Ian Walker, Santiago.

Material provided for inclusion, courtesy of Ian Walker & Chilean Cricket.

COSTA RICA

Cricket is the national sport of Great Britain and has been played for 400 years. It has been dominated by countries with historical British ties: England, West Indies, Australia, New Zealand, India, Pakistan, Sri Lanka and South Africa. Cricket's World Cup dates from 1975, the last being won by India in 2011, and Women's World Cup since 1973, was won by Australia in February 2013. Cricket is the second most played and watched sport in the world. It has been played in Costa Rica since the end of the Nineteenth Century. In the late 1870s, construction began on the railway between the port of Limon on the Atlantic coast and San José in the Central Valley, and a significant number of Jamaicans came to work in the country. They started playing cricket later, both for recreation and to preserve their Caribbean culture.

The heyday of the sport was between 1910 and 1939 when there were 46 teams in the Province of Limon, connected by United Fruit's railway. In 1930, a West Indies team, including legends Learie Constantine and George Headley, played in Costa Rica on its way to Australia. During the 1930s teams from Limon went to play in Jamaica and matches were played against Bocas del Toro, Panama, and British Honduras, now Belize. In Kingston in 1936, in a historic event for Costa Rica Cricket, Lancelot Binns of Siquirres made 30 runs for Jamaica Schoolboys against the English professional team, Yorkshire, which included no less than eight English Test cricketers, the most famous being Len Hutton. Binns continued playing in Costa Rica until the age of 84. The Second World War almost finished off Cricket, and in 1942 the main Limon pitch became a hospital. Many of the Jamaicans' descendants gave up playing the sport of their grandfathers in favor of football, partly in imitation of Pelé, and their own language for Spanish, looking to become more integrated into Costa Rican society. But cricket in Costa Rica refused to die.

From 1970 until the end of the Century there were several attempts to revive cricket, mostly among English expatriates in San José and a number of Limon stalwarts. Peter Lyon and Teofilus Foster arranged games at Estrada in 1973; the Cavaliers CC, with Ambassador Hamilton-Jones, beat a Royal Yacht team during HRH Prince Philip's visit in 1975, and Costa Rica beat Nicaragua in 1976, both reported in La Nación. Matches were also played in the 1970s in Nicaragua and El Salvador. Modern era CR Cricket restarted during the watch of Ambassador Daly and teams came to play from Panama (1986), Cayman Islands (1988), New Zealand (1993), and California (2001). Costa Rican side travelled to Panama and Nicaragua in 2002. A San José-Limon rivalry was maintained, with continuing patronage of the British Embassy.

Towards the end of 2000, a group of players formed the Costa Rica Cricket Association (CRCA), later inscribed as *Asociación Deportiva de Cricket* in the National Registry, in 2003. Costa Rica became an Affiliate of the International Cricket Council (ICC), the global authority for the sport, in 2002. ICC has 105 member countries at three levels: Full ("Test"), Associate and Affiliate. There are eighteen members in the ICC Americas region: Full - West Indies; Associate - Argentina, Bermuda, Canada, Cayman Islands and USA; and Affiliate - Bahamas, Belize, Brazil, Chile, Costa Rica, Cuba, Falkland Islands, Mexico, Panama, Peru, Surinam and Turks & Caicos. ICC Americas' RDM Martin Vieira chose Costa Rica for the 2005 Development Forum, and later for Coaching, Umpiring & Scoring courses. ICC gave two CR volunteers Development awards (2004/05) and five Gold Medals for service to Cricket in its Centenary year (2009). In Cricket development, CR has received encouragement from the Costa Rica sports institute ICODER, a succession of British Ambassadors, schools, newspapers, broadcasters, television, hotels, restaurants, with corporate and private sponsors. Articles on Cricket in Costa Rica were published in England in The Cricketer (*) and Wisden Almanack, in the ICC Americas NewsFlash, and domestically in the Tico Times and national press. It is also featured regularly on the leading Cricket websites: www.iccamericas.com

In 2005, the first Costa Rica Cricket League was established with four teams, Limon, Corsairs, Raleigh and CCCCR, competing annually for the Lance Binns Cup. Costa Rica played in the First Central America Cricket Championships (CenAm) in Belize 2006, finishing in third place behind Belize and Mexico. In 2007, the Second CenAm was held in Mexico, which won, with CR second, ahead of El Salvador. The Third CenAm Championships were staged successfully in Costa Rica at the prestigious Los Reyes Polo Club grounds in April 2009. Panama, Mexico, Belize, Costa Rica and El Salvador took part, finishing in that order. This event set a new standard for CenAm and was covered by Repretel TV, Radio Nacional and 99.5, La Nación, Al Día, La Republica, Tico Times and ICC Americas NewsFlash. Costa Rica received two tournament awards: Best Batsman (Shane Catford) and Spirit of Cricket (Sam Arthur). Recently, Costa Rica entered its first ever eligible team in an official one-day international tournament, the Pepsi World Cricket League ICC Americas Division IV, in Mexico City, against Mexico and Falkland Islands, from June 14-18th 2010. CR won one and lost three, coming second in one category and third in the other. Mexico became the champions, but CR's Ben Smith was Best Batsman and MVP of the tournament.

In addition to these international events and principal teams, in its ongoing Cricket Development Costa Rica has been adding new clubs, including Women's, and has broadened its schools program, mainly in Limon, but also in the central valley. Since 2008, thanks to increased ICC funding, it has enjoyed the services of development officer Sam Arthur, originally from India. With active participation of Limon president Armando Foster and others, cricket values have been promoted among boys and girls in eight Limon schools; also at the Roble Alto Home above Heredia, where cricket was introduced in 2003 and is continued by sports director Gerardo Montiel. Their combined efforts have resulted in the annual Under-19 schools cricket tournament played in Limon, competing in October 2008 and 2009 for the Standford Barton Cup, dedicated to that outstanding former president of Cricket Limon. A seminar on Introduction to Cricket & Coaching for Limon province male and female PE instructors was held in May 2009, and replicated in June 2010 as a four-day Seminar, backed by the Ministry of Education, for twenty PE instructors by ICC Americas Regional Development Officer, Wendell Coppin. These are very positive auguries for the future of cricket in Costa Rica.

The Association's status was upgraded to the *Federación de Cricket* (FEDECRIC), formed in November 2008, inscribed at the *Registro* in March 2009, and now Costa Rica's official cricket authority. Its two founding members were CRCA (*Asociación Deportiva de Cricket*) itself and CCCCR (Croquet & Cricket Association), subsequently joined by the Caribbean (December 2008) and Corsairs (June 2009) Cricket Associations, with equal standing. FEDECRIC started operations on July 28th 2009, holding its first General Meeting, and CRCA was wound up.

By Richard Illingworth, President, Federacion de Cricket, Costa Rica. Acknowledgements to T.A. Willasey-Wilsey, A Hundred Years of Costa Rican Cricket 1890-1990 – An Untold Chapter of Caribbean History, published April 1992 in The Cricketer magazine (Cricket Outposts) as Costa Rica: Playing Across The Lines (*).

Material provided for inclusion, courtesy of Richard Illingworth.

PERU

ricket has been played in Peru for over 150 years at the splendid Lima Cricket & Football Club, and is now undergoing resurgence as a recently-admitted Affiliate Member of the *International Cricket Council* (ICC) and a founder member of *Cricket South America*, along with Argentina, Brazil and Chile.

Lima Cricket Club was founded in 1859 and cricket has been played in Lima, on and off since then. The club moved to its present site with a cricket ground in Magdalena in the 1920s. The first match to be played against a foreign team by the Peruvians was against Sir Pelham Warner's MCC side, who were on their way back from Australia via Chile and Peru in 1927. Former England captain, Freddie Brown, was born in Lima and his father took five wickets against the MCC. Only internal cricket was played between then and the 60s and, sadly, we have little record of this. Between 1967 and 1980 there was a surge of interest in the game, largely based on workers from British textile firms. As well as intense local competition, tours were arranged to Argentina three times, as well as to Colombia and Venezuela, and there were visits by teams from Argentina, Australia and England, as well as the Derrick Robbins XI, which included future England internationals Bill Athey, Chris Cowdrey and Andy Lloyd.

ON THE VOYAGE TO SOUTH AMERICA IN 1926
Left to right—Back row: L. C. R. Isherwood, G. O. Allen, H. P. Miles, J. C. White, G. R. Jackson, M. F. S. Jewell, R. T. Stanyforth. *Middle row:* T. O. Jameson, P. F. W., G. J. V. Weigall. *Front row:* T. A. Pilkington, C. Levick, Lord Dunglass.

The 1980s proved to be another quiet time for cricket in Peru, but it recovered in the early 90s when the short, vibrant seasons in February and March raised interest; and during Easter of 1995, a tournament was arranged in Lima between teams from Chile, Brazil and Peru. Chile won with Peru coming in second and contact was re-established. The first *South American Cricket Championship* (SAC) took place soon after, in December that year featuring Argentina, Brazil, Chile and Peru. The Championship has taken place since then, at roughly two-year intervals, in Buenos Aires, Santiago – and Lima in 1999 and 2007 (at *Lima Cricket & Football Club* and *Markham College*). The most recent South American Championship, the 8th, was held in Brazil for the first time, in April 2009, at the Sao Paulo Athletic Club; and will be held again, in Santiago, Chile in Dec 2011.

After a promising season in 2006 and following a Twenty20 tournament between four local Lima teams, we made our successful application for Affiliate membership to the ICC (*International Cricket Council*) in 2009. This has injected new life and investment into Peruvian cricket. It also means that Peru is now part of a worldwide cricket league system, with the possibility, albeit unlikely, of qualifying for the World Cup.

We currently have some way to go to reach that lofty pinnacle as, having competed in three official, international tournaments, we are still in the ICC Americas Division III and (unofficially) ranked 85th in the world! Nonetheless, there have been some notable scalps in the process: Brazil in 2008, and Chile, Mexico, Costa Rica and the Falkland Islands in 2011.

With an eye to the long-term future, cricket has now been reintroduced to four schools in Lima, who competed for the first *Lima Inter-Schools Trophy* in Nov, 2010. Both boys and girls are included in these school programs. In 2009 the first women's cricket match was held between Markham College and San Silvestre Girls School. We were also proud to host a triangular Cricket South America Under-13 tournament between Peru, Chile and Argentina in April 2010 and again in 2011. Following the success of these junior tournaments, 2011 also saw Lima play host to its first ever official ICC tournament, the ICC Americas (South) Under-15 Championship, at Markham College. Argentina won the forty-over tournament with ease; but Peru created a massive upset to win the T20 competition. Back in the early 40's there used to be matches against the Chalacos, a very mixed bunch from Callao, some of whom had good eyes and did not disgrace themselves. But in those days there were several British companies in Callao and the old social British Club founded in the 1880's, I believe. Everyone came and went by ship, thus the British influence was much stronger.

Material provided for inclusion, courtesy Peter Relton, Asociacion Peruana De Cricket, Peru.

URUGUAY

The Montevideo Cricket Club's most immediate precedent was the Victoria Cricket Club, founded by a group of British citizens in October 1842 with the purpose of playing cricket. Its location was in the vicinities of the Arroyo Pantanoso, where the meat storage establishment of Samuel Lafone —one the club's founders— was situated. One year later, the club and local cricket practices did not seem to have many followers. At the time, the people of Montevideo were more focused on Spanish-rooted sports such as bull fighting, sack races and soaped pole competitions. The siege of Montevideo in 1843 interrupted all social and sport activities within the city. On July 18th 1861, barely 31 years after the first Uruguayan constitutional oath, the Montevideo Cricket Club was founded in the Confitería Oriental, a place well-known for high society and business gatherings, located in the area currently occupied by the Hospital Militar. Its founders were the same people behind the Victoria Cricket Club's foundation, men linked to different activities in Uruguay, mainly trade.

Uruguayan historian Eduardo Acevedo asserts in his Historical Annals that the first cricket competition between the Buenos Aires Cricket Club and the Montevideo Cricket Club was supposed to take place in 1864, however, the political turmoil occurring at the time led to its suspension. First it was the Cruzada Libertadora headed by Venancio Flores north of the Río Negro, and later the collapse of Bernardo Berro's government, the Paysandú siege and the war between Uruguay and Paraguay.

In 1862, the club made its first import purchase of cricketing equipment such as bats and balls (there are no records of previous sport-items imports in Uruguay before this). One year later, the Bank of London opened a branch in Montevideo and all of its employees became members of the Montevideo Cricket Club. In 1865, the Venancio Flores government called for tenders to provide Montevideo with drinkable water, a service which was finally taken over by the British company Montevideo Waterworks. This led to an increase of British citizens in Uruguay, all of which became members of the Montevideo Cricket Club.

The postponed cricket competition between locals and Buenos Aires finally took place in 1868, an event which marked both the first sports encounter in the Río de la Plata and the first international registered cricket match, played in South America and took place on MVCC's ground in La Blanqueda. A year later, the Montevideo Cricket Club and the Buenos Aires Cricket Club played the first international cricket match in Argentina. A very close bond was formed between both institutions and reached all sports practiced at the time (cricket, football, rugby, tennis, etc.). The number of competitions organized by both clubs was unmatched by any other institution at the time and the opening of the English High School in 1874 and the British Schools in 1885 contributed towards the mingling of the British community with Uruguayans. The latter would gradually enroll in sports circles once considered exclusive, thus increasing competitiveness and promoting the origin of new sports institutions. One of them was the Montevideo Rowing Club, founded in 1874 mostly by the Montevideo Cricket Club members. The following year, the Montevideo Cricket Club played as local the first international rugby match against the Buenos Aires Cricket Club.

Another significant British flow of immigrants occurred after Uruguay purchased English railway equipment for the first time in 1876. A very important institution that resulted from this was the Central Uruguay Railways Cricket Club (CURCC), which would later become the seed for the Club Atlético Peñarol. Sports in Uruguay definitely consolidated after the opening of the British Schools, which encouraged the formation of Uruguayan sports clubs such as the Club Nacional de Regatas in 1888. Previous to this, all sports clubs in Montevideo had been established by foreigners.

In 1878, the Montevideo Cricket Club played their first football game in Uruguay against the crew of an English ship. That same year, the club also organized the first Uruguayan championship of athletic games. In 1881, the Montevideo Cricket Club and the Montevideo Rowing Club played the first football game involving different clubs in Uruguay. In 1888, the Montevideo Cricket Club introduced tennis and velocipedist practices (the origins of biking) in Uruguay. In 1889, the Montevideo Cricket Club moved to its new headquarters in the intersection of Cardal and Larrañaga streets. For the opening of its new football court, a game between the national teams of Uruguay and Argentina was held (this event constituted the first of its kind in the Río de la Plata). Henry Stanley Bowles –a well-known Montevideo Cricket Club athlete– scored the first goal. The celebration took place on the 70th birthday of Queen Victoria, whose portrait was placed on one of the VIP seats. Our team was formed by players from the Montevideo Cricket Club and the Montevideo Rowing Club.

In 1894, Montevideo Cricket Club members began to feel like outcast by cricket, rugby and football, and thus introduced golf in Uruguay after finding good links in the area of Punta Carretas. In 1945, the club moved for the third time to the area of Sayago. That same year, the club participated in the first Argentine rugby championship of provinces. In 1951, the Uruguayan Rugby Union was formed and Montevideo Cricket Club's distinguished member and former president Carlos "Charlie" Cat was elected to be its first president. In 1955, the Montevideo Cricket Club moved to its fourth headquarters in Carrasco and in 1961, it celebrated an uninterrupted 100-year existence.

In 1996, the club moved to its fifth and current headquarters in the location of Solymar. The Montevideo Cricket Club is a key milestone in the movement of sports in Uruguay as a result of its leading position in this area from the very beginning. The institution introduced and practiced cricket, rugby, football, Hockey, athletics, velocipedist practices and tennis, and encouraged many of these sports after our country was affected by wars. It also had a direct influence on the introduction of several other sports in Uruguay.

Central Uruguay Railway Cricket Club, known as CURCC, was a sports club from Uruguay, founded on September 28, 1891 in Montevideo, the country's capital. CURCC was the result of the decision of the British railway company in Uruguay to have a sports club and the grounds were located at Casavalle, Villa Peñarol . As a matter of fact, the colors of the club were inspired from the railway signs.

The club reached important achievements in the 1890's and in the first decade of the twentieth century founding of the league and the AUF, but then entered political conflicts. This aspect is the cause of endless discussions between Uruguayan sports fans: On one hand, those who claim that CURCC disappeared in 1915 and on the other hand, those who claim that CURCC only changed its name and began to be known as C.A. Peñarol. The real facts behind the change of name was as follows: the English "section" of CURCC wanted to quit the practice of football and return to cricket as in 1891-92, mainly because of the numerous fans that were destroying the trains during the weekends and cost so much money to the club. The Uruguayan "part" insisted that cricket was not popular among the people, and also that the club made a name by playing football, not cricket. By votes, Football won over Cricket and the English directives decided to leave, and thus, during the season of 1913 the club started playing as "CURCC" and ended as "CURCC Peñarol". Later, on 13 December that year, the name changed to the actual denomination of Club Atlético Peñarol (Athletic Club Peñarol-as the club already had athletics and other sports along with football). People (mostly Club Nacional) who say CURCC and Peñarol teams co-existed in time, argue that CURCC as an institution existed until 1915. The truth is that, the field of CURCC did indeed exist until that year, but only symbolically, as the ex-directives of CURCC (English) continued paying the rent and they didn't want other clubs of the area to take the field as their home stadium (even Peñarol), but no team named CURCC played any game in that place in 1914. The supposed (not clear) matches of CURCC (apparently near 4 friendlies) would have been played in Rivera, north of the country. Peñarol then moved to new (still existent) field Las Acacias. More information can be found at www.bacrc.com, which is "Buenos Aires Cricket and Rugby Club" considered as our sibling.

Material provided for inclusion courtesy: Henry M. Frederick VP MVCC & President of the Uruguayan Cricket Association.

FIRST CRICKET HALL OF FAME
IN THE WORLD

In February of 1981, a group of visionary cricketers in Hartford, Connecticut, established the Hall of Fame, after a year of frustration and disappointment.

At the outset, the organization was named the "United States Cricket Hall of Fame," but that name was short-lived because of proprietary considerations. The initial attempt to start the institution was buoyed by verbal encouragement of team representatives from Toronto, Canada to Los Angeles, California. An Executive Committee which was given the task to get the organization off the ground established a formula by which every participating organization would share equally in the business of the Hall of Fame. With some apprehension though and much enthusiasm, the ensuing document was mailed to those organizations and a select board of regents (geographic representatives).

After much tedious work and some expense, the results that followed, proved to be disastrous. Not a single organization or individual responded. Unmoved by the lack of real interest, the Executive Committee at its February 1981 meeting, agreed to recommend to the membership of its parent body, the Sportmen's Athletic Club, Inc., that the program be instituted on an in-house basis. The optimism of the Executive Committee was reflected by the support of this new phase from those members who thought that it was an idea whose time had passed. Faced with the pitfalls of new ideals and stinging criticism, the committee stuck to its convictions. The rest is now history.

The first Annual Cricket Hall of Fame Induction Dinner was held on October 17, 1981, at the Hartford Holiday Inn Hotel. The affair was well attended. The capacity of the facility (330 dinner guests) was exceeded and the festive nature of the program prevailed. The inductees were James Gabriel, John Law, Lloyd Walford, Alfred Valentine, Lance Gibbs and Wesley Hall. A decision some years later to move the induction ceremony to New York resulted in it not coming off as expected. This led to the total inactivity of the Hall of Fame. After a five-year stagnation, a bold effort by Linford Miller (in 1997), who had become president of Sportmen's, to bring the institution back on track, paid off.

Under the leadership of former Sportmen's president Michael Chambers, the Hall of Fame became active again and has since regained the respect that it previously had among cricket players and lovers of the game. Since its revival, the Hall of Fame has inducted former Test stars Sir Vivian Richards, Alvin Kallicharran, Joel Garner, Michael Holding and Andy Roberts of the West Indies, Sunil Gavaskar, Gundappa Viswanath, Bhagwat Chandrasekhar, Syed Abid Ali and Farokh Engineer of India, Gregg Chappell and Kerry Packer (posthumously) of Australia and Tony Greig of England. The Hall of Fame also took over Hartford's Six-a-Side tournament for a period of time.

The institution has also aided some deserving charities, which included the raising of more than 400,000 surgical gloves for care givers in Jamaica working with AIDS infected children. Through its Humanitarian Award program, the Hall of Fame has raised funds for organizations like the Boys' Town project and Boy Scouts movement in Jamaica, a youth hotline project in Barbados, the Alvin Kallicharran Foundation and a children's home in St. Lucia.

The Cup pictured on the next page that ended up at the Hall of Fame, did not come with any information but the inscription on it, tells a story. It's called the *John J. Heys Challenge Cup* of the Massachusetts State Cricket League, founded in 1906 and now in continuous operation since the 1960s, according to their website. The cup may have been instituted in 1915, with the 'USMAA Whites' as the inaugural winners and the last cup winner was from 1951, they are listed as:

The U.S. M.A.A Whites won it in 1915, 16, 17, 18, and 1932.
West India Wanderers Cricket Club Inc. 1919, 20, 22-27, 29-31, 33, 41, 42, 48-50
Standard Cricket Club 1925, 1930
Windsor Cricket Club 1927-28, 35, 37, 38, 39
Arlington Mills C.C. 34, 36, 40
Hartford W.I.C.C 1951

Official schedules of the league were also printed and at one time were part of the K.A. Auty Library of Cricket collection.

Article provided for inclusion, courtesy: Stan Walker, Cricket Hall of Fame Hartford, Connecticut.

NOTES ON THE CHAPTER

Chapter 1. Colonial Cousins, the Yankee Game of Wicket

1: "Bristol, Connecticut" 1907, published by Eddy N Smith & George B. Smith. That Strange Yankee Game, Wicket - By Frederick Calvin Norton.

2: Cricket: A history of its Growth and Development throughout the world by Rowland Bowen. p.72.

3: Baseball in the Garden of Eden, The secret history of the early games, John Thorn 2011

4: ibid

5: Muzzy Field: Tales from a forgotten Ballpark, Douglas S. Malan 2009.

6: Brentano's Monthly, Devoted to the interest of all pastimes by field and water. Volume III-New Series. Brentano's Literary Emporium, Publishers, New York. Aquatic monthly and sporting gazetteer, April to September 1880: Vol. 3 p. 647 Reprint of the article by H.C.

7: John Thorn's blog: The Old-Time Game of Wicket. Ourgame.mlblogs.com

8: Early days on Boston Common, Mary Farwell Ayer, privately printed 1910. p. 7

9: Cricket: A history of its Growth and Development throughout the world by Rowland Bowen p. 30.

10: A Treatise on the Law of Trespass in the Twofold Aspect of the Wrong and the Remedy by Thomas W Waterman 1875
Reports of Cases Argued and Determined in the Supreme Judicial Court of Massachusetts Luther S. Cushing Volume 1 (Little Brown & Co, Boston, 1854) p. 453-457

11: Cricket: A history of its Growth and Development throughout the world by Rowland Bowen p. 269.

12: Retrosheet at "www.retrosheet.org".

13: Cricket: A history of its Growth and Development throughout the world by Rowland Bowen p. 72.

14: The Old-Time Game of Wicket and Some Old-Time Wicket Players by George Dudley Seymour. [A paper read before the Connecticut Society of Colonial Wars and reprinted from the Second Volume of the Proceedings of the Society)

15: Rev. Samuel Robert Calthrop. Compiled by His Daughter, Edith Calthrop Bump. Syracuse, New York. April 1939.

16: The Nation, A Weekly Journal devoted to Politics, Literature, Science, Drama, Musci, Art, and Finance. July 1, 1910 to December 31, 1910, New York. Albert Matthews, Wicket in America, p   8-9.

17: History of New Britain with sketches of Farmington and Berlin, Connecticut 1640-1889 by David N. Camp 1889.

18: The International Peace Movement, 1815-1874, Wilhelmus Hubertus Linden, 1987.

19: A Brief History of Hurling www.ancientsites.com/aw/Post/33637

Chapter 2. Cricket in Canada

1: JE Sullivan of the New York Athletic Club, as mentioned in "The Americana" a Universal Reference Library, by Frederick Beach and Edwin Rines.

2: Canadian Cricket website

3: The pleasure of the Game, Stanley Fillmore, History of Toronto Cricket, Skating and Curling Club 1827-1977

4: The Cultural bond: sport, empire, society by JA Mangan 1992, p. 169

5: Journal of a second Voyage for the discovery of a North-West passage from the Atlantic to the Pacific, performed in the years 1821-22-23 in his Majesty's ships FURY and HECLA, under the orders of Captain William Edward Parry p. 415

 6: Canadacricket.org

7: Seventy One not out – William Caffyn

8: Geo Wright's Cricket Guide mentions 6 matches being played, England winning 5 & drawn 1.

9: Cricketing Reminiscences and Personal Recollections, W.G. Grace 1899. p.38.

10: ibid p. 44

11: ibid p.49

12: A Century of Philadelphia Cricket – edited by John A. Lester 1951, p. 80

13: An Aspiration to Cosmopolitanism, Cricket in 19th Century St. Louis.

14: Cricket: A History of its growth & Development throughout the World – Rowland Bowen. Pg.122/123

15: Sixty Years of Canadian Cricket p. 407 Ch, XXI

16: Dreamcricket.com

17: Trinity College School Record, March 1922 to December 1924.

18: The Story of the Toronto Cricket Skating and Curling Club – Stanley Fillmore

19: Ridley College Scrapbook with various Newspaper cuttings.

20: Canadian Cricket.

21: The Don Meets the Babe, 1932 Australian Cricket Tour of North America. Ric Sissons 1995.

22: English Team in Australia 1932-33

23: Ten Great Bowlers, Ralph Barker 1967.

24: The Don Meets the Babe, 1932 Australian Cricket Tour of North America. Ric Sissons

25: ibid

26: Unknown newspaper article, information provided by State Library of South Australia.

27: The Don Meets the Babe, 1932 Australian Cricket Tour of North America. Ric Sissons

28: A Century of Philadelphia Cricket – edited by John A. Lester 1951, p. 290

29: Kevin Boller, Public Relations Officer, Canada Cricket Association.

Chapter 3. Prelude to Cricket in the Colonies

1: The Westover Manuscripts: containing the history of the dividing line between Virginia and North Carolina; a journey to the land of Eden, a. d. 1733; and a progress to the mines. Written from 1728 to 1736, and now first published. By William Byrd, of Westover.
Petersburg: printed by Edmund and Julian C. Ruffin. 1841.

2: David Block, 2005. *Baseball before We Knew It* (p. 101). Translated and excerpted in: Waldo, A. 1977. *The True Heroes of Jamestown* (p. 128). The original volume: Stefanski, Z. 1625. *Memorialium Commercatoris* (Amsterdam: Adreasa Bickera).

http://ourgame.mlblogs.com/2011/06/19/polish-workers-play-ball/

3: David Block, "An Early hint of Continental Europe's Influence on Baseball" MLBlogs Network

4: J Tillman Hall, School recreation: It's organization, supervision, and administration 1966 – "1621 – Governor William Bradford stopped a primitive game of Cricket in Plymouth Colony". p.7

5: A manual of the Reformed Church in America (formerly Ref. Prot. Dutch Church) 1628-1902: by Edward Tanjore Corwin 1902. P.36. Laws and Ordinances of New Netherland p. 258-263

David Block in his book writes, *"According to Mr. Spalding, "tcheque" was imported into America by the French Huguenots, who settled in the Dutch colony of New Amsterdam".* p. 11

This was the game identified in the French-Norman dictionaries as 'tèque" or "thèque', an old Norman ball game played in the nineteenth century. Was this mistaken for Cricket? They also played with an uneven sphere stuffed with horse hair – what kind of a ball game was this?

6: The Secret Diary of William Byrd of Westover, 1709-1712, ed. Louis B. Wright and Marion Tinling (Richmond: The Dietz Press, 1941).

7: Dr. Thomas L. Long, Thomas Nelson Community College, Hampton, Virginia. (tncc.edu)

8: History of Coffeehouses, The Colonial Williamsburg Foundation website

9: Ibid

10: Cricket in America, 1710-2000. P. David Sentance. 2006 p.7 (Lord Frederick Sackville of Knole's head gardener Romney captained a match)

11: Ibid 6

12: Derek Birley, *A Social History of English Cricket*, Aurum, 1999

13: H S Altham, *A History of Cricket*, Volume 1 (to 1914), George Allen & Unwin, 1962

14: Cricket – WG Grace 1891 Ch1 p. 3.

15: Timothy J McCann, *Sussex Cricket in the Eighteenth Century*, Sussex Record Society, 2004

16: Sports and Games of the Renaissance – Andrew Leibs 2004 – p. 157

17: Encyclopedia of Ethnicity and Sports in the United States: George B Kirsch, Othello Harris, Claire Elaine Nolte. 2000 p. 142/143

18: Information provided by Rhode Island Historical Society. «Colonials at Play: Leisure in Newport, 1723, by L. Douglas Good (Rhode Island History, February, 1974.)

19: A Century of Philadelphia Cricket – edited by John A. Lester 1951, Chapter 1.

20: Deamcricket.com

21: Chronological History of Savannah, from its settlement by Oglethorpe down to December 31, 1899. Together with a complete record of the City & County, and Savannah's Roll of Honor, A Roster of the soldiers who have In Three Wars gone forth at their Country's Call, from this city. A.E. SHOLES, compiler. Savannah, Georgia; The Morning News Print, 1900.

22: Georgian Encyclopedia.org Carol Ebel, Armstrong Atlantic State University 2007.

23: The Journal of William Stephens 1741-1743, Edited by E. Merton Coulter. University of Georgia Press 1958.

24: 'The Manly Game': Cricket and Masculinity in Savannah Georgia in 1859, Timothy Lockley, University of Warwick. The Journal of William Stephens.

25: ibid 23

26: (*Maryland Gazette*, 14 November 1754) South River Club Collection, Maryland Historical Society, Baltimore.

27: Ibid 19

28: Some Reminiscences of Cricket in Philadelphia before 1861, by William Rotch Wister, 1904. p.5. Also mentioned in 'A Century of Philadelphia Cricket', p. 5.

29: Cricket in America, 1710-2000. P. David Sentance, 2006, p.6.

30: Printed in the *Essex Gazette*, December 6 to 13, 1768 p. 81. Retrosheet.org

31: When London was Capital of America, Julie Flavell, 2011.

32: Anglophilia: deference, devotion and Antebellum America, Elisa Tamarkin 2008.

33: "In Pursuit of Refinement: Charlestonians Abroad, 1740-1860 by Maurie D, McInnis, Gibbes Museum of Art (Charleston, S. C.), Historic Charleston Foundation (Charleston, S. C.) 1999.

34: Ibid 32

35: From an article written and compiled by Karin Andrews – Thehouseandhomemagazine.com

36: Editorial in Connecticut Courant from 1850s

37: *Hartford Daily Courant* of September 25th 1858.

38: Cricket in America, 1710-2000. P. David Sentance. 2006, p.8

39: John Thorn, from Phelps-Stokes, Vol. VI, Index—ref. against Chronology and Chronology Addenda (Vol. 4aA or 6A); also, Vol. V, p.1068 (6/13/1778): Royal Gazette, 6/13/1778 – Retrosheet.org

40: ibid

41: A Century of Philadelphia Cricket – edited by John A. Lester 1951, pg. 5. Also, A Warm Bucket of Spit: Personality and the Vice Presidency, James C. Alexander Vanderbilt University. David Sentance in his book says that it was the Connecticut Senator Oliver Ellsworth who, *'complained that even fire companies and cricket clubs had presidents'*. p.9

42: The Journal of Lieut. William Feltman of the First Pennsylvania Regiment 1781-1782. Including March into Virginia and the siege of Yorktown. First published in Philadelphia, 1853.

43: A Century of Philadelphia Cricket – edited by John A. Lester 1951. p.5

44: Retrosheet.org/Protoball/Sub.USCricket.htm http://www.illinoisancestors.org/fulton/1871_canton/pages95_126.html Compiled by Janine Crandell. Cricket ball games banned on Sabbath in Canton, Fulton County, Illinois.

45: Dartmouth College Library Bulletin, Anyone for Cricket? Kenneth. C. Cramer, Nov 1992. David Sentance attributes the engraving to George Ticknor even after referring to the same article, which mentions the second oldest depiction of the college was a drawing by Ticknor in 1803, not the one depicting the Cricket scene.

46: http://www.ellenjaye.com/pub_publicker.htm

47: http://www.libraryindex.com/encyclopedia/pages/cpxktm064h/philadelphia-city-feet-street.html

48: Old Historic Germantown, an address with Illustrations presented at the Fourteenth Annual meeting of the Pennsylvania German Society, by Naaman Henry Keyser, 1906. p. 4

49: Colonial Families of Philadelphia, Editor John W Jordan Vol. II, 1911. p, 102

50: ibid 48, p. 43

51: John Thorn (Chadwick Scrapbook, Vol 20 & Boston Gazette, November 17, 1808). Source: Retrosheet. org.

Chapter 4. Growth and Development

1: A Century of Philadelphia Cricket – edited by John A. Lester 1951. P.7

2: An Anxious Pursuit: Agriculture Innovation and Modernity in the Lower South, 1730-1815 – Joyce E. Chaplin, 1993. Levi Sheftall Family Papers, January 13, 1801. See chapter: Petticoats & The Manly Game of Cricket.

3: NY Gazette & General Advertiser, March 18, 1801. Retrosheet.

4: Reprinted in NY Times issue of April 11th 1909.

5: John Thorn, Retrosheet.org

6: Richard Hershberger, American Beacon, Norfolk, Virginia, October 25th 1816. Retrosheet.org.

7: Two Year's Residence in the settlement on the English Prairie, in the Illinois Country, United States. With an account of its' animal and vegetable productions, agriculture and a description of the principal towns, villages with the habits and customs of the Back-woodsmen by John Woods, 1822. p. 148 & 295

8: Cricket in America, 1710-2000. P. David Sentance 2006, p. 10

9: Baseball and Cricket, the creation of American Team Sports, 1838-72, by George B. Kirsch

10: A Century of Philadelphia Cricket – edited by John A. Lester 1951. P.5 and Jennie Holliman, American Sports, 1785-1835. 1951, p.68 and retrosheet.org

11: Richard Hershberger in Retrosheet.org. New York Daily Advertiser, June 19, 1820, a box score was also provided on June 21. Also reported in New York Columbia June 19, 1820, players were described as all Europeans.

12: A Century of Philadelphia Cricket – edited by John A. Lester 1951. p.11

13: John Thorn in Retrosheet.org, citing Chadwick scrapbooks Vol. 20

14: The Tented Field, a History of Cricket in America, Tom Melville, 1998. p.15

15: Some Reminiscences of Cricket in Philadelphia before 1861, William Rotch Wister 1904. p. 6

16: Cricket in America, 1710-2000. P. David Sentance. 2006. P.14. Tom Melville puts the date at 1840.

17: Ibid 14 p, 11

18: The Book of Sports, by Robin Carver 1834. Boston: Lilly, Wait Colman & Holden.

19: Swinging Away, How Cricket and Baseball Connect. Beth Hise, 2010. p. 30

20: Abraham Peirsey of Jamestown Virginia

21: Chadwick's American Cricket Manual also A Manual of LaCrosse, New York, 1873. Robert M. DeWitt Publisher, p. 85.

22: The Tented Field, A History of Cricket in America, Tom Melville, 1998. p. 11

23: A Century of Philadelphia Cricket – edited by John A. Lester 1951. p.15

24: ibid p. 16.

25: The Tented Field, A History of Cricket in America, Tom Melville, 1998. p. 12

26: A Century of Philadelphia Cricket – edited by John A. Lester 1951. p.11

27: Some Reminiscences of Cricket in Philadelphia Before 1861. William Rotch Wister, 1904. p. 8.

28: The Tented Field, A History of Cricket in America, Tom Melville, 1998. p. 14

29: Ibid 26 p.12

30: Outing Vol. 5 October 1884 – March 1885. Cricket in America by George M. Newhall p. 49.

31: A Century of Philadelphia Cricket – edited by John A. Lester 1951. p.16 and Some Reminiscences of Cricket in Philadelphia Before 1861. William Rotch Wister, 1904.

32: The Tented Field, A History of Cricket in America, Tom Melville, 1998. p. 15

33: Some Reminiscences of Cricket in Philadelphia Before 1861. William Rotch Wister, 1904. P.8. An old newspaper article also corroborates the use of the term 'notches' as shown in "The Morning Post", London. Wednesday July 17ᵗʰ 1793.

> The married women and maids of Bury, in Suffex, are to play their return match of cricket, before the commencement of harveſt; and we hear that confiderable bets are depending on their ſhow of Notches, which at the concluſion of their laſt game, the umpires declared to be much in favour of the ſturdy matrons.
>
> Monday Evening Mr. Harris of Hampſtead was ſtopped in his carriage by three foot-pads, in Green-lane, Highgate, who robbed him of his watch and money.
>
> Yeſterday the ſhop of Mr. Honn, Hoſier in Mary-le-Bonne, was broken open, and robbed of ſundry articles of confiderable value.

34: Cricket in America, 1710-2000, P. David Sentance 2006, p. 14.

In, 'Some Reminiscences…by Wister' he refers to Mr. Robert Waller's recollection of early cricket in Philadelphia. *"That in 18839 the St. George's Cricket Club was formed, which was christened on St. George's Day, April 23ʳᵈ 1840, on the open space in the rear of a tavern on the Bloomingdale Road, now Broadway, where 32ⁿᵈ or 33ʳᵈ Street now is".* p. 140-141.

35: Some Reminiscences of Cricket in Philadelphia before 1861. William Rotch Wister, 1904. p.10

36: ibid p.141

37: ibid p. 12.

38: Jones Wister's Reminiscences, 1920. p.114

39: ibid p.115

40: Walter S. Newhall, A Memoir, Philadelphia. Published for the benefit of The Sanitary Commission, 1864.

41: The Tented Field, A History of Cricket in America, Tom Melville, 1998. p. 15

42: ibid. p. 19

43: Some Reminiscences of Cricket in Philadelphia before 1861. William Rotch Wister, 1904. p.13

44: ibid p. 15

45: The Tented Field, A History of Cricket in America, Tom Melville, 1998. p. 16

46: Some Reminiscences of Cricket in Philadelphia before 1861. William Rotch Wister, 1904. p.23

47: ibid p. 29

48: ibid p. 31

49: ibid. p. 71.

50: ibid p. 74 and New York Clipper.

51: American Cricket: Players and Clubs before the Civil War, George B. Kirsch. Journal of Sports History, Vol 11, No. 1 (Spring 1984). Spirit July 17ᵗʰ 1858

52: ibid 41, p. 127/128

53: ibid 41, p. 136 & Porter's Spirit 1860, Vol 9, November 6ᵗʰ. p. 165

54: Walter S. Newhall, Sarah Butler Wister. A Memoir, published for the benefit of The United States Sanitary Commission, 1864.

55: Jones Wister's Reminiscences, 1920. p.115-116

56: ibid 41. p. 85

57: The English Cricketers Trip to Canada and The United States, Fred Lillywhite, 1860. p. 43

Chapter 5. Petticoats and the Manly Game of Cricket

1: http://www.officialsavannahguide.com/category/75816-attractions

2: 'The Manly Game': Cricket and Masculinity in Savannah Georgia in 1859. Timothy Lockley. Warwick. ac.uk The International Journal of the History of Sport, Vol. 20, No 3 (September 2003) pp. 77-98. Published by Frank Cass, London.

Also, An Anxious Pursuit: Agricultural Innovation and Modernity in the Lower South, 1730-1815, Joyce E Chaplin 1996.

3: http://www.jewish-history.com/occident/volume1/nov1843/savannah2.html also http://mickveisrael. org/index.php?option=com_content&view=article&id=13&Itemid=18

4: http://www.exploresouthernhistory.com/gullyholecreek.html

5: Ibid 2

6: Ibid 2

7: ibid 2

8: Ibid 2

9: Ibid 2

10: Ibid 2: Also, Cricket in the Religious World in the late Victorian Period, Patrick. G. Scott, 1970.

11: Ibid 2: Also, Nancy L. Struna, 'Gender and Sporting Practice in Early America, 1750-1810

12: The Atlanta Constitution, April 19, 1896. "Cricket in Petticoats, Newest Fad for Girls".

13: The San Francisco Call, Saturday May 2nd 1896

14: Ibid 12

15: Ibid 2 and J.A. Mangan, Athleticism in the Victorian and Edwardian Public School / The Games Ethics and Imperialism: Aspect of the Diffusion of an Idea.

16: Ibid 2

17: Ibid 2 and 'Spirit of Times, November 26th 1859.

18: Some Reminiscences of Cricket in Philadelphia before 1861. William Rotch Wister, 1904. p.22.

19: Ibid 2 & http://en.wikipedia.org/wiki/John_Brown's_raid_on_Harpers_Ferry

20: The Century Illustrated Monthly Magazine Vol. LX May 1900 to October 1900. P. 16 under Schools (p.470)

21: p. 170 The School Journal Vol 57, July 1, 1898 to December 31, 1898.E.L. Kellogg & Co, 1898.

22: The paragraph talks about the girls from the class of '97 who were going to raise $1250 for the field. This appeared in the October 14, 1893 issue of The Wellesley College magazine, Vol 2

23: American Women's Track and Field: A History, 1895 through 1980, Vol 1. Louise Mead Tricard. 1996. p. 40.

24: ibid p. 18.

25: Girls and Athletics, edited by Mary. C. Morgan. Spalding's Athletic Library 1917. p. 11. Also, Sports: The First Five Millennia, Allen Guttmann, 2004

26: ibid p. 100. The girls at Smith may have played baseball as early as 1880.

27: The girls spelled it as 'Criquet', someone might wonder if it was 'croquet'. It was definitely Cricket as we see in the pictures; it's just a simple spelling mistake.

28: Choate Rosemary Hall

29: HistoricPelham.blogspot Blake Bell Town Historian NY Times May 24, 1896 refers to 'Mrs. John Cunningham Hazen's School' & also in 'Tented Field' while the Historic Pelham calls her,'Emily Hall Hazen'. The Morning Herald, Baltimore calls her Edith Hazen.

30: ibid

31: The Bachelor of Arts: A monthly magazine Devoted to University...Vol 3 June-December 1896.

32: The New York Times, November 15, 1896.

33: Ibid

34: Ibid 31

35: Yale Medical Journal, Volume III November 1896 – June 1897. Connecticut State Medical Society. New Haven, Conn: Published at the Yale Medical School, by the Editors 1897. Mentioned under the Alumni & School Notes, there is a F.W. Hulseberg listed at 276 Elm St (New Haven) from London, England. p. 48.

36: The archives at the Andrew Mellon Library at Rosemary Hall have scrap books/albums with lots of cricket pictures of Rosemary Girls playing against Pelham Hall take during 1896 timeframe. One picture shows a man standing on the field and the caption reads, 'Cricket Coach', I infer that would be Henry Canby.

37: After Glow, Lelia Caperton Stiles, 1898.

38: The Evening Telegram, St. John's, Newfoundland, Monday June 27, 1898.

39: The American Cricket Annual and Golf Guide for 1898. Compiled & Edited by Jerome Flannery. (This was the first time where records for Golf were included and this led to the name being changed to 'American Cricket Annual *and* Golf Guide')

40: ibid

41: Parisian Illustrated Review – Volume 9, 1900 p. 152.

42: Cricket in America, 1710-2000, P. David Sentance, p. 195.

Chapter 6. First Family of Cricket, Baseball – The Wright Brothers

1: Harry Wright – The Father of Professional Base Ball 2003 - Christopher Devine.

2: Henry Chadwick Scrapbooks, & Devine, p. 28

3: Devine, p.28 & Ryczek, When Johnny Came Sliding Home, p. 72

4: Harry Wright, Devine p. 10

5: ibid p. 60

6: ibid p. 86

7: "I feel frosty" wrote Harry Wright to his friend William Cammeyer September 15, 1874, after the tour, it was also a financial failure. SABRE

8: Harry Wright, Devine p. 110

9: American Cricketer, May 13, 1891.

10: Athletic Sports Illustrated 1889 p.228

11: ibid 9

12: ibid 9

13: ibid 10

14: Harry Wright, Devine, p.170

Chapter 7. Antebellum Cricket in America, the Civil War Era

1: Social Class and the Sport of Cricket in Philadelphia, 1850-1880, by J. Thomas Jable, William Paterson College in Wayne, New Jersey. Journal of Sport History, Vol 18, No. 2 (Summer 1991).

2: Philadelphia Historical Society

3: ibid 1. p. 215

4: A Century of Philadelphia Cricket – edited by John A. Lester 1951, p.207 taken from "The American Cricketer". and p. 90

5: Ibid

6: Baseball before we knew it, a search for the roots of the game, David Block 2005, p. 1. 1856 Porter's Spirit of the Times, "We feel a degree of old Knickerbockers pride, as the continued prevalence of Base Ball as the National Game of the region of Manhattanese".

7: This was Henry Chadwick writing to the American Cricketer (August 18th 1884) on return of the Gentlemen of Philadelphia after their first tour to Great Britain that met with unpredicted success. The Tour of the Gentlemen of Philadelphia (GOP), in Great Britain in 1884. John P. Green published in 1897. p. 44

8: Baseball and Cricket, The Creation of American Team Sports, 1838-72. 2007. p. 264

9: BBC September 2006 and Dreamcricket

10: The Tented Field, A History of Cricket in America, Tom Melville, 1998. p. 25.

11: American Cricket: Players and Clubs before the Civil War, George B. Kirsch. Journal of Sports History, Vol 11, No. 1 (Spring 1984).

12: Michigan Cricket Academy

13: ibid ref 10 p. 29

14: http://www-distance.syr.edu/SamCalthropBoyhoodStory.html
The Boyhood of Rev. Samuel Robert Calthrop. Compiled by his daughter, Edith Calthrop Bump, Syracuse, New York, April 1939. From Retrosheet: "Lee is reported to have become Superintendent of West Point in September of 1852, and had been stationed in Baltimore until then, did Calthrop get his dates wrong?"

15: Sward - A poetic term for an expanse of turf, often used when describing a closely cut lawn.

16: Just as Society in London was known as the ton, Society in New York was known as the Four Hundred. The name came about because of a statement of Ward McAllister. He said there were only about 400 people in New York who were at ease in a ballroom. McAllister even went so far as to make a list of names. There were not quite 400 people on the list, but folklore had it that only 400 people could fit into Mrs. Astor's ballroom, and the term the Four Hundred stuck.

17: A Backward Glance O'er Traveled Roads, Being an historical sketch of May Memorial Church (Unitarian Congregational Society in Syracuse) on the occasion of its Centennial Anniversary 1838-1938. October, 1938 Syracuse, New York.

18: The Tented Field, A History of Cricket in America, Tom Melville, 1998. p. 29

19: American Cricket: Players and Clubs before the Civil War, George B. Kirsch. Journal of Sports History, Vol 11, No. 1 (Spring 1984).

20: ibid

21: ibid

22: The Tented Field, A History of Cricket in America, Tom Melville, 1998. p. 30

23: The New York Times, August 30, 1863.

24: Old Boston Boys and The Games They Played – James D'Wolf Lovett (250 limited copies). Privately printed at the Riverside Press 1906. P202/203

25: The Tented Field, A History of Cricket in America, Tom Melville, 1998. p. 31

26: Baseball & Cricket, The Creation of American Team Sports 1838-72, George B. Kirsch. 2007. p. 80

27: ibid p. 83. Wilkes' Spirit.

28: ibid p. 85

29: ESPN cricinfo

30: 'Walter S Newhall, A Memoir. Published for the benefit of The Sanitary Commission, 1864, by Sarah Butler Wister. Picture of Newhall also taken from the same memoir. p. 17.

31: Merion Cricket Club

32: The Executive Documents, Senate of the United States, 1859-60, Vol 7-8 Mechanical Patent Office Report, p. 231

33: Patents for Inventions. Abridgements of Specifications relating to Toys, Games, and Exercises A.D. 1672-1866. London. Printed by George E. Eyre and William Spottiswoode, 1871 p. 55. B. Woodcroft. (here the patent number is given as 818 which does not correspond to the actual patent #23,017) Also, US Patent Office Specifications of Letters, Patent No. 23,017, dated February 22, 1859.

34: Scientific American, A Journal of Practical Information in Art, Science, Mechanics, Agriculture, Chemistry and Manufacturers. Vol V – No. 6, New York, August 10, 1861.

35: Report of the Commissioner of Patents for the year 1861, Arts and Manufacturers Vol I, 1863. p. 431

36: The English Game of Cricket, Charles Box 1877, p. 383

37: Historical Society of Pennsylvania

38: Bats, Balls and Books: Baseball and Higher Education for Women at Three Eastern Women's Colleges, 1866-1891," by Capt. Debra A. Shattuck, Department of History, U.S.A.F. Academy, in the Journal of Sport History, Summer 1992.

39: Ethnicity and Sports in Northern American History and Culture, by George Eisen and David Kenneth Wiggins p. 166

40: Cricket in America, 1710-2000. P. David Sentance. p.11

41: A Century of Philadelphia Cricket, Edited by John A. Lester, 1951. p. 378-383

42: ibid p. 380

43: The New York Times, May 22, 1881

44: A Century of Philadelphia Cricket, Edited by John A. Lester, 1951. p. 379

Chapter 8. Cricket's Ambassadors

1: The English Cricketers Trip to Canada and The United States, Fred Lillywhite, 1860. p. 1, 2

2: ibid p. 31

3: An estimated 20-25,000 spectators, watched the match in New York over the 3 days.

4: A Century of Philadelphia Cricket, Edited by John A. Lester, 1951. p.19

5: ibid

6: ibid ref 1 p. 38

7: ibid ref 4 p. 19

8: The English Cricketers Trip to Canada and The United States by Frederick Lillywhite 1860. p. 44

9: ibid p. 50

10: Tented Field, p. 46 & Oswego Commercial Times, October 1, 1860.

1868 Willsher's XI

11: ibid ref 4 p. 35

12: The New York Times, September 3rd, 1868. Also - Notice the emphasis on the 'old game' and 'old citizens', on what authority did the reporter opine. Clearly an ignorant and improper observation, and the situation is further exacerbated, as thousands form their opinion of the game solely by reading and forming a pre-conceived notion that it *must be* an old man's game. This constant 'drubbing' and emphasis on 'our national game' would affect the psyche of the public and erode their interest in cricket. Another reason to the bigger issue of why Cricket could not thrive.

13: The New York Times, April 13, 1870

14: Talks with Old English Cricketers, Alfred William Pullin 1900, p. 194. William Blackwood & Sons, London. George Kirsch in his book (P. 217) reports an income of $50 in gold and $7.50 per day + all travel expenses.

15: Baseball and Cricket, the Creation of American Team sports, 1838-72, p.217 and Clipper, September 19,26, 1868.

16: Talks with Old English Cricketers, Alfred William Pullin 1900, p. 195

1872 GRACE 3rd English visit

17: Cricketing Reminiscences, W.G. Grace 1899. p. 53

18: ibid p. 55

19: ibid p. 58

20: ibid p. 59

21: A Century of Philadelphia Cricket, Edited by John A. Lester, 1951. p. 41

22: ibid p. 43

23: ibid p. 54

24: A Century of Philadelphia Cricket, Edited by John A. Lester, 1951. p. 366/367.

25: Macmillan's Magazine, edited by David Masson, Sir George Grove, John Morley, No. 452 June 1897, Ch. 3, p. 106 Americans at Play. Also, The Living Age, sixth series, Volume XV, 1897.

26: ibid

27: ibid

1878 1st Australian Tour

28: South Australian Chronicle and Weekly Mail, Adelaide, SA. Saturday 7th December 1878.

29: A Century of Philadelphia Cricket, Edited by John A. Lester, 1951. p. 57

30: ibid p. 64.

31: ibid p. 64

32: ibid p. 57

33: <u>Cricket Archive</u> shows A. Bannerman did not bat in the 2nd innings which contradicts William B. Morgan's account in Lester.

34: Murdoch's score for 2nd innings match both in Lester's & Cricket Archive

35: <u>cricketarchive.com</u>

<u>1882 2nd Australian Tour</u>

36: Inangahua Times, Volume VII, Issue 1213, 29 December 1882, NewZealand paper.

37: On losing for the first time at home, the English press (Sporting Times) put out a satirical obituary, that English cricket had died and the body will be cremated and the ashes taken to Australia. Thus began the fight for the ashes as the next English tour to Australia in 1882-83 was a fight for the inaugural ashes. It was captained by Ivo Bligh and the English won 2-1 in a three match series, though a fourth was won by Australia which remained in dispute.

38: Ten Great Bowlers, Ralph Barker 1967, p. 26

39: A Century of Philadelphia Cricket, Edited by John A. Lester, 1951. p. 73

<u>1879 Lord Harris's Tour</u>

40: The New York Times, April 30, 1879

41: The New York Times. May 9th 1879

<u>1879 Richard Daft's XII</u>

42: Kings of Cricket, reminiscences and anecdotes, with hints on the game, by Richard Daft 1879. p. 168

43: <u>CricketArchive</u> Arthur Haygarth's Cricket Scores and Biographies Volume 16

44: James Lillywhite's Cricketers' Annual 1880, on page 5 match dates are given as 15, 16 & on page 10 match dates are given as 16, 17!

45: ibid p. 5

46: <u>Sports Illustrated</u>

47: The Sportsman's Yearbook for 1880, edited by J. Keith Angus. p. 160 and James Lillywhite's Cricketers Annual 1880

48: Dictionary of National Biography, edited by Sir Sidney Lee. Second supplement, Vol. 3 Neil – Young. 1912. p. 301/302

49: James Lillywhite's Cricketers' Annual 1880. p. 3

50: ibid p. 4

51: ibid p. 7

<u>1881 Shaw's XI</u>

52: Wisden on the Ashes: The Authoritative story of Cricket's greatest rivalry, edited by Steven Lynch. 2009 p. 11

53: James Lillywhites' Annual 1883. p. 45-46

54: ibid p. 47-48

<u>1879 1st Irish Tour</u>

55: The Irish Cricketers in the United States, 1879, by "One of Them" (Henry Brougham)

56: ibid

57: New York Herald, September 12th, 1879.

58: The Irish Cricketers in the United States, 1879, by "One of Them" (Henry Brougham)

59: ibid

60: ibid

61: ibid

62: ibid

63: Ethnicity and Sports in North American History and Culture, edited by George Eisen and David K. Wiggins, 1994. p. 61.

64: American Cricketer, Vol. XV. October 19, 1892.

65: October 10th 1888 – The Horae Scholasticae – St. Paul's School newsletter.

66: New York Herald, September 12th 1879. (The newspaper incorrectly identified the state as Massachusetts)

67: Harper's Weekly, New York, Saturday October 15th 1892.

68: ibdi 64

69: ibid 64

70: The American Cricketer Vol. 38 January 1915. p. 245

1884 GOP in England

71: The Tour of the Gentlemen of Philadelphia (GOP), in Great Britain in 1884. John P. Green published in 1897.

72: A Century of Philadelphia Cricket – edited by John A. Lester 1951, p.77

73: Green reported the paper as, 'The London Sportsman' while Lester calls it, 'The Sporting Life'

74: Ibid 72, p. 78

75: ibid 72

76: ibid 72, p.77

77: ibid 72. p. 284

78: ibid 71. p. 25

79: ibid 72, p. 79

80: ibid 71 p. 9/10. Also Century of Philadelphia Cricket, p. 80

81: ibid 71. p. 28

82: ibid72. p. 82 + ibid 1. P.43

83: ibid 71 p.32 + International Tennis Hall of Fame & Museum Rhode Island

84: ibid 71 p. 32 + http://www.wimbledon.com/en_GB/history/index.html

85: ibid 71 p. 36

86: ibid 72, p.83. ESPNcricinfo puts it at 110 wickets.

87: ibid 72. p. 83

88: ibid 71 p. 37

89: ibid 71. p. 66-67

90: ibid 71. p. 63

91: Encyclopedia-Titanica.org

92: ibid

93: Thayer Families Association/Titanic Historical Society

94: ESPNcricinfo Wisden Obituary 1913 edition.

1889 2nd GOP visit to England

95: A Century of Philadelphia Cricket, edited by John Lester 1951. p. 101

96: ibid p. 103

97: ibid p. 108

98: James Lillywhite's Cricketers' Annual 1890, p. 35

1897 3rd GOP visit to England

99: ibid 95 p. 146

100: ibid 95 p. 151

101: Spalding's Official Cricket Guide with which is incorporated The American Cricket Annual for 1904, Compiled & Edited by Jerome Flannery. p.9

1903 4ᵗʰ GOP visit to England

102: A Century of Philadelphia Cricket, edited by John Lester 1951. p. 184

103: ibid p. 197

104: ibid. p. 185

105: Spalding's Official Cricket Guide with which is incorporated The American Cricket Annual for 1904, Compiled & Edited by Jerome Flannery, p. 13.

106: ibid p. 13

107: ibid. p. 49

108: ibid p. 17

109: ibid. p. 17 and Century of Philadelphia Cricket. p. 190

110: The New York Times 26ᵗʰ July 1903.

111: Spalding's Official Cricket Guide with which is incorporated The American Cricket Annual for 1904, Compiled & Edited by Jerome Flannery. p. 18/19.

1908 5ᵗʰ GOP visit to England

112: CricketArchive

113: A Century of Philadelphia Cricket, edited by John Lester 1951. p. 222

114: ibid p. 224/225 and CricketArchive

115: ibid p. 226

116: ibid. p. 228

117: ibid. p. 229

118: ibid. p. 232

1886 1ˢᵗ West Indians tour to America

119: The First West Indies Cricket Tour, Canada and the United States in 1886, edited and with an introduction by Hilary McD. Beckles, 2006. p. xv

120: West Indian Cricket, Christopher Nicole. The Sportsman Book Club, 1960.

121: ibid 119

122: ibid 23, p.46 "The Tour of the West Indian Cricketers, August & September, 1886. 'A Memory' by One of Them, L.R. Fyfe.

123: ibid p. 13

124: ibid p. 16

125: The American Cricketers in the West Indies 1887-88, by Henry Robert Holmes, 1975. p. 6

126: ibid p. 7

127: ibid, introduction

128: Cricket Nurseries of Colonial Barbados: The Elite Schools 1865-1966, Keith A. P. Sandiford, 1998. p. 8

129: ibid ref 127 introduction

130: West Indian Cricket, Christopher Nicole. 1960. p. 33.

131: Tented Field, p. 137

132: Log of the Old Un, from Liverpool to San Francisco 1886. Peter Wynne-Thomas.

133: ibid

134: James Lillywhite's Cricketers' Annual of 1887, p. 193

135: www.statenislandcc.org – A Brief History

136: James Lillywhite's Cricketers' Annual of 1887, p. 192

137: Log of the Old Un, from Liverpool to San Francisco 1886. Peter Wynne-Thomas.

138: James Lillywhite's Cricketers' Annual of 1887 gives the score as 'innings and seventeen runs', (p. 196) though the individual scores match exactly with the Log of the Old Un – a simple mistake in addition or printing. The match dates are also different; Lillywhite puts it at September 23, 24 & 25th, whereas the dates in the book are given as September 24th, 25th & 26th.

139: Log of the Old Un, from Liverpool to San Francisco 1886. Peter Wynne-Thomas. p. 27 & 29. Also, from James Lillywhite's Cricketers' Annual of 1887, p. 196 & 198.

140: In the second match against Philadelphia, K.J. Key's score is shown as 30 in Lillywhite's, whereas in the Log of the Old Un it shows 60, one of them is correct! The scores in the book are referenced from Lillywhite.

<u>1891 Lord Hawke's XI visit USA</u>

141: The Illustrated American, Volume 8, August 22 to November 14, 1891. p. 391.

142: Outing an Illustrated Monthly Magazine of Sports, Travel and Recreation, Vol. XIX October 1891 to March 1892 Henry Chadwick, p. 33

143: ibid

144: The Illustrated American, Volume 8, August 22 to November 14, 1891. p. 393

145: James Lilywhite's Cricketers' Annual of 1895, p. 38/39

1897 Pelham Warner's visit

146: 1897 Article in Macmillan's Magazine Vol. 76 p. 110 'Americans at Play' talks about a trip during the Centennial Year Celebrations in Philadelphia, 1876, by a group of useless Cricketers.

147: James Lillywhite's Cricketers' Annual 1898, p. 207.

148: A Century of Philadelphia Cricket – edited by John A. Lester 1951, Chapter VIII p. 131/132

1893 AUSTRALIA visit to Philadelphia

149: Letter from a Melbourne paper, 'The Argus Tuesday, September 19, 1893.

150: A Century of Philadelphia Cricket- – edited by John A. Lester 1951, Chapter VIII p. 130

151: The Prince and Doctor: The 1893 Australian Tour to England and North America, 2007. Peter Sheppard.

152: Australian Town and Country Journal, Saturday October 14, 1893.

153: ibid (scores from other records vary slightly – always an issue with old records)

154: Score is from Cricket Archive, while the Philadelphia Record Almanac of 1890 shows the Australians winning by an innings and 70 runs)

<u>1896 4th Australian visit</u>

155: A Century of Philadelphia Cricket – edited by John A. Lester 1951, Chapter VIII p. 133 and Cricket Archive

156: ibid p. 133 – Lester writes that Philadelphia won by an innings and 99 runs while Cricket Archive gives he score as an innings and 60 runs.

<u>1912 Australian visit</u>

157: ibid 155 p. 24/241

<u>1913 Australian visit</u>

158: ibid 155 Chapter XVI p. 247

159: Cricket Archive

160: "The Queenslander" Sydney May 10, 1913

161: A Century of Philadelphia Cricket - – edited by John A. Lester 1951, Chapter XVI p. 244

162: ibid p. 245.

Chapter 9. A Prince and the King

1: Ten Great Bowlers by Ralph Barker, 1967 p.136.

2: A Century of Philadelphia Cricket – edited by John A. Lester 1951, Chapter XIII

3: Ten Great Bowlers by Ralph Barker, 1967 p.136.

4: Ranjitsinhji – His record Innings by Innings from the Famous Cricketers Series No. 12, p. 15. Published by the Association of Cricket Statisticians.

5: Obituary of John Barton King – Cricket Quarterly 1966 p. 61. (CC Morris Library website)

6: Ranji: The Strange Genius of Ranjitsinhji by Simon Wilde

7: ibid

8: ibid

9: ibid

10: ibid

11: Wisden Cricketers' Almanack. 1897. England Vs. Australia 1896

12: ibid 6

13: Ranjitsinhji – His record Innings by Innings from the Famous Cricketers Series No. 12, p. 12. Published by the Association of Cricket Statisticians.

14: ibid 6

15: ibid 6

16: A Century of Philadelphia Cricket – edited by John A. Lester 1951, Chapter XI.

17: ibid

18: ibid

19: Ten Great Bowlers – Ralph Barker 1967. Chapter 5.

20: Lee Allen in MLB.com Blogs

21: A Century of Philadelphia Cricket – edited by John A. Lester 1951, Chapter XI.

22: ibid

23: Ten Great Bowlers – Ralph Barker 1967. Chapter 5

24: A Century of Philadelphia Cricket – edited by John A. Lester 1951, Chapter XI.

25: ibid

26: ibid

27: ibid

28: ibid

29: ibid

30: ibid

31: Ten Great Bowlers – Ralph Barker 1967. Chapter 5

32: ibid

33: ibid

34: ibid

35: ibid

36: A Century of Philadelphia Cricket – edited by John A. Lester 1951, Chapter XIII

37: Ralph Barker referring to King notes that, 'but did not bowl in the second innings' pg. 140. There was no second innings as Gloucestershire were defeated by an innings and 26 runs.

38: A Century of Philadelphia Cricket – edited by John A. Lester 1951, Chapter XIII

39: ibid

40: Ten Great Bowlers – Ralph Barker 1967. Chapter 5

41: A Century of Philadelphia Cricket – edited by John A. Lester 1951, Chapter XIII, p. 195.

42: Obituary of John Barton King – Cricket Quarterly 1966 p. 61. (CC Morris Library website)

43: A Century of Philadelphia Cricket – edited by John A. Lester 1951, Chapter XIII

44: Ten Great Bowlers – Ralph Barker 1967. Chapter 5

45: A Century of Philadelphia Cricket – edited by John A. Lester 1951, Chapter XIII

46: Ten Great Bowlers – Ralph Barker 1967. Chapter 5

47: ibid

48: A Century of Philadelphia Cricket – edited by John A. Lester 1951, Chapter XV

49: ibid

50: Ten Great Bowlers – Ralph Barker 1967. Chapter 5

51: ibid

52: ibid

53: Martin Kettle The Guardian, Tuesday 8 August 2000.

54: A Century of Philadelphia Cricket – edited by John A. Lester 1951, Chapter XII

55: James (Red) Lillywhite's Cricketers' Annual – 1900

56: The New York Times, September 25th 1899.

57: They Made Cricket – G.D. Martineau 1957, The Sportsman's Book Club, Ch. 35

58: Cricket in America, 1710-2000. P. David Sentance, Chapter 4.

59: The Biography of Colonel, His Highness Shri Sir Ranjitsinhji by Roland Wild.

60: A Century of Philadelphia Cricket – edited by John A. Lester 1951, Chapter XII

61: Martin Kettle The Guardian, Tuesday 8 August 2000

62: They Made Cricket – G.D. Martineau 1957, The Sportsman's Book Club, Ch. 36, referring to Bart's pioneering effort in perfecting the art of swing bowling, though George Hirst of Yorkshire has been given the credit of discovering it but did not reveal till early 19th century by which time King was the undisputed pioneer for in-swingers.

63: H.V. Horderns autobiography, "Googlies: coals from a test-cricketer's fireplace".

Chapter 10. Waning prospects on the Green, the 20th Century

1: A Century of Philadelphia Cricket – edited by John A. Lester 1951, p. 206

2: ibid

3: Century of Philadelphia Cricket was printed in 1951, and, p. xii

4: The Tented Field, A History of Cricket in America, 1998. p. 126

5: ibid 1 p. 209

6: ibid 1 p. 235

7: ICC-Cricket.com

8: ibid 1 p. 238

9: ibid 1 p. 247

10: ibid 1 p. 247

11: ibid 1. p. 253

12: ibid 1, p. 254

13: ibid 1, p. 257 & *Cricketer* April 1923.

14: ibid 1, p. 258

15: ibid 1, p. 262

16: ibid 1, p. 264

17: ibid 1, p. 266-67

18: ibid 1, p. 269

19: ibid 1, p. 266 and from Scrap book of Arthur W. Norris, captain of Fordham C.C.

20: *Stiff Upper Lips and Baggy Green Caps, A Sledger's History of the Ashes* (Quercus) by Simon Briggs. The Telegraph, August 4th 2009.

21: ibid

22: 1938 Cricket and Rugby Annual and Directory of Clubs and Societies, published by KA Auty, President, Illinois Cricket Association Inc. & Illinois Rugby Football Union Inc.

23: The Cricketer, edited by Pelham Warner. Spring Annual 1945, p. 48.

24: Information provided by Richard White who played for the British Commonwealth CC in Washington DC during the 60s and currently resides in Tennessee. 1964 Yorkshire visit to America:

25: Worcestershire CCC World Tour, 1965. Official booklet gives the score as:

WCCC 184 for 5 declared & Honolulu CC 48. WCCC won by 136 runs. The score in the book is from an article by John Gardiner who was on the tour, hence taken as the correct score. All information provided by Tim Jones, Chairman of the Heritage Group at WCCC.

Chapter 11. Demise of Cricket in America, a Victim of *Propaganda*?

A premature obituary about baseball had appeared in the editorials of New York Times in 1881. *"There is really reason to believe that baseball is gradually dying out in this country. It has been openly announced by an athletic authority that was once called the national game is being steadily seceded by cricket...Our experience with the national game of baseball has been sufficiently thorough to convince that it was in the beginning a sport unworthy of men and that it is now, in its fully developed state, unworthy of gentlemen"* (The Dickson Baseball Dictionary – p572 Paul Dickson).

1: The Tented Field, A History of Cricket in America, Tom Melville 1998. p. 147

2: A, Century of Philadelphia Cricket, edited John Lester, 1951, p. 273

3: ibid 1, p. 147/48

4: ibid 2, p. 273

5: Major League Baseball's official historian - John Thorn

6: Baseball & Cricket, the creation of American Team Sports, 1838-72, George B. Kirsch 2007, p. 262

7: ibid p. 263

8: Harpers Weekly 1858

9: American Baseball: From Gentlemen's sport to the commissioner system – David Quentin Voigt 1983.

10: *Cricket: A History of its growth and Development throughout the World, Rowland Bowen, p 120.*

11: The Tribune Book of Open-Air Sports, Edited by Henry Hall, 1887. p. 128

12: Cricket Guide by George Wright, 1894.

13: Old Boston Boys and The Games They Played – James D'Wolf Lovett (250 limited copies). Privately printed at the Riverside Press 1906. p.78

14: Spirit of Time/Tented Field p. 18

15: Chadwick's American Cricket Manual 1873 p. 3,4.

16: Captain Crawley's Handbook of Outdoor Games – Cricket, Base Ball & Rounders' 1877 or 1878

17: *North American and United States Gazette* 1857, The Tented Field, A History of Cricket in America, 1998. p. 33

18: Baseball and Cricket, the creation of American Team Sports, 1838-72. George B Kirsch 2007. p. 262

19: Ibid p.51

20: The Tented Field, A History of Cricket in America, 1998. p. 2

21: Ibid 18

22: Ibid 18 p. 263

23: Baseball & Cricket, The Creation of American Team Sports, 1838-72. 2007. Preface

24: *1893 Dominion Illustrated Monthly, Cricket in Canada*

25: St Paul's School Archives, Concord, New Hampshire, pictures & reference material, courtesy of David Levesque, Ohrstrom Library, SPS.

26: A Century of Philadelphia Cricket – edited by John A. Lester 1951, p. 88

27: Baseball before we knew it, a search for the roots of the game'. David Block, 2005. p. 181

28: Article provided by Baseball Hall of Fame Library, Cooperstown, NY.

29: A Century of Philadelphia Cricket – edited by John A. Lester 1951, p. 89

30: Century of Philadelphia Cricket, Lester puts it at 1888, p. 89. He further writes that Sam Morley was a coach at Oxford Club and grounds man at Merion & a contract copy signed by him in 1886 still exists with the Philler papers at Merion! A handwritten note in pencil by Sam reads, 'shall I rekwire a Capp?".

31: The Tribune Book of Open-Air Sports, Edited by Henry Hall, 1887. p. 131

32: The New York Times, June 6 1893

33: St Mary's Church

34: The Encyclopedia Britannica. Vol. 24 p.78. 1911

35: The Churchman, An Illustrated Weekly News Magazine Vol 74, October 17, 1896.

36: A Century of Philadelphia Cricket – edited by John A. Lester 1951, Chapter XII

37: ibid

38: ibid

39: ibid

40: The New York Times, July 13, 1900.

41: The Gentleman's Magazine and American monthly review, William Evans Burton Vol V 1839.

42: Baseball before we knew it, a search for the roots of the game, David Block. 2005. Foreword XIV

Chapter 12. Cricket in Hawaii

Chapter 13. The Latin Flavor in Cricket
Mexico

1: Photograph taken by François Aubert, probably in 1865, which is in the collection of the Musée Royal de l'Armée in Brussels:

2: Games and Empires: modern sports and cultural imperialism, Allen Guttmann. 1994. p. 83.

3: Across Mexico in 1864-5. By W.H. Bullock, Macmillan and Co, 1866. P. 143. Author is also identified as William Henry Hall.

4: ibid. p. 144

5: ibid 1a & Judas at the Jockey Club and other episodes of Porfirian Mexico by William H Beezley. 2004. p. 18

6: Judas at the Jockey Club and other episodes of Porfirian Mexico by William H Beezley. 2004. p. 18

7: Information on Mexican History was provided by the Mexican Cricket Association with contributions from Prof Michael P. Costeloe and others, plus an article by Craig White which is re-produced in full with their permission.

Also, Ref 3a

Argentina

1: A Book of Argentine Cricket 1920 (Don't have further information on this book) AND, Gleanings and Remarks, collected during many months of residence at Buenos Ayers, and within the Upper Country, with a prefatory account of the Expedition from England, until the Surrender of the Colony of the Cape of Good Hope, under the joint command of Sir D. Baird and Sir Home Popham, by Major Alexander Gillespie, 1818, p. 139, 184.

2: A Guide to first class and other Important Cricket matches in North and South America, compiled by C. J. Clynes. Published by Association of Cricket Statisticians, 1987.

3: A Book of Argentine Cricket 1920

4: A Book of Argentine Cricket 1920

5: www.britishempire.co.uk

6: Encyclopedia Britannica

7: A Guide to first class and other Important Cricket matches in North and South America, compiled by C. J. Clynes. Published by Association of Cricket Statisticians, 1987.

8: A Book of Argentine Cricket (article by J. McG.) 1920

9: A Book of Argentine Cricket 1920, article written by J. McG.

10: A Guide to first class and other Important Cricket matches in North and South America, compiled by C. J. Clynes. Published by Association of Cricket Statisticians, 1987. p. 26.

11: ibid.

12: ibid

13: Cricketarchive

14: A Guide to first class and other Important Cricket matches in North and South America, compiled by C. J. Clynes. Published by Association of Cricket Statisticians, 1987. p. 27.

15: Cricket Argentina

16: 'The Sketch' dated August 4th 1897, Argentinian paper.

Chile

1: Did the Argentines play in Santiago or carry on to Valparaiso where Cricket had been established first and had better teams.

2: A Guide to first class and other Important Cricket matches in North and South America, compiled by C. J. Clynes. Published by Association of Cricket Statisticians, 1987. p. 27.

BIBLIOGRAPHY

A *'Bawl' for American Cricket, dedicated to the American Youth,* Jones Wister, 1893. Philadelphia.

A *Bibliography of Cricket,* compiled by E.W. Padwick, 2nd edition 1984, Library Association, London.

A *Book of Argentine Cricket* 1920.

A *Century of Philadelphia Cricket,* edited by John A. Lester, 1951 University of Philadelphia Press.

A *History of Cricket,* Volume 1 (to 1914), George Allen & Unwin, 1962. H.S. Altham.

A *History of Yale Athletics 1840-1888,* giving every contest with Harvard, Princeton, Pennsylvania, Columbia, Wesleyan, and others in Rowing, Foot Ball, Base Ball, Track Athletics, Tennis, by Richard M. Hurd, Yale '88. New Haven, Connecticut. 1888.

A *Manual of the Reformed Church in America (formerly Ref. Prot. Dutch Church) 1628-1902*: by Edward Tanjore Corwin 1902.

A *Record of 143 Cricket Matches played by Australian teams in Canada and the United States of America, 1878 to 1995,* compiled by Alfred James, 1999.

A *Social History of English Cricket,* Aurum, 1999, Derek Birley.

A *Sporting Time, New York City and the Rise of Modern Athletics, 1820-1870.* Urbana, 1986.

A *Treatise on the Law of Trespass in the Twofold Aspect of the Wrong and the Remedy,* Thomas W Waterman 1875.

A *Yankee looks at Cricket,* as told to Gerald Brodribb, by Henry Sayen. London, 1956.

An *Anxious Pursuit: Agriculture Innovation and Modernity in the Lower South, 1730-1815* – Joyce E. Chaplin, 1993.

Across Mexico in 1864-5. By W.H. Bullock, Macmillan and Co, 1866.

After Glow, Lelia Caperton Stiles, 1898.

American Women's Track and Field: A History, 1895 through 1980, Vol 1. Louise Mead Tricard. 1996.

American Baseball: From Gentlemen's sport to the commissioner system – David Quentin Voigt 1983.

Anglophilia: deference, devotion and Antebellum America, Elisa Tamarkin 2008.

Anyone but England. Cricket and the National Malaise, Mike Marquesee, London, 1994.

Athletics at Princeton, A History. Compiled and Edited by Frank Presbrey '79 and James Hugh Moffatt '00, Frank Presbrey Company New York 1901

Athletic Sports in America, England and Australia, 1889. Palmer, Fynes, Richter and Harris.

Barclays World of Cricket, the game form A-Z, General Editor, E.W. Swanton, 1986

Baseball before we knew it, A search for the roots of the game, David Block, 2005, University of Nebraska Press.

Baseball and Cricket, the Creation of American Team Sports, 1838-72, George B. Kirsch, 2007. University of Illinois Press, Chicago.

Baseball in the Garden of Eden, The secret history of the early Games – John Thorn 2011

Beadle's Dime Book of Cricket, New York, 1860, 1866.

Beyond the Boundary, C.L.R. James, 1958. London.

Brentano's Aquatic Monthly and Sporting Gazette 1879 + Various Issues/Editions

Bristol, Connecticut 1907, Published by Eddy N Smith & George B Smith, City Printing Company: That Strange Yankee Game, Wicket - By Frederick Calvin Norton.

Captain Crawley's Handbook of Outdoor Games – *Cricket, Base Ball & Rounders'* 1877 or 1878.

Chadwick's American Cricket Manual also A Manual of LaCrosse, New York, 1873.

Cricket and Cricketers, including an introduction by George M. Newhall, Ashley-Cooper Philadelphia, 1907.

Cricket Guide, George Wright, Spalding's Athletic Library, American Sports Publishing Co, New York, 1894.

Cricket in the Religious World in the late Victorian Period, Patrick. G. Scott, 1970.

Cricket: A History of its Growth and Development throughout the World, Rowland Bowen, 1970.

Cricket in America, 1710-2000, P. David Sentance, 2006. McFarland & Co.

Cricket Nurseries of Colonial Barbados: The Elite Schools 1865-1966, Keith A. P. Sandiford, 1998.

Cricket, Edmund Routledge, London.

Cricket, WG Grace 1891, Bristol, London.

Cricketing Reminiscences and Personal Recollections, W.G. Grace 1899.

Dictionary of National Biography, edited by Sir Sidney Lee. Second supplement, Vol. 3 Neil – Young. The Macmillan Company, London, Smith Elder & Co. 1912.

Draper's Self Culture, Vol. VI, Sports, Pastimes and Physical Culture. 1907. Andrew Sloan Draper, NY.

Early days on Boston Common, Mary Farwell Ayer, privately printed 1910.

English Cricket, Neville Cardus, London 1945.

English Sports and Pastimes, Christina Hole, 1949 London.

Ethnicity and Sports in Northern American History and Culture, by George Eisen and David Kenneth Wiggins. 1994.

From Ritual to Record, The Nature of Modern Sports, Allen Guttman, 1978. New York. Columbia University.

Gender and Sporting Practice in Earyl America, 1750-181, Nancy L. Strauna.

Googlies: coals from a test-cricketer's fireplace, H.V. Horderns autobiography. 1932.

Green Shadows, Abdul Hafeez Kardar 1958. Account of 1957-58 tour to WI, Bermuda, USA & Canada Padwick 5696.

Harry Wright – *The Father of Professional Base Ball* 2003 - Christopher Devine.

History of New Britain with sketches of Farmington and Berlin, Connecticut, 1640-1889, by David N. Camp 1889.

How to Play Cricket, A Manual for American Cricketers, George M Newhall, 1881. T.S. Dando & Co, Philadelphia.

BIBLIOGRAPHY

In Pursuit of Refinement: Charlestonians Abroad, 1740-1860 by Maurie D, McInnis, Gibbes Museum of Art (Charleston, S. C.), Historic Charleston Foundation (Charleston, S. C.) 1999.

James Lillywhite's Cricketers Annuals 1872-1899. London. James Lillywhite Frowd & Co.
Jones Wister's Reminiscences, 1920.
Judas at the Jockey Club and other episodes of Porfirian Mexico by William H Beezley. 2004.

Kings of Cricket, Reminiscences and Anecdotes with Hints on the game, Richard Daft. 1879 Bristol, J.W. Arrowsmith, London.

Log of the Old Un, from Liverpool to San Francisco 1886. Peter Wynne-Thomas.
Long Innings, the Autobiography of Sir Pelham Warner, 1951 George G. Harrap & Co, London.
*Lord's 1787-1945,*Sir Pelham Warner, 1946, London.

Muzzy Field: Tales from a forgotten Ballpark, Douglas S. Malan 2009.

North America in International Cricket, Rowland Bowen. M.S. Morris Prints Ltd 1960.

Old Boston Boys and The Games They Played – James D'Wolf Lovett (250 limited copies). Privately printed at the Riverside Press 1906.

Ranji: The Strange Genius of Ranjitsinhji by Simon Wilde. 2005.
Ranjitsinhji, his record Innings-by-innings, Simon Wilde. ACS Pub, Famous Cricketer Series No. 12.
Ranjitsinhji Prince of Cricket by Percy Cross Standing, JW Arrowsmith London, 1903.

Seventy One not out, the Reminiscences of William Caffyn. 1899.
Sixty Years of Canadian Cricket. John E. Hall & R.G. McCulloch, Toronto, Bryant Publishing Co, 1895.
Some Reminiscences of Cricket in Philadelphia before 1861, by William Rotch Wister, 1904.
Sport in England, A History of two thousand years of games and pastimes, Norman Wymer, 1949.
Sports and Games of the Renaissance, Andrew Leibs 2004.
Sports: The First Five Millennia, Allen Guttmann, 2004.
Sussex Cricket in the Eighteenth Century, Sussex Record Society, 2004. Timothy J McCann.
Swinging Away, How Cricket and Baseball Connect. Beth Hise, 2010.

Talks with Old English Cricketers, Alfred William Pullin 1900, William Blackwood & Sons, London
Ten Great Bowlers, Ralph Barker 1967 Chatto & Windus, London.
The American Cricketers in the West Indies 1887-88, by Henry Robert Holmes, 1975.
The Badminton Library of Sports and Pastimes.
The Biography of Colonel His Highness Shri Sir Ranjitsinhji Vibhaji, Maharaja Jam Saheb of Nawanagar, G.C.S.I., G.B.E., K.C.I.E. 1934. Roland Wild.
The Book of American Pastimes, Charles A. Paverelly, 1866. New York.
The Book of Sports, by Robin Carver 1834.
The Cricket Field, Rev. James Pycroft, London, 1922.

The Cultural bond: sport, empire, society by JA Mangan 1992.

The Don Meets The Babe, the 1932 Australian Cricket Tour of North America, Ric Sissons, with a foreword by Sir Don Bradman, published J.W. McKenzie, 1995.

The English Cricketers Trip to Canada and The United States, Fred Lillywhite, 1860.

The English Game of Cricket, Charles Box 1877.

The First West Indies Cricket Tour, Canada and the United States in 1886, edited and with an introduction by Hilary McD. Beckles, 2006.

The Golden Age of Cricket, 1890-1914, David Frith, London, 1984.

The History of Cricket, Eric Parker, Seeley Service & Co, London, 1950 (Completely ignores American History!)

The International Peace Movement, 1815-1874, Wilhelmus Hubertus Linden, 1987.

The International Series, The Story of the United States versus Canada at Cricket, John Marder, 1968.

The Irish Cricketers in the United States, 1879, by "One of Them" (Henry Brougham).

The Jubilee Book of Cricket, Prince Ranjitsinhji, 1897. William Blackwood, Edinburgh.

The Larwood Story with Kevin Perkins. The Sportsman's Book Club, 1967.

The Merion Cricket Club, 1865-1965. Privately Printed.

The Old-time Game of Wicket and some Old-time Wicket Players. Reprinted from the second volume of the proceedings of the Connecticut Society of Colonial Wars. 1905.

The Phoenix Dictionary of Games, how to play 487 games, compiled by J.B. Pick, 1952.

The Pleasure of the Game, the story of the Toronto Cricket, Skating and Curling Club: 1827-1977. Stanley Fillmore, 1977.

The Prince and Doctor: The 1893 Australian Tour to England and North America, 2007. Peter Sheppard.

The Record Almanac for the year 1885, published by The Philadelphia Record.

The Sportsman's Yearbook for 1880, containing a digest of information relating to the origin and present position of British sports, games and pastimes. Edited by J. Keith Angus. Cassell, Peter, Galpin & Co. London.

The Tented Field, A History of Cricket in America, Tom Melville, 1998, Bowling Green State University Popular Press, Ohio.

The Tour of the Gentlemen of Philadelphia (GOP), in Great Britain in 1884. John P. Green. Philadelphia, Allen, Lane and Scott, 1897.

The Tribune Book of Open-Air Sports, Edited by Henry Hall, 1887.

They Made Cricket – G.D. Martineau 1957.

Tom Richardson, A Bowler Pure and Simple, Keith Booth, 2012, ACS Publications.

Two Year's Residence in the settlement on the English Prairie, in the Illinois Country, United States. With an account of its' animal and vegetable productions, agriculture and a description of the principal towns, villages with the habits and customs of the Back-woodsmen by John Woods, 1822.

West Indian Cricket, Christopher Nicole. The Sportsman Book Club, 1960

When London was Capital of America, Julie Flavell, 2011.

Wicket in America, Albert Matthews. The Nation, Vol. 91 July 7, 1910

Wickets in the West, or the Twelve in America, R. A. Fitzgerald, London 1873.

Wisden on the Ashes: The Authoritative story of Cricket's greatest rivalry, edited by Steven Lynch. 2009. John Wisden & Company.

With Bat & Ball, twenty-five years' reminiscences of Australian and Anglo-Australian Cricket, George Giffen. London 1898.

Wisden Cricketers Almanack.

NEWSPAPERS, MAGAZINES, JOURNALS & PERIODICALS

American Cricket: Players and Clubs before the Civil War, George B. Kirsch. Journal of Sports History, Vol 11, No. 1 (Spring 1984).

Australian Town and Country Journal.

Athletic Sports Illustrated.

An Anxious Pursuit: Agricultural Innovation and Modernity in the Lower South, 1730-1815, Joyce E Chaplin 1996.

Athleticism in the Victorian and Edwardian Public School / The Games Ethics and Imperialism: Aspect of the Diffusion of an Idea. J.A. Mangan.

A Guide to first class and other Important Cricket matches in North and South America, compiled by C. J. Clynes. Published by Association of Cricket Statisticians, 1987.

Bats, Balls and Books: Baseball and Higher Education for Women at Three Eastern Women's Colleges, 1866-1891," by Capt. Debra A. Shattuck, Department of History, U.S.A.F. Academy, in the Journal of Sport History, Summer 1992.

Brentano's Aquatic Monthly and Sporting Gazette (London)

Cricket Guide by George Wright, 1894.

Cricket and Rugby Annual and Directory of Clubs and Societies, published by KA Auty, President, Illinois Cricket Association Inc. & Illinois Rugby Football Union Inc. 1935-40.

Cricketer (London)

Chicago Tribune

Chronological History of Savannah, from its settlement by Oglethorpe down to December 31, 1899. Together with a complete record of the City & County, and Savannah's Roll of Honor, A Roster of the soldiers who have In Three Wars gone forth at their Country's Call, from this city. A.E. SHOLES, compiler. Savannah, Georgia; The Morning News Print, 1900.

Colonial Families of Philadelphia, Editor John W Jordan Vol II, 1911.

Colonials at Play: Leisure in Newport, 1723, by L. Douglas Good, Rhode Island History.

Dominion Illustrated Monthly, Cricket in Canada.

Encyclopedia of Ethnicity and Sports in the United States: George B Kirsch, Othello Harris, Claire Elaine Nolte.

Frank Leslie's Illustrated Magazine

Harpers Weekly.

Journal of a second Voyage for the discovery of a North-West passage from the Atlantic to the Pacific, performed in the years 1821-22-23 in his Majesty's ships FURY and HECLA, under the orders of Captain William Edward Parry.

Lippincott's Magazine.

Macmillan's Magazine.

New York Times.

New York Herald.

Oswego Commercial Times.

Outing an Illustrated Monthly Magazine of Sports, Travel and Recreation

Parisian Illustrated Review – Volume 9, 1900.

Philadelphia Enquirer

Porter's Spirit of the Times.

Ranjitsinhji – His record Innings by Innings from the Famous Cricketers Series No. 12, Published by the Association of Cricket Statisticians.

San Francisco Chronicle

San Francisco Examiner

Savannah Republic

Scientific American, A Journal of Practical Information in Art, Science, Mechanics, Agriculture, Chemistry and Manufacturers. 1861.

Social Class and the Sport of Cricket in Philadelphia, 1850-1880, by J. Thomas Jable, William Paterson College in Wayne, New Jersey. Journal of Sport History, Vol 18, No. 2 (Summer 1991).

Spalding's Official Cricket Guide

Sporting News

The American Cricketer, a Journal devoted to the Noble Game of Cricket, Philadelphia, June 28, 1877 to April 1929.

The American Cricket Annual and Golf Guide for 1898. Compiled & Edited by Jerome Flannery.

The Century Illustrated Monthly Magazine.

The Cricketer.

The Churchman, An Illustrated Weekly News Magazine.

The Gentleman's Magazine and American monthly review.

The Illustrated American.

The Living Age.

The Journal of Lieut. William Feltman of the First Pennsylvania Regiment 1781-1782. Including March into Virginia and the siege of Yorktown. First published in Philadelphia, 1853.

The Journal of William Stephens 1741-1743, Edited by E. Merton Coulter. University of Georgia Press 1958.

'The Manly Game': Cricket and Masculinity in Savannah Georgia in 1859, Timothy Lockley, University of Warwick. The Journal of William Stephens.

The Nation, a Weekly Journal.

The Old-Time Game of Wicket and Some Old-Time Wicket Players by George Dudley Seymour.

The Secret Diary of William Byrd of Westover, 1709-1712, ed. Louis B. Wright and Marion Tinling Richmond: The Dietz Press, 1941.

The Sportsman's Yearbook.

Walter S. Newhall, A Memoir, Philadelphia. Published for the benefit of The Sanitary Commission, 1864.

Yale Medical Journal, Volume III November 1896 – June 1897. Connecticut State Medical Society. New Haven, Conn: Published at the Yale Medical School, by the Editors 1897.

INDEX

Brooklyn Cricket Club 94, 272, 276
Brooklyn Eagle 8
Brooklyn Ferry 95
Brooklyn Sons of St. George 275
Brooklyn Wicket Club 8
Brougham, Henry 193, 195, 197, 348, 360
Broun, Miss Madeline 131
Brown, Frederick 322, 327
Brown, George (Baltimore Mayor during the Civil War) 291
Brown, H 206, 207, 228, 229, 230
Brown, Hazen 201
Brown, J 313
Brown, John 128, 343
Brown, J.M. 11, 21
Brown, Reynolds D 210, 234
Brown Stockings (1st professional Baseball Club of St. Louis) 54
Brown, Thomas 122
Brown University vii, 98
Browne, E 58, 59
Browning, F.H. 199
Buckland, E.H. 229, 230
Buenos Aires Cricket and Rugby Club 331
Buenos Aires Cricket Club 312, 313, 329, 330
Bufford, J.H. 115
Bullock, W.H. 303, 355, 357
Bunch of Grapes Tavern 103
Burke, J.M. 218, 219, 225, 226
Burnup, C.J. 267
Burritt, Elihu 25
Burritt, John 7, 24
Burritt, William 7, 26
Burton, William Evans 100
Burwell, James 86
Bushnell, Horace 92
Butler, Fred 227
Butler, Thedeus 7
Bevington, T.A.D. 214, 215
Byrd, William 85, 88, 91, 338, 339, 362

Cadwalader Family Papers 164, 180

Caesar, Julius 40, 175
Caffyn, William 30, 40, 41, 42, 43, 174, 175, 176, 338, 359
Cahn, Sir Julien 313, 314
Calcutta ix, xii
Calder, J.F. 16
Caldwell, R.N. 182, 187
California Cricket Club 151
Callender, Roy 81
Calthrop, Samuel R. 21, 22, 151, 152, 337, 345
Calvert, C.B. 54
Camac's Wood 119
Cambridge Long Vacation Club 210
Cambridge University 202, 213, 241, 243, 244, 254, 260, 272
Cameron Cricket Club 275
Camp, David N 337, 358
Campbell, G.C. 239, 240
Campbell, H.J. 30, 54
Campbell, J.A. 314
Canada Cricket Association xiii, 69, 29, 81, 338
Canadian Cricket Club 52
Canadian Cricket Guide 34, 53, 57
Canadian Monthly and National Review 55
Canadian Pacific Railway 74
Canby, Henry 133
Cannavan Mr. 122
Cannon's Tavern 95
Cape of Good Hope 312
Cardus, Neville 358
Carelton Cricket Club 36
Carkeek, W. 238
Carpathia 209
Carpenter, Robert 40, 120, 174, 175, 176
Carpenter, William 6
Carr, Arthur 274
Carroll, Anna Ella 155
Carter, J.T. 221, 223
Carter, P.A. 16
Carter, Sammy 76
Carver, Robin 105, 107, 341, 359
Carvill, William 111
Casey, G.D. 193, 196, 197, 207

www.ingramcontent.com/pod-product-compliance
Lightning Source LLC
Chambersburg PA
CBHW080605090426
42735CB00017B/3338